Cities
Surround
The
Countryside

Urban
Aesthetics
in
Postsocialist
China

Robin Visser

Duke

University

Press *Durham & L(*

2010

Designed by Jennifer Hill
Typeset in Scala by Keystone Typesetting, Inc.

Library of Congress Cataloging-in-Publication Data
appear on the last printed page of this book.

Duke University Press gratefully acknowledges the support of the Chiang Ching-Kuo
Foundation for International Scholarly Exchange, which provided funds toward the
production of this book.

For Qingguo

Contents

Acknowledgments

I depended on a great many people for the completion of this book, but there are several to whom I owe a special debt of gratitude. David Der-wei Wang motivated this project and so much more through his unstinting support and guidance throughout my education and career. Wang Xiaoming, who generously hosted two research leaves at the Shanghai University Center for Contemporary Cultural Studies, inspired this book with his insightful direction and passion for social change. Direction provided by Chen Xiaoming of Peking University was instrumental in each stage of my research. Critical input from Judith Farquhar, William Olmsted, Sandra Visser, and Stephen Westin proved essential during the writing process.

I am grateful for the support of an American Research in the Humanities in China Award provided by the American Council of Learned Societies, and particularly thank Sandra Bradley and Zhu Shanjie for so capably facilitating visiting scholar logistics. My research was further supported by programs at the University of North Carolina, Chapel Hill, including a Grier/Woods Presbyterian China Initiative Fellowship in Chinese Studies administered by the Carolina Asia Center, and a Faculty Research and Study Leave provided by the College of Arts and Sciences and the Department of Asian Studies. I received generous summer research funds from Valparaiso University. A University of North Carolina Research Council Publication Grant and a Scholarly Publications, Artistic Exhibitions, and Performances Grant helped defray costs.

I thank J. Reynolds Smith, Sharon Torian, and the Duke University Press staff for their assistance. I am grateful to the anonymous readers of the manuscript, especially the seemingly tireless one, whose generous suggestions were invaluable. My first teachers of modern Chinese literature, Xiaobing Tang and Howard Goldblatt, helped shape my work, and I am indebted to other mentors at key stages, especially Gang Yue, Judith Farquhar, Ursula Heise, and David Eng. In addition to the many Chinese academics, artists, and professionals who graciously allowed me to interview them and are named within this book, I thank Daniel Abramson, Sahar Amer, Jan Bardsley, Yomi Braester, Thomas J. Campanella, Lingchei Letty Chen, Claire Conceison, Piper Gaubatz, Amy Goldman, James Hevia, Robert Hymes, Thomas D. Kennedy, D. Sabina Knight, Haili Kong, Charles Laughlin, Jianmei Liu, Jie Lu, Luo Gang, Bonnie McDougall, Ni Wenjian, David Michael Owens, Mark Schwehn, Yan Song, Mina Choi Tenison, Michael Tsin, Wu Hung, Xue Yi, and Yin Liyu. Each of these fine teachers, scholars, and friends contributed, perhaps unwittingly, to this project.

Finally, my deepest gratitude goes to Qingguo Ren. His love, humor, support, and our shared delight in Takoda Lei, Jordan Shan, and Zoe Ahn sustain me.

Introduction

Cities Surround the Countryside

Chairman Mao creatively laid down the general line and general policy of the new democratic revolution, founded the Chinese People's Liberation Army and pointed out that the seizure of political power by armed force in China could be achieved only by following the road of building rural base areas, using the countryside to encircle the cities and finally seizing the cities, and not by any other road.

"Text of Announcement Issued by Peking Reporting Death of Chairman Mao," *Xinhua*, 10 September 1976

Mao's mandate that the countryside encircle the cities has been irrevocably reversed during the past three decades in China. Although Deng Xiaoping's economic reforms started in the countryside, in 1978, with the household responsibility system, policy shifted to urban development with the establishment of the first Special Economic Zones, in 1980. Urbanization is now dominant in China, both demographically and ideologically. The question that first provoked my inquiry into postsocialist urban aesthetics is a simple one: what happens culturally when those in a historically agricultural civilization start to identify primarily with the city? China has maintained a rural population of nearly 90 percent for millennia, its poets rhapsodizing on glad retirements to rural abodes, its culture characterized by an "attachment to the soil." Yet both the soil and the values associated with it are swiftly transforming. The modern urban-rural dichotomy, a legacy of nineteenth-century imperialism, is being rapidly reconfigured in a

Skyscrapers are supplanting village forms in China. Pudong, Shanghai, was once farmland. Courtesy Marilyn Shea.

postsocialist, global environment. The capitalist city—denounced as parasitical under Mao and devalued by the norms of traditional Chinese ethics —now functions in China as a site of individual and collective identity.

Take the soil. The central government's decision, in 1990, to develop Pudong transformed sparsely populated farmland in eastern Shanghai into an urbanized zone seven times the size of the old city of Puxi. Beijing has likewise been ballooning concentrically since the Second Ring Road was first situated along the contours of the former city wall, in the 1980s; a Sixth Ring Road has been completed, and planners have even proposed a Seventh Ring Road, which would exceed the city limits and not only link very distant districts and townships but expand into neighboring provinces and cities. Throughout China, municipal officials pushing lucrative development projects confiscate rural land by guile, fiat, or force, with tens of millions of farmers having lost their land in the past decade. Qin Hui, a leading authority on rural China, contends that "if the government wants to take land, it can take it more or less at will. Farmers often not only haven't benefited from the process of urbanization, they are losing out because of it."[1]

Hong Village, Anhui Province, 2005. Photo by author.

Take culture. While claiming that we can bid "farewell to peasant China," as some scholars assert, may overstate the extent of China's urbanization, there is no question that cities increasingly envelope the countryside, not only geographically and demographically (40 percent urbanization in 2005), but in terms of cultural influence.[2] In 1994 Kam Wing Chan, a geographer who has been analyzing China's urbanization for decades, predicted accurately that "if an annual urban population growth rate of 4% to 5%, similar to that of the 1980s, is maintained in the coming decades, China's urban population will be hitting the 50% mark around the year 2010. In less than one generation's time, China will be transformed into a primarily urbanized society, both in demographic and occupational terms. Not only will these changes have a profound effect on the way of life of most Chinese people and the way Chinese society is organized but the outcome of such a mammoth transformation will also create a drastically different dimension in the future global political economy."[3] The way of life for "most Chinese people" is undergoing fundamental transformation because even everyday life in the countryside is impacted by urbanization. A noted ethnographic study demonstrates, for example, that new rural housing designs, directly influenced by exposure to urban markets, are radically altering life in the countryside by fostering youth autonomy, individual rights, and privacy while enervating patriarchal power structures.[4] The cultural effects result in part from a structural change in administration called *shidaixian*, literally, "cities leading counties," a program first deployed, temporarily, in the 1950s and reestablished in 1983 to effect the economic dismantling of the urban-rural dichotomy. In abandoning prefectures and transferring their subordinate counties to the leadership of cities, "the leading role of the city has been explicitly established to usher in an epoch of city-led regional development for the first time in Chinese history."[5] Despite China's limited urbanization during the twentieth century, it fully embraces urbanization in the twenty-first.[6]

By all accounts, the sustained economic, ideological, demographic, and material priority of the city in China is a very recent development. In this book I examine how the transformation of Chinese cities over the past three decades informs the cultural imagination as manifest in fiction, cinema, visual art, architecture, and urban design. Following Guy Debord's interpretation of aesthetics as new ways of seeing and perceiving the world, "urban aesthetics" refers to how the city is envisioned, experienced, and assessed. Proceeding from the premise that the built environment is not an autonomous realm, but rather an economic and social field with important political implications, I consider how the aesthetics of the urban environment shape the emotions and behavior of individuals and cultures, and how individual and collective images of and practices in the city, whether consciously organized or not, produce urban aesthetics. Drawing on interdisciplinary tools of urban studies, literary and cultural theory, and field research (empirical observations and interviews), I situate postsocialist urban aesthetics within broad economic, historical, ideological, and material contexts. My method for elucidating the urban imagination is to first analyze its general manifestations in postsocialist urban planning, economics, and critical inquiry, and then interpret its particular expressions in works of fiction, film, and art.

I exclude Chinese cities such as Taipei, Hong Kong, and Singapore from my analysis. In addition to a practical need to limit the scope of my examination, the theoretical thrust of my analysis examines the cultural ethos created by capitalist urban transformation in the wake of socialist modernity. The central dynamism of social and intellectual life in the People's Republic of China (PRC) in the 1990s was, as Xudong Zhang points out, due to the new social and power relationships produced by a market economy initiated and administered by the state bureaucracy.[7] Socialist systems and sentiments not only constitute the historical basis for urbanization in the PRC, they also continue to inform, in part, its ongoing processes and policies. The hybrid state of many of China's postreform sectors is epitomized, for example, in the mixture of socialist, market, and globalization rhetoric informing the "New Housing Movement," a self-described "urban real-estate development market cooperative network" that nonetheless uses the socialist mechanism of a "movement" (*yundong*) to mobilize itself.[8] The urban aesthetics produced under such conditions often engender a distinctive psychic lacuna, an aporia resulting from the coupling of socialist monumentality rhetoric with the quotidian ethos of consumer culture.

The tripartite structure of this book establishes the major epistemological paradigms that govern my inquiry into postsocialist urban culture. In the first section I examine what Henri Lefebvre called the "urban question" of late capitalism, both in how it is formulated by urban theorists and in how it is resolved by urban practitioners and intellectuals. In particular, I attend to dynamics of neoliberal globalization in building the new Chinese city, in inciting critiques of urban consumerism by literary and visual artists, and in enabling alternative intellectual strategies in the academy. Like Lefebvre, many Chinese intellectuals are particularly critical of how enlightenment rationality is used to justify spatial conquests by global capitalists. These intellectuals are particularly well positioned to confront the issues posed by neoliberal discourse and developmental strategies in part because China's search for modernity was shaped from the start by the historical context of imperialist expansion and a crisis in capitalism. The legacy of socialist egalitarianism in popular thought, coupled with the increasing influence of market-embedded activism, is starting to reverse the tide of indiscriminate ecological and heritage destruction that characterized China's first two decades of postsocialist urban development. The phenomenon of public-minded artists and intellectuals enacting social critique via commercial venues is itself constitutive of a new urban cultural aesthetics informing urban governance. Because urban development dominates questions of global sustainability, Chinese intellectual inquiry now extends beyond saving the nation (*jiuguo*) to saving the world from its present untenable developmentalism.

In the second section of this volume I explore how the city, and how specific cities, figure in the contemporary cultural imagination, as aesthetic depictions are often at odds with portrayals by sociologists or urban geographers. For example, while the scholar Paul Knox argues that global cities have more in common with each other than with features of their own state, Wang Anyi's literary evocation of Shanghai contrasts that city with the dominant, male-gendered, political culture represented by Beijing, rather than with other global cities. Again, while geographers such as Victor Sit argue that Beijing's recent development as a global city at the center of finance and corporate decisions mirrors its traditional role as the national center of communication and control, they fail to fully address the impact that capital, rather than political symbolism, is assuming in urban planning. Beijing writers, filmmakers, and artists depict the ruins predicated on development, protesting the commercial exploitation of traditional culture while appropriating market devices for their ends. Although prevailing theories of globalization continue to portray cities as spaces of cultural homogenization where place and community are disappearing, most cities are characterized not so much by homogeneity as by unevenness in places which anchor concrete social, political, and spatial projects. The disparate urban aesthetics of China's two major cities—Beijing as a space for performing identity, Shanghai as a space to be consumed—arise from distinct local urban histories and spatial forms that produce unique cultural identities. For example, urban aesthetics fostered by Internet literature (*wangluo wenxue*)—which includes conventional literary works uploaded to cyberspace and writings enabled by technology (such as hyperlink-packed articles, and material written specifically for posting on the Internet)—promote nationwide fantasies of the *xiaozi*, or "petty bourgeois" urban consumer.[9] Yet the use of local dialects and region-specific terms in online rap music, blogs, and literature continues to promote local urban identities.

In addition to examining cultural production that features the city as subject, I analyze works that portray the subject in the city. In the third section of this book I draw on urban sociology, psychoanalytic theory, and philosophy to query how urban subjectivities are produced by—and produce—urban space. Urban subjectivity in the fiction of the late 1990s is closely associated with the flux of metropolitan crowds, patterns of destruction and urban renewal, altered economic configurations, and the introduction of new technologies of transportation, communication, and socialization. In a rapidly transforming metropolis, the "walking through the city" so vaunted by de Certeau becomes, for some, less an exercise in staking spatial claims than the gendered experience of melancholy-inducing loss. The persistent metaphor of "flying" invokes a sense of breathtaking freedom and empowerment in some works, reckless speed and rootless disorientation in others. The waning influence of the work unit (*danwei*) and local street committee (*jiedao banshichu*), which were the socialist organizational mechanisms that had once circumscribed nearly all forms of urban life, provoked widespread reflection on autonomy, as urbanites came to make their own decisions about livelihood and lifestyle. The fiction of the 1990s attends in particular to the formation of the moral subject and new forms of citizenry as the logic of the marketplace supplants earlier ethical and regulatory paradigms. These narratives query the ethics of market utilitarianism in the wake of the radical deconstruction of the moral dictates of Confucianism, May Fourth Enlightenment, and Maoist socialism. The late twentieth century was a transitional period characterized by postrevolutionary dystopia and urban ambivalence, indicative of residual identifications with rural forms of social organization.

In the past decade social scientists, historians, and geographers have produced an impressive array of detailed English-language scholarship on economics, sociology, planning, architecture, and housing reforms in the new Chinese city.[10] I offer an aesthetic dimension to these historical and sociological studies. My approach is informed, in part, by interdisciplinary methodologies in Chinese-language scholarship which more broadly characterize urban culture.[11] In the growing English-language scholarship on Chinese urban fiction, cinema, and art, this volume is distinguished by its close attention to the built environment, offering a sustained analysis of cultural production relative to new material, economic, intellectual, and psychic forms of organization in the postsocialist city.[12] This study aims to situate postsocialist Chinese urban aesthetics within a nexus of local and global economic and intellectual trends that inform literary, cultural, and urban studies more generally. For example, it identifies the emergence of cultural studies in Chinese universities as a form of urban aesthetics, whereas few studies of Chinese critical inquiry focus on the city.[13]

A historical overview of the shifting connotations of the city in the cultural imagination of modern China may be useful. Perhaps the most remarkable cultural change wrought by new identifications with urban market values is in relation to China's unique experience of modernity, in particular, that experience governed by the ubiquitous question "whither China?" This question, which has plagued Chinese intellectuals since the mid-nineteenth century, may very well become irrelevant in the near future. Not in the real sense—as an epistemological inquiry the question of China's fate is more pressing than ever—but as a philosophical hermeneutic guiding everyday life. Consider, as a minor but telling example, the

Tourists pose in front of Olympic venues, proud to be on an equal footing with other nations. Beijing, 2008. Photo by author.

demeanor of the Olympic track star Liu Xiang, in 2004, after each qualifying stage of the 110 meter hurdles event. The Shanghai native breezily dismissed innuendoes by the Chinese media that he might feel the burden of becoming the first Asian male to medal in a short-distance track event. Instead of expressing cautious optimism about his success in the qualifiers, he affected an air of blithe confidence. While undoubtedly patriotic, Liu Xiang's drive for success, like that of many in his generation, derives as much from his personal goals as from his desire to gain glory for the nation. Such cosmopolitanism is also exemplified by Wang Liang, a twenty-nine-year-old Beijing native and principal oboist for the New York Philharmonic, who expressed genuine shock to learn that people identified him as "Chinese" before "musician": "The thing I don't understand is why it should make a difference. I am a Chinese guy when I look in the mirror, but I'm a world citizen of music."[14] Among many young urban Chinese there is a sense of being modern, a taken-for-granted quality embedded in everyday thinking and behavior. Marx's characterization of China as the "sick man of Asia" is defunct. The schizophrenic inferiority-superiority complex epitomized by the prominent writer Lu Xun's depiction of the

Chinese national character in "Ah Q" is replaced with a prevailing sense that one is a member of a global community of modern urbanites, that one is on an equal footing with other nations and cultures. This is not to suggest that nationalism is on the wane in the People's Republic of China—far from it—but rather that its valences are shifting in relation to alternative narratives of identity.

China today is a hybrid society where traditional agricultural practices coexist with postindustrial cities that coordinate worldwide production and consumption, where state-run institutions and private enterprises operate side by side in most sectors and regions. Older Chinese who have lived most of their lives dominated by a "native soil" (*xiangtu*) mentality have a mixed sense of fascination with, and hostility toward, the spatial, social, economic, and political mutations within their cities. The literary critic Li Jiefei speaks for many when he discusses the unanticipated "raising of [his] urban consciousness" in the 1990s.

> From my personal history I had no knowledge of anything outside the city, but that doesn't mean I knew the city. That confused me and I began questioning this. The city had failed to inspire me even during the 1980s —I never gave it a second thought. For years I simply had no incentive to reflect on the city. After consideration I realized that my only impressions of the "city" had been formed by watching films set in New York, Rome, London, Tokyo, or Hong Kong. But in 1993 and 1994 I suddenly became fascinated with urban space. I began to pay attention to the city landscape and urban events. Better put, the city started to change in such a way that I *had* to notice it. In the second half of the 1990s the trends in literature seemed to support my observations. Of all the new literature written since 1995, probably 80–90% is on the topic of the city. This is not to say that rural literature is dying out, but that the real vitality is clearly to be found in urban literature.[15]

The predominantly rural aesthetic featured in much of the cultural production of the 1980s—Fifth Generation film, root-seeking and avant-garde literature, and post-Mao pop art—represented place not chiefly for what it was, but for what it signified. By the 1990s, however, the city had become a subject in its own right, examined without recourse to rural values or national allegories. This altered mentality is encapsulated, in Qiu Huadong's novel *Yingyan* (Fly eyes, 1998), by a character who insists that "we need to return to our roots."[16] She is not referring to the countryside imagined by root-seeking writers and artists in the 1980s; rather, this new transplant to the capital concludes that her "roots" are in Beijing. The postrevolutionary generation that comes of age in the city feels itself to be firmly ensconced in the metropolis.

The rejection of metaphors of the nation-state, the main aesthetic strategy from the May Fourth period until the 1980s, is a key aspect of postsocialist urban aesthetics.[17] To understand the significance of the radical *absence* of nation-state metaphors in the urban aesthetics I analyze, it is necessary to briefly review how these images played out in the cultural geopolitics of national identity in modern China. It was to an earlier generation of urbanites that Fei Xiaotong addressed his classic account of Chinese society, *Xiangtu Zhongguo* (Rural China, 1947).[18] In it, he uses the rural-urban contrast as a rhetorical device to enable his urban readers to understand their cultural roots, long since severed. Fei characterizes fundamental aspects of Chinese society in relation to its uniquely rural features, in opposition to Western culture, which equates civilization with the metropolis. Although Fei's account exaggerates the contrast, cultural historians have long pointed out the etymological distinctions between Western and Chinese notions of the city. The English term *city* is derived from the Latin *civitas* (city-state), closely associated with *civilization*, whereas the term *country* is derived from *contra* (against, opposite side), referring to land which is set off from the observer. The closest approximation to a city in ancient China was the walled town seat (*guo*) at the head of a fief during the early Zhou dynasty. Frederick Mote points out that while the walled town may have represented civilization in that it was an island surrounded by hostile peasantry, the sharp division into distinct urban and rural civilizations disappeared in China altogether following the breakup of the Zhou dynasty. Rather, geographic and social mobility was achieved very early in Chinese history, a fact which "must be related to the existence of an urban-rural continuum, both as physical and as organizational realities, and as an aspect of Chinese psychology."[19]

The lack of any single great urban center strengthens awareness of rural China. Mote asserts that "the rural component of Chinese civilization was more or less uniform, and it extended everywhere that Chinese civilization penetrated it. It, and not the cities, defined the Chinese way of life. It was like the net in which the cities and towns of China were suspended."[20] Chinese cities were never separate and discrete from the rural areas that supported them. Both rich people and poor often moved to the city and later returned to villages. Inside the cities, social structures were often arranged along the lines of native place and common dialect, which helped reinforce ties to rural origins. Thus the Chinese terms for *city* and *country* refer to various levels of activity or administration on an urban-rural continuum. Furthermore, these terms have taken on affective associations which are the reverse of those in the West. In his study of early-twentieth-century urban literature and film, Yingjin Zhang points out that *cheng* (walled administrative city), *zhen* (unwalled market town), and *shi* (market) are terms which denote the more impersonal functions of administration or commerce, as opposed to the term *xiang* (an administrative unit ranking between county and village), a word which has strong personal connotations when used in combination such as *xiangtu* (native soil) and *xiangsi* (homesickness). On the other hand the term *shimin* (city dweller), far from implying the sense of the English word *civilized*, became a derogatory term used in phrases such as *xiao shimin* (petty urbanite) or *shikuai* (Philistine), "connoting a contempt on the part of the speaker for the 'lower' taste the majority of city dwellers display in their everyday practices."[21]

If an urban-rural continuum best describes the relationship between city and country for most of China's history, this continuum was disrupted at the approach of the twentieth century; the reasons for this schism remained under dispute. A widespread view, which informed Mao's opinion of cities as "parasitic," was that the pronounced polarization between urban and rural occurred after the Opium Wars (1839–42, 1856–60), due to the establishment of treaty ports, cities whose development resulted solely from Western exploitation and at the expense of the hinterlands.[22] Rhoads Murphey concurred that treaty ports never built effective ties with the hinterland, but merely drained the provinces of goods for export abroad, to the detriment of national self-esteem: "London and New York stock exchange reports were more important in Shanghai than news from Sichuan or Hunan. Treaty ports never functioned as an operative part of a larger system, and many Chinese suffered from foreign arrogance, treated as inferior or 'uncivilized.'"[23] Indeed, the conventional Western view held that Shanghai had been merely a fishing village prior to its opening to the West, in 1843, and that its subsequent development as a treaty port incorporated it into the modern world to the benefit of the nation as a whole. Ernest Hauser, for example, who wrote "Shanghai: City for Sale," a regular series in the *New York Times* in the 1920s and 1930s, promulgated such views by stating that "when it came into English hands Shanghai was a third-rate market town."[24] While this idea has been thoroughly discredited, its stereotype persists, even in Shanghai's contemporary promotional literature. A recent feature on Pudong quotes a foreign investor who states, "Shanghai is solidly based, and in addition it has the *blessed virgin land* of Pudong. It is rare for a big city to have such a large area of *exploitable land*. This will undoubtedly make it attractive to investors."[25] The fact that the Shanghai municipal government welcomes such imperialist rhetoric recalls Rey Chow's argument that processes of global commodification continue to inform discourses of ethnicity, as China gladly offers its physical capital (labor and land) to the West in order to secure better trade agreements in the international marketplace.[26]

Other images of cities emerged as well. Rather than accepting that Shanghai, for example, was a city bred exclusively of Western influence, which either greatly contributed to or irreparably damaged China's attempts at modernization, subsequent historical scholarship argues along other lines. Some scholars consider Shanghai to be representative of an "other China" which has always existed as a marginalized sector alongside the dominant, rural, and bureaucratic tradition resuscitated under the Nationalist Party and later under Mao.[27] The historian Li Tiangang, on the other hand, contests the idea of Shanghai as "other," stating that "if one must think in terms of centers and margins Shanghai has to be in some senses situated near the center," given its location in Jiangnan, the most developed cultural area of the Ming and Qing dynasties.[28] Characterizations of Shanghai as "marginal," says Li, erroneously insist on rigid dichotomies either between China and the West, or between the provinces and the coast. In addition to its complex fusion of Eastern and Western culture, he argues, Shanghai must be understood in terms of its larger situation in a network of Jiangnan towns and cities where market economies had flourished since the Song dynasty, creating cultural differences between commercial practices in the south, with its mix of high and low culture, and the officialdom of the north. This is the way that Wang Anyi understands Shanghai as well, conveying its "essence" in her novel *Song of Everlasting Sorrow* in terms of its long-standing contrast with northern official culture, rather than as an inauthentic, exotic Western creation.

Even if intricate ties between city and countryside existed prior to the twentieth century, the cultural and economic gaps between former treaty ports and rural locales, particularly during the pre- and post-Mao eras of decentralized economic growth, became greatly exacerbated during that century. In the wake of Western infiltration the concept of the city became increasingly problematic in China, acquiring a number of predominantly negative qualities. Like the long-standing anti-urban tradition in India, which derives from the same anti-imperialist roots, anti-urbanism in China assumed political as well as cultural priority. In 1927 Zhou Zuoren ridiculed Shanghai culture in his essay "Shanghai qi" (Shanghai style), reasoning that Shanghai was a "culture of compradors, hooligans, and prostitutes, fundamentally deprived of rationality and elegance."[29] In 1934 another Beijing-based writer, Shen Congwen, culminated a year-long series of cultural debates between *jingpai* (Beijing-style) writers and *haipai* (Shanghai-style) writers by lambasting the latter for their crass opportunism.[30] And in 1946 Fei Xiaotong barely conceals his resentment toward compradors in treaty ports that "live in, and take advantage of, the margin of cultural contact. They are half-caste in culture, bilingual in speech, and morally unstable. They are unscrupulous, pecuniary, individualistic, and agnostic, not only in religion, but in cultural values."[31] It is not coincidental that these provocative comments were penned by Beijing intellectuals during the two decades in which Shanghai had attained the height of its cultural glory. They reflect, among other things, anxieties about Beijing cultural identity, as the national center of culture shifted to Shanghai and the capital shifted to Nanjing, in 1928. Similarly, the marginalization of intellectuals under the commodification of culture in the 1990s resulted in a desperate attempt to mine the legacy of Chinese tradition in hopes of regaining a humanist spirit that had been "lost" in urban fiction and film. Those writers esteemed as advocating humanist spirit amid the cultural "ruins in the wilderness" include Zhang Chengzhi, Zhang Wei, and Shi Tiesheng, whose spiritual narratives were invariably set in rural locales.

In addition to the fear of cultural pollution, the fact that treaty ports were dominated by industry and trade leads Yingjin Zhang to conclude that early-twentieth-century Chinese cities underwent a recategorization from that of continuum to that of dichotomy: "On the one side is the traditional 'administrative city' (like Beijing) where space is highly managed and where politics and culture prevail, and on the other side is the modern 'economic city' (like Shanghai) where time becomes an increasingly important factor and where industry and trade dominate."[32] Although Republican Beijing was a large metropolis, Zhang situates it "in the middle of the urban-rural continuum," as its lifestyle, architecture, and aura reflected those of the traditional Chinese city. He concludes that in Beijing, with its emphasis on nature, traditional rural values prevail in its residents' mentalities. In such essentials as design, materials used, style, and ornamentation, Chinese urban structures were indistinguishable from rural structures, and "the typical Beijing 'sihe yuan' (a compound of four houses built around a courtyard) bears little difference from a typical country house in that both are one-story, spacious, natural, and accessible to interpersonal communication."[33] Rather than simply indicating a certain population density, the "urban" that dominated early-twentieth-century cultural debates referred primarily to the China of the treaty ports—to a China that was changing, either by corrupting Chinese patterns or by rejecting them altogether in favor of adopting an artificial Westernized society. Such polemics cast the urban as inauthentic, implying that rural China was a metaphor for genuine Chinese society.

Although the notion of the modern city remained suspect in the Chinese cultural imagination, the pace of urban change increased dramatically in the twentieth century; to interpret the cultural aesthetics of the contemporary Chinese city one must trace its material and social development in addition to understanding its history as a cultural construct. Piper Rae Gaubatz describes how the historic structure of cities was eroded by the abandonment of traditional institutions that accompanied the fall of the Qing dynasty, by the rapid introduction of foreign methods of building and city planning, and by the need for urban change to accommodate the implementation of modern transportation systems such as automobile and rail transport.[34] During the Republican Era "the points and lines of urban China grew and thickened," and "one sign that cities had come to exist as a separate category of thought, policy, and culture [was that] municipal studies emerged as a scholarly and administrative discourse."[35] As urban residents became consumers of public services and private housing, their "urbanite" (*shimin*) consciousness was raised, the new media providing outlets for expressing opinions on urban design. As early as 1912 a newspaper editorialist blamed the "mentality of tearing down walls" (*chaicheng de sixiang*) on "great political reformers" who believe that "because a dictatorial form of government has been overthrown, nothing in China that is old may be left standing."[36] This historical perspective highlights that the incredible destruction of urban fabric today is not only a function of global capital, but of longstanding practices appropriated by new Chinese regimes attempting to forge their own symbols.

Chinese life under socialism also privileged urban modernization, although in a highly regulated and circumscribed manner. Cities, according to Communist Party ideology in the 1940s, were to serve the people and the economic objectives of "New China" as productive entities that accelerated the growth of industrial output. The economic activities of cities were to support the population of the country, and the city as a social system would be leveled, with the stratification of neighborhoods eliminated in favor of classless spatial structures. Differences between countryside and city were to be reduced, and the frivolous urban activities associated with high rates of personal consumption and lavish living were to be expunged. Mao especially reviled the commercial, trading, and service activities associated with capitalist market economies. His legacy at death remained champion of the rural, his victory based on "encircling the cities from the countryside," his revolutions aimed at leveling urban-rural distinctions, his campaigns enforcing the reeducation of urban elite by the peasantry. Mao on the one hand called for his comrades to learn about the management of the urban economy and, on the other hand, feared that urban amenities would corrupt the spirits of revolutionaries like "sugar-coated bullets."[37]

Although the Chinese Communist Party tried to adjust its attitude toward cities after it attained the power to rule the country, the disdain for large, sophisticated cities was clearly revealed by the categorization of most metropolises as "consumer cities," where urban life was perceived as parasitic and unhealthy. A major tenet of Maoist socialism was that cities be cast in the mold of producers, rather than of consumers living off the surplus of the rural economy. Heavy industry was viewed as the sign of economic strength and consequently received the largest allocations of capital through the state plan, with urban infrastructure, particularly urban housing, remaining vastly underfunded. In the dictum "On the Correct Handling of Contradictions among the People" (1957), Chairman Mao censures cities as parasitic and consumption-oriented, a characterization with potent ideological force in evolving party policy on city development. While Shanghai's industrial output was the largest in the nation, for example, 90 percent of its enterprise earnings went to the central government, leaving the municipality perennially cash-poor. By 1982, due to the growth in urban population and lack of investment in housing stock, nearly half of all urban Chinese families had inadequate housing, and one-fourth were virtually homeless, with married couples forced to squeeze into parents' apartments or to live separately in work-unit dormitories. These abysmal conditions set the stage for the unprecedented speed at which housing and city centers transformed in the 1990s, in what Rem Koolhaas has called a "maelstrom of modernization," which has led to the creation of a completely new, and still evolving, urban substance.

During the first half of the 1950s, hundreds of thousands of professionals and workers were relocated from older industrial cities to new key cities (*zhongdian chengshi*) planned as important producer cities. Shanghai "ceased to be a 'world city' with diverse functions and became instead an

industrial workhorse for a plan-bound economy."[38] The Ministry of Construction Engineering, established in 1952, took charge of building new
cities and decreed that Beijing was to be restructured from a traditional
cultural and administrative city into a heavy industrial city. The imperial
North-South axis shifted to a socialist East-West axis in Beijing's urban
structures. Under the socialist slogan "eliminate the old in order to build
the new" (*pojiu lixin*), ancient city walls and buildings nationwide were
relentlessly torn down to make way for new structures: "Nearly one-fifth of
the existing buildings and dwellings in Taiyuan and Lanzhou were taken
down to make way for new construction, although these buildings were
still in good condition."[39] From 1954, when rental fees for land usage were
waived, to 1984, when they were restored, land was considered free resource rather than a commodity, and large-scale industry developed hap-
hazardly, without the coordination of urban planning. Jieming Zhu points
out that it was "not uncommon to see factories located in a city's central
business district, even in the 1980s in Shanghai. . . . [L]and squandering
was prevalent, and many [key cities, such as Lanzhou, Luoyang, and Har-
bin] uneconomically adopted great squares in their city plans."[40] The excessive land supply in such "new industrial cities" contrasted sharply with the
parsimonious land-use plans applied to "old industrial cities," those traditional manufacturing bases denounced as "consumer cities" by Mao. Socialist monumentality, where "bigger" is deemed "better," continues to
dominate municipal design in China, to alienating effect.

Despite the fact that socialist modernization relied on urban industrialization and that most PRC leaders and cadres moved to the cities, during
the Maoist era ideological identity was planted firmly in the countryside, its
cultural values fundamentally informed by the customs of rural society.
Mao Zedong's Yan'an talks, in 1942, formalized the primacy of rural literature and other cultural arts for the next four decades, as he mobilized
intellectuals to "go down to the countryside" (*xiaxiang*) to carry out cultural
work in direct contact with the rural masses. Mao also called for arts whose
"source" (*yuan*) derived from "national forms," as opposed to following the
"current" (*liu*) of foreign influences.[41] What had begun as cultural debates
in the 1930s between the nativist aesthetics of *jingpai* writers and the cosmopolitan *haipai* became explicitly politicized in favor of indigenous forms
with rural content. The rare literary depiction of the city during the Maoist
period, such as in Zhou Erfu's *Shanghai de zaochen* (Shanghai dawn, 1958),
is fanatically intent on depriving the urban space of its capitalistic functions
(Zhou's novel concludes with the entrepreneurs donating all of their capital

Socialist monumentality. Shanghai University Baoshan campus (est. 1994), 2006. Photo by author.

to the peasants, as their infrastructure has collapsed). It is only in the late 1970s that remnants of a merchant economy are reintroduced in literature, and then only cautiously, in terms of a town rather than a metropolis, such as in Gu Hua's *Furong zhen* (A town called Hibiscus, 1979).

For all the symbolic rebuilding that followed the collapse of the Qing dynasty and that continued under Mao, the material expansion of Chinese cities and destruction of historic fabric was greatest during Deng Era decentralized urban reforms, when market mechanisms were introduced into urban development, and cities accelerated the replacement of their "old and dilapidated housing," the vast bulk of which were located in the cities' historic centers.[42] The neorealist urban fiction, gritty documentaries, and "Sixth Generation" urban film produced concurrent to such material developments convey an immediate sense of the complex interactions between spatial configurations and subjectivity. Two of the earliest post-Mao urban novels, Fang Fang's *Fengjing* (Landscape, 1987) and Liu Heng's *Hei de xue* (Black snow, 1988), set in traditional neighborhoods in, respectively, Wuhan and Beijing, express deep-seated ambiguity about modernity relative to topological change. The Beijing author Chen Jiangong claims that in reorienting Beijing's visual landscape from horizontal courtyard houses to vertical high-rises, municipal leaders have engendered "a city where it's impossible to find a spot to hang up one's birdcage."[43] The Beijing gentleman and his birds, the shadow-puppet plays, the bathhouse culture, the cricket fights, the "rice-sprout" dances, and other traditional urban hobbies had virtually disappeared by the late 1990s for, as a character in Zhang Yang's film *Xizao* (Shower, 1999) states, "to raise crickets you need to live close to the earth." These sentiments are further examined by the aesthetics professor Cheng Xiangzhan, who draws on Kevin Lynch's theory of urban elements to analyze profound cultural differences between the village and city image ("urbanization"), the traditional and modern city image ("modernization"), and the Western and Chinese city image ("globalization"). In one example, Cheng analyzes Lynch's element of "path" in relation to "major roads" (*dalu*) in Chinese villages and traditional cities, where they are sites for inauspicious activities, such as funeral processions, which are conducted on public routes so as to not contaminate private space. Yet, as lanes and alleyways are destroyed in traditional cities so are their sacred spaces, leaving taboo forms to all but define the postsocialist city.[44]

In addition to the extreme makeovers of urban landscape and housing during the Reform Era, the privatization of Chinese enterprises, and concomitant debilitation of the socialist work unit, is a key contributor to the new cultural logic of China's postsocialist urban space, as increasing numbers of individuals become responsible for their own livelihood and lifestyle. The work unit had comprehensively circumscribed urban life under socialism by regulating, controlling, and providing for its members. Lu Feng indicates that the work unit functions much like a lineage or clan organization: it exercises patriarchal authority over members; the responsibility of individuals to the group is more important than individual rights; the group is responsible for the care of its members; relations are based on connections (*guanxi*); public opinion and moral condemnation forces individuals to adhere to accepted norms of conduct.[45] The postsocialist fiction and cinema analyzed in the present study reveal that in the absence of the regulation provided by the state-owned work unit, the individual is afforded so much autonomy that he is almost at a loss. Not only must he determine his daily routines and coordinate his social activity, but with the deterioration of ethical norms inherent in socialism it becomes incumbent on him to develop an entirely new value system.

With the increase in entrepreneurialism and rural-to-urban migration given the loosening of certain restrictions on the *hukou*, or household-registration system, Chinese society is reorganizing as a class system based on wealth, rather than maintaining its "caste system" composed of urban and rural residents.⁴⁶ Just as "the Dutch, more than anyone else, made making money respectable" during the mercantile modernity of the seventeenth century, the Chinese, under accelerated market reforms in the 1990s, "became willing to state openly that the reason they worked so hard was for financial gain, no longer considering it immoral to do so."⁴⁷ Commercial advertising began to blatantly flaunt class difference. For example, in 1994, an advertisement for Kangxing Park, an exclusive complex in southwest Shanghai, directly appealed to elitism via economic status by linking success to desirable professions: "A paradise for successful entrepreneurs, scientists, and artists, the key to the main gate of Kangxing Park will be the symbol of a successful man [*chenggong renshi shenfen*]."⁴⁸ The ubiquitous use of the phrase "successful man" in advertising came under attack in a series of articles by Leftist intellectuals such as Cai Xiang and Wang Xiaoming who argued, following Althusser's notion of ideology, that promoting the myth of the "successful man" serves to mask the social realities of the widely divergent classes.⁴⁹ In the past decade Chinese intellectuals have reengaged class analysis, not merely as a way to remind the party of its socialist roots, but to stem what many consider immanent social threats posed by vastly increasing gaps in income levels, sanctioned under the umbrella of "modernization."⁵⁰

Writers, filmmakers, and artists have also been probing the class contradictions inherent in China's "urbanization" and "modernization" rhetoric, starting with neorealist fiction and art in the 1980s. Powerful paintings, photographs, performance, documentaries, and installation art have contrasted prevalent forms of glitzy urban "renewal" with the government's irrational inattention to a livable urban infrastructure. Neorealist film, documentary, and fiction have tended to focus on neglected spots and isolated individuals in the modernizing city. These works eschew the didacticism that characterizes earlier (critical and socialist) realist aesthetics in the PRC, while still enacting a powerful social and political critique. Ban Wang insists that film aesthetics featuring the fraying social fabric of the city "make us share with the characters an unabridged, prolonged interval in their daily life and force us to take a long, hard, estranged look at the space they move in, until the space's intrinsic, unredeemed, untold banality and triviality leaves an indelible imprint in our consciousness."⁵¹ As one of several prevalent aesthetic strategies in the postsocialist era, neorealism challenges commonsense assumptions about the efficacy of modernization. While the documentary realism that typifies much postsocialist urban cultural production shares a drive to address anxieties relative to dislocation, most artists deconstruct the present with a conspicuous absence of nostalgia. The fact that so many unique urban forms and their corresponding life-styles have been indiscriminately uprooted in Chinese cities, compounded by the urgent and understandable need to modernize, has resulted in cultural production best characterized by what Ackbar Abbas, drawing on the work of Paul Virilio, has termed an "aesthetics of disappearance." The renewed preoccupation with "reality" in urban aesthetics, in addition to its function as counter-Maoist discourse, can also be attributed to a rising skepticism about the massive commercialization of culture and about the drive by the transnational cultural industry to turn reality into simulacra. In contrast, the new realism engages with the neglected, concealed strata of the city, spurning the portrayal of perfect bodies and venues in commercial ads as much as it rejects the idealized heroes and vibrant settings of socialist realism.

Main ——
scope

PAR. I

To analyze the synergies of global capital, class distinctions, and realism in contemporary urban aesthetics, the three sections of this volume each illuminate one aspect of how the postsocialist city functions in the cultural imagination. In part I I consider the question of urban image-making in relation to urban design, providing historical background on urban planning and architecture in postsocialist China, and analyzing salient aspects of cultural debates relevant to urbanization. The frenzied and often opportunistic development of cities in China today is creating social and political ruptures to which literary and visual artists are particularly sensitive. Edward Soja and Henri Lefebvre both tend to theorize the production of space to the exclusion of place, yet a primary source of modern ambiguity derives precisely from the merger of these two processes, in what Peter Taylor calls the "place-space tension" between the producers of space and the makers of place. In part I I theorize dynamics underlying this tension.

THEORY

———>

In chapter I I discuss dynamics between three decades of urban-planning practices and urban art which conveys cultural sentiments running counter to official discourse on Chinese urbanism. After addressing the particular challenges posed by the urban question in China today, I examine works from collaborative exhibitions that have fostered dialogue between artists and architects on contemporary Asian urbanism, such as "Cities on the Move," the Vienna Secession exhibit of 1997. These works expose contradictions inherent in the speed of demolition and urban renewal and seek resolution to these problems. Even as experimental artists depict a city that erases individual and cultural identity under global capitalism, experimen-

tal architects attempt solutions that enable culturally specific urban practices and provide aesthetic continuity despite the rapid demolition of new
structures due to shifting market priorities for space. They are creating
innovative designs as alternatives both to kitsch, with its stock emotions and
instantly identifiable themes, and to a global architecture devoid of local
characteristics. In hastily transforming cities where architectural images are
rapidly reproduced and circulated, experimental Chinese architects focus
more on the spatial and temporal effects than on the monumentality of the
architectural edifice. In chapter 2 I discuss debates over urban aesthetics
that emerged as the market increasingly defined cultural production. I trace
the global and domestic impact of neoliberalism, to contextualize the cultural debate over the "loss of humanist spirit" in the 1990s and the birth of
urban cultural studies in late-twentieth-century China as a means of recov-
ering it. I attribute the rise of cultural studies to a Leftist rejection of
Weberian specialization and depoliticization of the intellectual in an urban
market economy.

The subsequent sections address three dimensions of the postsocialist
"urban subject": the city as subject, urban subjectivity, and the subject as
citizen. In part 2 I examine how China's two major cities are imagined in
very different ways: Beijing as a space for performing identity, and Shanghai
as a space to be consumed. The disparate aesthetics of these two major cities
suggests their very different histories and characters. Shanghai, like Taipei
and Hong Kong, is best described as a hybrid "glocal city," a city which
attends simultaneously to the forces of globalization in identity formation
and to what Roland Robertson describes as the reconstruction of "locality"
in the same process. Beijing, on the other hand, is seemingly organic and
unitary, identified with its long history as the imperial and national capital of
an ancient civilization. Where the aesthetics of both cities converges is in
their profound ambivalence vis-à-vis urban modernity.

In chapter 3 I discuss the Wang Shuo and Wang Xiaobo phenomena that
engender a postsocialist "xin jingwei" ("New Beijing flavor"), informing an
aesthetic which performs Beijing identity on behalf of the nation. After
sketching the transformation of Beijing's urban fabric and demographics, I
analyze the performance of postsocialist national identity in Qiu Huadong's novel City Tank (1996), Wang Xiaoshuai's film Frozen (1997), and
late-twentieth-century works by conceptual and performance artists. Beijing cultural production of the 1990s exhibits a gradual shift away from
preoccupation with conceptual conflicts between artifice and nature, tech-

nology and spirituality, modernity and tradition, West and East, to identity grounded in the hybrid effects of these cultural admixtures. In chapter 4 I examine a corpus of works—including the artist Shi Yong's *Shanghai Visual Identity Project* (1997–2007), the filmmaker Lou Ye's *Suzhou River* (2001), and the novelist Wang Anyi's *Song of Everlasting Sorrow* (1996)—that reveal an aesthetics of simulacra. I trace how the post-Mao resurrection of the Shanghai dream of middle-class consumption exploded during the city's post-Deng transformation into virtual forms of consumption that find aesthetic expression.

In part 3 I question how subjectivity is produced by space, examining cultural aesthetics that portray not so much the external signs of the city as the city internalized in the consciousness of the individual; in other words, these works explore the psychic rather than material topology of the city. I scrutinize the production of subjectivity in relation to psychic theories of ego and gender, and the impact of market utilitarian ethics on everyday life and notions of urban citizenry. In chapter 5 I examine complex dynamics between urban space and the construction of subjectivity and gender in four novels set in Shenzhen, Shanghai, and Beijing. Liu Heng's *Black Snow* (1988), Sun Ganlu's *Breathing* (1993), Chen Ran's *Private Life* (1996), and Mian Mian's *Candy* (2000) privilege an interiorized subjectivity where postsocialist urban history, memory, and space induce melancholy and loss, figured in relation to the gendered categories of the feminine, the homosexual, and the narcissist. Finally, in chapter 6 I analyze the narrative ethics in the urban fiction of the 1990s, wherein characters negotiate postsocialist ethical terrain defined by the utilitarian logic of the market. Novels by Qiu Huadong, Zhu Wen, and He Dun are dominated by one of the key questions debated by ethical philosophers: the relationship between individual morality and the social good. Although satisfactory ethical answers to their characters' foibles do not readily present themselves, these authors persistently probe a variety of thorny ethical issues dominating everyday life in postsocialist China.

During the course of this book I identify three major trends in postsocialist Chinese urban aesthetics. I suggest that despite neoliberal urban development's undeniable devastation of ecological systems and cultural heritage, it has also fostered new realms of agency by provoking creative solutions to urban development, new forms of critical engagement, and nascent civic governance. Chinese urban aesthetics (the practices of artists, intellectuals, and urban designers) increasingly underscore the importance of more holistic forms of design and intellectual inquiry that make explicit the dynamics between scientific and economic theories and the ethical, social, and environmental resources that sustain them. Ultimately I suggest that as urban development dominates questions of global sustainability, Chinese urban aesthetics and the dilemmas posed by the postsocialist city extend beyond the historical modern dilemma of "whither China?"

Conceiving the Postsocialist City

Designing the Postsocialist City

Urban Planning and Its Discontents

> Kublai Khan does not necessarily believe everything Marco Polo says when he describes the cities visited on his expeditions, but . . . only in Marco Polo's accounts was Kublai Khan able to discern, through the walls and towers destined to crumble, the tracery of a pattern so subtle it could escape the termites' gnawing.
>
> Italo Calvino, *Invisible Cities*

Italo Calvino's classic montage on the character of cities opens with the eloquent insight that urban essence lies in the intangible. The aptly titled *Invisible Cities* suggests that a city is not so much its physical structure as the movements of its inhabitants, the impressions it imparts to its visitors, the odors and hums oozing from its cracks, its timeless pattern so subtle it can escape the termites' gnawing. Identifying the urban, embedded in but ultimately transcending the material, is the subject of this chapter. Defining the quality of the city has become one of the most pressing issues in China today, and it has global consequences. A civilization that has for millennia maintained a population that is nearly 90 percent rural, China's physical and cultural attachments to the soil are visibly transforming as its urban population moves into the majority by 2010.

To contextualize the roles of urban cultural studies, literature, film, and art in the modern urban landscape, I begin with a broad overview of the issues involved in urban development in China. I examine what Henri Lefebvre theorized as the "urban question" of late capitalism, conditions whereby urbanism rationalizes space as a neutral object to be acted on, rather than as a lived realm with social and political implications. Accordingly, I attend to the capitalist dynamics of *chaiqian*, or "demolition and relocation," with its attendant domestic and international demographic flows and concomitant creation of civilization mixes in the new Chinese city. I also address the manifest challenges of planning the postsocialist Chinese city, which are partially due to the city's function as a capital accumulation fix in the transition from a planned to a market economy. Finally, I detail the critiques such forms of urban development have incited among artists and intellectuals, as well as the new forms of civic agency they have engendered among activists.

Edward Soja and Henri Lefebvre theorize the production of space to the exclusion of place, yet a primary source of conflicted sentiment over postsocialist urbanism derives precisely from the merger of these two processes, in what Peter Taylor calls the "place-space tension" between the producers of space and the makers of place.[1] Do the tensions infusing China's new urban spaces harbor new civil possibilities or exacerbate social conflict? Do they create opportunities for creative aesthetic continuities or threaten to annihilate local cultures? How does the conflict between the panoptic representation of the city promoted by modernist planning, "the obsession . . . with appearances that are *zhengqi* (uniform and orderly)," and a Lefebvrian anthropological vision of the city as a socially constructed "space of representation" that is shaped, experienced, and transformed through everyday practices play out in China?[2] To answer such questions my analysis of urban aesthetics is informed by observations and material from site visits and interviews with urban artists, intellectuals, and practitioners, including architects, planners, and officials.

Identifying the Urban

One reason to redefine the Chinese urban is physical necessity. In 1997 China's registered urban population was 350 million (30 percent of the total), but "by the year 2030, when China's population is expected to be between 1.7 and 2 billion, China will have reached the urbanization rate of semi-industrialized countries (30% rural and 70% urban), and 1 to 1.3 billion rural people will have reorganized their lives in an urban way."[3] Although China's urbanization remains limited relative to industrialized nations, the absolute volume of the urban population is extremely large. These demographic realities led former Minister of Civil Affairs Doje Cering to announce in 2000 a plan to build four hundred new cities in twenty years.[4] Qiu Baoxing, Vice Minister of the PRC Ministry of Construction, remains adamant that "China's urbanization is good for the world" because it absorbs hundreds of thousands of rural migrants who might otherwise emigrate elsewhere, "but we certainly cannot develop like the U.S. or we will need three globes to support China."[5] Given that China already supports 22 percent of the world's population with only 7 percent of its arable land and water resources, its accelerated urban development is occurring at a time in history when new understandings of the urban are required.

The urban question also arises from the unique social and material forms of China's postsocialist cities. For example, globalization has introduced into China the concept of free-standing housing, with its concomitant notions of autonomy and privacy. Yet studies by David Bray and others suggest that the highly regulated spatial forms of the walled socialist work unit are replicated to a degree in gated communities.[6] Again, much has been written about new spaces of consumption in the postsocialist Chinese city, which have proliferated in size, scope, and functions vastly different from the more highly regulated market areas in imperial and socialist urban layouts.[7] Yet Duanfang Lu concludes in her study of Chinese urban form that "scarcity seems to be forever haunting modern society" despite the "world of boundless desire" provoked by the material abundance of the postsocialist era.[8] She cites, as an example, the national campaign of building "a conservation-minded society" (*jieyuexing shehui*) launched in 2004. Economic privatization also incites questions about social privations from resultant urban forms that destroy communal life. Recent translations into Chinese of classics in urban sociology, such as *The Death and Life of Great American Cities*, attest to an intensifying question in China: what is it about the city that gives it its lifeblood?[9]

There is no absolute way to define a city. A human settlement becomes more "urban" as it becomes more dense and, often, more diverse in its population. Density causes dissimilar people to interact, often radically challenging conventional views. Most urbanites must either abandon their traditional ways or increase their knowledge of and commitment to them by becoming more creative and skillful. While the synergy of human potentialities in a vibrant city can lead to advances in governance, science, technology, education, the arts, and culture, too much innovation too quickly can result in disorientation and destruction. A team of Swiss and Chinese planners involved in modernizing Kunming thus succinctly queried, "How much innovation is needed to accommodate the new needs and values of urbanites? How much of the existing must be preserved for the city to keep its identity and keep its inhabitants from becoming homeless?"[10] In the team's bilingual report, the Chinese planners translated "prevent homelessness" as "retain a sense of belonging [*rengyou yizhong guishugan*]." This drives the point home with force. The urban is more than the "housing" and other structures that form the tangible features of a city; it is ultimately a question of "home," a question of where people not only situate themselves physically, but identify with spiritually. The legendary architect Liang Sicheng clearly recognized the organic character of the city. Lying on his sick bed, in 1970, after having been persecuted, during the Cultural Revolution, for his "bourgeois plan" to preserve the old city of Beijing, he lamented to his wife, Lin Shu, "People today don't understand that a city is a living organism with a circulatory system and nervous system; if we don't treat it as such it will die."[11]

Italo Calvino was similarly concerned that his readers recall the animate nature of the city. *Invisible Cities*, published in 1972, imagines a semiotics of space which places late-capitalist urban developments, precedents for China's postsocialist urbanization, in sharp relief.[12] Calvino constructs his theory of city life through eighteen dialogues between the emperor and the traveler which explore many positions, ultimately undermining the dogmatic certainty of Enlightenment knowledge structures. In one dialogue, Kublai Khan says, "And yet I have constructed in my mind a model city from which all possible cities can be deduced. It contains everything corresponding to the norm. Since the cities that exist diverge in varying degrees from the norm, I need only foresee the exceptions to the norm and calculate the most probable combinations."[13] Marco Polo proposes an alternative: "I have also thought of a model city from which I deduce all the others. It is a city made only of exceptions, exclusions, incongruities, contradictions. If such a city is the most improbable, by reducing the number of abnormal elements, we increase the probability that the city really exists. So I have only to subtract exceptions from my model, and in whatever direction I proceed I will arrive at one of the cities which, always as an exception, exist. But I cannot force my operation beyond a certain limit: I would achieve cities too probable to be real."[14]

The emperor's belief that it is possible to categorize all cities relative to a comprehensive master plan replicates claims to scientific rationalism that dominate urban planning in China today. Polo repeatedly exposes the epistemological limitations of totalizing models by revealing the faulty logic on which they are based. As H. S. Becker points out in his analysis of the urban sociology of *Invisible Cities*, "The dialogical format encourages this indeterminacy. We are not reading a treatise which comes to a conclusion, but rather a discussion in which alternatives are considered, weighed, tried out, rejected, surpassed, and returned to. The dialogues explore but do not resolve the 'methodological' problem of how to understand a city."[15]

Calvino's sociological fiction was strongly influenced by the Italian architect Aldo Rossi, who, in *The Architecture of the City* (1966), criticized contemporary architectural practices that failed to value the city as an entity constructed over time, as a repository of "collective memory." For many twentieth-century planners and architects, the abstract notion of space as tabula rasa took precedence over place as socially constructed through historical practices and cultural memory. Leftist intellectuals theorized the late capitalist city as fluid, transient, and abstract, giving rise to Lefebvre's provocative notion that capitalism found new inspiration in the conquest of space rather than of territory. Critical of the long-held belief, perpetuated by Georges Haussmann (1809–91), that one could change society by transforming the urban environment, Lefebvre was especially attentive to the new ways in which such Enlightenment rationality was used to justify spatial conquests by global capitalists. In his essay "The Urban Illusion" (1970), a precursor to his opus, *The Production of Space* (1974), Lefebvre denounces the oft-repeated notion that urbanism refers to the "physical trace on the land of human dwellings of stone, cement, or metal," defining it instead as "a superstructure of neocapitalist society, a form of 'organizational capitalism,' which is not the same as 'organized capital'—in other words, *a bureaucratic society of controlled consumption*."[16] Scott Lash and John Urry later theorized this late stage of capitalism as a transition from "organized capital" to "disorganized capital," while Manuel Castells saw it as a movement toward the "space of flows" of the "informational city."[17] Under such conditions, where space was becoming objectified as a disembodied other to be acted on, Lefebvre saw urbanism as pernicious: "Urbanism appears as the vehicle for a limited and tendentious rationality in which space, deceptively neutral and apolitical, constitutes an object."[18] It is precisely the pseudo-rationalism informing the urban economy of controlled consumption that Chinese cultural critics target today.

In 1970 Lefebvre predicted that the problematic of urbanism would far surpass our understanding of it. Three decades later the Dutch architect Rem Koolhaas declared with characteristic rhetorical flourish that a "maelstrom of modernization is destroying everywhere the existing conditions in

Asia and creating a completely new urban substance [while] the urban seems to be least understood at the very moment of its apotheosis."[19] Defining the urban in China, in particular, is complicated by several factors. The first is that China's urbanization is occurring during the height of global capitalism, and the vexing issues addressed by Leftists such as Lefebvre and Calvino are thus more relevant than ever. The dynamics governing China's postsocialist urban transformation are firmly embedded in interrelated global processes extending far beyond local systems, a consequence of the interplay of exogenous and endogenous forces that include the shift from Fordist to post-Fordist modes of production, the emergence of flexible accumulation systems, the spread of transnational corporations as a consequence of "time-space" compression, and the rise of neoliberalism.[20] The economists Martin Hart-Landsberg and Paul Burkett argue that, as a result of these global capitalist dynamics, China's market reforms can no longer be contained by the elites.[21]

While its prevalence is contested, there is no question that many of the ideologies and structures attributed to neoliberal urbanism have been influential in China for over two decades. With the proliferation of global neoliberalism, theorists have turned their attention to articulating the neoliberal city.

The neoliberal city is conceptualized first as an entrepreneurial city, directing all its energies to achieving economic success in competition with other cities for investments, innovations and "creative classes." Second, it is a city in which municipal bureaucracies, dedicated to social missions, are progressively replaced by professionalized quasi-public agencies empowered and responsible for promoting economic development, privatizing urban services, and catalyzing competition among public agencies. Decisions are increasingly driven by cost-benefit calculations rather than missions of service, equity and social welfare. Third, it is a city whose residents are expected to behave responsibly, entrepreneurially and prudentially. They are made responsible for their own successes and failures, with the social obligation to make their expected contribution to the collective economic welfare alongside their hard-working fellow citizens.[22]

Each of these characteristics—entrepreneurialism, quasi-privatized public services based on cost-benefit analyses, and an increasingly self-sufficient citizenry—defines the new Chinese city.

The second difficulty in characterizing urbanization in China arises from the fact that it presents historically unprecedented scenarios. Demographic, geographic, social, and economic pressures, coupled with China's history of top-down planning and autocratic social engineering, have engendered a central-government policy that stipulates the building of four hundred new cities with populations of nearly one million or more by the year 2020. The idea that government officials and planners would locate a plot of land, then attempt to build a city from scratch sounds wildly utopian—a Corbusian dream—but it is happening in China at the rate of about twenty cities per year. For all the theoretical debates about whether cities are planned or self-generate organically, most are a combination of the two growth modes. Yet, in China, a significant number of new cities are entirely planned entities, with the question of population a mere afterthought. Some cities are even appearing where nothing but marine life previously existed. In the words of a planner for Lingang, a port city being developed on reclaimed land and designed to support a population of 800,000 by 2020, "If we build it, they will come."[23] Further, as the environmental fallout from shortsighted growth is, belatedly, becoming acknowledged worldwide, China feels increasingly pressured to build these cities and expand existing cities by adopting the latest technology in sustainable development. Additionally, a logistical challenge to defining the Chinese city comes from Reform Era (1978–89) administrative changes which incorporated a city's surrounding counties into its municipality. Ambiguity about the concept of the urban in China exist in part because the area and total population of a municipality often incorporates an area many times larger than that contained within the city's former boundary and the registered nonagricultural population.[24]

The third challenge involves the question of cultural identity. China's cities are once again becoming more diverse ethnically and socioeconomically. Ethnic and class differences are nothing new; China has a long history of synthesizing foreign cultural influences and of resilient social hierarchies. Instead, the most unprecedented cultural challenge will come from its massive demographic transformation from rural to urban. In less than thirty years China will metamorphose from a society organized around the collectivist, agrarian values which had also dominated its urban socialist work units, to a competitive, service-based, postindustrial urban culture. Its cities are increasingly populated by former rural dwellers—a growing minority in existing cities and the majority in newly forming cities—who are rapidly reorganizing their lives in urban ways. The renowned urban theorist John Friedmann suggests that "the most dramatic story of China's transformation during the past twenty-five years has been how significant portions of the country's rural areas have become 'urban' in the many meanings of this elusive term," noting that China's "*in situ* urbanization," as Yu Zhu terms it, "happened only in China and practically nowhere else in the developing world."[25]

Finally, as global exchanges escalate, the challenges presented to officials and planners of China's cities are compounded by competing epistemological models. Limited Maoist era education in the wide variety of planning theories and practices being developed worldwide, over-reliance on the advice of "foreign experts" unfamiliar with local conditions, and crude imitations by local planners of nontransferable plans have resulted in what some have characterized as "chaotic planning practices" in China. These practices have resulted in eyesores and irrational use of resources as well as the needless eradication of valuable heritage architecture. Erratic conservation practices are due in part to the Maoist legacy of condemning the preservation of ancient buildings as "architectural classicism." Further, although Western conservation discourse now circulates in Chinese planning institutes and architectural schools, ideas of "permanence" and "authenticity" continue to play out differently in Chinese culture. In art conservation, for example, Chinese museums tend to prefer reconstruction to conservation, and to favor the freedom to reinterpret the original over slavishly accurate replication. According to Daniel Abramson, this cultural aesthetic dominates Chinese urban planning as well, especially for capital cities: "In reinterpreting the original, [Chinese curators] did not care to distinguish what was new from what was old. The construction of capital cities in China seems to confront a similar problem. While it is important to reaffirm that the current regime is part of an orderly sequence of regimes, i.e., is following certain purportedly-timeless principles, it is just as important to start anew. Only by *rebuilding* the capital, and demonstrating its economic and political might by doing so, can the current regime live up to the glory of its ancestors."[26] This may explain why a significant proportion of Chinese intellectuals and of the public affirm radical redevelopment as progressive and take pride in the new image of their cities even when, or precisely because, it eradicates all that was old and familiar.

The inability to fully comprehend the urban in China today is well illustrated by the ambiguity of the opening sentence in Wu Hung's book *Remaking Beijing*: "As soon as Beijing was made the capital of the People's Republic of China this ancient city reached a fatal moment in its survival."[27] Does "fatal" mean "lethal" or "crucial"? Was Beijing dealt its death blow or set on the path of salvation? Wu Hung never clarifies his position, and urbanists are divided on the subject. While many, such as the urban historian Wang Jun in his bestselling *Chengji* (City records, also translated as *An Evolutionary History of Beijing City*), suggest that Beijing's urban essence has been irrevocably destroyed, others, such as the geographer Victor Sit, see recent developments as perpetuating its traditional social role. In his overview of Beijing city planning from its inception to the late twentieth century, Sit characterizes the traditional Chinese urban form as a utilitarian social setting which also provided a symbolic function for the state in informing and guiding human behavior. Beijing's traditional role as the national center of communication and control, Sit argues, is mirrored in its recent development as a global city at the center of finance and corporate decision making, providing communication and financial controls over material production and consumption, rather than engaging in productive activities.[28] From another perspective, the architectural historian Wu Huanjia, of Tsinghua University, harshly criticizes the Qing emperors' stewardship of Beijing for leaving it essentially unchanged, seeing it as an abdication of their responsibility as rulers.[29] "According to [Wu's] logic," says Abramson, "it is precisely the current destruction and remaking of Beijing that affirms most strongly its permanence as the seat of China's national government."[30] These contradictory interpretations of the remaking of Chinese cities derive from competing perspectives on the meaning of urban forms, which inform ambivalence over urban relocation and identity.

Chaiqian: Demolition, Relocation, and China's Emerging "Civilization Mix"

"The majestic trains roared past, casting beams of dazzling snow-white light over Father's tiny shack. What would the world be like without Father's little shack?"[31] This question, posed by the deceased infant narrator as his body is exhumed for reburial in a place safe from the impending demolition, haunts Fang Fang's award-winning novella *Fengjing* (Landscape, 1987). Her poignant vignette of a dock coolie raising his ten children in the slums of Wuhan spans the eventful years from Mao Zedong's political campaigns through Deng Xiaoping's modernizing reforms in the 1980s. Although the children achieve more material success than their parents, eventually moving out of Henan Shantytown to more respectable locations in Wuhan, something is irrevocably lost in the modernization process. Remarkably, the infant narrator exalts the intolerable conditions wrought by grinding poverty because his question about modernity endures: what *is* the world like without Father's little shack?

Stories expressing similarly ambivalent sentiments abound during the past quarter century of urban development. In Beijing, where over 7,000 lanes (*hutong*) once made up the Old City, most courtyard houses (*siheyuan*) have been systematically destroyed, including the destruction, in 2005, of 800 "old and dilapidated houses" (*weifang*) on legendary Coal Street in the historic Dazhalan area in front of Qianmen. Coal Street is now an access road to the west of the major artery of Qianmen Street, which was transformed into a pedestrian commercial area prior to Beijing's hosting of the Olympic Games in 2008. Hundreds more courtyard homes on the east side of Qianmen, whose history stretches back seven hundred years, through the Ming and Qing dynasties, were bulldozed to make way for an eastern access road. Nanchizi, a pilot project next to the Forbidden City, razed nine hundred ancient homes and relocated thousands of people in 2003. Despite loud protests over low compensation and a formal expression of concern by the United Nations Educational, Science and Cultural Organization (UNESCO), the government forced the project through. Many residents relocated for such projects are willing to move into better housing. Yet some of the elderly, such as Chongwen District resident Fu Zhizheng, who lived for half a century on Defeng Dongxia, a small lane 100 meters long with fifty courtyard houses and several hundred families, resisted. He refused to leave his convenient, familiar neighborhood in a now alienating megalopolis.[32] Similarly, Tanziwan, one of Shanghai's last shantytowns, which covered four million square meters with a mere 3.9 square meters of living space per person, was demolished in 1999, after the government scheduled a $280 million relocation of residents to better constructed and more spacious housing, with an average of 12 square meters per person. Although "not one of the ten thousand families to be relocated refused to move," former resident Yu Jiaotai displays his former house-number plaque in a prominent position in his new house as a reminder of fifty-two years of life in Tanziwan.[33]

Such poignant responses to relocation were featured in China Central Television's documentary series, in 2004, on urban-housing reforms. Like Sixth Generation urban films, new realist fiction, and contemporary urban art, such stories tend not to overdramatize the radical changes experienced by urban residents. Most of the fiction, art, films, and documentaries depicting China's urban demolition share a gritty documentary aesthetic which

Dilapidated *siheyuan* (courtyard houses). Drum Tower, Beijing, 2004. Photo by author.

addresses dislocation anxieties by deconstructing the present with a conspicuous absence of nostalgia. In postsocialist Chinese urban culture, nostalgia itself gets called up, exploited, and treated ironically. Jia Zhangke's
award-winning film *Sanxia Haoren* (Still life, 2006) features a villager
dislocated by the Three Gorges Dam project who jests, "We don't fit into
today's society because we're too nostalgic." When a Hong Kong developer

built a "city of commerce" (*shangcheng*) on the prime downtown real estate of the Central Academy of Fine Arts, the sculptor and instructor Sui Jianguo quipped, "This is not a protest because we are no longer there," in reference to *Ruins* (1995), his installation of chairs, a desk, and bookcases of broken bricks on the demolition site.[34] In *Xiangchou* (Nostalgia, dir. Shu Haolun, 2006), a documentary about the impending "urban reconstruction" of his Shanghai alley neighborhood (*shikumen lilong*), the director-narrator Shu Haolun scoffs at the idea of preservation. "If Da Zhong Li has any chance of being 'preserved' it will only be as a Xintiandi-type yuppie place," says Shu, recoiling at the thought of his three-generation home being redeveloped into a gentrified "New Heaven and Earth" so that tourists can commercially consume Old Shanghai.

The fact that so many unique urban forms and their corresponding lifestyles have been indiscriminately uprooted in Chinese cities, driven by the urgent and understandable need to modernize, has resulted in cultural production best characterized by what Ackbar Abbas (drawing on Paul Virilio) has termed an "aesthetics of disappearance."[35] The detached, raw aesthetic in much contemporary urban literature, film, and art displays what Abbas calls "achronicities," where past and present disappear in each other. Many examples of postsocialist urban art critique the highly contingent, culturally destructive features of China's urban development not by displaying wistful longings for the past, but by demonstrating that the past, as human sentiment, is nonexistent. Other forms of urban art, such as Shi Yong's decade-long *Shanghai Visual Identity Project*, playfully engage the hypermodern urban images and discourse propagated in various municipalities. Very few forms of Chinese urban art unabashedly celebrate urbanization, as did the work of the Italian futurists in the early twentieth century. Whether tongue-in-cheek or austere, an uneasy sense of foreboding pervades most Chinese urban art. The degree to which such works represent popular sentiment is debatable; however, their increased circulation in the mainstream media and public forums is raising general consciousness of the issues at stake in China's urbanization.

The question of forced evictions aside, scenes of relocation convey an emotional connection to home and neighborhood regardless of their material condition. Attachment to home may be a universal sentiment, but it is especially prevalent in a Chinese culture traditionally dominated by strong ties to place.[36] These cultural characteristics are reinforced by historical circumstances, particularly the material deprivations and overcrowding suffered by the older generation, which induced something akin to a "squat-

Gentrified *shikumen* (alley houses). Xintiandi, Shanghai, 2007. Courtesy Steve Mushero.

Ironic nostalgia: Shu Haolun documents the impending demolition of his *shikumen lilong* neighborhood in *Nostalgia* (2006).

Communal life in an alleyway
demolished in 2008. Taixing
Road, Shanghai, 2005.
Photo by author.

ter's mentality," where tiny spaces are fiercely defended, and a "Depression-
era mentality," where nothing with use-value is discarded. Most elderly
urban Chinese have lived alongside the same neighbors for decades, in the
tight-knit communities of dense alley housing. Shu Haolun's *Nostalgia*
documents the loss of communal lifestyle habits that were based on Shanghai's *shikumen* layout: children perambulating from rooftop to rooftop,
breakfast peddlers, communal television viewing, mahjong parties, people-
watching in narrow alleys. Likewise, Zhang Yang's film *Xizao* (Shower,
1999) laments the destruction of community ties and Beijing *hutong* practices such as cricket fights, communal bathhouses, go (*weiqi*) matches,
moxibustion treatments, massages, and rice-sprout (*yangge*) fan dances.
Both films intimate that when the elderly are forced to relocate to high-rises,
dementia ensues.

Middle-aged children, meanwhile, often placate their "rooted" elders
while escaping to their modern lifestyles in the suburbs. Even those who
appreciate the aesthetics, history, and convenience of China's older neighborhoods can feel uncomfortable settling there. Many middle-aged Chinese long for the comparatively quiet, orderly, spacious, secure, clean, and,

Award-winning renovated courtyard housing still lacks privacy. Chrysanthemum Lane, Beijing, 2005. Photo by author.

above all, private lifestyles afforded by residence in high-rise, townhouse, gated, and villa communities. The experience of He Hongyu, a Beijing native and Tsinghua School of Architecture graduate, and her husband, Joe Carter, a Canadian-born architect and long-term Beijing resident, is illustrative. Although they lived from 1993 to 2003 in the courtyard-style houses in Chrysanthemum Lane (Ju'er Hutong), for which the Tsinghua professor Wu Liangyong won a UN Habitat prize for innovative design in 1998, He Hongyu insisted on moving to a high-rise apartment near the Third Ring Road. Carter explained her sentiments: "While it allowed my children and I to enjoy the *hutong* of old Beijing, my wife, who had grown up on Gold Earth (Holy Land) Lane, not far away, was tired of the cramped conditions and lack of green space."[37]

While some of the elderly, known as "stubborn nails," may resist relocation, many younger residents "go willingly, glad to swap a cramped life of foul communal toilets and smoky coal stoves for spacious flat with private bathrooms and central heating."[38] Western media reports tend to play up human-rights abuses, but circumstances governing relocation can be quite complicated. In some cases residents are eager to move but resist, hoping to generate media coverage in order to negotiate more favorable compensation packages. For example, in December 2006 National Public Radio (NPR) aired a story on residents evicted from the 1928 Art Deco Capitol Building (near the Bund on the corner of Huqiu Road and South Suzhou Road), the first edifice in the city to accommodate offices and apartments over a theater (the air-conditioned, 1,000-seat Capitol Theatre).[39] Rockefeller Group International (a Mitsubishi subsidiary) and the government-affiliated New Huangpu Group Real Estate Company planned to reopen the theater and redevelop the rest of the building as high-end retail property. The NPR correspondent Louisa Lim reported that a handful of residents refused to move because they were being offered a mere one-sixth of the market value as compensation. As she later learned, Huangpu Group had initially offered residents compensation of 20,000 to 30,000 yuan per square meter, which most accepted as a reasonable package, but a minority stonewalled, hoping to get a higher offer. Their tactic backfired, and these holdouts were offered a mere 6,000 yuan per square meter in compensation.[40] Nonetheless, even the higher compensation figures were below market value, and this shady real-estate transaction is allegedly one of many illegal schemes orchestrated by Shanghai Communist Party Secretary Chen Liangyu, deposed for corruption on 25 September 2006. Further, the most vocal activists went into hiding to avoid arrest by the police when they were forcibly evacuated on 2 January 2007.[41] Evictions are complicated, and conflicts more often arise over economic benefit than over attachments to "home," "history," or "neighborhood." For example, residents of historic West Street in Quanzhou, Fujian, "actually prefer the favorable compensation that accompanies large-scale redevelopment, and do not share the planning authority's view of the street's historic value."[42]

On the other hand, compensation is a vital issue. Many residents of older neighborhoods are unemployed, elderly, and ill, often on fixed incomes. If the compensation does not allow them to relocate to an affordable apartment with convenient access to hospitals and markets, their very survival is jeopardized, and yet many new housing developments lack the necessary transportation and services infrastructure to create a livable community. As a result, many refuse to move. As of 7 February 2007, for example, only 60 percent of the residents in the Da Zhong Li neighborhood in Shanghai's Jing An District had accepted the developer's compensation package, nearly half resisting for reasons of financial and emotional security.[43] While artists and the media reveal the social and economic costs incurred by market-driven urbanization, the "official" representation claims that residents relo-

Bas-relief celebrates relocation to a Greco-Roman–style gated community. Shanghai Urban Planning Exhibition Hall, 2007. Photo by author.

cate cheerfully. Government propaganda slogans slung prominently over demolition sites encourage residents to rise to the task patriotically, glossing over the profit motive for such projects.[44] A graphic illustration of the government's one-sided portrayal of the controversial issues surrounding relocation is displayed in the lobby of the Shanghai Urban Planning Exhibition Hall. Large bas-reliefs depict the demolition of old neighborhoods, with grateful residents and their modern appliances relocating out to upscale housing signified by the Greco-Roman gates at the entrance to their new estates.

Another social dynamic created by urban relocation is the formation of new socioeconomic and ethnic relationships. Residential mobility rates in urban China are substantially lower than the American rate of 20 percent per annum, but in the more open economies such as Guangzhou and Shenzhen they have approached Western Europe's rates of 7–9 percent per annum.[45] This leaves a rather eclectic mix of residents living in the traditional housing stock that remains in China's major city centers. The majority of these residents are elderly, low-income locals who are unable to move and migrants living many to a dark, cramped, rented room, along with a small minority of foreigners and Chinese who purchase and reno- vate older homes to reside in, work in, or rent out.[46] Many expatriates, some alienated from their own experiences of growing up in sterile suburbs and therefore appreciative of mixed-use urban communities, are eager to live in historic neighborhoods. A growing number of Chinese urban professionals are starting to move back to the city center because they find the urban lifestyle more hip, stimulating, and convenient. The result is highly diverse cultural and socioeconomic neighborhoods, although these communities are in constant flux due to a transient population and rampant development.

The residential mix in a 1930s Western-style (*yangfang*) apartment building on Yanqing Road, formerly Route Mayen in the French Concession in Shanghai, illustrates this diversity. The following figures are close approximations that demonstrate the differences in scale and price structures in 2006. Half of the building is owned by a European family who purchased the three-story, 300 sq m (3,252 sq ft) flat for $800,000 in 2004 and resided there before renting it to a South Asian family in 2007. The first two floors of the other half are occupied by long-term Shanghai residents— extended families share the several rooms on each floor—who rent from the state for $12 per month per 30 sq m (325 sq ft). An American family rents for $500 per month the partially renovated top floor, which is 80 sq m (865 sq ft), from its former residents of thirty years, who purchased the apartment from the state well under market value in 1994 and moved in 2004 to a high-rise in Minhang District. A small building addition in the alley and its tiny loft (*gelou*) is occupied by a young family and their fellow villager from Anhui Province, who rent from a local resident for $40 per month to operate a hair salon, which charges fifty cents per hair cut.[47] Most of the migrants' domestic activities, such as washing, cooking, eating, socializing, television viewing, are conducted in the open air of the alley. Other migrants, who operate a breakfast stall in a cramped alley down the street, set up shop later in the day in this more spacious alley to sell rice, socialize, and relax. Yanqing Road also includes renovated *shikumen* alley houses populated by middle-class Chinese and foreigners; Western-style houses transformed into law firms, art studios, business offices, fashion boutiques, and restaurants; storefront massage parlors cum brothels that house young migrant women and hair salons that house young migrant men; bed-sized living spaces in cloistered alleys rented to migrant domestic workers; 1930s garden homes (designated by the municipality as "heritage housing"), some still occupied by their state-owned *danwei* (such as an operative pulmonary clinic), some privately owned, purchased for around $2.5 million by expatriates whose children are bussed to exclusive international schools.

A migrant family resides in a tiny loft next to longtime residents and foreigners in a diverse neighborhood. Yanqing Road, Shanghai, 2006. Photo by author.

Migrant workers, generally portrayed as having been "cleansed" from the global Chinese city, are far more integrated into this downtown neighborhood community.[48] They are sometimes bullied in typical fashion as "outsiders" (*waidiren*), but, given the shifting context of who now constitutes an "outsider," they are increasingly defended from such attacks by their neighbors and the local police. On an autumn day in 2006 I witnessed a confrontation between an Anhui barber (a one-year resident of Yanqing Road) and a long-term resident across the street who bullied the barber without cause, slandering him as an "outsider," punching him in the face and hurling a brick through the glass door of his salon. A large neighborhood crowd of mixed classes, ethnicities, and nationalities poured into the street to assess the drama. In the end the long-term resident was roundly denounced by neighbors as a "hooligan" (*liumang*), was arrested by the police, and was forced to pay 2,200 yuan ($280) in compensatory damages. Early the next morning the bully, having lost face, demanded a haircut from the badly bruised barber, but an elderly Shanghainese neighbor immediately intervened, calling on her son to haul the "hooligan" away from the wronged migrant. While this incident certainly does not discount the prevalence of

Migrant workers mix with longtime residents. Yanqing Road, Shanghai, 2006.
Photo by author.

social and systemic prejudice and injustice suffered by migrant workers, it
does call attention to specific identity formations within the city in question.
In global cities, as Jennifer Jordan suggests, "there is a spectrum from the
highly homogenized and interchangeable spaces of consumption and capital to pockets of meaning, memory, and moral narratives about right and
wrong."[49] And, indeed, the incident in question turns the conventional
depiction of migrants on its head: a member of the "floating population"
(*liudong renkou*)—with its negative connotations in a traditionally rooted
society—is defended by long-term urban residents against one of its members who is, in turn, labeled a *liumang*, literally a "floating commoner."[50]

Stereotypes in the media and popular discourse tend to portray migrants
as lowering the quality of life in the city by making it less safe, less sanitary,
and less cultured, characterizing them as a vast and unkempt horde of
ignorant outsiders who pour "blindly" into the cities, bringing dirt, disor-
der, and crime. However, as the Yanqing Road incident illustrates, long-
held notions of "insider" and "outsider" are slowly breaking down, at least
in certain neighborhoods, as the Chinese city becomes more mobile and
diverse. Demographic shifts and renovations in neighborhoods such as the
Yanqing Road area, which is in Shanghai's former "upper quarter" (*shang-
jiao*), do not comply with conventional understandings of globalized gen-

trification, in that "inner-city neighborhoods were never 'downtown' in a socialist city despite the signs of urban decay in certain parts . . . and have retained the self-image of being in the 'upper quarter' (uptown) since the 1949 revolution."[51] Residents, regardless of class, share a certain social status from the historic prestige of their neighborhood, yet many also retain the memory of being oppressed themselves (due to "wrong" class backgrounds, the ubiquity of colonial forms, etc.), and thus do not necessarily lay claim to their neighborhood in the strict terms of exclusivity.

The transprovincial and transnational, if transitional, socioeconomic cultural mixes forming in the older sections of China's cities have not been much theorized. Instead, most scholarly attention has been devoted to a more prevalent development, the unprecedented degree of suburbanization that has taken place since the mid-1990s.[52] In contrast to the more fluid socioeconomic diversity present in many urban neighborhoods, China's new suburban developments feature more highly segregated spatial arrangements, resulting in "golden ghettos" for the very rich and "migrant enclaves" for rural workers.[53] The concomitant psychological segregation of rural "outsiders," some argue, replicates the "internal colonialism" that occurred during the late Qing, whereby the interaction between the core and periphery results not in a reduction but in an increase in regional inequalities.[54] Gated communities allow a wealthy community to be built contiguous to dilapidated migrant housing, leaving economic classes sharply delineated. Migrants sometimes live in temporary accommodations built to house construction workers, but more often they reside in houses within "urban villages" (*chengzhongcun*, "village within a city") that are rented from the local "rural" population as urban sprawl overtakes formerly rural villages.

The complex identity formation among these new urban dwellers has been explored by a number of scholars. Some have found that, hardships notwithstanding, first-generation migrants express optimism about their experience, their perseverance fostered by pride and satisfaction at gaining a degree of independence, by their improving social status, and by their ability to accumulate greater social capital than their rural peers. Arianne Gaitano argues that although migrant domestic workers remain outsiders in the city, "these women begin to form new relationships in urban areas while strengthening ties to the village, accruing *guanxi* with employers, migrant peers, and co-villagers alike, and thus are never wholly social outsiders."[55] Similarly, Tiantian Zheng concludes that rural women working as bar hostesses feel empowered by their urban profession: "Their manipulation of rural women's images not only enables hostesses to be-

A migrant worker cycles past Viscaya, a Spanish-motif gated community. Pudong, Shanghai, 2005. Photo by author.

come active commodity consumers and debunk their images as country bumpkins, but also gives them access to their clients' social networks in order to reap cultural capital, social advancement, and economic security."[56] Social integration of migrants in the cities has been aided by initiatives such as UNESCO's "Together with Migrants" project, carried out from 2002–2007 in partnership with the Chinese Academy of Social Sciences to provide vocational training, career counseling, family planning, health training, and rights-awareness training for migrant workers nationwide. The project also addressed urban poverty, social and economic exclusion, national and local policy making, human rights, and discrimination against migrant workers, by raising public awareness of their plight and rights as citizens through the media, debates, exhibitions, and film screenings.[57]

While the social integration of first-generation migrants to the city poses tremendous challenges, the identity formations among their children—second-generation urban dwellers—are perhaps even more sobering. Preliminary research on teenagers enrolled in migrant schools in Shanghai, for example, indicates that these youth have internalized the prejudice to which they are regularly subjected. Those born in villages no longer identify with their rural roots, having absorbed the pragmatic consumer values of the city, while those born in Shanghai remain "outsiders" in the city, yet have no emotional attachments to their parents' village homes. The social implications of this identity crisis are profound. The teens do not consider a return to the countryside to be an option, but they hardly aspire to the lives of their parents, who take the hardest jobs with the lowest pay to eke out a living for themselves, their children, and their rural relatives. Unlike their rural peers, who are motivated to study hard in order to one day achieve success in the city, migrant teens are perceived as, and perceive themselves to be, the dregs of urban society. Cynical and devoid of utopian fantasies, they seriously underperform and are lacking in goals, ideals, and motivation.[58]

The national government is attempting to remedy the problem in part by enacting structural change. Although the children of migrant workers were previously barred from attending public schools in the cities where their parents work, a national mandate issued in 2006 required that cities provide public education for these children. This has created its own problems, however, as hundreds of "illegal" schools have closed down without ensuring proper placement of their students in public schools. Beijing schools were earmarked for closings in 2006, but the process stalled due to public complaints and charges of human-rights violations by nongovernmental organizations (NGOs) and legal experts. Guangzhou adopted a strategy of having the municipality purchase migrant schools and convert them into public schools, while Hangzhou is extending technical assistance to its schools in order to bring them up to standards. In 2006 Shanghai quietly closed 16 of its 293 schools, squeezing some schools out of the central city into the periphery, with an aim of integrating 70 percent of migrant workers' children into public schools by 2010. But a high-profile closing of its largest migrant school resulted in widespread criticism in the national media. On 8 January 2007, after school had started for 2,000 primary students, over one hundred police officers and local security officials stormed the school's courtyard and cordoned off the site, terrifying the children and staff.[59] If the intent of the new law is to provide migrant children with improved conditions for their education and to integrate them more fully into urban society, better procedures for actualizing these aims are clearly required.

As neoliberal market priorities for space result in the rapid demolition of neighborhoods and structures, complex spatial practices that both deconstruct and reinforce postcolonial geopolitical categories are forming from the attendant demographic flows. These flows create new cultural identifications among rural migrant workers that can cut across class lines.

Real estate advertisements promote cosmopolitan identities. Pudong, Shanghai, 2005. Photo by author.

New spatial forms and demographic flows also induce transnational cultural identifications manifest in material and nonmaterial forms among the new rich. Most middle-class Chinese relocate to high-rise communities in districts bordering the city center, with the richest living in apartments, townhouses, and single-family homes within luxury villas developed on prime downtown real estate or in outlying suburbs. Gated communities house wealthy Chinese from mainland China, Hong Kong, Taiwan, and Singapore, *haigui* (mainland Chinese who have returned from overseas), and corporate expatriates on short-term contracts. Residents have private drivers or drive their own cars, send their children to private or international schools, shop at hypermarkets (such as the French chain Carrefour), and frequent on-site sports clubs and golf courses.

Property developers in these locales promote cosmopolitan identities to attract buyers. For example, in 2005 upscale communities in a three-block section of Pudong's Jinqiao development zone posted the following street signs, development markers, and property advertisements: "Build First-Class Projects and Contribute to the International Biyun Fashionable Community," "Love Nature, Love Life," "Viscaya, A Living Resort," "Greenhills: A Healthy Villa of Great Worth," "Green Court: A Villa You Can Breathe In,"

"Diamond Villa: A Classic Collectors Item for the Ages," "Relish Biyun Slowly," "Elegant Silence," "A Truly Elegant and Relaxing Lifestyle," and "Fairylike Shanghai: Charm the World." Urban property managers nationwide market nature, peace, clean air, health, relaxation, luxury, connoisseurship, community, fashion, exoticism, and cosmopolitanism. Some housing developments highlight their foreign design principles, such as the "Orange County" townhouse community in northern Beijing, designed by "three genuine American architectural firms who 'inject many brand new and advanced international design *linian* [concepts] into the project.' "[60] Many buy into, both literally and figuratively, the rhetoric promoting new housing developments, embracing the identities expressed in the ads. What types of identities are forming in gated communities throughout China?

Similar to the eclectic cultural mix in older neighborhoods, but without the corresponding mix of socioeconomic classes, is an emerging "civilization mix," studies suggest, in the interpenetration between globalized culture and local civilization in upscale communities in China. Girard Giroir describes the Fontainebleau Villas (Fengdan bailou bieshu) in the Nanhui District of Shanghai as a mélange of architectural styles such as American Victorian, Royal Dutch, Portman, and the Mies, situated in Song dynasty garden settings. Giroir gives two possible readings of the cultural mix of this microterritory. One is that it offers an expression of multiform postmodern urbanism by combining the best of Western and Chinese traditions: "Truly exceeding each other, they may be a favorable synthesis between the Western art of building and the Chinese cosmological conception, between Western individualism and Chinese metaphysics."[61] Such aesthetic interpretations are fairly common. Liu Xinwu, for example, cites the China World Trade Center in Beijing as evidence of a successful cultural synthesis: "As long as the location is favorable, and foreign architectural language is used fluently, it enhances the appealing 'solid poetry' of China's vast land."[62] Giroir's second reading of Fontainebleau Villas sees the diversity of the architectural elements as lacking coherence.

> The naming of the housing complex, clashing with the nature of the architectural style, the absence of a dominant model of villas, and a patchwork scenery on a micro-scale sustain deep confusion and result in a true palimpsest. . . . The whole lot is part of the general trend of the "disneylandization" of urban forms. The Fontainebleau Villas are based on a dual amnesia. Enhancing the image of France makes one forget the colonial past, present in the French concession for a long time. Likewise,

the reference to the France of the Ancien Regime is politically incorrect in a Marxist-Leninist context based in part on the break with feudalism.[63]

While rhetorically suggestive, what Giroir overlooks in such a reading is that China has long since moved past the ideological purity that dominated socialist aesthetics and has, during its postsocialist era, returned to a syncretism that recalls its long history of Sinocizing foreign cultural elements. Further, in accordance with naming conventions everywhere, the villa name resonates on multiple levels at a remove from the original site. The term "Fontainebleau" became associated with Western luxury in Shanghai as early as 1979, when a painting exhibition of School of Fontainebleau masters was held in the former China-Soviet Friendship Hall. To use this term in naming the villa, rather than "clashing with the nature of the architectural style," is a calculated market strategy intended to manipulate Occidentalist connotations of opulence.[64] As Fulong Wu points out, "The motifs of classical European architecture and townhouse landscaping are selective and imagined" by necessity, because the extreme competitiveness of China's housing market forces developers to invent ostentatious estates, brand their products, and romanticize the discourse of property advertisement to exploit the niche market of the upwardly mobile urban rich.[65]

Whether one views new urban forms such as Fontainebleau Villas as a harmonious synthesis of Western and Chinese traditions or as a demonstration of identity crisis, such eclectic aesthetic mixes extend beyond housing complexes to China's overall urban planning. The question of what constitutes authentic "Chineseness" emerges repeatedly in critiques of urban planning, landscaping, residential developments, architecture, art, film, literature, drama, fashion, music, and cuisine. Many sources feed the tension over definitions of identity, from Orientalist prescriptions of culture, to a sense of postcolonial belatedness, to feelings that China's urban and social fabric has changed so rapidly it can barely be remembered, let alone historicized. In a climate of economic growth and devolution of power to localities, cities are building central business districts, commercial malls, office complexes, research and industrial parks, museums and libraries, educational facilities, recreational parks, and landmark architecture, with much of this effort aimed at creating a manifestly new identity.

Planning the New Chinese City

The field of urban planning has exploded in the postsocialist era. The sheer amount of building in Chinese cities—approximately a 250 percent increase in total built floor space since 1990—has required rapid restructuring of urban-planning functions, staffing, and relations. Over the past quarter century the number of Chinese universities with planning departments increased over thirty fold, from three in a thousand in 1980 (0.3 percent), to thirty-six in 1990 (3.6 percent), to one hundred in 2006 (10 percent).[66] At the same time, the number of personnel in planning departments increased 400 percent, from a technical staff of 20,000 in the early 1980s to 100,000 in 2006.[67] The stated goals of the Ministry of Construction, which oversees urban and rural planning throughout the country, are to implement strategies for sustainable development; to achieve a well-off society (*xiaokang shehui*); to adopt a scientific view of development; to construct a harmonious society (*hexie shehui*); and to develop a new socialist countryside (*xin shehuizhuyi nongcun*). To achieve these goals the ministry assigns full-time inspectors at national and provincial levels to supervise work in the localities, and requires formal approval of local plans at the provincial level. In practice, however, most planning decisions are made at the level of the municipal urban-planning department and sometimes at the submunicipal level of district, often with very little oversight. Although nominally there is a hierarchical process by which plans are to be approved, "the more detailed plans are often tightly integrated with the development process itself, leaving little distinction between regulation and implementation; local governments often compromise the former in order to achieve the latter."[68] In addition to the difficulty of implementing their plans, planners in China face tremendous challenges in other realms.

A report published in 2004 by China Development Press states categorically that China's urban-planning theory, skills, law, and practice are grossly underdeveloped.[69] The report goes so far as to quote an article by the Tianjin writer Feng Jicai in which he fiercely deprecates officials for destroying China's urban cultural heritage.

> Whether superficially pursuing instant modernization, frenetically accumulating political accomplishments, or purely fixated on economic gain, city administrators have wantonly handed over piece after piece of urban real estate to developers. The vast majority of these officials have absolutely no knowledge of the cultural heritage of these cities, and no

desire to learn about it. So in a mere decade the unique features, historical ethos, and cultural attractions of many cities have been utterly destroyed. The cultural losses are enormous! How many cities in the world preserve their ancient features as a source of pride? We, on the other hand, show off the appalling "marvel" of "changing the map every three months"! It is no exaggeration to state that every single minute a significant portion of our historical cultural heritage is destroyed by an excavator. Yet the distinctiveness of each city is only formed after hundreds and thousands of years of accumulated human creativity.[70]

Many share Feng Jicai's assessment. John Barber, for example, acerbically characterizes the horrors: "In China urban renewal is a Richter-scale event, utterly destroying the past and heaving up proud, sometimes bizarre skylines as the most visible evidence of the country's equally seismic upward eruption in economic activity and living standards. It has already swept away the quintessential imagery of dowdy socialist China, with its crumbling courtyard housing and bleak Soviet-style walkup apartment blocks, its walled work units and tinkling-bell bicycle traffic jams. Now, it is turning the country into the world's most boisterous architectural funhouse."[71]

Hyperbole notwithstanding, the earthquake and funhouse imagery are well worth considering. In an overview of modern Chinese architecture, Peter Rowe and Seng Kuan criticize Chinese municipal officials for destroying the city fabric and obliterating old patterns of life by succumbing to the temptations of global capital: "The pursuit of architectural novelty as more or less an end in itself, a pursuit driven by the very new experience of competitive market forces, ran counter to a long tradition in which outmoded structures were often simply renovated with no attempt to change them. Forced to take on so much, so soon, and with so little preparation, architects in China frequently created buildings uncouth, garish, and incoherent in their appearance and form, as well as downright ugly."[72] Foreign architects, meanwhile, often revel in their unprecedented opportunities to freely experiment in China.[73] A common complaint among Chinese architects and urban planners is that municipal officials, believing that "monks from afar are better at chanting the scriptures" (*yuanlai de heshang hui nianjing*), give the most visible projects to foreign design and planning firms, which lack knowledge of local conditions but charge ten times more than domestic firms.[74]

An alarming result of postsocialist cultural commodification has been the excessive investment in prestigious public-works projects aimed at

Controversial architecture. Top: CCTV Headquarters designed by Rem Koolhaas (model upper left); bottom: National Theatre, a.k.a. "Big Duck Egg," designed by Paul Andreu. Beijing, 2008. Photos by author.

catapulting various cities and towns into international prominence. Cities too often base their claims to be modern on their repertoire of readily recognizable architectural symbols in what Rowe and Kuan call the "theming" of urban environments for local commercial and political gain.[75] In the process municipalities often pursue private (mainly foreign) development interests that, regardless of national goals, behave according to the same patterns that "growth coalitions" have exhibited in cities around the world: "These patterns, as described by urbanist scholars such as M. Christine Boyer, Manuel Castells, Mike Davis, Susan Fainstein, David Harvey, and Saskia Sassen, include most prominently the trivializing and commercializing of local history, the fragmentation and privatization of the public realm, and the catering to business elites and tourists at the expense of local communities and less empowered members of society."[76]

Because it is believed that distinctive architecture and urban design sell and because many of these projects have been contracted to a small elite of internationally renowned architects, the resulting aesthetic tends to be that of "hyper-" or "global" modernity rather than one conceived of in terms of local architectural traditions. Arif Dirlik argues that while "colonial architecture was under some obligation, if only for political reasons, to legitimate itself by answering localized aesthetics[,] . . . global architectural practices . . . seem to derive their aesthetic legitimation not from some commitment to the local but from their ability to represent global capitalism and the consumer clientele they are in the process of creating."[77] Even projects which attempt to answer to local conditions can turn into easily commodified packages, as happened with the award-winning yet controversial Xintiandi project in Shanghai, traditional housing developed for commercial use by the Hong Kong Shui On Group and designed by the American architect Benjamin Woods. Although designers have insisted that the project should not, and cannot, be replicated elsewhere given its basis in Shanghai's *shikumen* lane houses (colonial tenements blending Western and Chinese design elements), cities near (Hangzhou) and far (Ningxia) have begged architects to give them their own "Xintiandi."[78] The American architect Christopher Choa quips that Xintiandi "has become a verb. Developers come to architects and say 'can you Xintiandi this project for me'?"[79] Similarly, local news reports of "Xining's Wangfujing" or "Lanzhou's Pudong" in provinces such as Qinghai or Gansu, led the urban geographer Piper Gaubatz, a specialist in China's western "frontier cities," to question the pursuit in such dissimilar landscapes of isomorphic urban forms established in Beijing and Shanghai.[80]

Domestic scholars blame the chaos in urban planning and architectural style on a series of factors including corruption, lack of proper training, and too superficial an understanding of rapidly imported Western theories. Yan Xiaopei, deputy director of Zhongshan University's Center for Urban and Regional Studies, in Guangzhou, denounces capricious urban officials: "Decision-makers tend to be keen on quick success and instant benefits, so that irrational behavior by developers is allowed, which prevents the enforcement of urban planning."[81] Effective urban planning is further undermined by the limited skills of Chinese planners, who are adept at physical planning but pay less attention to socioeconomic factors. Huang Yan, deputy director of the Beijing Municipal Planning Commission, criticizes comprehensive planning processes for being too static, too focused on physical and land-use plans, and too one-dimensional, without considering other social goals.[82] As for China's minimal conservation of existing urban forms, the Tsinghua University professor Wu Liangyong laments a lack of understanding of restoration among government leaders and the populace: "For many the best that can be done to 'respect tradition' is to use fragmented traditional motifs as decoration on essentially modernist urban designs."[83] As a result, China's most celebrated preservation projects to date have been executed by foreign firms. Further, China's rapidly changing economy and real estate regulations require architects, planners, developers, contractors, and other urban design professionals to adapt to unstable conditions. Ivana Benda, vice president of the Shanghai branch of Allied Architects International, identifies the major challenges to effective urban design in China as "abrupt changes in rules governing the real estate market, a lack of professional knowledge and experience, the limited capabilities of the construction industry, and highly demanding preparation and construction time frames." As a result, she says, "much of the architectural creation in China seems to lack the sophistication of Western counterparts on one or another level."[84]

Legacies from China's own tradition of urban planning also restrict civic culture in the postsocialist Chinese city. Sociologists and historians have long elaborated on the lack of an explicit legal and cultural notion of the public realm in Chinese cities. Wu Hung cites a famous, and misinterpreted, passage by the Ming historian Jiang Yikui, who describes Beijing's Qipanjie (Chessboard Street), an east-west avenue running along the southern Gate of the Great Ming, where "all types of people under Heaven— gentlemen and commoners, workers and merchants . . . with official credentials . . . all gathered here so the place becomes extremely crowded[,] . . . an extraordinary scene of prosperity at the gate of the state." While scholars have read this as an incipient public sphere forming in the marketplace, Wu argues that "in actuality it internalizes a perception that frames the place as a highly politicized space, where an idealized ruling authority is juxtaposed with an idealized subject . . . [and] the 'extraordinary scene of prosperity' [Jiang] describes, while supposedly spontaneous and unmediated, is actually under state surveillance."[85] Daniel Abramson would agree, arguing that "the public embellishments in Chinese cities today do not so much reflect civic pride as symbolize Modernist statism, and also hark back to periods of China's imperial history when planning practice favored symbolic structures and spaces at the expense of small-scale commercial activity and gathering places for a diverse citizenry."[86]

Anne-Marie Broudehoux is especially critical of these state priorities, reflected in the eradication of informal markets such as Beijing's Silk Alley, in the construction of remote, monumental municipal buildings surrounded by vast, empty plazas, and in the attention given to resource-wasting "nightscape" projects. Beijing's demise, she argues, can ultimately be traced to the communist leadership's adoption of Haussmann's "Grand Manner urbanism" and his "blind faith in the power of architecture and urban design."[87] By reducing urban diversity into an easily packaged urban product, she says, urban beautification projects not only alter the meaning and identity of place, but have a depoliticizing effect, distracting attention from inequities by reducing the city to an apparently transparent surface. Concern for face causes cities to squander their limited budgets to meet the expectations of potential investors and visitors rather than those of the more needy local population. She concludes that "the centrality of consumption to the contemporary urban experience has resulted in the neglect of other aspects of city life in urban governance, including the role of the city as a home, a place for self- and collective-representation, and a public sphere where local politics are debated."[88]

One problem with Broudehoux's conclusions is that, while partially true, they fail to historicize contemporary capitalist planning within long-standing Chinese practices of designing urban social space for surveillance and displays of power. David Bray notes that "the basic spatial unit of the new planning regime is the so-called small district (xiaoqu), which in many ways bears an uncanny resemblance to the danwei (socialist work unit) residential compound (shenghuoqu)," social spaces which in turn inherit hierarchical and governance features of China's imperial wards and Confucian walled family compounds.[89] In none of these historical contexts does Chinese urban social organization conceive of the city as a breeding ground for a civil society where representation can flourish. Even the public parks and squares introduced in the twentieth century were intended to display elite and state privilege and power rather than to function as spaces for popular recreation and diverse social expression.[90] Broudehoux also fails to account for the fact that modern Chinese planning practice stems almost exclusively from the design professions, unlike planning in the West which is "derived from two streams or traditions, a rationalist stream flowing from the design professions (architecture, engineering, systems theory) and shaped by positivist thought, and a critique coming from the social sciences . . . that stresses the need for negotiating trade-offs between social and institutional forces in the allocation of public goods."[91]

The rationalist tradition of professional planning, which first took root in China in the early twentieth century through the efforts of Republican Era reformers, has reemerged with a vengeance in the post-Mao period. Most official rhetoric about urbanization continues to perpetuate the idea, denounced in the 1970s by social planning theorists such as John Friedmann and Henri Lefebvre, that urban renewal creates an efficient, productive, functional social order. Take, for example, the general introduction to *A Comparison of Chinese and Foreign City Culture*, a four-volume academic series published in 2002. It begins by establishing the volume's scientific methodology: "Chinese and foreign urban cultures . . . are compared in order to minimize errors in China's urbanization and urban modernization"; it then continues its Enlightenment discourse of progress: "Changes in human society have resulted in two types of groups: groups that walk forward toward the world and the future, and those that conserve the old and preserve the past."[92] The implication of this division, stated explicitly elsewhere, is that the former group progresses by urbanizing, and urbanization equals civilization. Further, this equivalency rigidly quantifies cultural civilization in terms of the level of urbanization. "If the development of Chinese urban culture is to achieve that of developed Western countries, a great deal of effort is still required. In 1848 the level of urbanization in both China and the West was about 10%, however by 1949 China's urbanization remained at 10% while U.S. urbanization was already near 70%. In 2002 the U.S. already completed its urbanization process, surpassing 90%, such that the entire society had entered the stage of post-industrialized suburbs."[93] Such statements imply that China is civilized to the degree that it becomes urban, and urban in a Western, "end of history" sense.

The Czech-Canadian architect Ivana Benda, who is based in Shanghai, elaborates on planning problems resulting from the interplay between Euclidian orthogonal plans and the ward layout of the imperial city.

It is very common in China that urban planners base layouts of vast city areas on regular, rectangular blocks without any reaction to specific features of the local environment and specific roles of streets in the city structure. The resulting extremely wide, straight, and long roads, subdivided into many separate paths for cars, bicycles and pedestrians, create "wide rivers of asphalt." They are very difficult (and sometimes forbidden) to be crossed by foot. Such design affects the city on many levels. It may be seen as the only solution to traffic problems but it does not provide a satisfying urban environment for its citizens and does not offer suitable conditions for many urban functions including commerce. Although the original idea of wide roads and a simple rectangular concept is based on a proper observation that narrow, winding streets cannot handle increasing amounts of cars, when only very wide streets are used the city loses its prime role as a pleasant, lively urban environment. Allowing for very heavy traffic, the streets act as serious barriers for pedestrians. Further, the vast areas of asphalt without any green cover absorb heat from the sun and help to increase temperatures in our cities several degrees during every summer season. That in turn accelerates demands for electric energy for cooling in the worst period of the year.[94]

Such modernist, statist ideals govern much of the planning of new Chinese cities, both in the satellite cities emerging on the outskirts of major metropolises on the eastern seaboard, and in cities in the less-developed western provinces. One example is Lingang New City, located at the southeast tip of Shanghai Municipality in Nanhui District. Not unlike Dubai, which (in "the conquest of space" posited by Lefebvre) created valuable real estate on its man-made Palm and World Islands, Shanghai is building a utopian city on 300 square kilometers of reclaimed land.[95] Lingang aspires to be a worthy complement to its neighboring mega projects, the newly constructed Yangshan Deepwater Port and the East China Sea Bridge which connects Big Yangshan Island and Little Yangshan Island to the mainland, projects jointly "believed to be one of the two largest man-made constructions in the world today, the other being the Three Gorges Dam."[96] The neighboring Lingang New City debuted in March 2006 to much fanfare, with the first phase of construction scheduled to be completed by 2010. It comprises an integral part of the Shanghai Municipality's urban-

Model of Lingang New City. Shanghai Municipality, 2008. Photo by author.

planning system, code-named "1966" for 1 central city, 9 new cities, 60 towns, and 600 key villages.

Lingang's planners are proud of the city's allegorical layout, a small strip of land encircling a perfectly round, manmade freshwater lake said to cover the exact area as the famed West Lake in Hangzhou, with the rest of the city spreading fanlike, inland, away from the lake. Scenic spots surrounding Lake Dishui include Qingdian Square, Qingdian Musical Fountain, Number One Port, and Ocean Viewing Park at the Mouth of Nanhui, which boasts a huge metallic sculpture of a whale. In a fascinating instance of cultural legitimization, the development company memorialized its accomplishments for posterity much as imperial prefecture officials carved their deeds onto ancient steles. At the entrance of the Ocean Viewing Park, two large stone markers in the shape of open books commemorate the locale by situating the megaprojects in the long history of Chinese place lore. Unlike the Monument to the People's Heroes on Tiananmen Square in Beijing, which rewrites traditional Chinese history according to socialist ideals, these local monuments revive myths of place and seamlessly incorporate contemporary feats of capitalist construction into centuries-long tradition, as is clear in excerpts from the books monument, which is titled "A Record of Ocean Viewing Park at the Mouth of Nanhui."

The *locus classicus* for "Nanhui" is the *Former History of the Tang Dynasty*. . . . As the shoreline shifted and land amassed, its shape changed countless times over the centuries. . . . Now, at the start of the twenty-first century in the tide of reform and opening up, the Shanghai International Shipping Center of Yangshan Deepwater Port, the East China Sea Bridge, and Port City were built on this spot, presenting Nanhui a rare opportunity in its one thousand years of growth. As its developers, we brimmed with pride when gazing at our blueprints for Century Embankment, Surround the Lake Strip, the GIS [Geographic Information Systems] center of Dishui Lake, and Port City. At the border of the East China Sea we struggled at our duties like a veritable army. By applying our intelligence and strength to the task, we completed it in three-and-a-half years of arduous work. . . . Our reasons for installing this monument are twofold: first, to memorialize the history of building Port City for its descendents, and second, to entertain visitors. Erected by Shanghai Port City Development Group, Limited, December, 2005

Who these descendents and visitors will be, and whether they will exist decades from now, remains an open question. Situated a remote seventy-five kilometers from downtown Shanghai on reclaimed marshland, which was still drying when I and several urban specialists visited by special permit in November 2006, Lingang nonetheless boasts easy access to five modes of transportation: ocean, river, highway, railway, and air (it is just twenty-five kilometers from Pudong International Airport). Lingang is billed as an equipment-manufacturing base that will house automotive, shipping, logistic, electronic, and aerospace equipment; Liu Jiaping, a vice director of Shanghai Lingang New City Administrative Committee, claims that unlike the prescribed functions of other new cities around Shanghai, such as Anting (automobiles) or Songjiang (industry and education), Lingang is to be a "truly modern city," the sixty-six-square-kilometer central city planned to house financial, business, education, travel, leisure, and residential sectors in addition to industry. Yang Xiong, the vice mayor of Shanghai, said that to build the city, "developers are gunning for a total of 120 billion yuan (US$14.95 billion) in investments by 2010."[97] The truth is, however, that no matter how much foreign direct investment goes into Lingang's development, this megaproject, and others like it, has an "unlimited budget" from the Shanghai municipal government. Such showcase projects are designed to impress (both dignitaries on private visits and provincials on organized bus tours) and to serve as experimental testing grounds for hundreds of other new cities.

Such cities demonstrate how the function of the city post-Reform in China is transformed such that the physical environment is used as a means to overcome the constraint of accumulation in state-led industrialization. As Fulong Wu puts it, "The city is used as a fix to absorb capital."[98] Most of these new cities will serve as industrial bases to support the currently unemployed rural population. Despite all the talk of education, tourism, and culture, visiting urbanists remained skeptical about these functions. One Fudan University doctoral student exclaimed in disbelief, "Educated people won't relocate to such a remote area—they'll run right back to Beijing or Shanghai —we don't work as hard as we do only to end up in a cultural backwater!" Yang Xifeng, a vice director of Lingang New City Administrative Committee, conceded that most residents will be rural workers employed by the local industries, along with resort owners and a smaller number of transient young engineers and managers "willing to sacrifice a few years to contribute to nation-building."[99]

The question of who will inhabit satellite cities such as Lingang in Shanghai is pertinent to China's future social makeup. The eleven new towns around Beijing, for example, will house the 5.7 million urban poor relocated from the city proper, which aims to limit its population to 18 million, as well as rural migrants and local farmers.[100] Rather than creating a poly-nucleated urban form, as intended, the commuting distances and lower quality of life in the new towns will likely create two-tiered urban environments, intensifying pressure on the urban core. Nonetheless, each city is being branded to attract residents based on their particular aims and tastes: "Shunyi is being designed primarily for industrial workers, Yizhuang will accommodate white-collar employees, and Tongzhou may welcome migrant artists."[101] Considerable thought and expense went into the packaging of each satellite city, and each was prominently promoted in individual display rooms during the opening of the Beijing Planning Exhibition Hall, in 2005.

Although market forces have the potential to exacerbate earlier forms of Potemkinism through empty branding, they also can improve quality of life and sustainability. As municipal leaders begin to recognize the importance of market forces and social variables in planning, cities have begun to commission studies from outside experts and build a knowledge base from these intellectual and cultural exchanges. In 1994, for example, the 1,300-

year-old city of Quanzhou hired expertise from prestigious institutions throughout the country, including Tianjin University, the Jiangsu Provincial Planning Institute, Dongnan University, in Nanjing, and Tsinghua University, in Beijing. Such partnerships usually benefit both parties. The consultants on the Quanzhou redevelopment project wrote that "outside professionals, impressed by what they recognize as Quanzhou's strong local character, have more enthusiastically attempted to work that character into their new designs than what they might have done in projects closer to home . . . while the advice from planners in nationally-renowned institutes has carried more weight in the debates over planning policy than similar viewpoints presented by local factions."[102] Although 65 percent of Quanzhou's urban fabric was originally slated for demolition, only 17 percent was actually redeveloped by 1999, almost exclusively due to the influence of the outside professionals on the municipal government's understanding of the importance of preservation. Wang Shuangming, of the Quanzhou Urban Planning Bureau, told me that the municipality's initial approach to redevelopment was *jiucheng gaizao*, a term which implies complete rebuilding. "We razed entire areas and widened streets," he said, "but through the advice of the Tsinghua team and our observation that complete rebuilding had radically altered the density of the urban fabric and our way of life, we started to change our approach in late 1990s, when we adopted the policy of *gucheng baohu* [old city preservation]."[103] Wang explained that although the government initially permitted construction of new buildings six to seven stories in height, "it felt oppressive, so in 2001 a new regulation restricted buildings to five stories maximum, with three to four stories as the norm."[104] Now seriously committed to preservation, the city is actively restoring temples and vernacular housing, and in 2001 won a UNESCO preservation award for restoration of the historic business district of Zhongshan Road.

Similarly, the Kunming city government and Swiss planners formed a partnership from 1996–2002 to develop a more sustainable development plan. The synergy created by their work led to Kunming becoming, in 2001, one of four Chinese national pilot cities implementing innovative transportation and environmental initiatives. As in Quanzhou, the presence of "outside experts" was essential to convincing local municipal officials of the importance of preservation, even when the local planners already understood its significance. After a long period of "continued urging by Swiss experts," write the Kunming planners, the city government approved the protection of several historical city blocks in old Kunming, and established a

Zhongshan Road, Quanzhou business district, which won a UNESCO historic preservation award in 2001. Fujian Province, 2006. Photo by author.

formal preservation department.[105] The team also persuaded officials that the satellite cities being developed around Kunming should vary in character. By designating the historic city of Guandu as a focal point for culture and tourism, for example, the planning team convinced officials to forgo plans for two major roads that would have destroyed the built fabric, proposing instead that car parks be situated outside of the historic town, that the town's existing narrow lanes and traditional courtyard houses be preserved, and that vernacular architecture as well as monuments be restored.[106] While some residents of Kunming claim that the team's measures preserved too little too late, had such strategic partnerships not occurred the destruction of cultural heritage would have been even greater.[107]

Collaboration between experts on large- and small-scale planning projects are increasing nationwide; however, the degree to which outside advice is heeded varies greatly. In many cases consultants are merely hired for show.[108] The planning decision-making process is notoriously lacking in transparency throughout China, with Beijing topping the list for secrecy. In 2005 the Beijing Municipal Commission for Urban Planning (BMCUP), recognizing the need to fine-tune its 2020 plan to account for variables such as economic and population growth and market forces, commissioned a team of experts from the United States to assess alternative development futures. The scenarios generated by the task force indicated that the greatest environmental and lifestyle benefits would result from high density and contiguous urban development in the existing urban area (rather than building new satellite towns) and from developing a subregional job-housing balance along transportation corridors to encourage efficient commuting, improve employee productivity, and alleviate the current severe traffic congestion.[109] Yang Xinmiao, a professor at the Institute of Transportation Engineering at Tsinghua University, concurs that instead of adding a subway line that connects a residential area on the edge of the city to a business district in the center, the city ought to narrow the distance between workplace and home, eliminating the need for a commute altogether. "We need to learn how to make the city more compact," says Yang, stressing that Beijing's planning bureaus need to focus less on building and more on training and collaboration.[110] While BMCUP claims to be considering the task force's findings, its public commitment to developing satellite cities that function as "bedroom communities" will produce the worst possible outcomes. Yan Song, a professor in the United States and a member of the task force, anticipated that BMCUP would not heed recommendations to restrict Beijing's "pancake" development pattern of ring roads. It would be politically risky to raise car or fuel taxes or to restrict car ownership, she says, as decade-old policies that encourage the growth of road construction and the auto industry continue to prioritize the car above public transit: "This is how local officials get promoted to higher ranks; it's not a conspiracy theory; it's reality."[111]

Such examples illustrate that resistance to sustainable urban development in China is often due more to a lack of political will than a lack of knowledge. International collaborations between urban-planning experts, such as China Planning Network (CPN), initiated in 2004 by scholars at Massachusetts Institute of Technology and Harvard University, regularly partner with the Chinese Ministry of Construction to exchange knowledge. In 2006 CPN's commissioners declared that "China Planning Network has advanced from simply an academic interest group to an independent voice that can influence China's planning and development education, research, practice and policies. Though still in the preliminary stage, China Planning Network has moved forward on its mission to systematically introduce Western knowledge and experiences in planning and development to China."[112] These goals are closely aligned with those of a variety of innovative urban-design labs, networks, and collaborations, including the Rotterdam- and Beijing-based Dynamic City Foundation, the New York–based

People's Architecture, the Shanghai-based FAR Architecture Center, the Urban China Research Center at Cardiff University, the Urban China Research Network at the State University of New York, Albany, and so on.[113]

Studies also demonstrate that the urban-planning process in China is becoming democratized and increasingly represents public community interests in determining the form of cities, where the disposition of property is its ultimate subject.[114] Such democratization is aided, in part, by influential Chinese-language online forums on urbanization, such as that supported by the journal *Chengshi Zhongguo* (Urban China). Furthermore, most leaders in urban-planning bureaus—such as Zhou Lan in Nanjing, Wu Jiang in Shanghai, Huang Yan in Beijing, and Qiu Baoxing, the vice minister of the Ministry of Construction—are highly educated professionals with a clear sense of the cultural and social dimensions of effective urban design, although, for political reasons, those ideals do not always become actualized.[115] Nonetheless, specialists throughout the country are slowly facilitating the implementation of more rational, human-scale plans by educating municipal officials and future professionals. New generations of architects are being trained by talented professors with extensive theoretical training and design experience, and a real, if belated, debate about the cost and designers of landmark architectural projects has been launched nationwide.[116]

The Seer in the City: "Cities on the Move"

China's planners and municipal leaders have begun thinking creatively about questions of heritage and aesthetics in part due to two decades of consciousness-raising activities by a variety of activist intellectuals (artists, writers, performers, journalists, educators, preservationists, architects, etc.). These activists use their medium to unveil the unspoken assumptions underlying the discourse of urban modernization and to give voice to those disenfranchised under China's changing social contract. In the aftermath of the nationwide protests against rent-seeking and cronyism in the spring of 1989, which culminated in the massacre of students and civilians in Beijing on 4 June, the government silenced expressions of dissatisfaction with the social, ethical, and, above all, economic fallout of China's modernization. Although Chinese intellectuals reengaged class analysis of the vastly increasing gaps in income levels sanctioned under the umbrella of "modernization," such publications were heavily censored until the late 1990s. Experimental artists, on the other hand, managed throughout the

1990s to produce small-scale performances, installations, and video art that probed the contradictions inherent in "urbanization" and "modernization" rhetoric.

Artists have been particularly sensitive to the fact that the frenzied, contingent, and opportunistic development of Chinese cities creates major social and political ruptures rather than a predictable order evolving toward higher degrees of civility. Hou Hanru and Hans Ulrich Obrist, curators of a traveling exhibition on Asian urbanism, "Cities on the Move" (1997–99), described the theme as a dynamic of global capitalism: "Urban transformation inevitably causes contradictions, contestation, chaos, *and even violence*, laying bare the fundamental paradox behind the pragmatic conviction in the co-operation of Asian lifestyles and social orders and a globalizing liberal consumer economy. The impulsive and almost fanatical pursuit of economic and monetary power becomes the ultimate goal of development. In resistance to this new totalitarian power of hypercapitalism, new freedoms and social, cultural, and political claims are being made by the society itself. *The City is a locus of conflict.*"[117] If the artist is the seer of contemporary culture, the violence inherent in many of the Chinese works appears shockingly prescient from a post–September 11 perspective. Analysis of selected works from China from the 1990s, many of which were later exhibited in "Cities on the Move," illustrates ties between China's protests, in 1989, against economic and political disenfranchisement, and neoliberal development practices worldwide.

Avant-garde performance art was especially prevalent in Beijing in the early 1990s, with migrant artists living in the East Village (Dong Cun) because it provided some of the cheapest housing in the city. The resident art critic Karen Smith described the environment of that time: "In the shadow of the Metropolis many of the Village's indigenous population scrape a living by collecting and sorting rubbish. Waste accumulates by the side of the small ponds. This pollutes the water, generating noxious fumes in the summer. Raw sewage flows directly into the water. Slothful, threadbare dogs roam the narrow lanes between the houses. People stare with the blankness of the illiterate and benighted."[118] Zhang Huan, who studied classical painting in Nanjing, switched to performance art soon after his move to Beijing in 1992. On the scorching summer day of 2 June 1994, just prior to the fifth anniversary of the Tiananmen Square crackdown, he performed *Twelve Square Meters*. Zhang first sat naked on a filthy public toilet in the East Village, his body coated in honey. After an hour his body was coated with flies, and he ended his performance by dipping himself in

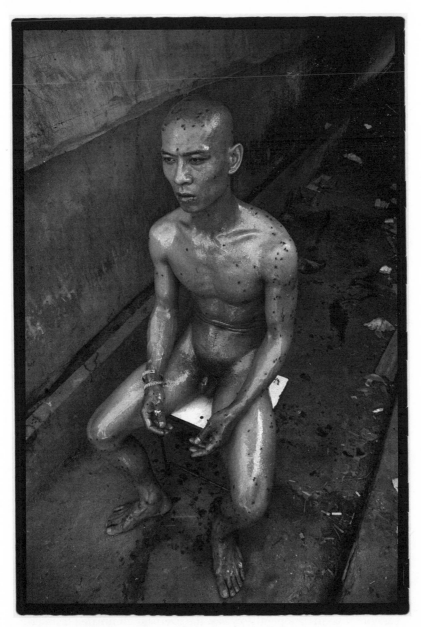

Zhang Huan, *Twelve Square Meters*, performance. East Village, Beijing, 1994.
Photo by Rong Rong. Courtesy Rong Rong.

a putrid pond, on the surface of which the fly corpses floated. This performance signifies, among other things, the intentional cheapening of the body (the human, the city) by sweetening its appeal to the craven flies hovering about (real estate developers, profiteers). Just as the protest of 1989 was incited by the actions of corrupt officials, so, too, the governmental neglect of infrastructure and human needs in Beijing for the sake of personal profit energized much of the avant-garde art of the mid-1990s. Zhang later explained the inspiration for his performance: "One morning I went to a public toilet near the Village which was impossible to set foot in. So I had to ride my bike over to the Village toilet. But as soon as I stepped inside it a swarm of flies assaulted me. I instantly conceived of this work, and tried my best to re-create the truth of that experience, but only understood what I was trying to express after performing."[119] Zhang's performance opposes prevalent forms of glitzy urban "renewal" that disparage other basic human needs.

Such performances give voice to public outrage at corrupt officials' irrational inattention to supporting a livable urban infrastructure, as illustrated by an incident in Nanning, the capital of Guangxi Province. I recall, from a visit in 1993, the pride of local residents after a traffic overpass (lijiao qiao) had been constructed downtown, which not only reduced congestion but was a key signifier of urban modernization at the time. To my surprise, during a visit in 2004 I learned from enraged local residents that the overpass had been torn down in response to a stipulation by developers who feared it would obstruct access to real estate purchased to build a Wal-Mart. Given that the population and car ownership had nearly doubled over the decade, this move created massive downtown traffic jams. When I asked about the decision-making process during an interview with a high-ranking official in the Nanning City Planning Administration Bureau, he answered, "There's a political explanation which wouldn't be advisable to voice. A deputy bureau chief is no longer at the bureau because he wasn't careful enough about what he said. Let's just say I didn't endorse the demolition of that overpass. I'm somewhat of a transportation expert but my proposal wasn't adopted. Anyway, the overpass eliminated traffic congestion. My approach to urban design is to build things well and let them serve their function, not to keep tearing things down and rebuilding them all over again. I believe you should carefully study the problem and then build according to a rational procedure."[120]

Lin Yilin contrasted such urban realities with irrational planning policies in *Safely Maneuvering across Lin He Road*, which he performed in Guang-

A traffic overpass is destroyed, irrationally, to ease access to Walmart. Nanning, Guangxi Province, 2005. Courtesy Xu Yiwei.

zhou in 1995; in this piece he attempted to cross this busy thoroughfare by constructing a movable brick wall for protection. Later, in "Cities on the Move," he juxtaposed a photograph of this attempt against newspaper reports of then Premier Li Peng's mandate to accelerate construction of a nationwide road-transportation network. Such policies not only repeatedly neglect pedestrian needs but have directly contributed to the traffic and environmental problems plaguing many Chinese cities today. Because of decade-old policies supporting special interests such as road construction and the auto industry, the development of human-scale, sustainable transportation is discouraged. Adherence to central policies that prioritize the car above public transit is, after all, "how local officials get promoted to higher rank."[121]

Welcome to China Southern Airlines (1997), Xu Tan's series of photographs in "Cities on the Move," represents similar contradictions of the modern metropolis. Using time-lapse photography, Xu captures the recurrent take-offs from Guangzhou's Baiyun airport from the perspective of a cyclist peddling past shacks of migrant workers and street hawkers. Xu's work foregrounds the new spatial and temporal layers into which Chinese cities are being reorganized, which can be measured by different speeds of displacement: by plane, by car, by bicycle, by foot. These disparate spatial and

Xu Tan, *Welcome to China Southern Airlines*, time-lapse photography, Guangzhou, 1997. Courtesy Xu Tan.

temporal zones in the city generate different notions of time, constituting different cultural experiences within the same city. Xu's caption for *Welcome to China Southern Airlines*—"This is a center for distributing money, myths, and power"—underscores the fact that classes experience the city in radically different ways depending on whether they are beneficiaries of the power and the money, or merely recipients of the myth. Most official representations of the Chinese city, especially in promotional material, urban-planning exhibition halls, and even published population figures, systematically preclude the urban underclass from representation, rendering invisible certain social classes in the city. The result is often violent protest, such as in Shenzhen, where disgruntled workers have threatened to leap from an unfinished skyscraper or set themselves on fire for not receiving promised pay.[122]

Some of the best-known images in "Cities on the Move" are the photographs of Cai Guo-Qiang's "explosions of gunpowder in landscape" performances, cumulatively titled *The Century with Mushroom Clouds: Project for the Twentieth Century* (1996). The performance scholar RoseLee Goldberg interprets Cai's works as manifestations of Chinese spirituality, but this reading fails to account for the political import of the particular landscapes in question, namely, the Nevada Nuclear Test Site and Manhattan.[123] Like the two cultural symbols targeted by terrorists on September 11, these sites signify American military and economic hegemony. In both of Cai's performances the performing subject appears to be an innocent bystander, and can be easily dissociated from the mushroom cloud he has produced, demonstrating how seemingly innocent image-making practices can easily obscure more pernicious interests.

A similar equation of urban violence with global capitalism appears in Chen Shaoxiong's *Fengjing* (Landscape), a series of hand-drawn sketches juxtaposed on forty-one stills from videotaped scenes of highway traffic, overpasses, bridges, parks, squares, high-rises, the airport, and panoramic vistas in Guangzhou. The sketches fall into three categories: military (tanks, fighter jets, rockets, submarines, helicopters), erotica (males and females in decadent poses), and wildlife (hedgehogs, crocodiles, bats, monkeys). The incongruity of the sketch and the video image invites semiological associations between the "imagined" signifier of the sketch and the "real" photographed scene it signifies. The speed of urban development leaves traces, and the sketches invoke an archaeological sense of the primitive layers comprising modern society. Chen's project uncovers cultural artifacts by unearthing the fossils of material culture and redeeming the historical meaning of contemporary urban landscapes.

Most striking in Chen's montage is the predominance of military images. Tanks roll through the streets and face off at Guangzhou Zoo while fighter jets encircle high-rises, clearly invoking the military invasion of civilian urban areas on 4 June 1989. Zhang Peili's exhibit in "Cities on the Move," a series of progressively blurred photographs of tanks rolling through Beijing, illustrates how the rhetoric and speed of modernization has obscured even such recent memories, the tanks signifying yet another archaeological layer to the Chinese city's modern history. The prevalence of the tanks motif in Chen Shaoxiong's series invokes not only domestic

Cai Guo-Qiang, *The Century with Mushroom Clouds: Project for the Twentieth Century.*
Top: "Manhattan," realized in New York City, looking toward Manhattan, 20 April 1996,
approximately three seconds, gunpowder (10 g) and cardboard tube; bottom: "Nevada Test
Site," realized at Nevada Test Site, 13 February 1996, approximately three seconds,
gunpowder (10 g) and cardboard tube. Photos by Hiro Ihara. Courtesy Cai Studio.

Chen Shaoxiong, *Landscape 2*, video stills. Guangzhou, 1996.

history, but also the numbing pressure brought to bear on the Chinese metropolis by the pervasiveness of global capitalism. Monolithic forces ubiquitous in the city, the tanks of Chen's sketches not only flatten the streets, but float with the clouds amid the high-rises on Huanshi Road. The idea of battling capitalist forces dominated the cultural imaginary of a number of Chinese artists in the mid-1990s. For example, the predominant image in Qiu Huadong's novel *City Tank* (*Chengshi zhanche*, 1996) is that of the free-spirited, idealistic, and dirt-poor artist flattened by the tank-like capitalist forces of the city.

Chen's photos of fighter planes attacking high-rise commercial buildings may be especially striking to Americans in the twenty-first century, but what is even more remarkable is the degree to which such images dominated the Chinese cultural imaginary in the late twentieth century. The Beijing writer Qiu Huadong's novel *Yingyan* (Fly eyes, 1998) features what has now, post–September 11, become a particularly poignant image of a pilot crashing his aircraft into a seventy-floor skyscraper in Beijing's commercial district. Qiu describes the pilot's crash: "Blinded by the sunshine glaring off the glass walls of a shopping center He Xiao closed his eyes and crashed into it. From a distance the remains of his helicopter looked like a tree branch sticking out of that seventy-floor building."[124] The impassivity of the shiny modern symbol of progress mocks any attempts by the free-spirited pilot "playing" in the city to alter the capitalist forces shaping the modern metropolis. Qiu and the aforementioned artists imagine an urban space where hegemonic images proliferate, replete with both imagined and historical referents.

By the twenty-first century Chinese experimental artists had moved from their highly marginalized position in Chinese society to center stage, largely due to their prominence in the international art market. Many, such as the performance artist Zhang Dali, contend that the move to the center of commercial culture in China allows artists to more actively engage the public, rather than compromise their social critique. In this sense, postsocialist urban aesthetics has broadened possibilities for civic engagement with China's urban development process. These seers in the city are increasingly being seen by the city.

Being Seen in the City: The Rise of Civic Activism

Chinese cities, which had been more culturally and visually homogeneous under socialism, are now, like cities worldwide, increasingly characterized by unevenness. Yet, as urban sociologists such as David Harvey and others have demonstrated, even those most disenfranchised in the city can engage in concrete social, political, and spatial projects. Saskia Sassen's recent work suggests, for example, that in many contexts those who lack power (migrant communities, environmental artists, gay activists, etc.) gain *presence* (hence political clout) in global cities due to the cross-border space that connects multiple cities.[125] This presence manifests in varied practices, from everyday life to organized strikes and protests, from mobile hawkers to grounded urban villages, from public acts of personal desperation to mediated expressions of injustice by the media, writers, artists, filmmakers, and performers. One could argue that recent policies enacted by China's central government, such as investments in the "new socialist countryside" aimed at enhancing rural quality of life to mitigate urban migration, or labor laws pitted against transnational corporations, are due in part to the increasing presence exerted by Chinese migrant workers.[126]

Civic awareness and activism is occurring in China in a wide variety of forums. Socially committed filmmakers such as Jia Zhangke continue to raise public awareness of the human cost of development. Journalists such Wang Jun publicize the consequences of redeveloping old Beijing into a modern socialist capital, rather than adopting the early 1950s Liang Sicheng–Chen Zhanxiang plan to locate the administrative center west of the old city. And while civil-society organizations (csos) and other grassroots communities remain structured and empowered from within the government, some argue that this system has favored the gradual growth of nonadministrative forces and mechanisms.[127] Meanwhile, the avant-garde art community of the twenty-first century is no longer poor and marginalized, having become far more integrated into the commercial and social fabric of urban China. Yet even from the center the artistic community continues to provoke the authorities and stimulate popular discourse.

The best-known venue for avant-garde art is the Dashanzi International Art District (or "798"), located in an old, Bauhaus-style complex in northeastern Beijing. Studios are situated alongside still operative state-owned factories, with some galleries located in defunct industrial spaces such as Factory 798, a munitions factory retaining its Cultural Revolution propaganda (retouched for postmodern effect). Though its "Soho-esque" image has created a tourist destination, fostered by events such as the annual spring Dashanzi International Art Festival, its activities turn enough media attention to the underside of politics that authorities still threaten to default on the lease or stop the festival. The artist Huang Rui, co-organizer of the festival "Beijing, Beijing" (Beijing and its background, 2006), said the festival's theme was chosen to provide a public forum for considering the possibility of developing a genuine urban culture in Beijing.

> Despite the fact that Beijing dates back to the Yuan dynasty, it has always been governed by peasants, from the Mongolians to the communists, who perceived a vibrant civic urban culture as a challenge to political authority. These days even government leaders realize they need to infuse culture back into the city's cells, given the destruction of the old urban fabric. But old habits die hard; despite their best intentions they habitually destroy the very sources of culture that they are now trying to nourish. The authorities need to stop thinking like peasants and start realizing that both the leadership and the populace would benefit from genuine urban culture, that it would actually enhance their political power. If Beijing cannot succeed in this, other Chinese cities are doomed as well.[128]

When Huang Rui directly voiced these ideas to Dashanzi District authorities, of course, they were highly displeased. "They hate that the media covered our festival. They hate the fact that we fail to 'obey.' The media and our international connections aid us in our quest for 'free speech'—otherwise 798 would have been demolished long ago."[129] On 9 November 2006, Huang Rui received a telephone call from the district head who once again threatened demolition, but two days later the decision was reversed, "because the central government policy had changed—they now want to 'do culture' [*gao wenhua*]. When people who are fundamentally opposed to culture start promoting it, you can imagine the results! So we continue to express through the arts and the media how such ridiculous understandings of urban culture play out in China."[130]

While such experiences demonstrate the local authorities' ambivalent attitudes toward urban culture, they also confirm that coalitions between artists, the media, and international interests can effect change. For example, when the land-use permits for Beijing International Arts Camp, founded in 2004 in Suojia Village, not far from Dashanzi, were suddenly revoked in 2005, an intensive international media campaign forestalled its demolition.[131] Similarly, the Moganshan Road studios located in the abandoned Suzhou Creek Japanese textile factories in Shanghai survived an attempt in 2004 to evacuate the artists through efforts coordinated by the artists and the media. Nonetheless, the nature and function of the media varies greatly between Chinese cities. The Shanghai playwright and art director Zhang Xian shares Huang Rui's sentiments about the importance of free expression, but insists that "it is absent in the Shanghai media, the 'sickest' in the entire nation. Incredibly rigid and petty, it lags far behind the media in Beijing and Guangzhou (Beijing due to its various political factions and interests, and Guangzhou because of the strong commercial competition). It is only through a tiny little arts festival" such as the Shanghai Fringe Festival, an annual alternative theater arts event launched in 2005, "that one can possibly air the disastrous effect of [deposed party secretary] Chen Liangyu's influence on Shanghai."[132]

Nonetheless, the media remains the most promising tool for probing the complexities of Chinese urban life. *Chengshi Zhongguo* (Urban China) is a prominent example. A monthly magazine which focuses on a variety of issues related to urban space and society, it has proved increasingly influential since its debut in February 2005. Glossy, cutting edge, and ubiquitous, the magazine is located in trendy coffee shops, restaurants, sports clubs, spas, art galleries, and bookstores in some forty-four cities throughout China. The journal focuses on a range of pertinent issues, including urban space, housing, governance, architecture, sculpture, culture, the impact of global urbanization on rural China, and everyday life in small Chinese cities. Packed with photos and catchy, attractive design layouts, the journal addresses sensitive issues in a sophisticated yet succinct fashion. Scholarly

Chengshi Zhongguo (Urban China), one of many new forums for civic discourse. Photo by author.

works such as Jane Jacobs's *The Death and Life of Great American Cities* are cited in passing, appealing to an educated readership that recognizes the relevance of such books to their everyday life.

The journal is sponsored by the Urban Planning Institute at Tongji University and is aimed at middle-class readers, especially those who wield social and political influence. Jiang Jun, the journal's thirty-eight-year-old chief editor, readily admits that the goal of his editorial team is to provide a forum in which urban innovators can network so that their collective authority will impact government policy. The son of provincial factory workers and an adherent of neoliberalism, Jiang insists that only by freeing entrepreneurial capital to create a material base and middle class can political liberalization can occur in China.[133] Operating offices in Guangzhou, Shanghai, Beijing, and Chongqing, the journal relies on its website, http://www.urban china.com.cn, to reach a much larger audience than its monthly circulation of 50,000. Prominent innovators comprise its advisory board, including the Dutch architect Rem Koolhaas, the Chinese-French art historian Hou Hanru, the Chinese-American dean of the MIT School of Architecture Yung-Ho Chang, the star architect Ma Qingyun, the cultural critic Zhu

Dake, the bestselling journalist and urban historian Wang Jun, and the prize-winning poet Han Dong. The journal also often includes high-quality articles from overseas contributors.

Civic activism in urban China is beginning to achieve tangible gains for citizens. In May 2006 the Chinese minister of culture, Sun Jiazheng, became the first high-level minister to apologize for the government's destruction of traditional Beijing as part of its relentless push to modernize. Sun admitted the government had broken its own rules in allowing redevelopment of the country's cultural heritage: "Some cities have unilaterally gone all out to get a new look and have not done enough to protect old buildings. . . . There are things that I should have done and did not do, meetings I should have attended and did not attend."[134] Jiang Jun credits effective consciousness-raising efforts, including his friend Wang Jun's influential book, *City Records*, for its impact on the attitudes of government officials: "Many officials confessed to Wang Jun that they were highly ashamed of their neglect of preservation."[135] With increasing public pressure, the cultural value of "face" and long-standing paternalistic notions (nurtured by Confucianism and communism) of the upright official's responsibility to the people may work to curb further destruction.

"What *is* the world like without Father's little shack?" The question lives on today. The narrator of Fang Fang's story asked his question in the mid-1980s, as China's urbanization was being launched, and as memories of the childhood "home" became embellished by the intense desire to imagine a sense of place. "Father's little shack" unquestionably needed renovation, but its indiscriminate demolition eliminated a former way of life and its associated values, resulting in a disconnection from roots and a lack of historical consciousness. That uncanny sense of the *unheimlich*, the feeling of not being spiritually at home anywhere, plagues the urbanite disconnected from her cultural roots. Although it is no longer possible in modern urban societies, even by taking deliberate steps, to regain a sense of rootedness, a sense of place can still be achieved. Yi-fu Tuan elaborates on the distinction.

> Rootedness implies being at home in an unself-conscious way, [whereas] sense of place implies a certain distance between self and place that allows the self to appreciate a place. . . . We all know the difference between a new town and an old village: the one denies history; the other embodies it in brick and stone. This fact, which seems so clear and obvious, is nonetheless a source of confusion. It confuses the difference

between "knowing" and "knowing about." There is a knowing that is the result of familiarity through long residence; and a knowing that is the result of conscious effort. The former kind generates a sense of stability and rootedness, the latter explicit knowledge. The longing to regain a sense of place through heightened historical consciousness is a modern venture.[136]

The work of the most innovative architects in China today attends to this modern need to incorporate historical and cultural memory into urban design. Fourth Generation architects such as Zhang Yonghe, Ma Qingyun, Paul Chen, Henry Wu, Cui Kai, Tang Hua, and Zhu Wenyi "are replacing the prior dependence on the figure of the building with attention to spatiality."[137] Thus, a middle school in Lijiang, Yunnan, designed by Li Xiaodong, the chair of architecture at Tsinghua University, carefully attends to locale by its utilization of local materials, in an elegant blend of local aesthetics with modern functionality.

Zhang Yonghe (Yung-Ho Chang), the dean of architecture at MIT, the former chair of architecture at Peking University, and atelier of Feichang Jianzhu (Extraordinary architecture), provides a succinct example of attention to time and space with his design, in 1996, of Xishu Bookstore in Beijing. Zhang acknowledges, as Walter Benjamin theorized in his analysis of the destruction of "aura," the historical transition from the representational priority of "surface" to that of "interface." Thus, he conceives of aura in terms of the spatial and temporal effects of its design, rather than in terms of the monumentality of the architectural edifice itself. Situated in a former traffic corridor through an office complex built in 1957, Xishu Bookstore employed a book-bike, a space-saving hybrid object created by placing bookshelves on top of bike wheels. The shelves revolved around the circular steel columns that supported the mezzanine above, recalling both the passageway and the bicycle street traffic via the motion of bike wheels. After Xishu Bookstore was torn down, in 2000, it was reconverted to a traffic corridor, so while the building itself was ephemeral, its design allowed the inhabited space to retain its historical character and function. This attention to the history of place, says Zhang, was the goal of his design: "The abstract movement of the space from a traffic corridor to a signifier of traffic (the book-bike) and back provides aesthetic continuity despite the rapid demolition of new structures due to shifting market priorities for space."[138]

Urban Chinese will never again be rooted. Yet aesthetic solutions can

Sustainable design: Yuhu Elementary School was built with local, low-cost, aesthetically harmonious materials. Lijiang, 2003. Courtesy Li Xiaodong.

Xishu Bookstore (Beijing, 1996–2000) attends to the history of place. Source: Zhang Yonghe, *Pingchang jianzhu* (For a basic architecture) (Beijing: Zhongguo jianzhu gongye chubanshe, 2002), 69.

create a sense of place through attention to lived, historical space, in turn mitigating the capitalist violence and "mechanical reproduction" so prevalent in the global city. The massive destruction of valuable heritage buildings and centuries-old urban fabric is a devastating cultural loss; the waste of public funds on private profiteering is unconscionable; the ignorance resulting in unsightly or substandard design is lamentable. Yet such developments were to some extent inevitable due to cultural and historical exigencies, and the mentality that propagated them is slowly but surely being altered. One point is uncontestable: this and the next generation of urban planners working in China will have more experience at solving global issues in urban design than anyone in the world, and their knowledge will shape future worldwide practices.

The Cultural Politics of Urban Aesthetics

> People only sense, to the point of terror, that things are not quite
> right in all aspects of their daily life.
>
> Zhang Ailing, "My Writing"

Alarmist denunciations of the devastation wrought by
China's exponential and chaotic urbanization abound.
From dislocated citizens, artists, writers, and filmmakers to architects, environmentalists, and cultural preservationists, the list of critics proliferates. As unin-
formed or shortsighted as China's policy makers may
appear, the decision-making process is extremely complex and varied. Yet one fact is undeniable: the dynamics governing China's postsocialist urban transformation are embedded in interrelated global processes.
This is why China's artists, far removed from Al Qaeda,
could "predict" with such clarity seemingly inconceiv-
able events such as aircraft crashing into seventy-story
skyscrapers in central business districts. Culture wars
are not limited to American identity politics or the
"clash of civilizations" predicted by Samuel Huntington at the end of the twentieth century. The new millennium also saw the convergence of efforts by a wide
variety of actors aimed at resisting global capital and the
neoliberal agenda legitimizing its international domi-
nation. By the end of the 1990s, as neoliberalism began
to falter—an effect of worldwide opposition to its policies, as well as of its evident failures—remarkably diverse organizations mobilized around interests such as

class, the environment, health, and the postcolonial subaltern. One of the most visible instances of such mobilization occurred when activists based in the United States "mobilized a stunning display of public fury" directed at global financial elites during meetings of the World Trade Organization (WTO) and International Monetary Fund (IMF) in Seattle from 28 November to 3 December 1999, in a "coming together and public coming-out of widely divergent and dispersed progressive forces."[1] The prominent Chinese intellectual historian Wang Hui, who was a visiting scholar at the University of Washington that fall, immediately saw the relevance of the Seattle protests to the outrage at unequal development and corruption in China that had provoked nationwide demonstrations in 1989. Both protests, he says, were "directed against a comprehensive system of political provisions having to do with ordinary life, a systematic program aimed at creating and expanding a comprehensive market society."[2]

In *A Brief History of Neoliberalism* David Harvey identifies a number of coalitions mobilizing against neoliberal policies. These diverse currents— which include traditional environmental groups such as Greenpeace, groups experimenting with new production and consumption systems such as Local Exchange Trading Systems (LETS), mass movements confronting the dispersed powers of the neoliberal order (which Hardt and Negri construe as "Empire"), and workers organizations (the Workers Party in Brazil or the Congress Party in India)—"now come together at the World Social Forum in an attempt to define their commonalities and to build an organizational power capable of confronting the many variants of neoliberalism and of neoconservatism."[3] While Harvey applauds these activists, he also intimates that such efforts will benefit from clear guidance in "more adequate lines of action" derived from the critical analysis of intellectuals like him.[4] In this sense he is not unlike many Chinese knowledge workers, who continue to see their role in society as standard-bearers for the way forward, no longer to merely save the nation (*jiuguo*), but to save the world from its present untenable developmentalism. Wang Hui pronounces "the principal task of the progressive forces in contemporary China" as urging the transformation of practical critiques and social movements "into a driving force seeking broader democracy and freedom in both China and the world."[5]

As conflicts over neoliberal globalization have become more prevalent, particularly in the wake of China's unprecedented urbanization and the fallout of the Asian economic crisis of 1997–98, a paradigm shift has occurred among many Chinese intellectuals. For scholars such as Qin Hui, Cui Zhiyuan, He Qinglian, Gan Yang, Wang Hui, Wen Tiejun, Lu Xueyi,

Sun Liping, Wang Xiaoming, Luo Gang, Xue Yi, Ni Wenjian, and countless others, "the China question" is no longer limited to China's ongoing search for modernity. Instead, a growing number of China's intellectuals believe that the resolution of China's problems may serve as a template for solving larger regional and global issues. These problems include rising gaps between the very rich and very poor, ecological degradation, resource shortages, escalating violence and authoritarianism, attenuated democracy, and the commercialization of the academy. Many believe that, given China's integration into the global economy, these problems derive from the worldwide proliferation of neoliberal political-economic practices and thinking since the late 1970s, evidenced by deregulation, privatization, and the withdrawal of the state from many areas of social provision. A fundamental tenet of neoliberalism is that human flourishing is best achieved by liberating entrepreneurial resources within an institutional framework characterized by strong private-property rights and free trade. Its core policies emphasize fiscal discipline, financial liberalization, reduced public expenditure and taxation, deregulation, decentralization, privatization, and a reduced role for the state. The state must preserve basic legal and financial institutions that allow markets to thrive, but should not intervene in markets once they are created.

Although neoliberal principles appear politically neutral, they in fact severely limit democratic participation, as Lisa Duggan explains in *The Twilight of Inequality? Neoliberalism, Cultural Politics, and the Attack on Democracy*: "Nominally pro-democratic, the neoliberal financial institutions have operated autocratically themselves, primarily through financial coercion. They have also consistently supported autocratic governments and plutocratic elites around the world to promote one kind of stability—a stability designed to facilitate business investment. The effects of neoliberal policy implementation have consistently included many kinds of instability, however, including unrest associated with dramatically increasing inequality, and political fragility resulting from reduced sovereignty for national governments."[6] Most theorization of neoliberalism to date has focused on its developments in the United States and United Kingdom under Ronald Reagan and Margaret Thatcher and on its coercive policies in Latin American economies. Only recently have a number of theorists elaborated on neoliberal structural transformations in East and Southeast Asia, particularly after the Asian economic crisis.[7] Neoliberal privatization in China has created multiple problems, the most visible being rent seeking and rampant corruption, especially at the local level, and social instability due to unemployment and lack of affordable social services such as health care and education. The economic, not to mention political, disenfranchisement of vast portions of China's rural population has created severe social unrest, causing Hu Jintao to modify earlier neoliberal policies by implementing social safety nets. While mainstream economists in China classify such problems as a historical inevitability of capitalist development intensified by China's accelerated transformation from an agrarian to an urban market economy, other scholars are not as sanguine about the assessment of China's current state as merely "transitional."

With China's urban fabric and demographics being transformed by the logic of market development, it is worth considering how scholars analyze the cultural effects of these urban transformations in relation to the economics and politics of global neoliberalism. Of particular interest is the shift in the Chinese academy away from traditional scholarship such as literary studies to the interdisciplinary critiques of cultural studies, and the degree to which this approach enables political agency bears study as well. Despite the anti-establishment foundation of cultural studies, its activities are perceived by many Chinese officials to be more conducive to state goals of urban market development, and its actors are thus allowed more autonomy than those in the more politically sensitive literary and fine arts.[8] This assumption may be justified. In other cultural contexts, particularly in advanced industrial nations, cultural studies has come under attack by progressives for its acquiescence to the norms of dominant consumer culture and the neoliberal agenda promoting it. I will examine why cultural studies was adopted by progressive Chinese intellectuals as the most effective means of comprehending the urban consumer culture dominating China, and the degree to which it aligns itself with state ideology. Of related interest is whether the professionalization of the Chinese academy is undermining belief in the power of intellectual labor to change social life. By probing the identity crisis among intellectuals in the humanities in China, and by examining the rise of cultural studies as literature fell from favor as a legitimate object of analysis among literary historians, I recharacterize the well-worn summaries of post-1989 intellectual debates (over radicalism, nationalism, "humanism" versus "postmodernism," and "neoliberalism" versus "neoleftism"), relating arguments over the effects of China's urban consumer culture to the politics and economics of neoliberalism. This diversity of intellectual opinion is, in its own right, an expression of the new urban consciousness in post-Reform China.

Whither the "China Question"?

The scholarly discourse of the 1980s "culture fever" (*wenhua re*) generally denounced socialism as "feudal" and antimodern, which led, for a time, to a widespread and fairly uncritical embrace of capitalism as the primary path to modernity. Many endorsed the "end of history" theory delineated by Francis Fukuyama, in which "the rest of the world is envisioned as moving on its own momentum toward a society modeled on Western capitalist democracies."[9] As the Shanghai literary historian Wang Xiaoming put it, "In the mid 1980s the extremely optimistic outlook of the academic community was widely diffused throughout society. . . . [N]othing could now ultimately thwart the dynamic of modernization. . . . [W]e were finally leaping into the new world of telephones, refrigerators, cars, and skyscrapers."[10] That China was to follow a "unique path" to this capitalist "end" (embodied by the government slogan "socialism with Chinese characteristics") became clear when the social movements during the spring of 1989 ended in bloodshed. Deng Xiaoping's "southern tour" (*nanxun*), in 1992, signaled the central government's firm commitment to continued economic liberalization sans political liberalization. Yet this did little to dilute enthusiasm for capitalist market reform: "Even after the terrible, bloody shock of June 1989, as soon as the top leaders proclaimed that economic reform would continue, people quickly recovered from their depression, as if nothing much had happened; at worst a slight detour. The tune of 'modernization' struck up again, and the rhythm of 'reform' beat even faster, as if China had more hope than ever. I can clearly remember how loud the clamor for modernization was in 1992, when the slogan was launched once again, drowning out all other sounds, filling everyone's ears with one ringing call: 'This is modernization—hurry up and hop on the bandwagon or you'll miss it!' "[11] Wang Xiaoming's cynicism derives not from his skepticism about the benefits of capitalist development per se, but from the means by which market reform was occurring in China in the mid-1990s. Just as Wang Hui attributed the 1989 protests not so much to popular aspirations for democracy as to anger over corruption and rent seeking by Chinese leaders after urban market reforms were launched in the mid-1980s, Wang Xiaoming concludes that the economic development policies of the 1990s aimed at yielding short-term advantages for China's political elite to the long-term detriment of the ecology and economy.

Wang Xiaoming's sarcasm is directed toward the many intellectuals and citizens who accepted uncritically the ideology promoted by the new rich for their own profit. Deng Xiaoping's slogan that all can earn a "decent living" (*xiaokang*) is a fallacy, he says, urging that special attention be given to the appraisal of China's future by its elites. "It might be thought that a new social class that gains power as a result of a modernizing system would be most eager to continue reforms. However . . . the new rich are for the most part very pessimistic about China's future. Almost every one of them has a foreign passport in his or her pocket, as if preparing to escape a dangerous situation."[12] The notion that elites charged with serving the public good intentionally abnegate responsibility resonates with David Harvey's view of U.S. political leaders: "If we ask the general question, 'Who has actually benefited from the numerous financial crises that have cascaded from one country to another in wave after wave of catastrophic deflations, inflations, capital flights and structural adjustments since the late 1970s?', the weak commitment of the current U.S. administration to fending off a fiscal crisis in spite of all the warning signs becomes more readily understandable. In the wake of a financial crash, the ruling elite may hope to emerge even more empowered than before."[13] Both scholars intimate that the ruling elite of transnational capital have no motivation to adjust failing economic policies, given that a financial crash will likely empower them even more.

Leftist intellectuals such as Wang Hui, Wang Xiaoming, and David Harvey attribute financial crisis and unequal development to the intentional manipulation of national resources and financial markets to the benefit of a small but powerful elite class. This assessment has been and continues to be contested from a variety of perspectives on both the Left and Right. Many development economists across the political spectrum celebrate China as the model for success. Both conservative and liberal neoliberals tend to depict a smooth and low-cost marketization of the Chinese economy, crediting its capital controls and expansionary macropolicies with the ability to insulate it from the worst effects of the East Asian financial crisis. Leftists, on the other hand, often see China's reforms as offering a "third way" between capitalism and centralized state socialism. Some denounce all of these positions as overly optimistic, yet do not attribute China's current social unrest and uneven development to greed alone, but rather to the vicious cycle of "contradictions" set in motion by market reforms in the 1980s. The economists Martin Hart-Landsberg and Paul Burkett, for example, take the Marxist position that China's market reforms have led not to socialist renewal, but rather to full-fledged capitalist restoration, an outcome driven by more than class interest: "Once the path of pro-market reforms was embarked upon, each subsequent step in the reform process was largely driven by tensions and contradictions generated by the reforms themselves."[14]

Critical inquiry by Chinese intellectuals into the conditions of urban market development developed in new ways after the traumatic crackdown on 4 June 1989. After this event, Chinese society changed palpably, the shock being qualitatively similar to the impact of September 11 on American society. Initially both the general populace (so-called *laobaixing*) and intellectuals (*zhishifenzi*) withdrew from broader social and political movements and focused instead on their private interests and advancement in society. The harsh political climate obviated organization; however, the paradigm shift stemmed also from a deep sense of disillusionment, betrayal, and confusion. The violent end to the 1989 protest movement induced a great deal of introspection. Gloria Davies points out that a cursory review of the literature indicates that " 'To what extent were *we* and the ideas *we* disseminated responsible for the tragedy?' and 'Where should *we* go from here?' were questions that were frequently raised or for which answers were proposed in Chinese critical inquiry of the 1990s."[15] Throughout that decade, Chinese intellectuals at home and abroad (many of whom decided to flee or to remain overseas after 1989), and a number of Sinologists, engaged in numerous debates about "radicalism," "neoconservatism," "consumerism," "Confucianism," "humanism," "postmodernism," "postcolonialism," "nationalism," "globalization," and "neoliberalism." These debates have been summarized by China academics such as Geremie Barmé, Timothy Cheek, Chen Yongguo, Rey Chow, Cui Zhiyuan, Gloria Davies, Gan Yang, Merle Goldman, Edward Gu, Huang Ping, Ji Zhe, Andrew Kipnis, Lau Chong-chor, Li Zehou, Liu Dong, Liu Qingfeng, Liu Zaifu, Suzanne Ogden, Chaohua Wang, Wang Hui, Wang Xiaoming, Ben Xu, Xu Jilin, Xudong Zhang, Zhang Yiwu, and Yiheng Zhao.[16]

One can see from the plethora of scholarship on Chinese intellectuals that their debates are deemed important by China scholars; yet their relevance to other regional contexts may not be immediately clear. In her discussion of how Chinese critical inquiry aligns itself with the theoretical concerns of Western thought, Davies goes so far as to refer to the status of the Chinese humanities as "perceived as or perhaps even demonstrably 'theoretically underdeveloped.' "[17] This sense of inferiority is echoed in the complaint among some Chinese intellectuals, heard particularly after 1989, that there are so few "genuine intellectuals" in China. The term *intellectual* has an elitist connotation to most Americans, who tend to see it as coterminous with *academic*, yet in twentieth-century China this group, inheritors of the earlier literati or scholar-official (*shi*) class, was very self-conscious about their ethical imperative to influence national policy. As Wang Hui indicates, for some Chinese intellectuals, their moral mandate now extends to the world.[18] One way to assess the cultural changes in China wrought by urban modernization and globalization is to evaluate whether solutions put forth by Chinese intellectuals attempt to move beyond the ubiquitous question "whither China?," which has dominated the Chinese intelligentsia since the mid-nineteenth century. Has the "China question"—or "obsession with China," to borrow C. T. Hsia's famous critique of twentieth-century Chinese writers for their exclusive focus on the nation—now permuted into scholarly inquiry into the welfare of the world?

Neoliberalism and the Rationalization of the Academy

To better understand the relationship between structural and cultural transformation in China, a brief discussion of global and domestic neoliberal developments is in order. One can identify a number of key periods in the development of neoliberal policies, which were first theorized in the late 1940s by the Austrian political philosopher Friedrich von Hayek and the Mont Pelerin Society, then popularized by von Hayek's *The Constitution of Liberty* (1960), and later validated when von Hayek received the Nobel Prize in Economics, in 1974. A crucial year for the institutionalization of neoliberal policies was 1979. That year Paul Volcker, chair of the U.S. Federal Reserve Bank, engineered a radical shift in U.S. monetary policy by shifting from Keynesian New Deal principles of embedded liberalism, with full employment as the key objective, to a policy designed to quell inflation regardless of consequences for employment. The "Volcker Shock" was subsequently applied in other national economies, especially in Latin America. China also began making political and economic adjustments conducive to neoliberalism in the 1970s, on the eve of the Reagan, Thatcher, and Helmut Kohl administrations. The People's Republic of China reestablished relations with the vast majority of world nations during the Cultural Revolution, and in 1972 replaced the Republic of China (Taiwan) in representing China to the United Nations. By the time Deng Xiaoping had launched economic reforms, in 1978, China's relations with the United States, Japan, and other advanced capitalist countries had become its principal focus. China's neoliberal policies began in earnest in 1984, with its urban reforms, through the process of "devolving political and economic power" (*fangquan rangli*) which gave rights to transfer and apportion state-controlled resources to the localities. Within one decade the income differential between city and country, which had greatly diminished due to the agricultural reforms of 1978–84, increased exponentially. Today China's urban-rural differential in real incomes is, according to some estimates, greater than in any country in the world.[19]

Subsequent to the neoliberal policies launched in the 1980s in the United States, the United Kingdom, the People's Republic of China, and elsewhere, the end of the Cold War brought about another shared historical moment. Widespread embrace of Fukuyama's end-of-history thesis provided momentum to the Washington Consensus in the West, while Deng's southern tour reinvigorated capitalist reforms in China. "Washington Consensus"—a phrase coined in 1990 by John Williamson of the Institute for International Economics, a think-tank based in Washington, D.C.—attempted to summarize the commonly shared themes of policy advice given by Washington-based institutions at the time, such as the IMF, the World Bank, and the U.S. Treasury Department. The Washington Consensus policies were considered necessary for Latin America to recover from the financial crises of the 1980s, and their rationale was adopted by key Chinese economists and policy makers in the early 1990s, gaining greater currency in the wake of the Asian financial crisis of 1997–98. The Washington Consensus identified the market as a universally efficient mechanism to allocate scarce resources and promote economic growth. During the 1980s, international financial institutions, particularly the IMF and the World Bank, actively encouraged governments to dismantle market controls. By the 1990s, the Washington Consensus had gained currency in mainland Chinese intellectual circles, best evidenced by the "Hayek fever" that ensued after von Hayek's *The Road to Serfdom* and *The Constitution of Liberty* were translated into Chinese, in 1997, and immediately became bestsellers.

Yet, by the turn of the millennium, neoliberal policies, subject to wide-ranging criticisms from a variety of social actors, had been replaced by the post–Washington Consensus, which underpins neoliberal policies with social safety nets in order to deal with market failure, recognizing cases in which government intervention in the market can play a positive role. While a number of Chinese liberal intellectuals continue to argue that a capitalist economy can be a free and spontaneous order without state intervention, Chinese leaders made a similar adjustment away from pure market neoliberal policies. After nearly two decades of decentralization and privatization, Premier Zhu Rongji and his top deputy and successor, Wen

Jiabao, began reinstating governmental safety nets such as reduced taxes and school fees, and subsidized healthcare, under the motto "new socialist countryside."[20] Such perceived failures in neoliberal theory have led many to argue that, as a viable guide to ensuring the future of capital accumulation, neoliberalism is already in trouble, if not actually dead. However, as a dominant mode of discourse neoliberalism continues to hold sway worldwide, especially in China.

One reason this form of thought has prevailed is its appeal to "commonsense" intuitions, values, and desires. In David Harvey's words, "The founding figures of neoliberal thought took political ideals of human dignity and individual freedom as fundamental, as 'the central values of civilization.' In so doing they chose wisely, for these are indeed compelling and seductive ideals."[21] The effective use of neoliberal rhetoric was exemplified in the garnering of a political base in support of the U.S. invasion of Iraq through appeals to liberty for American and Iraqi citizens. Although the initial justification for invading Iraq was to ensure the physical safety of U.S. citizens—Saddam Hussein was said to harbor weapons of mass destruction and to collaborate with terrorist groups such as Al Qaeda, claims later proven false—the Bush administration quickly shifted its rhetoric to emphasize instead the liberation of the Iraqis from a brutal dictator. Once Hussein was captured, "liberty" was to be achieved through the establishment of the "new sovereign Iraq"; however, in 2005 a U.S. senior official expressed, anonymously, that "the United States no longer expects to see a model new democracy, a self-supporting oil industry or a society in which the majority of people are free from serious security or economic challenges."[22] At the time of this volume's publication, Iraq's political and economic stability remains threatened. As complex as motivations for the invasion may have been, what is uncontested is that a major, yet rarely voiced, objective was the "freeing" of Iraqi markets for global capital investment and circulation. The invasion allowed Paul Bremer, head of the Coalition Provisional Authority, to enact policies such as "the full privatization of public enterprises, full ownership rights by foreign firms of Iraqi businesses, full repatriation of foreign profits . . . the opening of Iraq's banks to foreign control, national treatment for foreign companies and . . . the elimination of nearly all trade barriers."[23]

In addition to commonsense appeals to liberty and human dignity, neoliberal claims that market liberalization produces unrivaled benefits have been repeated so often that many people accept them as unchallengeable truths. Consequently, business and political leaders routinely defend their efforts to expand free trade as necessary to ensure a brighter future for all people. In 1997 Renato Ruggiero, the first director-general of the WTO, declared that liberalization efforts have "the potential for eradicating global poverty in the early part of the next century—a utopian notion even a few decades ago, but a real possibility today."[24] Nearly a decade later a senior fellow for the Institute for International Economics claimed that "if all global trade barriers were eliminated, approximately 500 million people could be lifted out of poverty over 15 years."[25] The sad truth, however, is that the income gap between the fifth of the world's people living in the richest countries and the fifth of world's people living in the poorest increased from thirty to one in 1960, to sixty to one in 1990, to seventy-four to one in 1997.[26] The trend is not encouraging. In India an estimated 26 percent of the total population, or 260 million, were living in poverty by the end of 2000, and in 2006 at least one in seven Chinese lived below the poverty line, a figure ten times worse than the official estimate of 20 million people earning less than $1 per day.[27] Particularly troubling in China is that the country's overall Gini coefficient, a measure of inequality in which a value of 0 represents perfect equality and 1 means perfect inequality, exceeded 0.5 in 2006, well over the 0.4 value generally considered to represent alarming levels of inequality.[28] Instead of reducing poverty, the past three decades of free-market structural adjustments, which have intensified since China's entry into the WTO, in 2002, have enabled economic and political elites to consolidate their wealth and power.[29]

It is important to realize that neoliberalism functions not as a scientific framework for maximizing economic well-being and efficiency, but as an ideological cover for the expansion and enhancement of corporate profit-making opportunities. In a recent article Martin Hart-Landsberg analyzes a number of WTO agreements explicitly designed to limit public regulation of economic activity by individual states in order to increase the profits of transnational corporations. The Agreement on Trade-Related Aspects of Intellectual Property Rights (TRIPS) limits state ability to deny patents on certain products, significantly increases the time patents remain in force, and restricts compulsory licensing to ensure affordability of critical medicines. The Agreement on Trade Related Investment Measures (TRIMS) restricts states from putting performance requirements on foreign direct investment (FDI), including use of local materials and labor. A proposed expansion of the General Agreement on Trade in Services (GATS) would force states to open national service markets (such as healthcare, education, public utilities, retail trade) to foreign providers, as well as limit public regulation of their activity. A proposed Government Procurement Agreement would deny states the ability to use noneconomic criteria, such as labor and environmental practices, in awarding contracts.[30]

Each of these agreements are based on the alleged virtues of free trade and free labor flows, a notion which holds enormous sway in many advanced industrial nations. In China as well, the ideal of achieving the equilibrium of perfect competition, perfect mobility of labor and capital, and perfect trade balances is considered by many to be realizable once China progresses through the transitional stage of "primitive accumulation." Andrew Kipnis cites a conservative Chinese MBA student who voices an assumption common in China about the process of capitalist development: "The stage of primitive accumulation can only be achieved through the stripping of rights from and the brutal exploitation of workers. Marx showed that to be the case for all European countries. Anyone who opposed the brutal exploitation of workers in China simply doesn't want China to develop and is anti-China."[31] While this is a dubious interpretation of the Marxist theory of primary accumulation, the student's remark is representative in assuming that inequity and violence are inevitable and necessary in this "transitional" stage of China's development. Wang Hui is especially critical of using the term *transition* to characterize China's development: " 'Transition' is the crucial unspoken premise of the contemporary discourse on Chinese society—it presupposes a necessary connection between the process of current inequality and an ultimate ideal."[32]

Chinese intellectuals are particularly well positioned to confront the issues posed by neoliberal discourse and developmental strategies in part because China's search for modernity was shaped from the start by the historical context of imperialist expansion and a crisis in capitalism. As early as the Qing dynasty, Chinese intellectuals questioned the Enlightenment assumptions governing modernization theory: Kang Youwei's one-world utopia (*datong*), Zhang Binglin's egalitarianism, and Sun Zhongshan's (Sun Yat-sen's) principle of the people's livelihood (*minsheng zhuyi*) all theorized forms of modernization that rejected instrumental rationalization. In the past decade a number of Chinese scholars have pointed out contradictions of the neoliberal process, notably rapid economic deregulation conjoined with a still highly intrusive and often authoritarian state. Many of these intellectuals have been labeled "neoleftist" (*xin zuopai*), implying they are unduly influenced by Western neo-Marxists. Yet the antecedents of China's critique of capitalism clearly precede its twentieth-century adaptation of Marxism and practice of socialist modernization.

Shijun Tong's study of the Chinese discourse of modernization, for example, historicizes three earlier alternative approaches to instrumental rationality.[33]

In his introduction to Wang Hui's essay "The 1989 Social Movement and China's Neoliberalism," Theodore Huters explains that Wang considers the Chinese case to be particularly revealing of how the neoliberal process works in the new global order as a whole, such that economic growth and development trumps every other concern, particularly democracy and social justice: "At its heart the essay is an impassioned plea for economic and social justice and an indictment of the corruption brought on by the explosion of 'unregulated' markets, a phenomenon that had become evident in China long before it did in the United States."[34] Like David Harvey, He Qinglian, Qin Hui, Wang Xiaoming, and others, Wang Hui argues that terms like *free* and *unregulated* are largely ideological constructs masking the intervention of highly manipulative, even coercive, governmental actions on behalf of economic policies that favor a particular scheme of capitalist acquisition, a process that must be clearly distinguished from truly free markets. In Wang's words, "The creation of today's market society was not the result of a sequence of spontaneous events, but rather of state interference and violence."[35]

Arguing in a similar vein, the liberal-leaning rural sociologist Qin Hui, like Hart-Landsberg and Burkett, dismisses the common views of China held by Western economists. One group, he says, adheres to the Washington Consensus of classical liberals and believe that by avoiding privatization China is making only temporary gains and will face grave consequences. Another group adheres to a Keynesian model and praises China for remaining a "quasi-welfare economy" that avoids the hazards of excessive marketization. "Both are under the illusion that the Chinese transition is more 'gradual' and 'socialist' than the East European ones. In reality, the process of 'dividing up the big family's assets' has been proceeding as relentlessly in China as in Eastern Europe. . . . [I]f privatization is an operation performed in the dark under authoritarian rule, whether by 'division' or 'sale,' it will inevitably be robbery of the masses."[36] The earliest blow to mainstream economic studies in China, which by the late 1990s were largely aligned with American academies, came from economic journalist He Qinglian's book *Zhongguo xiandaihua de xianjing* (Modernization's pitfall), first published in Hong Kong in 1997. A PRC edition published the next year became an instant bestseller and was widely pirated by street vendors. Chaohua Wang explains that "as an attack on the spread of social injustice and inequality in the PRC, the book was without precedent. ... [T]he strong social response to He's book struck a direct blow to public trust in mainstream economic studies, which typically presented the reform process in a bland and euphemistic light."[37]

During the post-Reform Era the Chinese academy became increasingly commercialized, rationalized, and privatized along with other social sectors. Thus the paradigm shift that has occurred among Chinese intellectuals since the 1990s is based, in part, on a need to redefine their relationship to society. As the Chinese state promotes capitalist development, a new bureaucratic and technocratic elite has replaced the Enlightenment intellectual of the New Era, a political-cultural designation for the decade of modernizing reforms launched by Deng Xiaoping in 1979. China's "intellectual power elite," situated in universities and research centers, the Chinese Academy of Social Sciences, and media outlets, are changing their social roles and adopting new objects of study. Intellectuals are often identified as antagonistic to the establishment, yet in China the historical role of the scholar-official (*shi daifu*) has been more complex. On the one hand, the *shi* saw himself as the moral standard-bearer of the empire and, as such, advised the emperor to conduct his affairs ethically so that his reign would flourish by bettering the lives of the people. On the other hand, as an "official," he was a member of the elite governing class, and his interests were closely aligned with those of the establishment. Yet, as Edward Gu and Merle Goldman point out, "within the ruling class, both the *literati* and the intelligentsia are dominated by other ruling elites—namely, emperors, courtiers, and even eunuchs in imperial times and politicians, militaries and Party-state bureaucrats in the modern era."[38] Chinese intellectuals enjoyed considerable political influence and social prestige during the May Fourth Movement (1915–25) and Reform Era (1978–89), but they also suffered the worst political repression in Chinese history under Mao Zedong's rule. In post-Reform China their social and political influence continues to be negotiated and contested.

According to Jerome Karabel, sociologists generally discuss intellectuals in two ways. The "realist-structuralist approach" perceives intellectuals as professionals who form a social group with a core and a periphery: the core comprises those who create knowledge (scholars, writers, artists, and sometimes journalists); then there are those who distribute and transmit knowledge (journalists, teachers, clerics); finally, there is a periphery of those who apply knowledge as part of their job (engineers, physicians, lawyers).[39] The second methodology, which focuses on the public role or political responsibility of the intellectual, is called the "phenomenological approach." These two approaches embody two competing definitions of intellectuals: experts versus critics. What one finds, with careful attention to the contours of the debates over urban cultural aesthetics in China, is that opposing sides often appeal to different understandings of the role of the intellectual. This has a great deal to do with the increasing privatization of the academy, the creation of semi-official and nonofficial institutions, and the commercialization of culture, all of which have had a profound impact on the relationship of Chinese intellectuals to the state and society. Gu and Goldman suggest that perhaps one of the most applicable formulations of the positions that intellectuals occupy in China's social structure is Pierre Bourdieu's notion of intellectuals as "a dominated fraction of the dominant class."[40] As dominance over capital increasingly determines power in China, Chinese intellectuals begin to share a social state similar to intellectuals in postindustrial societies. The challenge of how to wield power while remaining dominated, not so much by a totalitarian state as by instrumental rationality, underlies many of the contemporary debates in China today.

A challenge for all intellectuals, including those in China, is their situation relative to "state" and "society." One problem in advanced postindustrial societies is that the term *intellectual* has little substantive meaning because of the "degradation" of the intellectual-cultural enterprise into that of technocrats.[41] Steven Brint argues that since the 1960s in the West there has been a transformation from "social trustee" to "expert professionalism."[42] Many of China's critical debates in the 1990s were driven by a fear that the professionalizing trend would degrade the historically privileged status of the intellectual, the literati, the scholar-official in Chinese society. These rapid and disorienting social changes led scholars such as Wang Hui to reflect on the difficulty of "affirming who we are" (*queren ziji*): "Owing to the disintegration of the traditional social system and its ethical structure, no longer does our social role provide us with an objective foundation from which to make moral judgments or with the conditions that will allow us to understand ourselves."[43] Wang Hui sees self-definition as essential, in Gloria Davies's words, because of the "strong expectation (often explicitly expressed) that modern Chinese intellectual history, properly examined, will yield the necessary truth to advance China socially, culturally, and politically."[44] While many Chinese scholars have relinquished this expectation in the new environment of market rationalization and professionalization, some have redoubled their efforts to effect social and political change.

Intellectual Identity in Urban Consumer Culture

The disenfranchisement of intellectuals in the humanities was one of the most obvious cultural effects of China's rapid economic development. Scholars fell from their twentieth-century pinnacle of influence in the 1980s, when they led the nation in debates over culture and future ideology, to a position of irrelevance in matters of national import. In the 1980s intellectuals were reassessing the ideological orientation of a nation in the aftermath of the Cultural Revolution, and their role was crucial as a nation attempted to come to terms with its past. As individuals withdrew from social movements in the politically rigid climate after June Fourth and focused instead on private economic advancement, the role of intellectuals appeared far less relevant to the nation as a whole. Unlike academic discourse on *socialist* alienation in the 1980s, in the 1990s intellectuals lamented their *social* alienation and engaged in genuine self-examination devoid of the confidence and optimism characterizing their earlier introspective campaigns. Competing understandings of the new role of the intellectual in an emerging consumer culture informed a contentious debate over "humanist spirit" (*renwen jingshen*).

In early 1993, as the nation was applying itself to the task of commercialization under Deng Xiaoping's mantra "To Get Rich Is Glorious," the writer and former minister of culture Wang Meng published the provocative article "Avoiding the Sublime" in the influential journal *Dushu* (Reading). He extolled the bestselling author Wang Shuo's self-proclaimed "hooligan literature" (*wanzhu wenxue*) for its "perfect fit with the Four Cardinal Principles and the market economy."[45] Not coincidentally, it was Wang Shuo's "mocking" (*tiaokan*) urban literature and media productions that inspired "intellectual-bashing" in the first place. Wang Meng's article elicited immediate objections by eminent scholars such as Chen Pingyuan of Peking University. In mid-1993 a nationwide debate was launched when a group of Shanghai intellectuals, led by Wang Xiaoming, initiated a series of roundtable discussions on "the loss of humanist spirit" in the emergent culture industry.[46] Sponsored by *Reading*, the first dialogue was published under the title "Ruins in the Wilderness: The Crisis of Literature and Humanist Spirit," in which Wang Xiaoming harshly assesses the contemporary literary climate: "Today the crisis of literature is obvious, literary magazines are falling by the wayside, the quality of new pieces is declining, die-hard readers are diminishing daily, writers and critics realize they've chosen the wrong profession so more and more are 'casting into the sea' [*xiahai*]. . . .

Today's literature crisis is an obvious sign that the quality of public culture is on the decline and the spiritual quality of several entire generations is progressively worsening. The crisis of literature exposes the crisis of humanist spirit in contemporary China."[47] The term *renwen jingshen*, which has also been translated as "spirit of humanism" or "humanistic spirit," is essentially an Enlightenment concept of reason and informed consent, the civilized pursuit of Arnoldian "sweetness and light" in culture. It stands opposed to what it perceives to be the philistine elements of decadent popular culture. Matthew Arnold's ideal of culture, expressed in his nineteenth-century classic, *Culture and Anarchy*, conveys the spirit of the discussions: "Culture, then, is a study of perfection . . . and perfection which consists of becoming something rather than in having something, in an inward condition of the mind and spirit, not in an outward set of circumstances."[48] The idea of the discussions was to identify those spiritual aspects of culture worth nurturing, particularly in the face of vulgar urban commercialism.

Geremie Barmé summarizes the ensuing "humanist spirit discussions" (*renwen jingshen taolun*), an umbrella term for a variety of literary and cultural concerns.

> Among other things, leading thinkers and writers debated how they should respond to the extreme commercialization of the society. What, if any, were the abiding moral and intellectual values of the past? How should the concerned individual act in the face of the combined autocracy of politics and capital? They lamented the lack of a deep-seated intellectual skepticism and an independently critical spirit in the intelligentsia; they questioned whether the tradition of liberalism in twentieth-century China was dead or in its death throes. This group, it was argued, was paralyzed by an inability to articulate any "ultimate concerns," *zhongji guanhuai*, and literary criticism itself seemed flaccid and cast adrift from any moral or aesthetic underpinnings, its course set by the prevailing winds of fashion and squalls of political necessity. . . . The plethora of articles published on the "humanistic spirit" expressed a sense among many publicly active intellectuals that if none of the (revived) scholastic standards and traditions of the past could withstand economic imperatives, then thinkers and independent commentators as a whole would be shunted aside by the market just as previously they had been marginalized by politics.[49]

This fear of social irrelevance drove the discussions. Participants aimed at nothing short of reclaiming the grand mission of the May Fourth thinkers by updating a metaphysical paradigm for China in the twenty-first century. Wen Liping quotes nearly fifty writers and critics who participated in the discussions, and summarizes the content in seven topics: (1) definitions of humanist spirit; (2) characteristics of humanist spirit; (3) the crisis of humanist spirit; (4) the need to reestablish humanist spirit (given the absence of religion); (5) intellectual resources for restoring humanist spirit (to combat the self-interest of a free-market economy); (6) cultural resources for restoring humanist spirit (compatibilities between traditional Chinese culture and modern society); and (7) determining which "ultimate concerns" should serve as the foundation of the humanist spirit.[50] Such weighty topics notwithstanding, the round-table discussions failed to convert random suppositions into a systematically argued schema, much less an overarching world-view or belief system.

Predictably, a number of Chinese intellectuals considered their colleagues to be taking themselves far too seriously. One group, "represented broadly by the 'two Wangs'" (the writers Wang Meng and Wang Shuo), continued to celebrate the market economy as the best antidote to the "extreme leftism" of the Maoist past.[51] Another group of detractors were pejoratively labeled the "post-masters" (houzhu) for championing various forms of poststructuralism such as postmodernism and postcolonialism. Zhang Yiwu, Zhang Fa, and Chen Xiaoming, among others, interpreted mass consumer culture as a universal form of postmodern culture inextricably enmeshed with secular society. Postmodernism had first been introduced in China when Fredric Jameson lectured at Peking University in 1985; however, "when it was applied to Chinese conditions by Zhang Yiwu, Chen Xiaoming, and others a decade later," Wang Chaohua opines, "the caustic edge of Jameson's theory, which had described postmodernism as 'the cultural logic of late capitalism,' was abandoned for a contented or even enthusiastic endorsement of mass culture, which they saw as a new space of popular freedom."[52] As a whole, the "post" theorists affirmed the literary and cultural climate of the 1990s and hailed the increased globalization of ideas as the twenty-first century dawned, dismissing the so-called loss of humanist spirit as the fretting of intellectuals floundering in the newly emerging market economy, rather than being an indicator of cultural decline.

These two camps embody two competing definitions of intellectuals: critics versus experts. Post theorists focused on gaining international symbolic capital by acting as cultural pundits conversant in the latest critical theories. They, like many academics, judged critical prowess more in terms of its reception in the global academy (quantified by invitations to international conferences, translated works, overseas appointments as visiting scholars, etc.) than in its ability to challenge power structures operative within culture. They advocated the understanding of an intellectual as an expert or technocrat, not to mention one whose material lifestyle was improving as a result of market reforms. To academics such as Zhang Yiwu, a professor at Peking University, the posturing of the Shanghai intellectuals remained just that, nostalgia for the bygone role of literati as beacons of light guiding the flailing masses. With the rise of an urban middle class in the 1990s, the traditional Mencian dichotomy—between scholar-gentleman (*shi*) and people (*min*), between "those who use their minds [*laoxin*] and those who use their muscles [*laoli*]" (III, A:4)—became blurred, threatening the traditional role of intellectuals in Chinese society. From the perspective of the post theorists, the "people" no longer need someone to speak for them, obviating the need for an entire class to lead society. Enlightenment intellectuals, on the other hand, continued to adhere to a sense of broader social mission, convinced they should sustain their role as public intellectuals who enact change in the political and cultural sphere through their critique of noxious elements. The question for the latter group was how to regain social agency in the new context of urban consumer culture.

By reviewing how the market economy impacted Chinese scholars, one can better understand their assessment of urban cultural aesthetics. In the 1990s, particularly after Deng Xiaoping's southern tour, many citizens left the security of state positions to "take the plunge" or "cast" into the sea (*xiahai*) of entrepreneurialism, and to "stir-fry stocks" (*chao gupiao*) to make money on their money. Moneymaking was no longer the domain of the enterprising farmer or private peddler (*getihu*) of the 1980s; rather, individuals from diverse backgrounds began to play the market, form large-scale domestic businesses, become freelance artists, cooperate in joint ventures, and collaborate in profitable cultural enterprises. An increasing number of literary intellectuals, feeling the pinch of their meager teaching salaries or writing stipends, chose to cast into the sea of business, giving rise to the term "literati angling for profits" (*wenren xiahai*). The impact of this social change on literary culture was immediate. In an interview in 1997 the Nanjing writer Ye Zhaoyan assessed the change.

During the New Era, in the 1980s, literature was emphasized—even though writers couldn't make a lot of money, they had an especially high social status. However, as the 1990s progressed, the status of writers dropped to a more normal level. Also, the 1990s are very different than earlier periods of Chinese history in that that average Chinese person can openly admit to not being interested in literature. In the past, even if the average "Zhou" on the street didn't read much, he wouldn't admit openly that he didn't like books, but now Chinese culture is like any other, where only those who really like to read do so. I think this is a more natural situation—some people like pop music, some people like literature; you pursue what you like. So the status of writers has fallen to a more normal level—they are respected by those who really care about literature and who actually read their books. But some writers and literary critics feel threatened by this. They worry about the fact that writing is something that some people just don't care about anymore. They don't realize that the point of literature is that it is written for those who want to read it. They feel threatened so they feel the need to promote literature. Actually, I think this is a good trend, because it means that literature only rewards those who are truly interested in literature for its own sake. Literature no longer brings social status, so a lot of writers are giving it up. That's good. It means the question of what literature "does" is disappearing. China has come to understand this about literature.[53]

Like post theorists, Ye Zhaoyan affirms commercialization in the belief that market forces rationalize culture in a way that fosters rather than detracts from the possibility of "good literature," despite the fact it might be read by a smaller proportion of the population. Similarly, the Shanghai cultural critic Mao Shi'an attributed the "humanist spirit" debates to intellectual disorientation in an increasingly rationalized economy.

In the 1980s intellectuals were operating against the backdrop of ideological liberation, and they were still working out the problems left by the conclusion of the Cultural Revolution in the 1970s. So the role of intellectuals was essential—the whole country was trying to figure out what had happened to them. But in the 1990s everyone became interested in the economy, and didn't really care about ideology. Intellectuals were at a loss, as economic development brought about many cultural changes which troubled them. An impoverished widow could invest in the stock market and suddenly make several thousand yuan. Such radical changes in economic status shocked intellectuals. It seemed whoever was "brave" could "make money." Intellectuals felt that suddenly the "hooligan class" [liumang wuchan jieji] was controlling society. A popular saying of the early 1990s was "Better to sell tea-leaf eggs than make nuclear weapons" [*zizao yuanzi dande buru mai chaye dande*], meaning it is better to be illiterate and rich than brilliant and poor. So intellectuals started to discuss their position [*dingwei*] in the city. They were trying to figure out a way to tie their role into this developing economy since they were being increasingly marginalized. This led to the discussions [on humanist spirit] launched by Chen Sihe and Wang Xiaoming.[54]

While these scholars attributed the discussions to social disorientation, others saw the Shanghai intellectuals as avant-garde thinkers who perceived the nature of consumer culture most clearly, given their immersion in Shanghai's accelerated modernization after Deng's southern tour.

The initial strategy of Shanghai intellectuals to reset their moral compass was to mine the legacy of Chinese tradition in the agrarian roots of its culture. Just as "root-seeking" (*xungen*) writers responded to an influx of disorienting Western literary theory by probing the cultural potential of the countryside, Enlightenment intellectuals validated literature set in rural locales as "spiritual." They identified as exemplary such writers as Zhang Chengzhi, Zhang Wei, and Shi Tiesheng, who critiqued contemporary culture through recourse to nature and religion. Conversely, those works identified by scholars as indicative of a loss of humanist spirit were set in contemporary urban culture, namely, Wang Shuo's Beijing-based fiction and television screenplays, Jia Pingwa's first novel on urban themes, *Feidu* (Defunct capital, 1993), and "new state of affairs" (*xin zhuangtai*) urban fiction.[55]

In the first published discussion about "humanist spirit," Wang Xiaoming harshly denigrates Wang Shuo for debasing spiritual culture by writing "mocking" or "scoffing" literature. It is this tendency to "scoff at everything" (*tiaokan yiqie*) which most troubles Wang Xiaoming, since he finds that not only does such literature cater to base public morals, it is ultimately "an attitude opposed to life" (*fei shengming zhuangtai*).[56] Xu Lin describes the "Wang Shuo phenomenon" as a pernicious reworking of classics like *Rulin waishi* (The scholars, 1803) or Qian Zhongshu's novel *Weicheng* (Fortress besieged, 1940) because, despite their shared sarcasm toward ineffective scholars, Wang Shuo's literature has no ideology of redemption and instead "identifies with the ruins."[57] The filmmaker Zhang Yimou is also singled out as a harbinger of the general decline of contemporary Chinese humanist spirit. Zhang Ning and Xu Lin attack the renowned director for "failing to maintain a critical attitude toward the decrepit, filthy material he displays" and for "not pointing to possibilities for the existence of a new spiritual space."[58] Although Zhang's early films are set in the countryside, his detractors consider his works to be infused with the decadent sexual mores of the modern city. His critics also proffer the commonplace criticism of Zhang's works as pandering to foreign interest in Chinese exoticism in order to achieve international renown.

In 1994, in response to the first round-table discussions in Shanghai, the Beijing scholar Bai Ye provided Wang Shuo, Wu Bin, and Yang Zhengguang a forum in which to defend their occupational choices in China's commercial environment. These men had recently started a successful television- and film-production company, which intensified critiques that they were sacrificing artistic ideals by capitulating to market demands. In Bai Ye's interview the writers denied that moneymaking was their primary goal; instead, they said, they were motivated to contribute to culture and further develop their artistic interests. Wang Shuo defended screen media, claiming its artistic equivalence with literature in its ability to influence people. Wu Bin explained that they launched a television production because "society has given us an opportunity to adapt to the 'new state of affairs.' . . . [O]thers are envious if you're not poor like they are."[59] Yang Zhengguang claimed that his psychological state had improved due to his new creative horizons. Bai Ye argued that these writers felt artistically empowered by gaining financial autonomy. The question is, according to their critics, whether or not this "freedom" is merely another form of capitulation to the power and capital dominating Chinese society, this time in the guise of popular interests. Postmodernists came under attack by both liberal and Leftist intellectuals not merely because they celebrated decadent mass culture, but because, in their failure to critique power, they were seen to shirk their responsibilities as public intellectuals.

Ultimately it was the contested role of intellectuals in a culture dominated by neoliberal market reforms that stoked the passionate debates over humanist spirit. The literary critic Chen Sihe, now dean of humanities at Fudan University, argued that the real reason the discussions incited such national debate is that they hit too close to home: "Intellectuals have neglected their social responsibility and hoped this 'new state of affairs' would become the norm."[60] The term "new state of affairs," coined by the Nanjing editor Wang Gan, was used widely at this time to refer to urban consumer culture. Those who advocated the role of intellectual as "expert" were seen to be uncritically aligning themselves with the interests of a state intent on promoting economic reform without political liberalization. This led to the ironic position whereby postmodernists who were advocating the most cutting-edge critical theories were simultaneously accused of cultural conservatism. Postmodernists, for their part, accused the Enlightenment scholars of nostalgia for the utopian quality of 1980s culture, with its forward-looking beliefs in progress and enlightenment, which in fact masked the "radicalism" of the decade.[61] By and large, postmodernists concurred with the assessment put forth by Li Zehou and Liu Zaifu in their book *Farewell to Revolution* (1995), which blamed the violent outcome on June Fourth squarely on the long history of radicalism throughout the twentieth century. According to American-based critic Ben Xu, these postmodern "new cultural conservatives" happily bid farewell to China's twentieth-century history of "radical discourse" inherited from the May Fourth Movement, instead emphasizing "Chineseness" and "reality" as a means of addressing an economically decentralized but politically authoritarian postsocialist system.[62] Meng Fanhua, a Beijing-based critic, identifies three characteristics of the new cultural conservatism: "First, it rejects the radical critical spirit and opts for moderate and steady discursive practice; second, it gives up anxious concern about and questioning of the collective situation and turns its attention to the personal situation; third, it declines to quest for ultimate value, goal, or faith, and is concerned with solutions to local problems."[63] Ben Xu criticizes "new cultural conservatives" of creating an artificial contrast between radicals and conservatives, thereby downplaying the pro-Enlightenment and prodemocracy concerns of the cultural critique in the 1980s.[64]

Before assessing the degree to which postmodernist scholars capitulate to neoliberal global capital and a corrupt regime, it is sensible to assess their views on urban consumer culture. The oppositions between high and low culture, modernization and tradition, and urban and rural aesthetics, which had dominated cultural discussions of the 1980s, were further complicated when these binaries became subsumed by the global. Many cultural critics observed that, as evidenced by the reception of Fifth Generation films by Zhang Yimou and Chen Kaige, the most "indigenous" (i.e., rural) cultural products appeared to be those most "palatable" to international (i.e., Western) tastes. On the other hand, those values inscribed in urbanite (*shimin*) culture seemed to be most reflective of domestic reality, as evidenced by the popularity of Wang Shuo's works and Jia Pingwa's *Defunct Capital*. In the early 1990s Zhang Yiwu argued that the decade was marked by a new cultural logic, which he dubbed the *hou xin shiqi* (post–New Era), the aesthetics of which were encapsulated within urban culture.[65] Building on Fredric Jameson's theory of Third World national allegory, Zhang indicates the post–New Era is categorized by a rejection of metaphors of the nation-state, the main literary strategy from the May Fourth period until the 1980s. The *hou yuyan* (postallegorical) phase is marked instead by a new set of cultural dichotomies, especially that between elite and popular culture in the cultural context of globalism. He argues that "high culture" tries to "go out to the world" (*zouxiang shijie*, a term from the cultural discussions of the 1980s) and tends to exoticize and essentialize a traditional, rural-based China. These elite cultural products include films such as Zhang Yimou's *Dahong denglou gao gao gua* (Raise the red lantern, 1991) and Chen Kaige's *Bawang bieji* (Farewell my concubine, 1993). This is in contrast to "low" or "local culture," which is contemporary, urban-based, and intended for domestic consumption. Well-known examples include Wang Shuo's television series *Kewang* (Desire, 1993) and the popular play *Beijingren zai Niuyue* (Beijing native in New York, 1993). According to Zhang, whereas the internationally acclaimed Fifth Generation filmmakers merely "otherize" China for Western consumption, becoming "Third World slaves" in a "postcolonial climate of globalization," the soap operas, popular fiction, entertainment films, and pop music which have flooded the domestic market have "grasped the contemporary mentality."[66]

The term "new state of affairs" is essential for Zhang's theorizing of the post–New Era, as it differentiates the popular urban works of this period from the "allegorical" thrust of the highbrow rural works, which he claims continue the May Fourth practice of making the native soil "other." The concerns of "new state of affairs" works are neither the "nation" nor the "subject" (two key terms theorized during the culture fever of the 1980s); rather, they reflect an individual's concrete situation. Zhang views this new urban literature as nothing less than a new form of cultural expression which for the first time replaces stereotypical "Enlightenment intellectuals" and "feudalistic peasants" (in fiction of both the May Fourth era and the early 1980s) with an underclass of "lowlife" (*pizi*) heroes, disenfranchised intellectuals, and the middle class.[67] To counter the understanding of post-Mao cultural history put forth by the Enlightenment intellectuals, Zhang Yiwu and the Beijing writer Liu Xinwu published their own dialogue summarizing developments in the Chinese cultural and literary scene in the 1980s and 1990s. Liu and Zhang take issue with the fact that the Shanghai scholars adhere to the traditional notion of cultural enlightenment, where intellectuals enlighten the masses (" 'wo' qi 'ni' meng" ["I" enlighten "you"]), failing to recognize the new cultural patterns of social influence at the turn of the millennium where the line between "intellectual" and "the people" is increasingly blurred or irrelevant. They tie this development to the strengthening of urbanite culture, a trend which, just as in the seventeenth-century Ming dynasty, established new economic and social relationships between people operating outside the political and moral power wielded by intellectuals and the state. Zhang is especially critical of the humanist-spirit debate, pointing out that whereas Chinese Enlightenment intellectuals attempt to define "ultimate concerns," the roots of humanism in the West were opposed to those transcendental values posited by the church, and the entire movement was motivated by anti-ecclesiastical values. Further, they consider the bestselling novels by Jia Pingwa and Wang Shuo to exemplify the liberal values sought by Enlightenment intellectuals, namely, the search for autonomy. Wang Shuo's works, says Liu, express "*this* moment, *this* place, *this* self, *this* significance," private moments not intended to be generalized. "His 'hooligans' were never meant to lead Chinese society, instead they represent people who have stopped pursuing lofty goals and live in the present. . . . [I]t isn't about requiring everyone to become a 'hooligan' but about the individual's search for identity and status. The questions he explores are how do we become a self? How do we imagine the self?"[68] Liu believes that Wang Shuo's novella *Wo shi ni baba* (I'm your father, 1991), for example, is a serious, profound reflection on human relations despite its sarcastic veneer. Zhang agrees, seeing Wang Shuo's rise to prominence in the early 1990s as indicative of the irreversible state (*zhuangtai*) of China's contemporary urban culture.

Anyone conversant in twentieth-century critical theory should be familiar with the assumptions underlying these debates. One only need think back to the influential essays of the late 1930s—Walter Benjamin's "The Work of Art in the Age of Mechanical Reproduction" and Clement Greenberg's "Avant-Garde and Kitsch"—to recall early theories on the aesthetic changes effected by consumer society. The notion that humanist spirit is lost in a market society resembles Benjamin's theorization of the loss of "aura." Benjamin used the term to refer to the feeling of awe created by unique art works or relics of the past. According to Benjamin, earlier cultures generated auras around particular objects of veneration, while capitalist culture causes the decay of the aura due to the proliferation of mass production and reproduction technologies. Unlike the categorical critique of consumer culture by Chinese Enlightenment critics, however, for Benjamin this was an ambiguous historical development, a force for democratizing both access to cultural objects and a critical attitude toward them, but also for harboring the potential elimination of reflection and imagination. In this sense the arguments of Chinese Enlightenment critics more closely resemble those in Greenberg's article, where he criticized the "kitsch" produced by capitalist propaganda, arguing that modernist ("avant-garde") art was a means to resist the leveling of consumer culture. The arguments of the Chinese postmodernists resonate with those in Susan Sontag's well-known essay "Notes on 'Camp,'" which provided the groundwork for the popular understanding and reception of pop art in the 1960s. The aesthetic position maintained by the "two Wangs" is easily recognizable in number 41 of Sontag's fifty-eight numbered theses: "The whole point of Camp is to dethrone the serious. Camp is playful, anti-serious. More precisely, Camp involves a new, more complex relation to 'the serious.' One can be serious about the frivolous, frivolous about the serious."[69]

Yet there are several important differences between the recent debates among Chinese intellectuals and those waged earlier in Western contexts. First of all, the debates over cultural aesthetics in China are set against a context of neoliberal hegemony and global flows (as Manuel Castells has theorized it), as opposed to the economics of embedded liberalism (Keynesian limits on privatization) and the restricted capital and information flows prior to the 1970s. Because of the increasing porosity of state boundaries with respect to capital flows, exchange rates were allowed to float after 1971. Second, cultural specifics complicate the manner in which these debates play out in China. The intellectual tradition of the scholar-official, like the strong tradition of the politically engaged intellectual in France, results in a very different understanding of the role of the knowledge worker in shaping state policy and culture than in Anglo-American settings. Further, the collectivist roots of China's Confucian and agrarian culture result in subtle distinctions from aesthetic trends emerging in other cultural contexts. Although global media images and information flows profoundly influence Chinese culture, emerging cultural phenomena such as reality TV, text messaging, blogging, cosplay, and Internet literature take on very different contours in China than in Japan or the United States. The specificity of the new forms of autonomy manifest in contemporary Chinese culture has been analyzed in books by scholars in diverse fields such as literary history, ethnography, urban studies, and medical anthropology.[70] Conversely, as aspects of Chinese culture begin to influence other national cultures, just as Japanese *manga* and *anime* have become a constitutive part of the American youth experience, and Indian yoga a mainstream practice for young urban professionals worldwide, China's long history of absorbing and Sinicizing other cultures may well become manifest in a global context. As Samuel Huntington correctly pointed out, globalization does not mean Westernization.

As a "new state of affairs" defines global consumer culture, the underlying assumptions informing the past decade of debates in China between neoliberals and neoleftists increasingly define the culture wars in other national cultures as well. Just as the convergence of aims that extend across nation-state borders has led to unlikely coalitions among diverse interest groups, an alignment of coalitions around or opposed to neoliberal capital is occurring among scholars worldwide. One of many examples is the East Asian Regional Conference in Alternative Geography (EARCAG), established in 1997 during the Inaugural International Conference of Critical Geography to avoid "merely translating spatial theories developed in the Western context into local languages" while claiming "solidarity among critical and alternative geographers at the global scale."[71] Similar forums, such as the Inter-Asia Cultural Studies (IACS) project, initiated in the late 1990s "to provide a platform . . . to analyze urgent issues emerging in the Asia region," aim at more than polite scholarly exchanges.[72] The process of globalization has generated new intermediary conditions of knowledge production in regionalization. These regional coalitions challenge previous analytical frameworks bound by local society and enable Chinese scholars to study the local in relation to regional dynamics. As articulated by the Shanghai hosts of the 2007 IACS meeting, "[Such coalitions] enhance opportunities to work together beyond nation-state boundaries and call for a change in our mode of thinking if not intellectual life."[73] As the contours of regional and global debates between neoliberals and neoleftists begin to merge with the local, one must reexamine the question "whither China?" in the context of rising Chinese nationalism in the 1990s.

While intellectuals and the populace of China during the 1980s were generally favorable toward Western political, cultural, and economic theories, these sentiments began to change in the early 1990s, in large part due to more widespread media access, especially to Western news outlets. Chinese citizens began to see firsthand the biased manner in which China was discussed in other national contexts, and no longer accepted idealized notions that human rights and the rule of law were the operative policies in the United States. Instead, they saw how vested interests often worked against human betterment, and began to grasp how U.S. congressional politics was related to media representations of China as militaristic. In 1991 Chinese intellectuals—almost all of them liberal in the pro-Reform sense and still in the shadow of June Fourth—experienced their first collective shock, watching on television pro-Yeltsin troops bombard the Russian parliament. Xudong Zhang remarks, "That this antidemocratic violence went on as liberal democratic world opinion remained amiably silent stood in stark contrast to the boisterous protests and sanctions against the Chinese government after Tiananmen."[74] In 1994, despite the fact that most Chinese were cynical about the state's highly orchestrated bid to host the 2000 Olympics, its rejection at the hands of Western governments coalesced into what Zhang deems nationalism's "first popular channel of expression in the 1990s." Two years later, the editors of the provocative bestseller *China Can Say No* articulated this nationalism: "Certainly, the commercial greed and impotence before terror revealed during the Olympics in Atlanta should shake America from its illusion of being the sole world leader from here to eternity. This is especially noteworthy because the 'Anti-China Club' in the US vetoed Beijing's chance to host the Summer Olympic Games for the year 2000 in that city because 'we couldn't handle it.' At the end of the 20th century, China has once again become a world power in its own right. It need not play second fiddle to anyone. The next generation coming to power in China is prepared to say no and won't hesitate to do so when it is in our interests."[75]

Xudong Zhang details a number of subsequent incidents, in the 1990s, that further exacerbated nationalist sentiments. In 1995–96 the first Taiwan Strait crisis broke out following the visit to the United States of Lee Teng-hui, then president of Taiwan, which led to China's "testing" of missiles near the Taiwan coast and to the United States deploying two aircraft-carrier battle groups outside the strait. Not only did the crisis bring the two countries closer to the brink of direct military confrontation than at any time since the end of the Vietnam War, "it also opened a profound collective wound among Chinese intellectuals and the population as a whole, who learn by heart the history of humiliations of China by Western imperialism between the Opium War in 1840 and the Japanese surrender in 1945." Zhang continues,

> A belief in the American intention to divide and contain China out of both ideological difference and economic interest became a national consensus, its imperial design and the Chinese counter-strategy an open topic of discussion in the Chinese media. An entire generation of Chinese students, including many who went to the United States to study, became increasingly nationalistic in the sense that a smooth integration

with, if not an enthusiastic embrace by, the U.S.-dominated world system was cast in doubt. The intellectual world was deeply divided. While the government policy of pressing forward with the reform and open door policy, which required stable and constructive Sino-U.S. relations, remained unchanged, it was tinged with a wariness toward the United States and, at a more philosophical level, with a new anxiety over the emerging post–Cold War world order and China's place in it.[76]

This anxiety is best summarized in the bestselling book *Zhongguo keyi shuo bu* (China can say no: Political and emotional choices in the post–Cold War era, 1996), edited by Zhang Xiaobo and Song Qiang. Significantly, the editors directly relate the coalescing of anti–United States sentiment to its media images: "Examining the state of US-China relations, we are pessimistic about the future. The younger generation China can't stand America's disingenuous preachiness on human rights (haven't we all seen the video of Rodney King or of the immigrant workers being mercilessly beaten by police in Riverside, California?)."[77]

The nationalist slogans that pervaded the country in the build-up to the "return of Hong Kong to the Motherland" in 1997 were largely orchestrated from above, yet the ubiquitous banners declaring the end of China's humiliation by imperialist nations expressed deeply felt public sentiments. A decade of growing nationalist sentiment culminated with the war in Kosovo, in 1999, when the Chinese government, intellectual community, and populace were unified in their assessment that American cruise missiles intentionally targeted the Chinese embassy in Belgrade on 9 May, which resulted in the deaths of three Chinese journalists and destruction of the building. Although the North Atlantic Treaty Organization (NATO) categorically denied these claims, insisting the missile attack was accidental, a detailed investigative article published in October of that year by the London *Observer* and its sister paper, the *Guardian*, backed up the claims. These papers cited top NATO sources who asserted that the United States had deliberately bombed the embassy after discovering that it was relaying Yugoslav military radio signals. Yet the mainstream American media responded with strenuous denial.[78] Zhang summarizes the fallout from this event: "The Western rhetoric of universal human rights was thoroughly and perhaps irreversibly discredited and perceived as a mere cover for the exercise of raw power out of a sheer self-interest by an integrated West led by the United States in a world without a military and ideological rival such as the former Soviet Union."[79]

It is important to understand that the mounting nationalism of the 1990s redressed China's unchecked romance with Western theories and policies a decade earlier. Twenty-first-century debates over China's development and global positioning have been far more sophisticated and are increasingly posed in terms that transcend the dualist rhetoric that has dominated Chinese intellectual debates over modernization since the nineteenth century. The decade-long debate between neoliberal and neoleftist approaches to global capitalism, launched in 1997 with Wang Hui's essay "Contemporary Chinese Thought and the Question of Modernity," is a case in point. Granted, some accuse both camps of continuing to perpetuate rigid political categories. Andrew Kipnis, for example, suggests that by adopting the "line-drawing" rhetoric or "road metaphors" prevalent during the Cultural Revolution, Chinese intellectuals singularize the nation and present concepts such as "liberalism" as social wholes to be swallowed or rejected *in toto*.[80] However, China's most influential intellectuals are quick to reject simplistic modernization, Cold War, or Cultural Revolution formulations, and are far from viewing China as "a unified construct travelling the same course at the same speed" as Kipnis claims. Wang Xiaoming, for one, explicitly denounces such epistemological categories: "The extraordinary persistence of intellectuals in thinking in terms of such dichotomies as traditional/modern, closed/open, conservative/reformer, market/planned, socialism/capitalism, communist/anti-communist seems simple-minded."[81] Likewise, during a lecture in 2000 the liberal Qin Hui observed that the confrontation between liberals and the "New Left" seems misplaced given the radically uneven and polarized Chinese reality. For Qin, the problem is that the peculiar Chinese reality exists far beyond the parameters theorized in these positions and the real task is to "criticize Chinese neoliberals with classical liberalism and the New Left with Marxism."[82] Qin's notion that new formulations are necessary to theorize China's current socioeconomic situation is shared by Left-leaning intellectuals. Wang Xiaoming argued, in 1999, that "every generalization about China—that it is a communist-led socialist society as before, that at its core it is a society of traditionally centralized power, that it has virtually become capitalist, that it is a full-fledged consumer society, or even that it is already postmodern—can be supported with examples, as can its opposite. This causes people to reflect. Could it be that the long-standing query 'Whither China?' lacks purchase on the complexity of contemporary society? Perhaps all we can grasp are several, or even only one, of the many dissimilar 'Chinas' that now exist."[83] Wang goes on to suggest that only the methodologies engaged by local cultural studies will allow one to understand the many dissimilar regions that now constitute "China." Here is evidence that Chinese intellectuals have largely moved away from knowledge categories that Xudong Zhang identifies as "obsolete binary opposites—state versus society, 'official' versus 'nonofficial,' dictatorship versus democracy, communism versus capitalism, hard-liners versus reformers, government intervention versus a free market, etc.—opposites that still obstruct our [the West's] critical knowledge of the country."[84]

The problem, as posed by those who attempt to explain Chinese society today, is that there is no readily available theoretical paradigm, whether derived from China's intellectual tradition or from another national, cultural, or historical context. Does the turn to cultural studies maintain the same utilitarian logic and teleology commonly at work in contemporary Chinese scholarship, functioning merely as the latest means of "uncovering" or "creating" a holistic system for understanding the past and present? Scholars such as Gloria Davies see the frequent use in Chinese critical inquiry of terms such as *qingli gongzuo* (sorting out and putting things in order) and *ziwo pipan* (self-criticism) as an indication that "the establishment of the proper order of things (not its interrogation) and self-understanding (not its problematization) are [Chinese critical inquiry's] key goals."[85] Yet, at present, Chinese theorists on the Left and Right are stymied not so much by lack of political imagination, as Kipnis implies, or by neo-Confucian constraints on knowledge production, as Davies suggests, as by the extremely complex economic dynamics governing contemporary Chinese political and social culture. The recent collaborative activities of Chinese intellectuals—new initiatives by overseas Chinese academics to educate China's rural teachers, field research in China's interior by Beijing academics (such as Lu Xueyi, Sun Liping, Wen Tiejun, and Wang Hui) and their partnership with provincial scholars and journalists reporting on ecological devastation and rural corruption, collaborations between eminent geographers such as Wing-Sheng Tang and David Harvey in the East Asian Regional Conference in Alternative Geography, innovative educational and publishing initiatives by Shanghai scholars in cultural studies, regional strategies developed by groups such as the Inter-Asia Cultural Studies Organization—demonstrate creative approaches to the very real economic and political constraints faced by Chinese intellectuals. The development of cultural studies at Shanghai University offers a case study for assessing the potential for knowledge production and political agency in the contemporary Chinese academy.

Cultural Studies: Political Agency or Acquiescence?

In an address delivered in 2006, in Taiwan, to IACS, Wang Xiaoming, director of Shanghai University Center for Contemporary Cultural Studies (CCCS), traced the development of cultural studies in the People's Republic of China.[86] The following summary of these developments comes from Wang's IACS address, his "Manifesto for Cultural Studies" (1999), and a decade of my own observations and interviews with CCCS affiliates. While scholars such as the professor Dai Jinhua, of Peking University, have applied the methodology of cultural studies in their scholarship since the early 1990s, cultural studies was not institutionalized in China until the end of the decade. Within five years "cultural studies fever" had spread throughout China, particularly in Shanghai and Beijing universities. Its popularity stemmed from two sources. First, humanities scholars had, by the mid-1990s, identified cultural studies as one of the most cutting-edge fields in critical theory overseas. Second, this approach seemed particularly applicable to understanding the popular consumer culture dominating Chinese cities, which was also precisely why cultural studies had gained institutional authority in industrialized countries in earlier decades. Yet according to Wang, different Chinese intellectuals became attracted to cultural studies for starkly different political reasons. Some postmodern scholars who celebrate popular urban culture as a democratizing influence engage in cultural studies as a means of legitimating the ongoing market reforms. Neoleftist scholars, rather than perceiving China as moving inevitably toward capitalist democracy, interpret China's economic development more pessimistically, as it is not accompanied by the institutional reforms that occurred in Western democracies. These scholars, including Wang, consider China's current society to be autocratic, corrupt, and devoid of civil rights, and to defy all existing political-economy paradigms, particularly capitalism or socialism. Wang Xiaoming, and the group of Shanghai scholars whose activities he coordinates, self-identify as "pessimists" vis-à-vis China's present reform process, seeing themselves as public intellectuals positioned to critique deleterious social formations.

In "A Manifesto for Cultural Studies," a translation of an unpublished Chinese paper written in 1999, Wang Xiaoming argues that the most urgent task for China's intellectuals is to conduct empirical investigations into contemporary culture to understand China's monumental transformation to a market economy. This research, he says, must exceed the bounds of existing academic disciplines by integrating understandings of culture with its political and economic factors. Wang Xiaoming's study of the real estate market in Shanghai does just this, and although he has given formal talks on his research outside of China, he has yet to publish his book within China, due to the highly sensitive nature of his critique.[87] Xudong Zhang argues that China's recent economic and social developments defy control to such an extent that they threaten the legitimacy of the state. Because of the complexity, unevenness, and diversity of Chinese socioeconomic development, Zhang says, the Chinese state "needs a new ideological coherence to better identify, claim, or fuse with the emerging social-ideological center."[88] It is precisely this "new ideology" that Wang Xiaoming and his Shanghai cohort are interested in unmasking. "The more one understands the operations of various political and economic powers behind this new ideology," says Wang, "and the ways it responds to and constructs mass desires and public imagination, numbing and postponing any social awareness of crises, the more cultural studies should take the new 'thought' as its most important object of criticism."[89] The point of cultural studies, as Wang understands it, is not to further "self-understanding" or establish the "proper order of things," as Davies suggests is the norm for Chinese scholarship. Instead, such research aims to problematize the rhetoric legitimizing the interests of the new rich, which confuses its own class interest—the smooth, uninterrupted functioning of the global system of accumulation—with national or local territorial interest. Wang elaborates how scholars might probe the workings of such an ideology.

> Special attention should be paid to the ways in which this ideology enriches itself from economic and cultural exchanges between China and foreign countries, as restricted by the current pattern of globalization, and to the warm relationships between the new "thought," state power and the new rich. Another important area for research is the complex relationship between the new ideology and the official ideology of the Cultural Revolution, and the ways in which the former has been able to draw on the widespread social disgust toward the latter to create a unique dual identity, as a mainstream ideology that simultaneously poses as a bold heterodoxy. Here we would also need to clarify the extent to which the intellectual community itself has in some respects become an unwitting assistant of the new ideology, and what critical resources the last two decades of literature, art and theory have bequeathed us to resist it.
>
> Today the new ideology has seeped into every pore of social life. There cultural studies must track it, without undue respect for disciplinary

restrictions of specialized fields. Not only must we scan literature, music, painting, sculpture, and film. We must also pay special attention to commercial advertisements, entertainment magazines, popular music, soap operas, newspapers, TV shows, window displays and public decorations. We need to look not only at concrete cultural products, but also at abstract theoretical discourses, and the relationship between these two dissimilar cultural activities. Paper, canvas, screen; buildings, publishers, government bureaus; bars, dance halls, and coffee shops—all should be our province. Where necessary, each must be recalled to its social context: cultural studies in China should neither rigidly adhere to existing disciplinary confines, nor strive to become a new discipline itself. Its hope should be simply to grapple with the more disturbing questions of contemporary life in China, in conditions of globalization, and perhaps to suggest some timely and vigorous responses to them.[90]

Wang clearly adheres to an Althussiarian notion of ideology that permeates society yet derives from disparate, nonunified sources.

It is difficult, in all honesty, to know how to best characterize this new "thought" since it hardly qualifies as a system, jumbling together paradoxical propositions that are impossible to validate. Even though it pervades the majority of advertisements, it is not merely a capitalist product. It features so insistently in the media it could be a set of official slogans, but there is no clear evidence that it was ever intentionally designed by the government. It has no generally recognized spokesmen, and though it often surfaces in cultural and theoretical debates, no one is willing to stand up and take credit for it. But it is precisely this sort of ideology, of indeterminate origin and indistinct contours that feeds the appetite of influential powers in China—and not just the government.[91]

In order to reveal these subtle power relations and unmask the myths supporting this persuasive new ideology, in 2001 Wang Xiaoming established the Center for Contemporary Cultural Studies at Shanghai University (SU) (Shanghai Daxue Zhongguo Dangdai wenhua yanjiu zhongxin) while remaining director of the Chinese department at East China Normal University (ECNU). Wang insists that he initially offered this opportunity to ECNU and only approached other universities once ECNU rejected his proposal. These protestations notwithstanding, not only has Wang benefited financially from his joint appointment, he has been given more political leeway to pursue his agenda at SU. In addition to the fine line between using and being used by one's institution to gain social capital, public intellectuals today (in all geopolitical contexts) are increasingly subject to corruption by economic capital. In an insightful essay Gloria Davies and Geremie Barmé discuss the controversial Cheung Kong–*Reading* Awards, funded by Li Ka-shing, the Hong Kong–based billionaire who has become a highly influential benefactor of Chinese higher education and research since the late 1990s. The acerbic rhetoric feeding the debates between neoliberals and neoleftist largely derives from the fact that in 2000 the *Reading* editor Wang Hui was one of the first recipients of the award, which fed accusations of nepotism and, more importantly, of recriminations against Wang Hui for "selling out" the Leftist cause by accepting international acclaim and neoliberal mammon.[92] Similarly, most cultural studies departments and research centers are funded by the central government's "985 Project" (985 *gongcheng*), a funding initiative launched by Jiang Zemin in 1998 to raise China's higher education up to the world standards of top-tier universities worldwide.

In 2003 the sociology department and Chinese departments at su accepted their first doctoral students in cultural studies, and in 2004 Shanghai University established the first cultural studies department in the nation. Other universities in Shanghai quickly followed suit, including the Research Center of Urban Culture at Shanghai Normal University (Shanghai shifan daxue dushi wenhua yanjiu zhongxin), the Center for Modern Chinese City Studies at ECNU (Huadong shifan daxue Zhongguo xiandai chengshi wenhua yanjiu zhongxin), and the Cultural Criticism Research Center at Tongji University (Tongji daxue wenhua piping yanjiusuo). Some of the directors of these centers, such as Xue Yi at Shanghai Normal and Luo Gang at ECNU, have collaborated with Wang Xiaoming for over a decade. Many young professors now active in cultural studies in Shanghai, such as Luo Gang, Ni Wenjian, and Dong Limin of ECNU, and Ni Wei of Fudan University, were Wang Xiaoming's former graduate students at ECNU and participated in the humanist-spirit debates and biweekly scholarly forums (which I also participated in as a doctoral student in 1997). Others, such as Mao Jian of Shanghai University, Lü Xinyu of Fudan University, and Zhang Lianhong of the Shanghai Academy of Social Sciences, are prominent young voices in film and theater studies. The doctoral students of these affiliated universities compile readers (in Chinese and English) in cultural studies, organize conferences, invite nonaffiliated Shanghai graduate students and the public to their forums, and maintain an active website, http://www.cul-studies.com, through Shanghai University's Center for Cultural Studies. Other than the website, the most visible result of their collaboration in cultural studies is a book series, published in 2007, which analyzes eight aspects of Shanghai's local culture in the 1990s: the media, the real estate market and its advertising, visual culture and imagery on the streets, migrant workers' villages (urban villages), cultural history of factories and factory workers, Internet literature, new urban space, and fashion.[93]

These multidisciplinary and multiclass activities have generated considerable excitement, and draw on the model for cultural studies established in the 1960s by Birmingham Centre for Contemporary Cultural Studies (which trained Stuart Hall and Paul Willis). They adhere to principles that defined early cultural studies, as articulated by Richard Hoggart in his *The Use of Literacy* (1957) and Raymond Williams's *Culture and Society: 1780– 1950* (1958), namely, engagement (in the social, political, and ethical concerns of contemporary culture) and subjectivity (the recognition that cultural studies is personal and ethnographic, involving the observer as much as the observed). These cornerstones of cultural studies set the discipline apart from New Criticism, which dominated Anglo-American literary criticism in its privileging of the "autonomous text" defined by the transcendental, the objective, the long-lasting, and the nonpolitical. The approach is liberating for Chinese students in the humanities who have traditionally confined their studies to the classroom rather than the streets. As an su graduate student excitedly confessed, "Sitting in my room I had come up with this solution [pointing left], but after I helped the migrant workers establish their new school I realized the answer was here [pointing right]. I was completely off."[94] What this ad hoc remark suggests is that while Wang Xiaoming's goal for cultural studies may be the problematization of society, finding "the answer" remains the goal of intellectual inquiry for many Chinese scholars.

In addition to the need to adopt epistemological paradigms that break from heuristic understandings of scholarship, Chinese intellectuals face additional obstacles in that they are situated within an authoritarian regime which has decentralized its economic development. The first problem, and one familiar to scholars in other contexts, is how to pursue anti-establishment cultural studies in an authoritarian society. Wang Xiaoming comments,

> Although the foundational stance of cultural studies is anti-establishment, nearly all of the resources utilized by Chinese cultural studies derive from within the establishment, especially the educational system (upon which it depends for informational access and financial resources). The greater the

trend toward globalization, the more disenfranchised the lower classes of society become. And the educational establishment merely replicates the unequal social conditions prevailing in society. Thus an associated question is how to use the system without allowing it to use you. Once cultural studies becomes an established discipline, how do you keep it from losing its critical and experimental character? Who's using whom?[95]

Unlike his colleague Wang Hui, an intellectual historian at Tsinghua University who has devoted considerable scholarship to analyzing the workings of neoliberal capital, Wang Xiaoming tends to view the problem of intellectual autonomy as unique to China's transitional, and as yet untheorized, political economy. What Wang Xiaoming grapples with, however, is not merely the financial exigencies of institutional affiliation, but the ways in which the educational enterprise is embedded in processes of global capitalism, which, through privatization and rationalization, increasingly dictate the content of higher education.

To scholars in the United States and other industrialized countries, the problem as articulated by Wang Xiaoming is becoming all too familiar. To take but one of many examples, in 2000 Roger Bowen was forced to resign as president of State University of New York (SUNY), New Paltz, because he resisted the corporatization of the academy by aligning himself with the classic values of academic culture. In a speech he delivered in May 2001 Bowen reflected: "The prevailing mind set is: If something is not measurable, then it lacks value. It was only a matter of time before this ideology and its proponents began wresting control of the academy."[96] Given that higher education is increasingly governed by corporate values, some scholars have strategically acquiesced. In a creative attempt to theorize ways for the humanities to "use the institution" in a bottom-line culture, prominent academics such as Ien Ang suggest promoting cultural studies as an "applied humanities" particularly suited to making expert knowledge relevant to the "real world," an "institutionally practical" strategy which implies collaboration with, not defiance against, the university administration that speaks for the financial interest of the institution.[97] Ang's pitch resonates with the corporate agenda governing the SUNY system, articulated in 1997 as "putting in place a tightly drawn conservative curriculum throughout SUNY and reducing the university to a training school that prepares workers for jobs the corporate sector tells us they need."[98]

What is especially interesting about the SUNY case, as Lisa Duggan discusses in *The Twilight of Inequality? Neoliberalism, Cultural Politics, and the*

Attack on Democracy, is that the ostensible reason for pressuring President Bowen to resign was a highly publicized and seemingly manufactured scandal regarding the content of a women's studies conference. What very few Leftist activists in the academy have done, argues Duggan, is to make the necessary connections between the cultural wars and identity politics that tend to dominate cultural studies, and the neoliberal agenda driving corporatization of the academy. She cites Alisa Solomon, a City University of New York faculty member, as one of the few intellectuals who illuminates the relationship between culture, politics, and economics. Writing about the suny scandal in the *Village Voice*, in an article headlined "Sexual Smokescreen," Solomon begins, "When there's scant support for your campaign to downsize public institutions, seek out the sex—especially when it's female or gay."[99] Duggan goes on to make a compelling case for the subtle move in the 1990s by "Third Way" politicians and activists to denigrate identity politics in favor of "personal responsibility." When this move was replicated in the academy, she argues, it squarely aligned the scholarly aims of fields such as cultural studies with those of neoliberal capital and the neoconservative right.

The late-twentieth-century shift in the theoretical focus of cultural studies in the West illuminates dilemmas faced by its practitioners in China. Wang Xiaoming's center is beholden to global institutional capital, and thus not only faces similar economic influences and strictures on research, but borrows from cultural studies theories that gained currency during the economic neoliberalism of the late twentieth century. Simon During summarizes the effects of neoliberalism on cultural studies in the United Kingdom.

> The more the market is freed from state intervention and trade and finance cross national boundaries, the more the nation will be exposed to foreign influences and the greater the gap between rich and poor. Thatcherite appeals to popular values can be seen as an attempt to overcome this tension. . . . A homogenous image of national culture is celebrated and enforced to counter the dangers posed by the increasingly global nature of economic exchanges and widening national, economic divisions. . . . When cultural studies moved away from a Marxian [analysis based on class], it began to approach, if in a different spirit and register, certain Thatcherite themes. After all, both movements were strongly anti-statist; both affirmed, within limits, a decentered view of social organization.[100]

not natural!
It's designed!

The reason for these similarities, During continues, is that the new Right insists that no social institution stands outside particular economic interests, and the cultural studies that evolved in the 1980s and 1990s bases itself on the strong belief that there is no "metadiscourse" outside any discursive practice and that all theories must be engaging, subjective, and contemporarily relevant. As a result, says During, those areas of cultural studies with solid currency today, such as postcolonialism, subaltern studies, gender studies, visual studies, hybridity theories, and identity politics, enact cultural parallels with the neoliberal structural policies of decentralization, free trade (no borders), and privatization. On translating these recent theories in order to create a cultural studies reader for graduate students, the Shanghai scholars recognized that they had compromised their Leftist agenda. They immediately engaged earlier class-based theories, emphasized the importance of data from local empirical field research, and collaborated with other Asian scholars in cultural studies to develop more critical theories and methodologies.

The concern that much of the theory dominating cultural studies in advanced industrial nations is complicit with neoliberal capitalism may be well founded. In a recent article on neoliberalism and cultural studies in the United States, Gang Gary Xu cites the activities of David Horowitz, a notorious conservative commentator who is attempting to introduce an "academic bill of rights" in the legislature of twenty U.S. states. Xu argues that the premises and the rhetoric of the bill borrow liberally from concepts promoted by cultural studies. For example, the gist of the bill is "diversity" (claiming American higher education has been controlled by "liberals" who preach "anti-Americanism") and supporters of the bill, trained in cultural studies, emphasize that there is no privileged perspective, edification is unnecessary, and everyone's lifestyle deserves respect. Xu cites other examples—such as white students suing the University of Michigan over affirmative action, blaming the University of North Carolina for requiring them to read the Qur'an, and voting to retain the racist symbol "Chief Illiniwek" as the mascot for the University of Illinois—as cases in which "the 'American value' is given the uttermost importance, yet the rhetoric supporting such value has no difference from that of multiculturalism." Xu concludes, "If cultural studies is not responsible for the current turn to campus right-wing activism, it at least coincides with certain themes of this activism: social engagement, statism, subjectivity, equal and non-privileged multi-perspectivism, insistence on essential differences between American culture and other cultures, and so on."[101] Lisa Duggan also analyzes these cases, concluding that neoliberalism's most prominent characteristic is its claim of multicultural neutrality that separates the "natural" processes of capitalism from sticky issues of class, race, and identity.

It is this unwitting collaboration with mainstream ideology that Wang Xiaoming and his Shanghai cohort guard against vigorously. Hence he distinguishes their work from counterparts elsewhere in China who engage in poststructuralist approaches to cultural studies. Instead, the Shanghai group of scholars adheres to the class-based origins of cultural studies as developed at Birmingham University. In Wang Xiaoming's address in 2006 to the International Association for the Advancement of Curriculum Studies, the socialist underpinnings of his thoughts on cultural studies become clear when he lapses into Cultural Revolution (rather than deconstructionist) terminology: "We don't just want to destroy (po)—we also want to establish (li)." The Marxist rhetoric continues, suggesting that while Wang no longer sees China as a single entity, he has also rejected the theoretical assumptions of late-twentieth-century cultural studies. Given that the government policy of rapid urban development has created extreme class differences, the role of those in cultural studies is to identify new social change agents. Shanghai scholars, he says, have considered two possible targets: "The middle income class of urbanites (not the middle class) or the lowest income strata of society (the urban poor and most peasants)." He elaborates on the challenge of organizing pedagogical activities that can mobilize these two classes.

> The question is one of research materials—do you focus on material read by the middle class, such as essays, the college curriculum, the Internet, university presses, etc., or do you focus on unconventional educational materials such as those used in workers' night schools, migrant children's schools, and the town-village movement? If you focus on the latter class (I focus on the former) it creates another problem, namely, the gap between urban and rural culture. Many students have an unrealistic understanding of the countryside, and reproduce those fallacies in their work. Even if some of the students at Shanghai University come from the countryside, or have taught high school in the countryside, it does not mean they understand the countryside. So the challenge is providing them with materials that enable them to reflect on their experience in the countryside. And those materials do not yet exist. So ever since the "three rural" topics started in 2004 (rural industry, villages, and dwellers) we have tried to encourage our students to spend time volunteering to support rural education—either helping establish libraries and do part time teaching in the countryside (such as Shandong) or teach in migrant workers' schools in the suburbs of Shanghai. Obviously this has some

difficulties, including issues of safety, bureaucracy, or being used by local officials.[102]

At present, students of cultural studies at s u take theory courses (on sociology and cultural studies) and conduct fieldwork analysis, as taught by specialists in various fields of study. The problem, according to Wang, is that cultural studies data from fieldwork in mainland China is still in the initial stages; with very few studies having been completed to date, the materials can only be broad overviews, without enough detailed data, and remain unsystematic and arbitrary. As for theory, Wang's center developed an English reader in 2003 because they felt that the quality of existing translations was poor—but the selections are exclusively from Europe and North America. "Perhaps I haven't done enough research, but it seems to me that Cultural Studies practices in nearly every national setting proceed according to European and American methodology and theory."[103]

Have changes in Chinese humanities scholarship during China's intensification of capitalist urbanization, epitomized by a decade of developments in cultural studies, enabled Chinese intellectuals to reengage society and politics in a meaningful way? I argue, against Gary Gang Xu and Ben Xu, that Shanghai scholars' approach to cultural studies retains the possibility for political agency by revealing connections between power and capital and assumptions supporting promarket discourse. Wang Xiaoming and other intellectuals, such as media watchdogs, are trying to expose injustices in society and the power relations that enable them. What these efforts may end up doing, however, is to aid current developmental trends by defusing social tension through publicizing the voices of selective disenfranchised social groups. This cathartic function, whether or not it is intentional, ends up containing opposition voices from below as much as it struggles against the censoring power of the Chinese state and its new rich. This is one reason for the unprecedented latitude that institutional and party officials grant Wang and his colleagues in carrying out their research.

The changing role of the watchdog journalist provides a fruitful analogy to that of the establishment intellectual. In her insightful essay on the Chinese media, Yuezhi Zhao points out that "in contrast to Western media portrayal of maverick Chinese journalists challenging the Party line from below and from the outside by discussing hot social issues and exposing official corruption, the most significant step towards the rise of watchdog journalism was initiated at the top of the Party's propaganda hierarchy."[104] The party delivered a new direction in its 1993 propaganda guidelines, allowing Yang

Weiguang, president of CCTV, to set in motion the creation of CCTV's news commentary department, which has since produced the country's most celebrated watchdog programs: *Oriental Horizon* (*Dongfang shikong*, 1993), *Focus Interviews* (*Jiaodian fangtan*, 1994), and *News Probe* (*Xinwen diaocha*, 1996). Xu Hui summarizes the resulting reports: "Official corruption, excessive exploitation of farmers, fraud and smuggling, mismanagement of state enterprises, violation of citizen and consumer rights by local officials and businesses, and problems in education, healthcare and housing reforms, have been persistent themes in watchdog stories. Journalists assume a multiplicity of roles in these programmes: an advocate of state objectives, a voice of victims of power abuse and consumer fraud, and a social commentator, condemning 'unhealthy' social trends and upholding social morality."[105] As Yuezhi Zhao points out, "Rampant corruption and growing social tensions have forced part of the Party elite to replace paranoid and paternalistic thinking with a more functionalist view that media exposure can act as a social safety valve. In this view, media exposure plays a system-maintaining function."[106] The cultural studies activities of humanities scholars may be supported for similar reasons. Not only do the efforts of research students directly aid current stated government goals (such as alleviating pressures on migrant workers or educating the populace about urban real estate bubbles), the active support of government institutions and multinational corporations in such research deflects criticism that they are responsible for or unconcerned about such problems.

Scholars have attributed the demise of literary studies in Western scholastics to neoliberal policies that have led to the underfunding of the academy and thus to increased reliance on corporate funding, private capital, and entrepreneurial methods of survival. Yet some scholars see the success of neoliberal rhetoric deriving, in part, from their very efforts in the field of cultural studies. Cultural studies, they claim, has given rise to terms of the debate which have been appropriated by the conservative Right to claim dominance. By appealing to notions promoted by cultural studies, such as "difference," "diversity," and "marginalization," neoliberal interests have flourished. Yet in China the disillusionment with literary studies in the wake of the humanist-spirit discussions of the mid-1990s was due neither to the infiltration of corporate money into the academy, nor to institutional necessity whereby it is impossible to find a job without "diversifying" one's field of research. Rather, it was due to what was perceived to be a real dearth of quality in the field. The combined effects of consumerism and ongoing ideological control wielded by the China Writer's Association have led some to declare the "death" of Chinese literature and to urge high-profile writers to drop their membership in the association.[107] Thus, critical theorists decided to pursue cultural studies—the very target of attack among Western academics—in order to reveal the workings of society and to reestablish an audience for their scholarship by establishing blogs and other Internet forums, and by adopting the reportage style championed by He Qinglian and Li Changping. Many Chinese intellectuals continue to adhere to the belief in the power of intellectual labor to change social life via new media and methodological tools. Despite the many fast-paced intellectual shifts that have taken place in Chinese thinking since 1978, the moral purpose of Chinese critical thinking continues to be determined by nation-building and modernization priorities. Concern for one's country and culture should not, however, be too narrowly equated with nationalism.

Are efforts by neoleftist scholars such as Wang Xiaoming in danger of stirring up radical movements, as their detractors claim? I believe this is unlikely. Post-1989 denunciations of the legacy of May Fourth radicalism, which culminated in Li Zehou and Liu Zaifu's book *Farewell to Revolution* (1995), very negatively associated the term *Leftist* with the radicalism of the Cultural Revolution. Yet, as class analysis has proliferated in a postsocialist era characterized by extremely uneven economic development, its adherents have grown in number and appeal. In fact, research efforts by most neoleftists aim explicitly to avert social upheaval. The target of scholarship such as localized cultural studies or sociology of the "three rural problems" (*sannong wenti*, theorized by Wen Tiejun) is not liberalism or "capitalist roads," but rather the *lack* of freedom inherent in elite power structures governing development. Many Leftists argue that the social safety nets implemented by China policy makers adhering to the post–Washington Consensus, while temporarily mitigating instability, will ultimately fail to achieve liberal ideals. Rather than promoting Cultural Revolution radicalism, the empirical investigations of neoleftists such as Wang Hui, Sun Liping, Lu Xueyi, Wang Xiaoming, Li Changping, and Wen Tiejun aim to foster liberal ideals of civil rights, rule of law, and social justice. Given that political rhetoric about liberty and freedom often functions as a mask for practices that maintain, reconstitute, and restore elite power, the rise in scholarship that counters such myths and mitigates unjust developmental policies appears particularly urgent at this historical juncture.

In jettisoning their scholarly origins in literary criticism Wang Hui and Wang Xiaoming bespeak a disappointment with post-reform Chinese literature shared by many Leftists. The urban fiction, film, and art I will discuss move beyond a facile embrace of consumer culture to a critical interrogation of urban subjects. They parody the manufacture of desire, perform urban alienation, depict a citizenry set adrift, and reveal the barren ethical terrain on which urban modernity is constituted. It is art that reveals more than inspires, that queries more than declares, that frustrates more than celebrates. That the works I will discuss relinquish the incisive critical spirit of Lu Xun in favor of the author Zhang Ailing's measured depiction of the terror of everyday life marks them as "trivial" to those wed to more trenchant critiques of global modernity. Relinquishing "truth" in favor of the "real," these are trivialities well worth pondering. Ultimately, the empiricism characterizing urban cultural production mirrors the new methodological approaches in cultural studies championed by public intellectuals.

The City as Subject

3

Performing the Postsocialist City

Beijing Identity in Art, Film, and Fiction

In the thirteenth century Marco Polo declared that Beijing was so vast, rich, and beautiful that no one could design anything superior to it. Rich cultural qualities permeated its majestic layout, its ethos encapsulated in the "Beijing style" (*jingpai*) of its elite mandarin culture and the "Beijing flavor" (*jingwei*) of its folk popular culture. Unlike Shanghai, where a diverse social stratification and history of commerce produced, in its "mixture of high and low" (*yasu gongchang*), a popular "Shanghai style" (*haipai*) culture with refined tastes, Beijing culture has always displayed a strong contrast between high and low. Today, however, this ancient capital is metamorphosing to such an extent that most scholars and architects struggle to identify the city's essential energy and inspiration. The urbanist Anthony M. Tung describes modern Beijing as "a fractured environment of unrelated elements, and a conglomeration of undistinguished buildings," and Beijing now hires foreign consultants such as Celestino Soddu to "increase its identity."[1] The amalgam of elements that defines the capital's physical environment also characterizes its cultural production. In the 2006 edition of *Urban Vicissitudes: The Cultural Spirit of Beijing and Shanghai* (*Chengshi jifeng: Beijing he Shanghai de wenhua jingshen*), published over a decade after his bestselling first edition, Yang Dongping wrote, "In the conclusion to my first edition I wondered if [in the future] *jingpai* and *haipai* would continue to be a cultural topic worthy of scholarly attention. Today it is clear that this query in fact constituted an elegy."[2]

In the postsocialist era *jingpai* is but a memory, the culture of the scholar-official thoroughly discredited by the iconoclastic May Fourth Movement (1915–25), the anti-elitist tenets of Maoism, and the utilitarianism of global capitalism. *Jingpai* culture had represented the values of the elite, serious, traditional mandarin class of scholar-officials, while *haipai* reflected modern, popular, commercial, "entertaining" (*boxiang* in Shanghai dialect), middle-class interests.[3] As a result, *haipai* culture reflected the tastes of a broad spectrum of urbanites (*shimin*), whereas in Beijing urbanite culture was restricted to the lower social stratum described in *jingwei* fiction. While interest in regional urban culture has reemerged, structural, political, and demographic developments under Maoism and Deng-era market reform have given rise to postmodern forms of mass culture that convey alternative sensibilities born of, yet subverting, elite cultural norms. The "new Beijing flavor" (*xin jingwei*) that characterizes most contemporary Beijing literature, film, music, theater, and art eradicates distinctions between high and low culture, and in so doing attracts to the capital diverse creative talents who perpetuate its dynamic, if inchoate, energy and allure.

The renewed scholarly interest in the regional peculiarities of urban culture during the postsocialist era is not limited to aesthetic considerations. Many speculated on whether particular manifestations of urban culture might engender the type of civil society that encourages political liberalization. Mainland Chinese scholars first broached the concept of civil society through the notion of rights for urban citizens. Guobin Yang points out that "through ingenious reinterpretations of Marx's classical writings, Shen Yue, for example, argues that the term 'bourgeois rights,' a standard Chinese translation of Marx's German term *burgerliche*, should be translated as 'townspeople's (*shimin*) rights.' "[4] Overseas, scholarly interest in civil society in China arose in response to the student protests in China and the fall of the Berlin Wall in Eastern Europe in 1989, culminating in an influential symposium, in 1993, on civil society and the public sphere.[5] Guobin Yang surveys over a decade of scholarship on Chinese civil society, including titles such as *Urban Spaces in Contemporary China: The Potential for Autonomy and Community in Post-Mao China*, many of which analyze ties between urbanization and political liberalization.[6]

My primary aim here is not to predict whether Beijing culture in its current forms will give rise to democratic liberalization, but rather to describe how postsocialist Beijing identity is *performed* by its cultural practitioners. In particular, Beijing literary, film, and visual artists perform the *nation*, rather than the global or personal. Because performing the nation is commonly about reforming the nation, Beijing cultural production, whether by its long-term residents or so-called Beijing floaters (*Bei piao*), remains centrally dominated by political concerns. Newer residents may hail from apolitical regions where "Heaven is remote and the emperor is far away" (*tiangao diyuan*), but once in Beijing many migrant writers, artists, and filmmakers engage with the primary cultural ethos of the capital, namely, politics. Another reason for the eclectic cultural and political dynamism characterizing Beijing today is that structural developments under socialism centralized China's creative industries in Beijing. Maoist-era Beijing cultural production was indistinguishable from party propaganda generated nationwide, yet by relocating major cultural organs to Beijing (such as Commercial Press [Shangwu yingshuguan] and New China Books [Xinhua shuju], from Shanghai), the party constructed the organizational infrastructure for a centralized base of "cultural workers." Synergy between established cultural bureaus (such as publishers, museums, universities, research institutes, and media organizations, built by the party throughout its dictatorship) and the gradual loosening of residency restrictions since the 1980s, which has allowed independent-minded intellectuals to migrate to the capital, have energized postsocialist Beijing culture in unanticipated ways.

Beijing postsocialist literary, cinematic, and visual artworks, even if playfully postmodern, reveal anxieties about the capital's (nation's) international status, apprehension over self-positioning in an increasingly cosmopolitan and constantly transforming urban space, and uneasy acquiescence to the marketing norms that allow for global success. The Beijing cultural production engendered by rapid urbanization and economic empowerment is distinct from early-twentieth-century European aesthetics movements in dialogue with urbanization, such as German expressionism or Italian futurism, which respectively rejected or celebrated urban modernity.[7] It also differs from cultural movements that arose during earlier periods of urban transformation in China, such as the nativist Beijing School (*jingpai*) of the early 1930s and the root-seeking (*xungen*) movement of the mid-1980s, where artists depicted the countryside spatially, valorizing it as transcending historical change in opposition to a time-bound metropolis. Rather, postsocialist Beijing literary, film, and visual art have rendered obsolete the binary opposites (such as time-space, city-country, modernity-tradition, West-East) that still obstruct critical knowledge of China. Although many postsocialist artists initially explored questions of identity by positioning the subject in the nexus of local versus global culture, aesthetic versus commercial interests, and organic versus artificial constructs, by the end of the twentieth century they demonstrated increasing interest in examining the *effects* of such hybrid juxtapositions, rather than the *concepts* each embodied. Instead of merely protesting the commercial exploitation of cultural sites, for example, artists started to appropriate this trend for their own ends. Many self-consciously resist the tendency to privilege one aspect of culture (e.g., tradition versus modernity) over another. By expressing hybrid effects, rather than merely conceptualizing the tensions inherent in the global city, contemporary Beijing cultural production provides a site of resistance against the effects of global capitalism while simultaneously repositioning writers, filmmakers, and artists at the center of commercial culture, in turn expanding spaces for public dialogue and critique.

Bohemian Beijing: Postsocialist "New Beijing Flavor"

Much has been written on post-Mao cultural production in the 1980s, which with its new Beijing flavor injected vitality into art forms that had been largely devoid of regional characteristics throughout the Maoist era. As Beijing was transforming its urban fabric (a decade prior to Shanghai's building surge), nostalgia for "Old Beijing" was on the rise. In 1983 Wu Yigong adapted *My Memories of Old Beijing* (Chengnan Jiushi, 1969), a memoir by the Taiwanese writer Lin Haiyin, as a popular film of the same title.[8] The Beijing writer Liu Xinwu's highly acclaimed novel *Bell and Drum Tower* (Zhonggulou, 1985) won a Mao Dun literary award and was adapted for television in 1986. This lauded TV series was directed by Lu Xiaowei, who later directed popular Beijing-based television series such as *Kewang* (Yearning, 1991) and *Siheyuan* (Courtyard house, 2004).[9] Like each of these works, Chen Kaige's award-winning film *Farewell My Concubine* (Bawang bieji, 1993) prominently featured the courtyard alley life of Old Beijing, and Chen Jiangong and other writers described the social dynamics embedded in Beijing's traditional urban fabric. While the new Beijing flavor arose partially out of this nostalgia for the Beijing of the Republican Era, it is best characterized by art conveying the effect of post-1949 developments on the contemporary urban milieu.

Wang Shuo emerged as the notorious auteur of such works. The Wang Shuo phenomenon has been widely analyzed. His works catalyzed the mid-1990s humanist-spirit debates and came to epitomize, for Leftist scholars, the crass collusion with market forces that characterized overall cultural decline. Wang Shuo, along with Wang Xiaobo, profoundly influenced the ethos, style, and marketing mechanisms of subsequent Beijing cultural production. For example, the acerbic style of Han Han, a bestselling high-school dropout, reveals him to be, in part, Wang Shuo's cultural inheritor. Ironically, despite Wang Shuo's anti-elite persona, it was his elite revolutionary class background that enabled him to seamlessly navigate the emerging market economy as a "private operator." By adopting the street language of disaffected urban youth culture, Wang Shuo infused the local Beijing flavor, once the domain of the urban poor, with the mores of privileged classes.

The Maoist campaigns were intent on the reeducation of the elite by the proletarian masses. To some extent Wang Shuo's work is indebted to Maoist attempts to eliminate class distinctions by hybridizing high and low cultural values. Yet the poetics of suspicion in his work results primarily from postrevolutionary dystopia. As multinational capitalism began constructing Beijing in the 1980s, a postmodern aesthetics of dissent emerged there. Jean-François Lyotard identified in postmodern aesthetics an emphasis on the figural over the discursive, the impact of art over its meaning, its sensation over its interpretation. In privileging the signified over the signifier and the image over the narrative, postmodern aesthetics results in a loss of meaning, depth, and interpretation, because there is no longer an interplay between representations of reality (the signifier) and reality (the signified). Yet there is, to use Linda Hutcheon's term, a "complicitous critique" in postmodernism's aesthetic strategy of resistance. Despite the critique that postmodernism levels at globally comprehensive capitalism or system rationality, its cultural production cannot help but be integrated into a system of commodification and distribution that tempers any call for political change. Postmodern aesthetics necessarily operates within the system, never fully extricating itself from what it critiques, a characteristic shared by postsocialist Beijing culture.

Lao She is, of course, the foremost writer of traditional Beijing-flavor fiction, works which represent the interests, language, and lifestyle of Beijing alley (*hutong*) culture. Because of Wang Shuo's detailed descriptions of Beijing landscape and natives in his fiction, he is seen to further the tradition of Lao She and his successors of the 1980s, Deng Youmei, Liu Xinwu, and Chen Jiangong. His humor, however, contains a biting sarcasm not found in *jingwei* works. Whereas the humor in traditional *jingwei* fiction is a relatively mild form of telling tall tales or poking fun (*kan*), Wang Shuo is often criticized for his iconoclastic use of derision or scoffing (*tiaokan*), which he directs at nearly every institution traditionally held sacred. The derisive tone of his works led critics to accuse him of mindless nihilism and a loss of humanist spirit. Wang Shuo further departs from the *jingwei* tradition of depicting down-and-out figures of the Beijing *hutong*, characters such as Liu Heng's protagonist in *Hei de xue* (Black snow, 1988). Instead, for the most part, Wang Shuo's protagonists are the children of middle-class officials and intellectuals, so-called big courtyard children (*dayuan zidi*), who are bored and disillusioned with official paths to success and have opted to live a freewheeling life on the edge. Seldom financially destitute, they possess acumen and connections, which enable them to maintain housing in the city and engage in shady financial pursuits. The language in Wang Shuo's fiction is no longer limited to a subset of lower-class Beijing society, but represents the city slang of urban youth. With Wang Shuo, *jingwei* becomes hip, and represents a broader category of urbanites than those steeped in the customs and vernacular of Beijing's traditional back-alley culture. The Wang Shuo phenomenon was a sure sign that China's cultural center had shifted to Beijing, eclipsing the preeminent position that Shanghai had established in the early twentieth century. Interestingly, Wang Shuo was the first writer in the post-Mao era to become embroiled in legal battles over intellectual property rights; likewise, many of the early *haipai* writers, who depended on writing for their livelihood, often found it necessary to sue for the rights to their work to receive just recompense.[10]

Born and raised in Beijing, Wang Shuo drifted with minimal adult supervision during the Cultural Revolution (1966–76), inhabiting a youth subculture depicted in Jiang Wen's award-winning film *Yangguang canglan de rizi* (In the heat of the sun, 1994), an adaptation of Wang's short story "Dongwu xiongmeng" (Animal ferocity, 1991). Wang Shuo fought in street gangs as a teenager, had a stint in the navy in the post-Mao 1970s, worked in a state pharmaceutical company, and smuggled commodities in the early 1980s, during the Reform Era. He claims that most of his time, especially after he quit his job in 1984 to become an entrepreneur (*getihu*) and writer, was spent "hanging out" in the streets and alleys of Beijing, "lolling about the office, going to films, and chasing women."[11] Immersion in everyday urban life directly fed his creativity. Between 1984 and 1991, Wang Shuo published more than two dozen stories and novels about contemporary urban life, and his first four film adaptations came out in 1988 (which the media dubbed "the year of Wang Shuo"), including the box-office hits *Wan zhu* (Masters of mischief, directed by Mi Jiashan) and *Lunhui* (Samsara, directed by Huang Jianxin). Shuyu Kong describes Wang Shuo's catapult to fame: "Starting from the cultural margins in the early 1980s, writing 'entertainment literature' with political undertones that mocked the system in his unique and humorous 'Beijing hooligan' style, and at one point reviled by elite writers and critics as 'zui meisu de zuojia' (the most vulgar writer in China), by the 1990s Wang had moved to the center of the Chinese literary and entertainment scene and become a cultural hero."[12] At this point, the elite cultural establishment could no longer ignore him, and in 1993 critics launched the heated debate over humanist spirit (*renwen jingshen*), a debate initially fueled by the question of whether Wang Shuo qualified as a true writer or crass hooligan.

In an article detailing the sociopolitical class background of Wang Shuo and his privileged cohort, Yusheng Yao challenges the view that Wang Shuo represents the "common man," by demonstrating how the confluence of an elite political class background and Cultural Revolution priorities led to the birth of a unique urban youth subculture. The new Beijing flavor conveyed in Wang Shuo's fiction reflected social relations in the "big compounds" (*dayuan*) that housed the most prestigious category of the new elite in Mao's China: families whose heads served in the military general headquarters or institutions. "The intensified class bias and struggle during the Cultural Revolution further enhanced their status as children of one of the most admirable 'five red categories': 'revolutionary army personnel' (*geming junren*)."[13] "No matter how bad the Cultural Revolution was made out to be," says Wang Shuo in his autobiography, "it disrupted the ordinariness of everyday life and offered opportunities for individual development and freed the children from the bonds of an old and decaying education [system]."[14] Yao points out that Wang and his cohort were *particularly* liberated in that "they were more apt to rebel against authority and discipline than most others because their 'impeccable' class background protected them from serious consequences."[15] Many of the children of this prestigious revolutionary class used their elite connections to successfully negotiate the transition to a market economy in the 1990s. Wang Shuo remained a member of the elite despite his anti-intellectual persona; likewise, the drifters in his stories are rarely destitute or angst-ridden. As entrepreneurs in the new market society his characters always find a way to come out on top, and yet they operate outside the strictures of traditional elite cultural norms that venerate book learning and disparage merchant activity.

The forms, language, mores, and ethos of the subculture popularized by Wang Shuo in the late 1980s directly inform Beijing cultural production in the twenty-first century. The Wang Shuo phenomenon blends high and low Beijing culture to create works no longer restricted to depicting the life-style, language, and mores of the lower classes. Beyond the immediate impact of Wang Shuo's anti-elitist discourse on the popular lexicon nation-wide—for example, with expressions such as "mei jinr" (depleted) and "wanr" (messing around)—his long-term impact on postsocialist Beijing cultural production is a popular culture that blends a witty, cynical sen-sibility with clever cultural marketing strategies.[16] Wang was among the first of serious Chinese writers to publicly acknowledge that literature is a commodity, to treat writing as a private business rather than a public mis-sion, and to see the market potential of literature. His success as script-writer on the popular television series *Kewang* (Yearning) inspired him to adapt his own works in collaboration with the Beijing Center for Television Art (Beijing dianshi yishu zhongxin). His wildly popular television series *Bianjibu de gushi* (Stories from the editorial board, 1992), adapted from his story of the same name (published in 1988), caused his literary works to become bestsellers, with sales of the four-volume *Wang Shuo's Collected Works* quickly topping a million copies, not counting numerous pirated editions.[17] According to Yao, "In the past decade more than 10 million copies of his books have been sold, and most of his twenty-odd stories and novels have been made into movies or television miniseries."[18]

Today most Beijing artists actively embed their works within commodity markets. Zhang Xiaogang, a "Beijing floater" originally from Yunnan who studied in Sichuan, is the second-most-traded artist in the world, having earned $56.9 million as of 2007. High-school dropouts, such as the Beijing native Chun Shu (Xie Nan), prosper from domestic sales and international book deals. Liu Zhenyun, a writer who once spurned commercial culture, collaborated with the director Feng Xiaogang to produce television series such as *Chicken Feathers Everywhere* (*Yidi jimao*, 1994) and blockbuster films such as *Cell Phone* (*Shouji*, 2003) and *A World Without Thieves* (*Tian-xia wuzei*, 2005). For *Cell Phone*, Liu first wrote the screenplay, then, at Feng's insistence, adapted it into a novel that was published to correspond with the film's release. Feng's marketing strategy provided Liu with one of his bestselling works—sales quickly reached hundreds of thousands of cop-ies.[19] Conversely, Liu's previous work, *Homeland, Flour, and Flower* (*Gu-xiang, mian, he huaduo*, 1996), with which he "awed the literary circle with his professional piety after he secluded himself for eight years to write the four-volume novel," is "rarely read."[20]

Postsocialist Beijing cultural production stems from at least one other source, in addition to the Wang Shuo phenomenon, namely, the Wang Xiaobo craze. Wang Xiaobo was an American-returned writer and scholar who resigned, in 1992, from his teaching post at People's University to freelance as a fiction writer, film consultant, and news columnist, until his death, at the age of forty-five, from a heart attack, in April 1997. When I attended a special memorial service for him in the summer of that year, his widow, the prominent sexologist Li Yinhe, detailed his many accomplishments and introduced his newly published *Time Trilogy* (The Golden Age, The Silver Age, The Bronze Age; *Huangjin shidai, Baiyin shidai, Qingtong shidai*). Although a number of writers and other intellectuals attended the memorial service, Wang Xiaobo's talents were not widely recognized until the publication of *Time Trilogy*, when "his humor, his unique facility with language, and his penetrating criticisms of contemporary Chinese culture made him a cult figure among alternative writers."[21] Furthermore, every April since 1997 Wang's readers have organized activities to commemorate his passing. Heavily influenced by such Western intellectuals as Italo Calvino, George Orwell, Marguerite Duras, Milan Kundera, and Bertrand Russell, Wang's works advocate rational, scientific thinking that frees the mind from conventional frameworks and explores primal expressions of sexuality and power. According to Zhang Yiwu, of Peking University, "Wang writes in a hyper-free state of mind. He looks deep into the darkness and complexity of human nature. And almost at the same time, he churns out penetrating views about worldly affairs in a fast-changing China."[22]

The bohemian ethos conveyed by Wang Shuo's "anti-intellectual hooligans" and Wang Xiaobo's "alternative intellectuals" derives from elite culture, but popularizes this culture through the mechanisms of the market, the media, and the Internet. In a interview in 2007 Yang Dongping concurred that "Wang Shuo and Wang Xiaobo are two branches of new Beijing flavor [*xin jingwei*], and many young people today are developing a style based upon their linguistic and creative breakthroughs. . . . New Beijing culture is still very much in its developmental phases and will only continue to grow in scope and influence. You see evidence of it everywhere . . . even really young 'born in the 1990s' writers are writing fantastic *xin jingwei* stories, poems, and articles."[23] Since the late 1990s Internet blogs and chat rooms have become a means of both self-promotion and democra-

tization of cultural production. Bohemian artists who were culturally, politically, and financially marginalized in the early 1990s have moved to the
center stage of economic and political power in the twenty-first century.
Many of them have links to the film and media industry, its prestige embodied in the CCTV tower in Beijing's Central Business District, designed
by Rem Koolhaas, and in the Office for Metropolitan Architecture (with a
controversial $636 million budget).[24] As Beijing gains prominence in the
twenty-first century, its artists, situated in the cultural center of the nation,
play a significant role in performing national identity for the world.

Socialist and Postsocialist Beijing Urban Development

While Beijing experienced various modernizing stages throughout the
twentieth century, those of the last three decades were on quite another
scale. In the early twentieth century Beijing remained a city defined by
walls, walled-enclosures, and gates, unlike most other twentieth-century
cities in which broad avenues, parks, and public squares opened up the
metropolis to the mass assemblies essential to modern commerce, culture,
and politics. David Strand has thoroughly documented the unique ethos of
modernity in Republican Era Beijing, when new technologies only subtly
altered the speed, scale, and direction of city life. He observes that "Beijing
in the 1920s clearly preserved the past, accommodated the present, and
nurtured the basic elements of several possible futures. Few cities in the
twenties in China looked so traditional and Chinese and at the same time
harbored the essentials of modern and Western urban life."[25] As the nationalist government relocated to Nanjing for most of the 1930s, the veneer
of modernization in Beijing remained fairly static until the Communist
Party reestablished it as their capital midcentury.

Under Mao, the plan for developing a capital that suitably represented
the ideology of the newly founded People's Republic became embroiled in
controversy. Many know the details and aftermath of the party's decision, in
the 1950s, not to adopt Liang Sicheng's and Chen Zhanxiang's plan to
locate the administrative center to the west of the Old City.[26] The story of
how in 1952 Liang wept at the destruction of the ancient city walls (eventually replaced by the Second Ring Road) has entered the realm of urban
lore. But fifty years later, when the journalist and urban historian Wang Jun
revisited the debate in his bestselling book *Chengji* (City Records), Mao
Zedong's missed opportunity particularly resonates with Chinese citizens
suffering from pollution, congestion, and needless loss of cultural heri-

tage. Wu Hung insists that "the consequences of Mao's decision cannot be exaggerated: All the subsequent destruction and construction of Beijing were fundamentally determined at this moment. . . . In short, Beijing's fate was sealed by locating the government in the old city."[27] The "concentric circles with one center" pattern of development has resulted in endless downtown traffic jams in an area comprising 12 percent of the city but carrying a quarter of the total traffic flow to the four hundred government organs and institutions crowded within it. The incessant "ringing" of Beijing continues, with a Sixth Ring Road (on the outer fringes of Beijing Municipality) completed in 2009 and a Seventh Ring Road extending beyond the city limits in the works.

Efforts to modernize the capital under Maoism waxed and waned according to prevailing political movements. In keeping with the industrial requirements of the first five-year plan, land-use zoning in 1954 resulted in the development of several industrial districts in the eastern, southern, western, and northeastern suburbs. The original urban area was further expanded several years later, during the Great Leap Forward, when elimination of the "three differences," between worker and peasant, urban and rural, and intellectual and laborer, led to a "scattered collective" model for cities to parallel rural communes. The new urban plan was to result in an urban region twenty-eight times larger than the traditional area of the inner city, with the same target population. A generous number of parks and open spaces were to be designed, and the population was to decentralize into a number of "scattered collectives." While this plan was never fully implemented, Beijing became more dispersed and rural than urban in character, in keeping with Maoist ideology of leveling distinctions between urban and rural locales.[28]

The spirit of "Chinese yet new" (*zhong er xin*) dictated socialist architecture, a policy intended to retain historical Chinese characteristics while reflecting new socialist ideals. The ten Great Architecture projects planned for the tenth anniversary of the People's Republic exemplify this policy. The government widened and extended Chang'an Street, expanded and rebuilt Tiananmen Square, and constructed new buildings, such as the Great Hall of the People, the Museum of History and Revolution, and the Beijing rail station. In the 1960s and 1970s it improved public facilities by constructing libraries, museums, hospitals, and cinemas. In the post-Mao era, city planners largely eliminated Beijing's industrial function and directed the notion of *zhong er xin* toward the international community. In April 1980 a new set of policy guidelines specified that Beijing's primary function would be as a national political and cultural center. An unprecedented construction boom was launched in the 1980s, funded largely by the private sector and fueled by foreign capital. The city invested in development of the infrastructure, building highways concentrically from the Second Ring Road (which follows the contours of the former city wall) to the Sixth Ring Road (running twenty kilometers from the city center), and extending interurban superhighway links from Beijing to Tianjin and Shijiazhuang. Such incremental expansion outward from the core of a developed city center, "the pattern of making a pancake," is a typical model of Chinese metropolitan suburbanization.[29] Beijing developed a National Olympic Sports Center for the Asian Olympics of the 1990s, a direct highway to the international airport, an international convention center, an international silk boutique, a world park, a Chinese nationalities park, the Old Beijing miniature garden, and Olympic Park for the 2008 Beijing Olympics, most located on the central axis north of the Imperial Palace.[30] The 2020 plans for Beijing, unveiled to the public with the opening of the Beijing Planning Exhibition Hall in 2004, retain Tiananmen Square and the Forbidden City as the ideological center of the 16,410-square-kilometer metropolis. They feature plans for a twenty-one-line subway system to extend 680 kilometers and connect eleven "new towns" (*xincheng*) to the urban core, described by the municipal website as "bright pearls" that "ring" the Old City like a "jade necklace."[31]

In terms of urban migration, the population of Beijing swelled in the 1950s, as workers migrated to staff the new industrial factories established in accordance with the first five-year plan. However, in the 1960s out-migration prevailed as many industrial projects were canceled due to a new ideology in favor of the countryside. This trend was reflected in all of China's major urban centers. Thus, while the average rate of urbanization during the Maoist period was 4.5 percent in other developing countries, China's annual urban growth rate from 1949 to 1981 was restricted to 2.8 percent, only slightly higher than the 2.1 percent rate in developed countries.[32] Under loosened restrictions on rural-to-urban migration in the early 1980s there was an upsurge of migrants into the capital, followed by a leveling off for the rest of the 1980s as the government feared uncontrolled population growth. With the rapid escalation of the market economy in the 1990s, restrictions on migration were again lifted. By 1995 Beijing had swelled to include an estimated 3.2 million migrants from the countryside, over one quarter of its population.[33] By 2007 the capital included an estimated 4 million migrants in a total population of about 16 million, with

Prominent north-south axis from Forbidden City in the south (top) to Olympic Village in the north (bottom), as seen on a 1:750 scale model of Beijing. Beijing Planning Exhibition Hall, 2008. Photo by author.

many assisting in the Olympics building surge.[34] A key rationale for promoting the eleven new towns is to relocate some 5.7 million people from the city proper, which aims to limit its population to 18 million.

The government was slow to catch up with the need for housing and infrastructure to support Beijing's burgeoning population. In 1988, after the State Council decided to turn urban housing from a social good into a commodity, the majority of cottage stock houses in Beijing's alleys, comprising over 50 percent of its residential housing, were slated for redevelopment. Most residents opted for a lump-sum subsidy and agreed to move to outlying areas rather than buy the redeveloped residences.[35] This accorded with city plans to move industry and housing to peripheral constellations of Beijing by expanding 43 percent in area between 1987 and 2000, reducing the Old City and industrial patches in the suburbs by 46 percent.[36] In addition to allowing officials to capitalize on escalating real-estate prices, such planning intended to erase the old sores left behind by the Cultural Revolution, in which industrial plants had been deliberately located in a sporadic fashion. In turn, property prices in the Old City, especially around the Imperial Palace, have surged as property developers compete for prime real estate. Because there are few restrictions on the resale of developed land, speculation is rampant. While a number of important historic sites are marked for preservation, they amount to only a tiny proportion of the total building stock. The Beijing 2020 plan includes one of the most aggressive underground-development plans in the world, promoted as contributing to the sustainable ideal of a compact city, but meanwhile capitalizing on the sale of additional land-use rights.

Despite the manifest transformation of the urban fabric, some scholars still insist that Beijing maintains its traditional urban form. Victor F. S. Sit, for example, sees the traditional Chinese urban form as a utilitarian setting in which society functioned while also providing a symbolic function for the state to inform and guide human behavior. In this sense, he argues, Beijing's traditional role as the national center of communication and control is mirrored in its recent development as a global city at the center of finance and corporate decisions, providing communication and financial controls over material production and consumption, rather than engaging in productive activities.[37] Others locate Beijing's historical continuity in the symbolic import of Tiananmen Square. In their article "Beijing: The Expression of a National Political Ideology," Zixuan Zhu and Reginald Yin-Wang Kwok sanction contemporary Beijing urban planning, particularly in relation to the city center: "Positioned at the center of Beijing's traditional north-south axis and the new east-west axis, Tiananmen Square is the heart of the capital. Surrounded by carefully selected and designed structures, the square has taken on immense political and ideological meaning, symbolizing not only the authority but the historical continuity of the state, with the imperial dynasty replaced by the socialist republic. As Beijing moves toward the twenty-first century, Tiananmen Square is truly at the nation's center, in both symbolic and utilitarian terms."[38] In his book on the history of Tiananmen Square, Wu Hung agrees that the square remains the symbolic heart of the capital, yet he details how the introduction of performance, installation, and multimedia art to China has provided new possibilities for unofficial artists to engage with the square in ways that defy government intentions.[39] Zhu and Kwok, on the other hand, seem unaware of the new spatial and social formations engendered by globalization and market forces, including collusions between government officials and real estate developers. They acknowledge the pressures brought to bear on urban planners by market reforms, yet assume that governmental and economic spheres of activity remain separate, suggesting that "the new contest for urban space will be between state bureaucrats and private entrepreneurs."[40]

It is only by glossing over the fact that public bureaucrats aggressively pursue private interests that these scholars can posit Beijing's deliberate functional and aesthetic continuity into the twenty-first century. Those who traverse the city daily paint quite another picture, as they observe devastating upheaval and ruins predicated on modernization and development. The claim that planners are developing spatial strategies to combine the attractions of the ancient capital with the requirements of an international postindustrial metropolis is extremely tenuous. Not only are ideological concerns regularly trumped by financial interests, those architects who try to develop alternative approaches to city planning, such as by incorporating a dynamic relationship between the human body and urban architectural space, have been effectively excluded from positions of influence.[41] Indeed, a number of studies delineating details of urban real estate transactions indicate that while municipalities initially became entrepreneurs to meet social needs, they eventually come to be motivated by sheer profitability.[42]

The phenomenon of business interests driving out traditionally valued cultural institutions is poignantly illustrated by the fate of the Central Academy of Fine Arts in Beijing. In 1994, having been sold to real estate developers by the municipal government, the academy was informed of the impending destruction of its downtown campus. Mainly funded by the Hong Kong magnate Li Jiacheng, the plan for this multimillion-dollar project was to incorporate the land of the former academy into a "city of commerce" (shangcheng). To many of Beijing's artists and intellectuals this plan symbolized the overthrow of art and education in favor of a crass market economy, and many protested the government's action. Adding fuel to the protests, it became evident that the then mayor Chen Xitong and other high-ranking officials were benefiting greatly from this and other deals made with foreign investors.[43] Forced relocation and demolition abounded in Beijing and other Chinese cities in the mid-1990s, as traditional houses and cultural artifacts were replaced by hotels and shopping malls funded by investments from Hong Kong, Taiwan, Japan, and the West. Wu Liangyong, chair of Tsinghua University's School of Architecture and one of the central figures in debates over Beijing's urban planning since 1951, states that "from 1993 to 1996, due to special political conditions, Beijing suffered from an over-heated boom in real estate development. Market prices for real estate rose dramatically and remain unreasonable even now. The situation was most severe within the Old City proper, where, immune to local government control, large-scale commercial real estate development brought enormous profits."[44] Due to bureaucratic city planning and the desire to make a greater profit, however, much of the demolished housing stock remained in ruins. Because there are very few restrictions on China's secondary real estate market, which involves the exchange of land-use rights of semideveloped or developed land and commodified housing, "land in valuable locations is often underutilized or vacant purely for speculative purposes."[45] While cities worldwide are fully acquainted with the disruption of construction projects, the enormity of the demolition China has experienced in recent years has had a profound psychological impact on city residents. In many Chinese cities radical demolition has continued for more than a decade, keeping metropolises like Beijing in a state of perpetual destruction and disruption.

Qiu Huadong's *City Tank* and the Beijing Floater

In his novel *City Tank* (*Chengshi zhanche*, 1997), Qiu Huadong addresses the conflict between the ideals of the utopian global city that dominate urbanist discourse about Beijing and the realities of the city that people inhabit. Capitalizing on his experience as a business journalist with extensive social networks, Qiu, raised in Xinjiang Province and holding a degree in Chinese literature from Wuhan University, imbues his fiction with a strong ethnographic flavor. *City Tank* is peopled with a wide array of visual, musical, and literary artists in an attempt to convey the sensibilities of the Beijing artist subculture. With fewer restraints on mobility in the 1990s, Beijing became populated with what Qiu terms "new urbanites (*dushi xin renlei*), the so-called Beijing floaters (*Bei piao*), who, like Qiu himself, were newcomers to Beijing and who differed from the long-term Beijing residents described in Liu Heng's and Wang Shuo's fiction of the 1980s.[46]

In her analysis of *City Tank* Jie Lu argues that Qiu Huadong depicts a breakdown in the symbolism of Tiananmen Square, which urban geographers continue to depict as a unifying principle of politicized, homogenized everyday life. Rather than a defining symbolic order, Qiu instead represents Beijing as the fragmented "modern/postmodern metropolis of a globalized consumer culture."[47] As a chronicle of practices in the artistic community of the mid-1990s the novel convincingly illuminates the issues faced by artists in a postrevolutionary consumer society. While all fiction is informed by authorial experience, the tendency to construct fictional narratives transparently based on actual events is especially prevalent in urban fiction of the 1990s. This fiction shares the same documentary drive as Sixth Generation film, addressing the decade's postindustrial anxieties by blurring the lines between constructed and lived narrative. One should avoid interpreting these works as direct mimesis, yet it is clear that these accounts are continuous with common structures of everyday experience.

City Tank is written from the first-person perspective of Zhu Wen, a painter who befriends poets, novelists, documentary artists, filmmakers, painters, performance artists, concept artists, installation artists, playwrights, singers, musicians, sculptors, and art critics. Qiu's description of the artists' living quarters accurately represents the predominant lifestyle for artists in Beijing's low-rent districts. In addition to developing fictional characters, Qiu refers to well-known artists and events, such as the poet Gu Cheng's suicide, Gu Wenda's hair sculptures, Xu Bing's postmodern installations, Cui Jian's rock concerts, Zhang Yuan's documentary *The Square*, the Gao Brothers' *Midnight Mass* condom installation at the "China/Avant-Garde" exhibition, Su Tong's and Wang Shuo's *Collected Works*, and Jia Pingwa's novel *Defunct Capital*. Qiu complicates his character mix by using the occasional pseudonym for actual artists and the names of real artists for his fictional characters. For example, the protagonist's name is a homophone for the Nanjing writer and filmmaker Zhu Wen. One of Qiu's major fictional characters, a housewife whom Zhu Wen teaches to paint, shares a moniker with the acclaimed Beijing painter Yu Hong, a graduate, in 1984, of the Central Academy of Fine Arts. Qiu also uses the pseudonym Feng Yue to refer to Zhang Huan, and includes a description of Zhang's infamous performance, *Twelve Square Meters*. In addition, Qiu documents the historically accurate events of "Feng Yue's" arrest, the disbanding of the artist community in the East Village in June 1994, and Feng's pledge of defiant return.

Like many of Qiu Huadong's novels, *City Tank* opens with a panoramic description of the city. Zhu Wen, a young painter in his early twenties, who has recently moved to Beijing from Wuhan to make his mark on the avant-garde art scene, gazes south toward the city center from the northern loop of the Third Ring Road. "Looking from a distance, all of the people are trees. Especially as night falls the city is like a huge cancerous stomach ulcer floating amidst the lights, the shadows of scurrying inhabitants elongating and rapidly shifting under the lights."[48] The narrator depicts the city as neither heaven nor hell, but rather a sort of limbo—a shadowy place consisting of nondistinct souls with an indeterminate destiny. His subsequent description provides more graphic evidence of his equivocal attitude toward the city. After throwing up the contents in his stomach from a late-night party, Zhu Wen vividly describes the colors of his vomit floating on the river's surface: "That liquid looked like blood and brains mixed together, just like three years ago when I saw this sort of thing on the streets of Wuhan—someone who somehow split his head open and was lying in the middle of the street with all kinds of people surrounding him silently looking on, and I pushed my way through the crowd to see that blood and brain mixture thing that looked as pretty as ice cream. Many years later when I ate that kind of thing at an Italian ice cream shop on Jianguomen-wai Street in Beijing I didn't feel disgusted in the least."[49]

Qiu Huadong's aestheticization of urban filth is reminiscent of the New Sensationalist (*shinkankakuha*) writer Yokomitsu Riichi's descriptions of Shanghai in the 1920s: "Oil patterns floated on the surface of the sewer water beneath the fog, as duckweed sprouting on the side of the mortar lapped at the oil on the water's surface. Nearby, the yellow corpse of a chick laid its head among the rape leaves, stockings, mango peels, and scraps of straw, gathering the pitch black bubbles that welled up from the depths to form a small island in the middle of the sewer."[50] Yet Qiu's prose differs from both Yokomitsu's urban-grotesque style and from the Chinese avant-garde aestheticization of the decaying rural landscape in the 1980s, by introducing a humorous note of sarcasm lacking in these other genres. Qiu Huadong's characters acknowledge urban decadence—few of his characters revel unreflectively in the city's materialism and moral chaos—yet they embrace the possibilities of the city rather than shunning its corrupting influence.

The narrator's soliloquy on the cityscape ends abruptly when he is solicited by a young woman from the northern countryside, trying to "make it" in the city with wealthy gentlemen, one of which she presumes him to be. They wend their way out of the bright lights of the city into the harrowing depths of the back alleys leading to his "house"—a ramshackle room he rents alongside other artists in the garbage-filled Dongcun, or "East Village," section of Beijing. Zhu Wen's dilapidated housing sharply contrasts with the flashy nightclubs and hotels that he and his friends frequent when finances allow. Zhu Wen wavers between a sense of euphoria and despair about life in the city, denouncing his living "hell" yet captivated by the invigorating possibilities of "heaven" which he sees all about him; he's alternately depressed by his impotency in the urban context, epitomized by his relationship with the hooker (he fails to "get it up"), and exhilarated by the opportunities Beijing affords him. Gradually, however, his artist's enthusiasm for the city wanes, his dreams extinguished by grinding poverty. Zhu Wen comes to view the city as a voracious devourer that is never satisfied, leaving the idealistic individual famished, stripped clean of modest gains he may make there. The marginalization of starving artists within the city is mirrored by the identity of the capital itself, as it struggles to attain equal status among international powers.

After attempting various money-making schemes, such as painting imitations for a gallery owner to sell to unwitting foreigners, Zhu Wen returns to his ideals, refusing to "sell out." He answers an ad from a bored, wealthy young housewife, Yu Hong, soliciting private painting lessons. She pays him well, and while her husband is on business in Hong Kong, she invites Zhu Wen out on the town to dine at five-star hotels, bet on horses at the racetrack, and dance in lavish nightclubs. He thus witnesses the fact that in Beijing "each class lives a completely separate life at their own level." It dawns on him that the city has the same effect on rich and poor alike, leaving individuals hollow and empty in the loneliness of the crowds, since the exchange value of the market is operative in every relationship. Ultimately, Zhu Wen adopts the Marxist view of the city as a demeaning marketplace, and he struggles with placing a value on his idealism and poverty in such an environment, bitterly joking that perhaps even his poverty can be "exchanged" for something of financial value. *City Tank* may be a predictable tale of the alienated, starving artist in the metropolis, yet it provides valuable ethnographic details of the complex interface between art and Beijing's urbanization and consumerism in the 1990s.

The ostensible concern of the novel is how to locate the "independent" or "vagrant artist" (*liulang yishujia*)—living in Beijing without a residence permit (*hukou*), unattached to a work unit (*danwei*)—in the newly emerging exchange economy of Beijing, a locale that simultaneously entices and debases. In this sense *City Tank* resembles urban classics such as John Dos Passos's *Manhattan Transfer* (1925), wherein the city proves both stimulating and enervating to struggling individuals. Yet Beijing's late-twentieth-century status as a world-class city was less definite than New York's in the Roaring Twenties; hence, the novel also addresses issues of global identity politics. In keeping with a Beijing cultural aesthetic which performs the nation, Zhu Wen engages in debates over ethnic versus international art, and attempts to resolve (personal and national) identity issues through his sexual encounters with various "local" and "global" partners. In discussing aesthetics with Westerners, Zhu Wen passionately explicates the rationale for an aesthetic transition away from the root-seeking nativism of the 1980s. On one occasion he gushes, "I long for a new form for Chinese art—one which meets international standards and uses contemporary values to become a branch of global culture rather than merely promoting the nativist notion 'the more ethnic the more international.' "[51] The narrative is peppered with transparent references to academic debates, in the 1990s, that condemn "ethnic" art (such as films by Zhang Yimou), which is seen to manipulate stereotypical Chinese images to gain Western approbation. The artists engage in countless discussions of cultural theory, tossing off terms such as "postcolonial culture," "pastiche," "imitation," and "globalism," to demonstrate their grasp of contemporary terminology in Western cultural criticism.

The anxiety surrounding Chinese cultural identity in the mid-1990s is aptly characterized by one of Zhu Wen's encounters, with a European girl at an embassy party who questions the "Chineseness" of contemporary Chinese art, failing to recognize the cultural colonialism at play in such a question. Zhu Wen ends the conversation by madly kissing the girl, consummating yet another "global relationship" before abruptly breaking off relations because of his "low self-image" and "post-colonial inferiority complex."[52] Whether such scenes are intended to be farcical (Yu Dafu's short story "Sinking" ["Chenluo," 1921] comes to mind) or are sincere expressions of cultural schizophrenia in the face of new global pressures, the protagonist expresses undeniable frustration at the imposition of Western aesthetic standards to which Chinese feel bound if they are to be recognized internationally.

Representations of the "postcolonial subaltern" were prevalent in Beijing's cultural production of the 1990s, as means of performing national identity. As Liu Kang puts it, "By using postmodernism as a new lingua franca, Chinese intellectuals can partake in global intellectual communications without the intermediary of a powerful existing discourse of the West about China."[53] As noted in chapter 2, in the early 1990s Professor Zhang Yiwu of Peking University argued that the new decade, which he called the post–New Era (*hou xin shiqi*), expressed a new cultural logic characterized by urban cultural aesthetics.[54] In the context of globalism this cultural logic, Zhang contended, altered the valences of China's modern urban-rural dichotomy. Whereas cultural production since the May Fourth Era (1915–25) privileged allegories of the nation-state, and closely identified the nation with rural culture, under globalism rural culture is depicted not as a productive national force but as an exotic Other, packaged for western consumption. Elite cultural production under conditions of global postcolonialism, Zhang argues, capitalize upon depictions of Chinese rural culture as oppressive, stagnant, and debased. As a form of resistance to such developments, "low" culture, or the new "local culture," features contemporary realities in a rapidly urbanizing China. According to Zhang, whereas internationally acclaimed Fifth Generation filmmakers such as Zhang Yimou and Chen Kaige are "third-world slaves" in a "post-colonial climate of globalization," it is the urban cultural production for domestic consumption during the 1990s that truly "grasps the contemporary situation."[55] The irony, of course, is that the lingo of postcolonialism took on heightened usefulness precisely as a way of performing the nation. Although the nation-state is no longer represented metaphorically in postsocialist Beijing cultural production, its shadow remains.

Art critics use similar "post" rhetoric in the mid-1990s to discuss the dilemma of positioning the Chinese artist in a global context. For example, in Huang Zhuan's preface to the catalogue *The First Academic Exhibition of Chinese Contemporary Art 96–97*, the Guangzhou-based critic states,

> The international trend of postcolonialism in the 1990s has provided Chinese contemporary art with unprecedented opportunities to enter the global sphere. But because the position of Chinese art in this globalization process is determined by mainstream international art, it can only make a

passive entrance onto the international stage. Not only is Chinese art stripped of an opportunity to demonstrate its real significance to a global audience, it has been used as material to enrich a post–cold war and postcolonial discourse. In my view, the limitations of the current international discourse on art should make us realize the necessity of approaching Chinese contemporary art initially as an internal issue—how to come to terms with the self-positioning of our own domestic culture.[56]

It is clear that the move by scholars such as Huang Zhuan and Zhang Yiwu to privilege domestic urban culture as the true representative of "Chineseness" was partially an attempt to resolve the tension between catering to Western stereotypes, on the one hand, and sharing a language with the West, on the other. Beijing works such as *City Tank* depict conflicted characters in a fragmented capital attempting to overcome subaltern positions in a global market. The rise of Chinese nationalism in the 1990s should be understood in the context of such urban aesthetics, which attempt to place the nation on an equal footing with other powers, to gain as much respect as other modern nation-states, rather than forever be exoticized as other.

The anxiety about cultural identity that permeates the discourse on aesthetics in *City Tank* is not imagined. During the inaugural Shanghai Biennale in 2000, "the most relevant question—one much discussed by about forty seminar speakers over two long days at the show's inauguration—was whether [China's] art can remain, in any meaningful sense, 'Chinese' at all."[57] Such discussions call to mind Roland Barthes's decoding of "Italianicity" in a French pasta advertisement that draws on "a specifically 'French' knowledge (an Italian would barely perceive the Italianicity of tomato and pepper), based on a familiarity with certain tourist stereotypes."[58] In other words, definitions of cultural identity reside with those who name it rather than with those who embody it. By the late 1990s Chinese artists had begun to recognize the limitations of performing the nation by merely conceptualizing Cold War dichotomies. Instead, they shifted their aesthetic strategy, choosing an approach that expressed the effects of globalization on identity by playing with stereotypes of "Chineseness."

The Limits of Performance: Wang Xiaoshuai's *Frozen*

Books such as Thomas Berghuis's *Performance Art in China* (2007), and exhibitions such as "Photographs of Chinese Performance Art" (Zhongguo xingwei yishu sheying), curated by Shu Yang for the May 2007 Dashanzi Arts Festival, confirm the highly political nature of the art form in postsocialist China. For example, one of China's first performance art groups, Concept 21, comprising Sheng Qi, Zheng Yuke, Zhao Jianhai, Kang Mu, and Xi Jianjun, then students at the Central Academy of Industrial Arts (Zhongyang gongyi meiyuan) and the Central Academy of Arts (Zhongyang meiyuan), performed from 1986 to 1988 at historical venues such as Peking University, the Great Wall, the Ming Tombs, and Yuanmingyuan (the former Summer Palace).[59] For their performances, they often dressed in black and wrapped their bodies in white medical bandages, sometimes "attacking" each other with colored paint. Sheng Qi explains their choice of materials: "Colors were one of our tools, and we felt these tools could be weapons. We grew up listening to propaganda all of our lives. . . . [E]ven our art education indoctrinated us in military terms such as 'wage warfare' [dazhang], 'liberate' [jiefang], 'unify' [tuanjie]. . . . The bandages signified injury. Although Cui Jian hadn't yet written his song, we anticipated the sentiments in his lyrics: 'I'm wounded but I don't know where this wound comes from' [Wo yijing shoudaole shanghai keshi wo buzhidao zhege shanghai cong nali laide]. . . . Although we were so young, we all had this feeling of having been wounded."[60] That these young artists titled their Great Wall performances "The Human Series" (Ren xilei) exemplified the heightened attention afforded the human subject during the "high culture fever" (wenhua re) of the 1980s.

Other well-known performances during this first decade include the couple Tang Song and Xiao Lu, who shot bullets at their installation Dialogue during the "China/Avant-Garde" exhibition held in the National Art Gallery in February 1989, street performances during the student movement later that spring, and clandestine performances in Yuanmingyuan Artist's Village (late 1980s to 1994) and the East Village (early 1990s to 1994). A variety of sources document the precarious lifestyle within artist villages: the artists often shaved their heads so as to blend in with the neighboring criminal population; they lived a hand-to-mouth, unsanitary existence among wild dogs and vermin; many were arrested and imprisoned under very harsh conditions during police crackdowns in 1994 and 1995.[61] Zhang Huan, Ma Liuming, and Zhu Ming, for example, were each imprisoned for several months in 1994 after separate performances in the East Village.[62] Many (including the now internationally prominent artists Yue Minjun and Fang Lijun, as well as the influential art critic Li Xianting) moved in 1994 to Songzhuang, a rural village east of Beijing, avoiding politically sensitive areas such as Peking University to escape police raids.

Most performances at the time were considered politically sensitive, as they targeted irrational planning (and its inattention to human scale, health, welfare, infrastructure), corruption and profit-taking, and repression in the wake of June Fourth.

To some observers, however, the prevalent phenomenon of isolated performances viewed by a handful of other artists and photographed by the same for circulation among the same was far from political theater. Instead, it constituted nothing short of a highly introspective, narcissistic form of artistic expression anathema to China's strong tradition of moral censure and social consciousness. As Gao Minglu observed in 1998, "On the whole, avant-garde contemporary art in mainland China has turned from a serious concern with humanism and the criticism of reality and political authority to a more cynical or mundane approach."[63] The film *Frozen* (*Jidu hanleng*, 1997), directed and filmed by Sixth Generation filmmaker Wang Xiaoshuai (under the pseudonym Wu Ming, or "Anonymous"), critiques Beijing performance art along these lines.

Frozen's bleak narrative starts with a voice-over claiming that the film is based on a true story from 1994 and proceeds to convey a sense of the avant-garde art scene in Beijing through the life of Qi Lei, a performance artist whose ultimate work is the staging of his own suicide. The film, like Qiu's novel, transparently references actual people and events, including a Beijing drama student named Qi Li, who committed suicide in the early 1990s, and the influential art critic Li Xianting (Lao Lin in the film). Qi Lei is played by Jia Hongsheng, who went on to play the male lead in Lou Ye's *Suzhou River* (2000).[64] Qi Lei performs four seasonal events: an autumn earth burial, a winter water burial, a spring fire burial, and a summer ice burial. In the final event Qi Lei feigns death with the assistance of three accomplices: the art critic Lao Lin, his physician sister, and his sister's colleague, who produces a death certificate. The point of the exhibition, masterminded by Lao Lin, is to observe the effect of Qi Lei's "death" on his colleagues, and on the city populace in general. The reaction is disappointing, aside from that of his closest friends, who, in any case, only briefly argue about the efficacy of the morbid performance art which has dominated the 1990s. The voice-over states, in a monotone, that "everything went as planned and the debate about performance art gradually subsided, much faster than expected." Whereas performance art began in China in a highly charged environment of public-minded actors performing the social consciousness of the nation, it atrophied with the growing preeminence of a material culture in which attention to the human subject all but disappears.

Annihilation of the human subject in the city: Qi Lei (Jia Hongsheng) performs an "earth burial" on the first day of autumn. Still from *Frozen* (1997).

While all performance art attempts to blur the lines between life and art (hence its alternate designation, "live art"), it invariably implies negotiation between the two. The film, however, pushes the envelope by documenting an attempt to absolutely equate life, and its correlate death, with art. At the end of the film Qi Lei, who has retreated to a Buddhist temple in Xiang-shan, the "Fragrant Hills" west of Beijing, is unable to resist the pull of the city and his friends, and so he abandons the indefinite abode of the temple. Qi Lei's suicide performances—his attempts to conceptualize the attenuation and disappearance of the human subject in commercial urban culture —are symbolically reenacted for the film's audience. He enters the city in a taxi that displays an "empty cab" sign, then calls his sister from a payphone but refuses to speak. He gazes through a window at Lao Lin seducing his erstwhile girlfriend, Shao Yun, the only character shattered by Qi Lei's "suicide" and faithful to his feigned ideals. However, he disappears when Shao Yun, sensing a ghostly presence, stumbles into the night to look for him. The film ends abruptly with the chilling voice of the narrator: "Three months later they found the body with a slit wrist, under a tree, on the first day of autumn."

Immediately the viewer wonders with Shao Yun: was Lao Lin's treachery responsible for Qi Lei's death? As a self-interested art curator who manipulates idealistic youth with impotent theories about the power of art to trans-

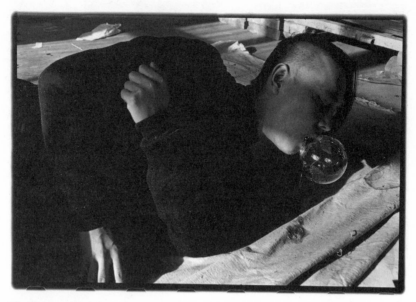

Zhu Ming, *12 o'clock December 27, 1994*, realized in Anjialou, Beijing.
The performance inspired the soap-eating performance scene in *Frozen*.
Photo by Xu Zhiwei. Courtesy Xu Zhiwei.

form society, Lao Lin seems to replicate the cycle of despair intimated by Lu Xun's famous story of the Iron House, where the sleepers are awakened by an enlightened intellectual only to suffocate. Yet reminiscent of Lu Xun's bitter self-referentiality as an artist, Wang Xiaoshuai's entire film becomes one long cynical voice-over, a postmodern undoing of each of the themes in the story. Such deconstruction is evident in multiple details: the all-too-graphic suicide of an artist jumping to her death outside Qi Lei's window, the mournful music predictably reinforcing a clock's insistent ticking throughout the film, the excruciating soap-eating performance demonstrating the concept of "revulsion" (voyeuristically consumed by the artists themselves), the camera frozen on the tree at film's end, stubbornly refusing to release the audience. Such an unrelenting portrayal of the post-industrial urban angst dominating the art scene in the mid-1990s is so extreme that the film calls attention to itself as performance.

The entire film frames the city of Beijing from the perspective of its outlying countryside. The opening and closing scenes feature a tree on a suburban hill overlooking the metropolis, the site of Qi Lei's apparent suicide (despite the solemnity of the narrator's voice we realize by the final scene that it, too, may be performance). While located in the city Qi Lei appears mired in inaction, effectively "frozen," whether attempting to starve himself in his sister's sparsely furnished two-bedroom apartment or contemplating his staged suicide in the dark confines of his claustrophobic room in run-down artists' quarters. The noise of city traffic is omnipresent outside his room, and he occasionally traverses the streets in cabs that whisk him between performances, yet he observes the high-rises without affect, a passive participant in the urban bustle. In one scene in particular, when Qi Lei and Shao Yun ascend from the underground residence of a soothsayer who predicts his death and rebirth, the camera pans up the steps to the fluffy clouds and blue skies providing a backdrop to the high-rises. Reminiscent of the opening and closing scenes in Yuan Muzhi's classic film about the urban underclass, *Street Angel* (Malu tianshi, 1937), where a vertical pan of Shanghai's heights dramatically situates its depths, Qi Lei's positioning in the liminal regions of Beijing is firmly established.

The protagonist is unable to escape the hold of the city by retreating to the countryside. Although he appears to slowly rejuvenate in the monastery, Qi Lei ultimately rejects the possibility of living there in anonymous bliss. He is vitally tied to Beijing, the most horrifying aspect of his "death" being the fact that he must leave the city and his friends there. As one of Qiu Huadong's similarly conflicted characters says in his novel *Yingyan* (Fly eyes, 1998), "We can't escape the city. As soon as we leave [Beijing] we'll want to return, because this is our stage, the place which nourishes dreams, and we depend on it for our very breath."[65] Such works tend to portray Beijing as exerting powerfully addictive forces on its inhabitants, forces which eventually enervate despite their promise of liberation. This bohemian Beijing aesthetic is prevalent in a variety of films and novels of the 1990s, including Zhang Yuan's *Beijing zazhong* (Beijing bastards, 1993), Wang Xiaoshuai's *Dong Chun de rizi* (The days, 1993), He Yi's *Xuan lian* (Red beads, 1993), Jiang Wen's *Yangguang canlan de rizi* (In the heat of the sun, 1994), and fiction by Wang Shuo, Wang Xiaobo, Ding Tian, Xu Kun, Chen Ran, and others.

While *Frozen* provokes multiple interpretations, it ultimately speaks to a certain impasse in the experimental art scene in the mid-1990s in Beijing. In many respects, the search for extreme "concepts" dominated mid-1990s experimental art. When Qi Lei explains his rationale for staging a suicide ("Performance art is a concept expressed through a human being rather than a medium. I want to mix the two and consider the result."), Lao Lin cautions, "You need to think carefully about this." Rather than condemning the manipulation of idealistic youth, the film highlights the notion of conceptual art gone awry. The Beijing artist and curator Qiu Zhijie argued against this trend among the avant-garde, indicating that art should instead focus on the construction of certain "effects," rather than externalizing some intrinsic "meaning" generated by an author's intentions.[66] Similar to developments among installation and performance artists in other cultural contexts, during the late twentieth century Beijing saw a movement away from conceptual art and political critique driven by the analysis of formal and cultural limits within which art exists and struggles.[67] In its place grew a concern with the techniques and effects of contemporary cultural practices as they circumscribe the definition, production, presentation, and dissemination of art, which become the sites of critical intervention.

Dialogue with Urbanization: Postsocialist Beijing Installation and Performance Art

Works such as *Frozen* suggest that attempts to merely conceptualize postmodern consumer culture are enervating at best, deadly at worst. By the mid-1990s, performance art had reached an impasse, as neoliberal capitalism changed the terrain of political critique; its target had shifted from a totalitarian state to a pervasive consumer culture in which artists were increasingly complicit. To address the increasing hegemony of global capitalism in Beijing, experimental art began to occupy new spaces, site-specific venues that served two interrelated purposes. First, they brought experimental art to the public by transforming unofficial art venues into public exhibition spaces. Second, these public art venues were more closely integrated into China's socioeconomic transformation by unambiguously relating the exhibition with its social environment.

Zhang Huan's *Twelve Square Meters*, which he performed in Beijing in 1994, opposed prevalent forms of urban "renewal" by demonstrating the disparagement of the human subject in such projects. The group installation *Property Development* (1995), by the Three Men United Studio at the Central Academy of Fine Arts, also engaged contemporary urban policy, after the dismissive relocation of the academy to the outskirts of the city. Two days after the academy was forced to move out, Zhan Wang, Sui Jianguo, and Yu Fan held their exhibition in the old classrooms of the department of sculpture, where they had studied and taught. Wu Hung describes Zhan Wang's *Classroom Exercise* and Sui Jianguo's *Ruins*: "[Zhan's installation] included a mass of rubble and dirt pouring into his former classroom

Zhan Wang,
Classroom Exercise,
installation. Beijing,
1995. Courtesy
Zhan Wang.

through a broken window. On top of the rubble lay small clay figures—classroom exercises left by the students. Through the window one could see the rising buildings of the future City of Commerce. . . . [H]ere the 'missing subject' is clearly identified as the teachers and students in the classroom. The same message became even more explicit in Sui Jianguo's installation: he cleared and paved the ground of a no longer existing classroom, then arranged rows of chairs, a desk, and two bookcases filled with broken bricks."[68] These political statements differ from those of post–Cultural Revolution "scar art" (*shanghen yishu*) or earlier avant-garde art in that they speak more to the lack of human subjects than to their wounds, and as such function as a silent but powerful marker of absence. In fact Sui Jianguo remarked about his installation, "This is not a protest because we are no longer there."[69]

In an interview conducted by the art historian Francesca Del Lago in

2000, several Beijing artists reiterated this sentiment of powerlessness in the face of municipal development practices. Zhang Dali disparaged the municipal authorities for their construction of Peace Avenue (Ping'an Dadao) in 1998: "They said they wanted to remake it as a Ming-Qing style street. But it was a Ming-Qing style street to start with. They tore it down then re-created it into a theater set, using old-style bricks and tiles." Zhan Wang adds, "There is a terrible contradiction here. On the one hand they oppose tradition and destroy the old culture; on the other hand, they attempt to revive it in a very artificial way. . . . [M]oreover, your oppositional voice has absolutely no chance to be heard. This brings you to a state of total helplessness. My *Ruins Cleaning Project* emerged from such a condition. I started cleaning and restoring a building during its demolition, when the bulldozers had stopped for a few days. This was not about nostalgia, but about my state of embarrassment and impotence, knowing that nothing I could do would change or stop this process."[70] Zhang Dali conveys this sentiment with his *Dialogue* series (*Duihua*, 1998), in which a distinctive silhouette of a male head forms an opening in a semi-demolished wall in Beijing, revealing the abandoned ruins within. Wang Jingsong's *Bai chai tu* (One hundred demolition drawings, 1999), are photographs of walls whitewashed with a large, circumscribed character, "chai" (demolition). Similarly, Zhang Nian features demolition in his video artwork *Chai Beijing* (Demolish Beijing, 1990–2000), juxtaposing images of the character "chai" engraved on ancient steles against U.S. dollars, excavators, models of the new city, and migrant workers, who move slowly around their shacks in Beijing's *hutong*, before speeding along its ring roads.[71]

Most of these works draw attention to development run amok. Others, such as Zhan Wang's *Artificial Mountain Rocks* series, highlight superficial understandings of Chinese aesthetics in contemporary urban design. Inspired by spatial changes in Beijing, Zhan reflected on how Chinese traditionally placed rockeries (gnarled stone) in gardens and in front of buildings for decoration and meditation purposes, as a means of connecting humans with nature. Yet Chinese consider these real stones to be "fake" or "artificial" (*jiashanshi* literally means "fake mountain rocks"). As Zhan explains,

This has to do with Chinese aesthetics. What is seen is not a rock, but a way to fulfill the imagined idea of a rock. In the modern city, we do not know where to put rockeries, and they end up clumsily placed in front of

Zhang Dali, *Dialogue* nos.
125A, 121, Beijing, 1998.
Courtesy Zhang Dali.

Zhan Wang, *Artificial Mountain Rocks* series, stainless steel. Beijing, 2004. Courtesy Zhan Wang.

modern buildings with which they have no relation. I started making the sculptures on stainless steel because it's very popular material in contemporary architecture. It's everywhere in China. The shine creates the impression of something precious, and at the same time it's relatively cheap. I used to hate steel and chose it as a negative reflection of Chinese cultural values. I use steel to replicate the stone and create a fake "artificial mountain rock"—a really fake stone. Negating a negation becomes an affirmation; it becomes something real.[72]

Because structures in traditional Chinese cities were constructed of wood, tile, and stone, rockeries, even if "artificial" in the cultural imagination, provided an aesthetic continuity between humans, nature, and the built environment. Rockeries invoked sacred mountains, and the most important aspect of landscape layout was its *shi,* or "inclination of nature."[73] Landscape, as a construct of the mind, was perceived to be "alive" and possessed of its own dynamism. As Li Xiaodong and Yeo Kangshua explain, "The [traditional Chinese] architectural landscape largely consists of symmetries that define a centre which in turn delineates motion and regulates symmetry. The core plot organizes space experientially, such as movement through the landscape implies one's progress to enlightenment or knowledge."[74] With the wholesale adoption of concrete and steel structures based on modern modular design requirements, the inherent symmetry of traditional structures using wooden joint brackets or interlaced glazed roof tiles is altered, necessitating a corresponding design shift in landscape architecture.

These late-twentieth-century installations and performances featuring ruins and artificiality clearly demonstrate that many Chinese artists were vehemently opposed to the lack of attention to cultural heritage and the human subject in Beijing's postsocialist urban development. These works challenge historical representation by engendering transient images of disembodied places. As spatial representations of disappearance, they evoke traces of the vanishing essence of the city, rather than invoking its history per se. In sharp contrast to the aesthetic of nostalgia that dominated urban art in Shanghai in the mid-1990s, in Beijing there is no attempt to lay claim to the city's rich historical past, and the uncanny effects of achronicity operate as a powerful cultural critique.

In her book analyzing moral agency in twentieth-century Chinese fiction, Sabina Knight notes the return, in the fiction of the 1990s, of Confucian and Enlightenment humanist values that contest the determinism of free-market capitalist fundamentalism, a reversal of the moral indeterminacy of the avant-garde fiction of the 1980s.[75] One observes a similar shift from indeterminacy to agency among Beijing avant-garde artists as they began situating their works in public space to critique inattention to the human subject. Song Dong's works are a case in point. For example, in 1995 Song set performances in his neighborhood *hutong* in Xisi, Beijing, pouring boiling water or writing his water diary in the lanes, performances that, at least initially, expressed a sense of impotence and insignificance. Reflecting back on that period, Song said, "You felt there was a lot to do, but no way to do it; all you could do was watch time pass you by."[76] To counter this sense of indeterminacy, Song initiated a series of site-specific performances to highlight the relationship between space, time, and place. In 1996, during his now famous performance, *Breathing*, Song Dong lay prostrate on Tiananmen Square, breathing on it for forty minutes on a freezing winter night with four puzzled People's Liberation Army soldiers as spectators, while his wife, Yin Xiuzhen, photographed the slow formation of a mass of ice. Similar to Sui Jianguo's installation on the demolished grounds of the Central Academy of Fine Art, and to Zhang Dali's graffiti art, Song forcibly inserts himself into the urban space despite the fact that his presence is largely ignored and that the traces of his presence (boiling water, water calligraphy, a block of ice) are transient. By exerting even this modicum of agency, these artists refused to succumb to numbing strictures on post-1989 public discourse and the ahistorical get-rich-at-all-costs narrative dominating urban development. Song Dong sums up the avant-garde attitude of the mid-1990s in a sentence I translate loosely as "Just do it" ("Bu zuo, bai bu zuo; zuo, ye bai zuo; bai zuo, ye dei zuo" [If you don't act, it's in vain; if you act, it's also in vain; despite acting in vain, you must act"]).[77]

Starting in 1997, Song Dong and Yin Xiuzhen, both Beijing natives, began working intentionally against the disappearance of site specificity and cultural memory by collecting material fragments of a vanishing present. They gathered relics along the controversial construction site of Peace Avenue, an enormous architectural project with a total budget of two billion yuan ($350 million in 1998). The avenue, running thirty meters wide by seven thousand meters long through the most populated section of the capital, forms the second-widest east-west road across central Beijing. The relocation phase was completed by early 1998, with the families silently displaced, their streets and lanes vanishing from the city's map. Song Dong saved "door plates" (*menpai*) from the demolished houses to create an installation, but he was initially unable to complete his project as government authorities confiscated his collection, accusing him, in an ironic twist, of gathering construction rubble to engage in profiteering.[78] Yin Xiuzhen used roof tiles to create her installations *Hanging Tiles Out to Dry* and *Transformation*, the latter comprising rows of roof tiles that filled an empty courtyard, each affixed with a photo of the house from which the tile came.[79]

While native Beijing residents perform personal attachments to the traditional urban fabric, its newer artists, including migrants, overseas returnees, and foreign artists, also perform Beijing identity in their art. In his documentary film *Beijing, Beijing* (2006), a television show produced for Swedish public television, Henri Seng (Sheng Hai), who returned to Beijing after an extended period abroad in Sweden, poignantly captures the ethos of the postsocialist capital from the perspective of its migrant artists. He features the prominent conceptual artist Zhang Dali, who returned to Beijing in 1995 after living in Bologna for six years; Zhu Ming, one of Beijing's earliest performance artists, who moved to Beijing in 1991, from

Hefei, Anhui Province; and the performance artist He Chengyao, who moved to Beijing in 2000, from Chongqing, Sichuan Province. Like the filmmaker Wang Xiaoshuai, the novelist Qiu Huadong, and the documentarians Wu Wenguang and Zhao Liang, Henri Seng portrays the lives of early performance artists as impoverished, angst-ridden, and oppressive. While each artist did in fact face tremendous financial, political, and psychological hardships in making his or her initial transition to Beijing, when I interviewed them in 2007 each expressed a sense of joy and freedom in performing in Beijing, a city where each plans to reside indefinitely. By 2007 each artist was also relatively (or in the case of Zhang Dali, extremely) financially secure, well known, well traveled, and afforded a considerable degree of creative license. In the words of Zhu Ming, the biggest struggle for artists in Beijing has always been to maintain one's ideals and not "sell out" to materialism and consumer culture.[80]

Zhang Dali's work provides a particularly interesting case of the attempt to situate art directly in urban space, outside of the isolation of the academy, gallery spaces, and avant-garde villages. Zhang was born in Harbin in 1963, moved with his family to Jingdezhen in 1969, returned to the small town of Jixi in Heilongjiang in 1977, and studied in the Central Academy of Arts in Beijing from 1983 to 1987. From 1987 to 1989 Zhang Dali lived in the Yuanmingyuan (the former Summer Palace) as a "vagrant artist" without a Beijing residence permit or work unit. In July 1989 he moved with his Italian wife to Bologna, but returned to Beijing in 1995. In interviews by Wu Wenguang, conducted over the course of twelve years and published in 2000, Zhang describes his intense attachment to the city: "You could say my life started in Beijing."[81] He goes on to explain that Beijing, unlike the other places he had lived (including Europe), was a place with an open-ended future, where he could fantasize about its fate. Indeed, this sense of possibility was what most defined the capital in the mid-1980s, when Zhang Dali first moved there, an ethos that continues to the present and draws ever-increasing numbers of intellectuals to the capital, even from overseas.

Zhang Dali's signature work, *Dialogue* (*Duihua*), featuring his bald silhouette clandestinely spray-painted by night throughout Bologna, was born out of his frustration at not being able to communicate clearly in a foreign land. When he continued his performances on his return to Beijing, however, he discovered new layers of meaning. Zhang was partially motivated by a fundamental need to communicate: "The Beijing environment was unfamiliar to me; I was at a loss about how to communicate with many people."[82] Although he had experienced a similar expressive impulse in Italy, he felt especially pressed in China to establish a direct connection between avant-garde art and society. Zhang wanted his work to further enlarge the urban public sphere.

When I started *Dialogue* in Europe I was influenced by their graffiti art, but when I returned to Beijing I found it was particularly suited to Beijing [where] there had been very little public space until the 1990s. . . . [W]hen people moved to other locales without a *hukou*, they had to depend on other urbanites to survive and enjoy themselves. So when I started doing this graffiti art in Beijing, people thought it was weird, or difficult to understand, but they basically could accept it. I painted buildings slated for demolition, so people were puzzled, but no one considered it vandalism. If I had done it earlier, it would have been impossible; if later, it would have been meaningless.[83]

In fact, Zhang did not reveal his identity as the anonymous graffiti artist until 1998, when a public controversy about the figures, which now numbered over two thousand, emerged in Beijing's newspapers. Zhang wrote his own explanation for the images for the group exhibition "It's Me," curated later that year by Leng Lin: "This image is a condensation of my own image as an individual. It stands in my place to communicate with this city. I want to know everything about this city—its state of being, its transformation, and its structure. I call this project *Dialogue*. Of course there are many ways for an artist to communicate with a city. I use this method because, for one thing, it allows me to place my work at every corner of this city in a short period."[84] In his discussion of *Dialogue*, Wu Hung astutely observes the unsettling dissonance between the artist's assumption of communication and photographs of the images themselves, which appear to evoke little response from passersby. The irony is that while this public-minded artist was genuinely motivated by a desire to bypass the established art system and engage the city in dialogue, most residents remained unaware or uninterested; a further irony is that photos of this series, which sell for exorbitant prices to foreigners, have nevertheless "come to symbolize a new image of this city."[85]

Although Zhang self-identifies as a conceptual (rather than graffiti) artist and continually strives to raise the public's awareness of social issues, most of his images of the city are consumed overseas. For example, his *Chinese Offspring* series, created from 2000 to 2003, both underscores and perpetuates the spiritually numbing, objectifying effects of urbanization on the

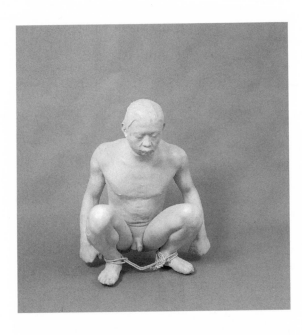

Zhang Dali, *Chinese Offspring* no. 5, mixed media (resin mixed with fiberglass), 2003. Courtesy Zhang Dali.

rural migrant laborers building China's cities. Zhang took resin casts of one hundred workers, substituted numbers for their names, signed the figures, and offered them for sale. Predictably, these works have circulated in overseas exhibitions and entered the global art market, defining the Chinese city more for foreigners than for its residents. While Zhang paid each worker the respectable fee of one thousand yuan ($120) per body cast, in 2007 the casts sold at £10,000 ($20,500) each, when Charles Saatchi purchased fifteen of them for his new gallery on King's Road in London.[86]

Zhang's growing prominence over the past decade typifies a general trend in Chinese experimental art summarized by a headline that appeared in the *Guardian* on 11 April 2007: "Once Hated, Now Feted—Chinese Artists Come Out from behind the Wall." The exhibit "It's Me," where Zhang first "came out" by displaying photographs of his graffiti, signaled an intentional shift by Chinese experimental artists from the margins to the center of global urban commercial culture, political risks notwithstanding. The exhibition of works by twenty-six artists was scheduled for 21–24 November 1998 and was to be held in the main ritual hall of the former Imperial Ancestral Temple in Beijing, but it was canceled by the authorities on opening day. According to Leng Lin, a researcher at the Chinese Academy of Social Sciences, whose preface to the exhibition doubled as the curator's representation of self, the works comprised "a conscious effort to ease the pressure [of globalization] by developing a new, transnational sub-jectivity."[87] A self-portrait by Zhu Fadong, for example, encapsulates a per-formance he conducted in 1994, after moving to Beijing from Yunnan; in the performance, he took long daily walks through Beijing's streets with the announcement "This person is for sale; please discuss price in person" on his back. The performance speaks to the reality of the so-called floating population of migrants in the capital, and the marginalized position of artists in particular.

On the other hand, many works in "It's Me" reversed the stereotype of the alienated artist by positing the artistic self at the center of global capitalism. Zhao Qin's and Liu Jian's *A Successful Day* (1998) is a painted photograph of the two exuberant artists impersonating businessmen, which flanks a paint-ing of four foreign businessmen with exaggerated smiles making phone calls to the artist-businessmen outside the frame. Hong Hao's photograph *Hello, Mr. Hong* (1998) shows the artist in a Western suit, being served wine in an elegant living room. Using computer-generated images, Zhou Tiehai pronounces himself "Man of the Week" on a mock *Newsweek* cover, while Zhao Bandi plays with Orientalist images by portraying his pajama-clad self cuddling a panda as a beautiful girl paddles his wooden skiff on a tranquil lotus pond. Whether satirizing China's hyped globalization or its gritty urban reality, what "It's Me," and exhibitions like it, demonstrated was a new negotiation of the impasse presented by the multiple concerns of global versus local ("Chineseness"), form versus function ("consumerism"), and nature versus artifice ("urbanization"), the very subjects that dominated aesthetic debates in Beijing in the mid-1990s. While individual works continued to conceptualize particular aspects of urban identity, their ar-rangement under a rubric of inclusiveness ("it's *all* me") marked a shift in artistic expression.

The hybridization of earlier conceptual dichotomies became evident at the level of curatorial decisions not only regarding content, but, perhaps even more importantly, regarding site. Many art critics have been troubled by the so-called globalization of contemporary Chinese art in the 1990s, where selected Chinese works are absorbed into Western cultures to satisfy foreign rather than domestic needs.[88] The site for "It's Me" was strate-gically chosen in an effort to counter the dual forces of the essentialization of Chinese experimental art in international art shows and the Orientalist portrayals of China by Westerners. Capitalizing on consumer trends, the artists in "It's Me" decided to rent the Imperial Ancestral Temple in the Forbidden City to exhibit their images of the self. This positioning functioned both as a foil to the Orientalist productions increasingly dominating this space and as a means of situating art in the unique nexus of traditional, modern, and postmodern aesthetics that dominate Beijing.[89]

Exhibitions began to highlight the fact that state hegemony is wielded through forms of capitalist development that threaten human dignity as much as totalitarianism. The exhibition "Departing from China: An Exhibition of Chinese New Art," scheduled to open 24 April 1999 (but canceled by authorities) at the Design Museum in Beijing, included many works suggesting the disappearance of the human subject in the capital.[90] For example, Zhao Liang's *Eye Assault* is a video installation of a young man walking aimlessly in Beijing's subway, his image unpredictably disappearing and reappearing, changing from solid form to blurred, speaking to the disorientation of the human subject in the vast metropolis. Tian Zizhong pieces together photos taken along Chang'an Boulevard in front of Tiananmen Square, the "central axis" of the capital, reinforcing the notion of Beijing's traditional political power. Song Dong's year-long, seven-city exhibition "Wildlife: An Experimental Art Project Held Outside Conventional Exhibition Spaces and Devoid of Conventional Exhibition Forms," was explicitly organized to decenter Beijing's dominance over art. His contribution, *Transposition of the Center Axis*, refigured the capital's symbolic political hegemony over its subjects. After mapping the respective central axes of the city of Beijing and his home in the city, he took photos along each axis, pieced them together in a linear composition, then transposed the photographs of one axis onto the other axis in reality, creating a complex transgression of the traditional relationship of individual subjects to the state by inverting public and private space.[91]

Other exhibitions situated themselves in the center of consumer culture and new urban construction. For example, the fashionable Club Vogue, in the Sanlitun District, hosted the exhibition "Food as Art" (17 February 2000), and basements of commercial buildings featured exhibitions such as "Persistent Deviation" (7 November 1998) and "Post-Sense Sensibility" (9–10 January 1999).[92] Both the club scene and the basements were closely linked to Beijing's urban development in the 1990s. With the construction of thousands of high-rise buildings, broad basements with intricate interiors added a new dimension to the existing urban spatial structure. Wu Hung elaborates on the dual attraction of basements as exhibition sites: "Practically speaking, a basement is cheap to rent, and an experimental art exhibition held in such an unobtrusive place has a better chance to evade the watchful eyes of the authorities. Symbolically, an art exhibition installed

Song Dong. *Transposition of the Center Axis*, performance and photo installations. Beijing, 1997–98. Left: photos of Beijing's central axis placed along the central axis of Song Dong's home; right: photos of the central axis of Song Dong's home placed along Beijing's central axis. Source: *Yesheng: 1997 nian jingzhe shi* (Wildlife: Commencing Jingzhe Day, 1997) (Beijing: Xiandai yishu zhongxin, 1997), 50–51.

in a basement can intentionally draw on the political and social connotations of 'underground.' "[93]

Less than a decade later, however, artists no longer need to go "underground," for better or worse. As Zhang Dali stated confidently in 2007, "Just think, five years ago contemporary art had to be exhibited underground, and artists would be driven out of places like 798 or artist villages like this one. But now the government accepts us, and even sees us as good social elements. And they're willing to go to places like 798 or even Venice to meet artists and try to understand contemporary art. This is important."[94] When I pressed him as to whether art really has the power to change society, he answered categorically in the affirmative, but acknowledged the challenge. Why, for example, had he introduced the "AK-47" mark into what had previously been an unarmed figure inviting dialogue? He answered, "My *Dialogue* drawings were vandalized [fandao], and I felt the deep level of violence in Chinese culture. In China if someone is sincere he'll be attacked by another."[95] This idea informs his latest sculpture series, *Man and Beast*, life-sized bronze statues, derived from migrant-worker casts, that depict in-

Zhang Dali, *Man and Beast*, bronze. Shanghai, 2007. Courtesy Zhang Dali.

dividuals with dull expressions who are pinned to the ground by or precariously balancing like acrobats on fierce animals.[96] "Confucius once declared that a cruel government is more ferocious than a tiger," Zhang stated. "These animals represent a spirit that oppresses people. Even the sculptures where people are riding on their backs represent an overwhelming force that these individuals are incapable of changing. They can only endure. . . . We all feel this sense of impotence. . . . Everyone knows what has to be done but no one dares act, no one dares name what has to be done."[97]

At the Dashanzi International Art Festival in May 2007, many artists displayed recent historical events and current social problems in uncompromising terms. The Gao Brothers' exhibit "Zhua xiaojie" (Arresting prostitutes) was a series of paintings and sculptures based on media images of police raids on prostitutes and their clients, that clearly reveal individuals' identities on television and the Internet. The most damning sculpture, prominently displayed outside their new studio space at 798, featured three policemen, each grasping a limb of a young woman, the folds of her

Gao Zhen and Gao Qiang, *Arresting Prostitutes*, painted bronze. Beijing, 2007. Courtesy Gao Brothers.

skirt opened to reveal her vagina, inviting repeated violations and humiliation by voyeuristic viewers.[98] Sheng Qi's oil painting series features the faces of innocent youth, especially women and children, smilingly gazing from the barrelheads of the tanks on Tiananmen Square. Another exhibit of oil paintings, by an anonymous artist surnamed Zhou, depicted tanks surrounded by miniature action figures or Peking Opera figurines, clearly powerless to halt their assault; a blindfolded dog on his hind legs, labeled "running dog" (*zou gou*); a blindfolded, eviscerated, bloodied hog, its innards protruding, held up by its hind legs by two white-gloved, black-sleeved arms, labeled "slaughtered pig" (*sha zhu*). As I was observing the exhibition, two stylish Chinese professionals in their early twenties walked into the (very small) space, and after looking carefully at the paintings, one commented "I just don't understand what these artists are trying to convey," a sentiment her partner shared. I asked hesitantly, "You really don't

Oil paintings reference the 4 June 1989 crackdown on Tiananmen Square. Dashanzi International Art Festival, May 2007. Photo by author.

Sheng Qi, *Five Angels*, oil acrylic on canvas, 2007. Courtesy Sheng Qi.

understand these paintings?" "Not at all," they answered. I mentioned the year 1989, pointed out that the miniature figures appeared powerless to stop tanks on a square, then gestured toward the disparaging slogans. "Oh," they said, nodding thoughtfully. "Oh, I'm beginning to understand."

I was their age and living in China on 4 June 1989, when People's Liberation Army tanks rolled into the streets of downtown Beijing toward Tiananmen Square, firing at civilians and students to end the weeks-long stand-off between the government and students who had been engaging in hunger strikes on Tiananmen Square, with over a million Beijing citizens demonstrating in support. The massacre was, for me, as for most of the artists, writers, and filmmakers I have interviewed, a life-changing event. And yet by July 1989 the party propaganda machine was in motion, and the youth nationwide were learning a very different version of events. Because those who contradicted the party line could be arrested or punished, the elders rarely informed the youth otherwise. Very few young people today have a clear picture of what happened that fateful spring. The paradigmatic symbol of a lone man defying tanks on Tiananmen Square, a photo that circulated worldwide and was featured years later on American billboards promoting values to which to aspire (such as "courage"), does not register in the visual memory of China's younger generation.

From this one example one can see artists' potential for reengaging cultural memory and political dialogue. Some artists unquestionably capitalize on foreign obsessions with the breaking of political and social taboos in China, but regardless of their financial aspirations, many remain highly sensitive to pressing social issues. In 1998 the art curator and critic Gao Minglu concluded that "the avant-garde artist in contemporary China is at a crossroads, faced with either jumping into the circle of the new middle class as a career artist or continuing to be an independent intellectual, the role that had been at the core of contemporary Chinese avant-garde."[99] Yet positioning and identity can no longer be so neatly delineated in Beijing or the nation. Instead, by situating themselves at the center of commercial culture, China's experimental artists attract more captive, interactive audiences. Neoliberal capitalism is provoking new forms of civic agency. Beijing artists, now numbering in the thousands and living in dozens of artist zones and villages around the city's suburbs, can exploit unique opportunities to perform the nation to its citizens. The most public-minded of these artists align their goals with those which have always energized avant-garde art, and, even as they gain material prosperity, by working to reengage the public, they hold out the possibility of effecting social change.

Consuming the Postsocialist City

Shanghai Identity in Art, Film, and Fiction

> The modern Chinese city is the product of contact between East and West. Those individuals who, through contact with Western culture, have changed their way of life and thinking will not find themselves able any longer to live in the country. A new parasitic man comes into being [in a] community of dependent consumers.
>
> Fei Xiaotong, *China's Gentry: Essays on Urban-Rural Relations*

Jan Nederveen Pieterse's study of globalization as hybridization identifies two concepts of culture. The first, which better characterizes Beijing and other (formerly) administrative cities, "views culture as essentially territorial, [and] assumes that culture stems from a learning process that is, in the main, localized," whereas the second, which better characterizes Shanghai and other (especially southern or former treaty-port) commercial cities, sees culture as a "translocal process" that "involves an *outward*-looking sense of place."[1] The first type of culture concerns itself with the language of nation, empire, and endogenous sources of identity and authenticity. The second type of urban culture relies more on the discourses of diaspora, migration, half-caste ethnicities, and heterogeneity. If postsocialist Beijing identity is performed on behalf of the nation, its centrality unquestioned, its adherence to master narratives supreme, even as artists claim to undermine them, postsocialist Shanghai identity eschews the national. Instead, it is produced for consumption by world citizens with whom Shanghai urbanites fully identify.

Host to the 2007 Special Olympics and the 2010 World Expo, Shanghai finds its cosmopolitanism is now a source of pride, with the Shanghai roots of the NBA star Yao Ming and the Olympic gold medal track star Liu Xiang regularly touted in the media. Yet the hybrid identity of the Shanghainese had regularly been, until quite recently, denounced by traditional literati and Maoist intellectuals.

In 1946, the sociologist Fei Xiaotong published an article in the *American Journal of Sociology* characterizing Shanghai's earliest "secondhand foreigners" as outcasts of the traditional structure who had lost their positions and sought their fortune by illegal means. He continued, "They live in, and take advantage of, the margin of cultural contact. . . . [T]hey are half-caste in culture, bilingual in speech, and morally unstable . . . , unscrupulous, pecuniary, individualistic, and agnostic, not only in religion, but in cultural values."[2] Today these culturally suspect urbanites aspire to no less than making Shanghai the "capital of the twenty-first century," a status held by New York in the twentieth, and Paris in the nineteenth. Fully embracing its cosmopolitan, semicolonial past as the breeding ground for China's earliest urban modernity and launching pad for its global future, Shanghai imagines itself as *the* city to emulate, not just in Asia, but in the world.

On 27 September 2004 *Time* magazine named Shanghai "the world's most happening city," but just how global a city it is remains a live question. If one uses the quantitative measures of world-city theorists, who calculate levels of advanced producer services such as accountancy, advertising, finance, and law, one finds that less than a decade ago Shanghai ranked as a third-tier "gamma" city, along with Amsterdam, Melbourne, Boston, Warsaw, Atlanta, and Kuala Lampur.[3] The historian Jeffrey Wasserstrom considers Shanghai to be in the early stages of its "reglobalization," as he characterizes the postsocialist development of former world-class cities, placing it in a category shared by Budapest, Prague, and Berlin.[4] During its first stage of development, from the thirteenth century through the first Opium War (1839–42), Shanghai emerged as a trading center of first local and then regional import, and eventually of certain international significance as a transshipment point for commodities circulating between China's provinces and Southeast Asia. It was forced to internationalize during its century-long treaty-port era, from the early 1840s through the 1940s. The city became more integrated within the national and political economic order during its socialist transformation (1950s through early 1980s). Postsocialist Shanghai image-making, however, tends to reject its socialist history, remaining far more enamored of the capitalist modernity

semicolonial past in order to embrace its postmodern future. "The 1990s cultural reversal," she writes, suppresses "imperialism, semicolonialization, [and] the profound wounding of the race. In the imagined nostalgic scenario, the historical Shanghai succeeds in becoming a cultural springboard that allows us to leap unscathed across [humiliating] experiences and to express new freedom."[13] Through the consumption of nostalgia the past disappears into the future, and quotidian forms of the treaty-port phase of Chinese modernity become ritualized in everyday life. Shanghai's selective memory of the past boosts confidence in its future. Sunny free-market ideals replace loaded epithets for old Shanghai, which had ranged from "Paris of the East" to "Whore of Asia." Although pundits such as John Ralston Saul declare the "death of globalism," Wang Xiaoming notes that its popular sentiments are alive on the streets and feed self-aggrandizing official discourse on Shanghai economic culture.[14]

The transmutation of colonial catchphrases into neoliberal mantras is due in part to the need to imagine a classical moment of Chinese bourgeois modernity, but a more mundane explanation for the rise of the Shanghai nostalgia industry is money. As a marketing strategy, glorifying Shanghai's heyday attracts consumer spending and investment in the city. The one constant of *haipai* culture is its pragmatic engagement in commerce, with consumerism providing the sociological link between old Shanghai and its postsocialist revival. In promoting particular modes of consumption as the "art of living," and in selling the idea that one defines one's identity through consumption, tantalizing, if illusory, forms of freedom are promised. Thus, propaganda strategies that play into insecurities about self-image are especially lucrative in Shanghai.

Certain postsocialist works by Shanghai visual, film, and literary artists play with and even capitalize on, but ultimately expose, the sociopolitical reality behind the Shanghai dream of middle-class consumption. These works from the late twentieth century anticipate the myth of the *xiaozi*, or "petty bourgeois" urban consumer. This fantasy has gathered strength in the new century through bulletin boards, chat rooms, and cyberliterature (*wangluo wenxue*) by writers such as Anni Baobei. The *xiaozi* embodies a taste, lifestyle, and imagination associated with transnational commodities, rather than a real class in a political sense. Xin Yang attributes this urban aesthetic to a combination of de-revolutionized daily life, an emergent class of white-collar professionals, and the circulation and consumption of global commodities, yet she underscores the fact that before the term *xiaozi* became a popular one, the media was already constructing the imaginary of alternative lifestyles and consumption.[15] Three artists offer particularly trenchant explorations of the commodified lifestyle as it has emerged in Shanghai: Shi Yong, a Shanghai artist who playfully deconstructs the imaginary *xiaozi* identity in *Shanghai Visual Identity Project* (1997–2007); Lou Ye, whose film *Suzhou River* (1999) illuminates *xiaozi* mythmaking; and Wang Anyi, whose novel *Song of Everlasting Sorrow* (1996) captures the postsocialist transformation of the commodity.

Shanghai Simulacra: Shi Yong's *Shanghai Visual Identity Project*

Born in 1963, Shi Yong studied commercial advertisement at the Shanghai College of Applied Technology from 1981–84, then specialized in oil paintings which infused classical realism with romanticism. The pragmatic turn of the populace in the aftermath of June Fourth impacted Shi Yong's idealistic generation. During the early 1990s, Shi Yong stopped painting and lived collectively with other artists and intellectuals in low-rent farmer's housing in the western suburbs of Shanghai, where they spent most of their time reading philosophy and literary theory by thinkers such as Roland Barthes, Michel Foucault, Jacques Derrida, and Martin Heidegger. This period of introspection ended after Deng's southern tour caused the Shanghai government to launch new promotional campaigns, which inspired the next stage of Shi Yong's artistic production. Since the mid-1990s Shi Yong has been creating a corpus of humorous conceptual art which constitutes a play on Shanghai's urban image-making.

In 1993 the municipality initiated a concerted effort to shed its forty-year image as a lumbering industrial workhorse for the socialist state in order to reclaim its former image as the cosmopolitan vanguard of East Asia. One of the first slogans launched by the government, sustained well into the twenty-first century, depicted Shanghai as a window on the world. This "window" was understood as a two-way portal, with Shanghai showcasing the latest international trends for the nation while the world peered in at Shanghai to gauge China's future. Refrains such as "window of the world" (*shijie zhi chuang*), "align with international trends" (*yu guojia jiegui*), "a new look every year; a huge makeover every three years" (*yinian yige yang, sannian da bian yang*), "attract FDI" (*xiyin waizi*), "keep in step with civilization, be an attractive Shanghainese" (*yu wenming tongxing, zuo ke'ai de Shanghairen*) were ubiquitous. These mottos, which appeared in ads, the media, and interviews with businesspeople and officials, were also posted in residential communities and work units. And the citizenry took these

"Window of the World." Shanghai Urban Planning Exhibition Hall, 2007. Photo by author.

mandates to heart. As Shi Yong explains, "In planning her career, the average urbanite (*shimin*) would consider how her vocation could achieve these goals: 'What can I do *personally* to give Shanghai its annual makeover, to bring it up to international standards.' "[16]

In 1997 Shi Yong launched a decade-long project titled *Shanghai Visual Identity Project*. The idea was inspired by his formal training in commercial advertisement and by the ubiquitous photo booths located in the shopping malls that had sprung up in the mid-1990s. He later, in 2005, recalled the ethos of those times.

> You could change your hairstyle, hair color, clothing, then take a photo of the new you. Then your friends could decide what style was best suited to you. I thought this was hilarious, but also very representative of our current cultural attitudes. On the one hand, the past forms and systems remained intact; on the other hand, all of these new images were flooding society. What were you to do? You felt conflicted. You didn't want to eradicate everything that was "you," but you wanted to be new. Just as you were mired in confusion a guide appeared, a photograph instructing you on how to partake in the new commercial culture without going to extremes. A flood of books on image hit the market telling people how to

Promoting subway civility: "Keep in Step with Civilization: Be an Attractive Shanghainese."
Shanghai Metro, 2005. Photo by author.

dress for success. Of course, as a city that functions as a "window on the world," its image is multifaceted. There's the architecture and its ethos. But the actual heart of the city is its people, its residents. And those *shimin* have two parts—a body and an image, it's never just a unified whole. So I decided to start from the body to explore body image, to confront the confusion presented by contemporary commercial culture.[17]

To "resolve" this identity confusion Shi Yong developed an interactive video installation for "Cities on the Move," the Vienna Secession exhibition in 1997. The idea behind Shi Yong's installation, *The New Image of Shanghai Today,* was to have exhibition visitors choose the most strategic image for an artist wishing to keep up with his city's grand ambitions. Replicating prevalent urban-design practices that contracted the most important projects to foreign firms, Shi Yong produced a concept sketch for the artist's backdrop with the requisite city landmarks (the Bund, the Pearl of the Orient TV Tower, the Nanpu Bridge, the Yan'an Rd overpass), but left the "design details" to the Europeans visiting the exhibition, who were asked to first assess twelve portraits of Shi Yong sporting various hairstyles and clothing, then vote online to help determine which image best aligned him with Shanghai's world-class aspirations. He provided this tongue-in-cheek explanation to the Vienna Secession voters: "Shanghai, at the front-line of China's opening to the outside world, is now developing at so rapid a pace that 'every year it looks new and every three years there is a tremendous change.' As an individual involved in the ever-changing urban environment, I feel that it is urgent to refresh my self-image to keep pace with the development of the city. Therefore I plan to revise and redesign my image strategically, standardizing and unifying it, with the hope of keeping up with the new appearance and fresh concept of my city."[18] A computer-generated statistical analysis tallied the "scientific" results that determined his new image: wavy dyed hair, shades, Italian leather shoes, and a crisp white business shirt under a Mao suit (known as a Sun Yat-sen suit in Chinese). As Shi Yong explained later, his project conveyed both genuine identity confusion and a powerful critique of cultural colonialism: "What is the appropriate image for a contemporary Chinese artist attempting to align himself with global trends? It was, of course, essential that the legislators be Westerners, as they continue to wield the power over international aesthetic standards."[19]

Shi Yong's simulated image, in turn, became the basis of his subsequent work in the *Shanghai Visual Identity Project,* such as in his conceptual piece *Adding One Concept on Top of Another* (1997), which doubly appropriates from Westerners in a parody of such legitimating processes. As Shi Yong explains, "I employed Joseph Kosuth's 'One and Three Chairs' as the starting point for my work, since it is not only a piece of conceptual art, but one which has been legitimized with the power of language in the context of contemporary Western art history. Adding the legitimized image of a contemporary Chinese artist to it adds an accepted (Western) concept of 'contemporary Chinese' to an accepted (Western) concept of the power of language. Therefore, the original concept that Kosuth's chair embodies inevitably transforms into a concept of the mutual relationship between the Chair and the Chinese sitting on it, offering a valid stage for producing legitimized performances."[20] Shi Yong's mimicry of a work of conceptual art legitimized by the dominant canon recalls Homi Bhabha's analysis of the shared discursive process of colonial imitation "by which the excess of slippage produced by the *ambivalence* of mimicry (almost the same, *but not quite*) does not merely 'rupture' the discourse, but becomes transformed into an uncertainty which fixes the colonial subject as a 'partial' presence [that is] both 'incomplete' and 'virtual.' "[21]

Cynicism about the need to be endorsed by Westerners dominated avant-garde art in Shanghai in the 1990s. The Shanghai artist Zhou Tiehai's black-and-white silent film *Bixu* (Necessity, 1995) comprises five humorous clips exposing the international politics behind Chinese identity, especially the subaltern position of the Chinese artist waiting to be "discovered" by a powerful Western Other. One clip features Chinese artists strategizing

Shi Yong, *The New Image of Shanghai Today*, interactive video installation. Vienna Secession, 1997. Courtesy Shi Yong.

how to shut domestic competitors out of the international art market, their gestures and scripted discourse mimicking early film footage of communists planning their military attack against the Nationalists. Another clip shows Chinese artists being diagnosed by Western doctors.

B Shares, Zhou Tiehai's "stock report" entry in "Cities on the Move," is an especially sardonic read of the mediated nature of the image of China-Shanghai-the Artist. The report, presented as a two-page layout, reads in part,

> If you want to know how the West views Shanghai, read *Time, Der Spiegel, The Asian Wall Street Journal*, etc. If you want to know the view of a Shanghai artist, see the next page.

> New Listing, Zhou Tiehai, Rises on Debut before Reaching Fair Value
> When first listed July 12 on the Shanghai Stock Exchange, Zhou Tiehai appeared undervalued, rising only slightly in the first hours of trade. But Class B shares* in the issue appreciated steadily over the next two weeks, as foreign investors learned more about the enterprise's fundamentals . . . The gradual appreciation accelerated into an all-out buying spree on July 26, when the unnamed European buyer discovered previously undisclosed assets in Zhou Tiehai. . . .
> * Shanghai has two stock markets. Class B shares are denominated in US dollars and tradable only by overseas investors; Class A shares, denominated in yuan, are available only to Chinese buyers.[22]

Zhou Tiehai's conflation of a Chinese artist with a stock spoofs the incredible hype that China's opening, particularly its potential for profit, has

The International Version of the 'vis' project:
The New Image of Shanghai Today ------The Logo and the settings

最佳发型评选范围
The best selection of hair styles

A D

B E

C F

2

The International Version of the 'vis' project:
The New Image of Shanghai Today ------The Logo and the settings

专用服装评选范围
The available selection of the clothing

❶ ❷

4

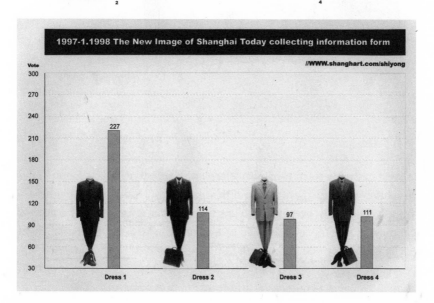

1997-1.1998 The New Image of Shanghai Today collecting information form

//WWW.shanghart.com/shiyong

Vote

Dress 1 — 227
Dress 2 — 114
Dress 3 — 97
Dress 4 — 111

Shi Yong, *Adding One Concept on Top of Another*, staged photograph, 1997. Courtesy Shi Yong.

created in the Western media. Western ardor for Shanghai, as Zhou Tiehai so astutely realizes, plays into colonizing stereotypes about the enlightened arbiter of taste discovering "previously undisclosed assets" in the heart of darkness. Only the enlightened Westerner can, via the Shanghai Stock Exchange, determine China's (the Chinese artist's) identity and value. The perpetual Western fascination with Shanghai, which is today no more exotic than global mall culture, is surely due to the colonizers' earlier success in dominating a small part of China's "inscrutable" culture, in their ability to perpetuate a modicum of Western mores to great profit. Deng Xiaoping, needing to reinstill trust in the investment climate after June Fourth, "rediscovered" Shanghai in the knowledge that the nation would profit by disseminating that illusion. Cognizant that Shanghai is typed overseas as the "window on China," the municipality capitalizes on this perception to attract foreign direct investment during a postsocialist era dominated, above all, by the logic of global commodification.

Zhou Tiehai, *Necessity* (1995), film stills.
Courtesy Zhou Tiehai.

Following this logic, Shi Yong next incorporated *The New Image of Shanghai Today* into the global supply chain by offering a doll-sized replica for sale as "art" in Supermarket ("Chaoshi," 1998), an avant-garde exhibition situated within a Shanghai shopping mall. For Supermarket, the performance artist Song Dong, spoofing prevalent commercial practices, used a megaphone to rally visitors off the street to view *Art for Sale*, where they first entered a supermarket selling replicas of the "real art" on exhibit. Once Shi Yong's new visual identity, a precursor of the *xiaozi*, entered the commercial sphere, it, like Chinese art generally, facilitated the circulation of global capital. The ironic result of such reproducible images is, of course,

Shi Yong, *Made in China—Welcome to Shanghai*, sculpture, 9.2 x 5.2 x 29 cm. A miniature version of *The New Image of Shanghai Today*, for sale at the Shanghai exhibition "Supermarket," 1998. Courtesy Shi Yong.

Shi Yong, *Dreamy Shadowboxing*, digital photo, 2002. Courtesy Shi Yong.

Shi Yong, *Continuous*, video still, 2004. Courtesy Shi Yong.

an absence of meaning and representation, quite the opposite of the traditional function of visual images, which in turn sabotaged Shi Yong's avowed intention of "locating" identity. *The New Image of Shanghai Today*, as Shi Yong cleverly reveals, is merely an endless unveiling of images whose only destination is more images. Subsequent works in his *Shanghai Visual Identity Project* feature the "New Image," the flattened image of the figure in *The New Image of Shanghai Today* emptied of signification, such as

You Cannot Clone It, but You Can Buy It (2003), a digitized photo of dozens of "New Images," and the video *Continuous* (2004), where the "New Image" morphs into the features of thirty-two other Shanghai citizens, blurring distinctions between the "real" and its sign.

Simulated identities can only be sustained by the flip side of commodity culture, consumer desire. The absence of meaning implies, as Nietzsche has argued, that one must create it. The market, in order to convince the public of the reality of the social, the gravity of the economy, and the necessity of production as an end, tells them to take their desires for reality. In order to explore this trend in Shanghai urban culture, Shi Yong created a series of works in 2002 that deconstruct the desires that sustain simulated identity. In the photograph series *Dreamy Shadowboxing*, Shi Yong digitally removes the body from *The New Image of Shanghai Today*, leaving the outline of the stylish clothes and hair to form a series of shadowboxing, or *tai chi*, poses. The image thus takes on a life of its own, separate from the body, which becomes expendable once desire dominates being. In the installation *The Moon's Hues Are Teasing*, Shi Yong not only disembodies but dismembers the "New Image," which remains under the influence of irrational desires akin to lunar (lunatic) gravitational pulls. An oversized pair of plastic hands, functioning as feet, emerges from the bottom of disembodied pair of "New Image" pants, which "stand" before a pink, glowing, artificial pet's bone a few feet away on the ground. The hands appear captivated by the vibrant bone and its enigmatic sounds (a recording of a dinner party inaugurating the Shanghai Biennale of 2002), suggesting the powerful attraction between animals and bones as an analogy for base desire. Similarly, in the video installation *You Can Fly Higher and Higher*, Shi Yong conflates animalistic imagery of a human on all fours, begging for a bone, with paws that transform into wings, propelling the "New Image" skyward. In each of these works Shi Yong accentuates the carnal desires that buttress dreams of unbridled success. In *Gravitation* (2003), Shi Yong installs lovely, sensual photographs of the tips of Shanghai skyscrapers in fifty-six lightboxes, evoking a prevalent disassociation between disseminated images of the Shanghai dream and its (hidden, brute, corrupted) base. *Gravitation* recalls the romance of Shi Yong's oil portraits of the 1980s, but the dreamy humanist ideals are now disembodied (base-less) skyscrapers, mechanically reproducible via the technological medium of the photograph and lightbox. Shi Yong plays with the empty signifiers fueling Shanghai's frantic development, in *Keep the Height by All Means* (2003), in which visitors can pump "hot air" into a 7.3-meter inflatable

Shi Yong, *Gravitation*, lightbox installation, 545 x 25 x 228 cm, 2003–2004.
Courtesy Shi Yong.

Shi Yong, *Keep the Height by All Means*, installation, 180 x 180 x 730 cm, 2003. Courtesy Shi Yong.

skyscraper; if it receives enough air to stand erect, an operatic aria celebrates the successful endeavor.

The decade-long evolution of Shi Yong's *Shanghai Visual Identity Project* documents what Baudrillard terms "the precession of simulacra" in consumer culture.[23] The new image of Shanghai today is one of readily reproducible and superficial surfaces. Shi Yong's work is playfully postmodern, implicating the subject, rather than critiquing culture from a transcendent subject position. He readily attributes "Shanghai superficiality" to inherent cultural characteristics: "The bad thing about Chinese people, including myself," he says, "is that we are very utilitarian. When it comes to development, we very rarely start from fundamental principles and build from the ground up. Instead we start from the superficial—from the outside. It is much easier to get instant gratification from superficial changes—you see it so can appreciate it—it's not a rational, internal revolution."[24] Similarly, he says, Shanghai residents readily acquiesce to municipal campaigns, because "it is an approach to social change which is all too familiar."

During every stage of our recent history we have adopted slogans to enact change. Even though it feels ludicrous [*kexiao*] it can also seem quite charming [*ke'ai*]. It's a very familiar part of our everyday life. Before the Central Government invested directly in Shanghai's urban development, life for Shanghai residents was very difficult. Shanghainese were always keenly aware of this inequity—previously it was the most flourishing city in China, and then became one of its poorest. So once Shanghai started to develop, people didn't really care whether the material and aesthetic effects were good or bad, they just got very excited about its future prospects.[25]

Like Beijing culture, Shanghai culture is postmodern, but in a different sense due to its postcolonial history and lack of imperial tradition. In Shanghai, which is more similar to Taipei and Hong Kong, historical depth, authenticity, and resistance are absent—the city calls for a makeover and the citizens follow suit. Its "feminine" character and "hybrid" history allows for flow, adaptation, and the rapid assimilation of "foreign" influences into identity.

If Shanghai urban culture has about it a sense of superficiality, it derives from its endless production of desire. When the reproduction of Shanghai images of bourgeois identity is momentarily halted, as happens during an air raid described in Zhang Ailing's short story "Fengsuo" (Blockade, 1943), "one wonders if the city existed at all, if the modern, with all its material monumentality and mundane concreteness, is nothing more than a fleeting sentimentality, a sham. . . . In a city at standstill, modernity finds its vivid allegory in the dispersal of urban middle-class reality into a daydream."[26] In her role as subversive allegorist Zhang Ailing, Shanghai's most celebrated writer, anticipates later generations of literary and visual artists: Shi Yong's visual parody of the desires that hollow Shanghai culture; Lou Ye's filmic exposé of its phantasmagoric dreams on the grimy margins; and Wang Anyi's literary detailing of the "plebian" or "petty urbanite" (*xiao shimin*) yearnings that exude from Shanghai's alleyway courtyard (*longtang*, or *lilong*) neighborhoods.

Imbibing the City: Lou Ye's *Suzhou River*

Shanghai is a city of flows. A former fishing village situated "on the sea," as its name implies, it is divided by the Huangpu River into its old city on the west bank, Puxi, and the new development zone of Pudong on its east. The Huangpu River is a branch of China's largest river, the Yangtze (Changjiang), which empties into the East China Sea at the Wusong Mouth in northern Shanghai. Suzhou River, better known as Suzhou Creek, originates in Lake Taihu near Suzhou and flows from west to east through the heart of Shanghai, emptying into the Huangpu River at the northern end of the Bund. Shanghai's situation as a port city, a "window of the world," orients her seaward, her back to the hinterland. But the flows within the city have been historically stagnant and rank. So beginning in the late 1990s the banks of Suzhou Creek, where dilapidated warehouses and factories once demarcated colonial spheres of influence, have been gentrifying to retrofit Shanghai as a neoliberal city.[27] In 1998 the Asian Development Bank described the Suzhou Creek Rehabilitation Project as follows:

> Suzhou Creek is about 125 km long of which about 24 km passes through the highly urbanized part of Shanghai. Up to 3,000 barges per day ply the creek, serving numerous landing stages along the banks. The Suzhou Creek has a long history, dating to the 1920s, of being the most polluted natural waterway in Shanghai. The [Suzhou Creek Rehabilitation] Project aims to promote economic, cultural and social regeneration of the area; and encourage urban renewal for mixed-use business, commercial, residential, tourism, and recreational activities. The immediate objective is to substantially remove the polluted water and improve its color and smell by 2000.[28]

The underbelly of the city, its network of ports and waterways once the stage for triad deals, drug traffickers, and houses of ill repute, is being sanitized to make its flows of capital more "transparent."[29]

Shanghai's fluidity metastasizes into her personification as a femme fatale, the enigmatic "Whore of Asia" whose seductive yin recesses ebb and flow. In the Chinese cultural imagination the south has long figured as "feminine" in comparison to the "masculine" north. In his comparison between Tang dynasty painting schools Dong Qichang (1555–1636) used adjectives that remain ensconced in the popular consciousness to this day, contrasting gu (ancient), pu (simple), and chun (pure) northern aesthetics with the southern sense of the xin (new), qi (exotic), and huan (illusory).[30] As literary movements in China have tended to originate in the politically dominant north and move south, the north historically has been considered the cultural "center" and the south "marginalized," resulting in a southern style characterized as sentimental and nostalgic.[31] In his study of modern Chinese fiction C. T. Hsia takes these contrasts for granted in

Overlooking the skyscrapers of Pudong Lujiazui financial district and the Waibaidu Bridge, where Suzhou Creek empties into the Huangpu River on the Bund. Photo by Aly Song. Courtesy Reuters.

comparing Lao She with Mao Dun: "Using the time-honored test of Northern and Southern literary sensibilities, we may say that Lao She represents the North, individualist, forthright, humorous, and Mao Dun, the more feminine South, romantic, sensuous, melancholic. . . . Mao Dun records the passive feminine response to the chaotic events of contemporary Chinese history; more concerned with individual destinies than social forces, Lao She shows his heroes in action."[32]

Historically, then, southern Chinese aesthetics have been typified as exotic, fanciful, sentimental, and nostalgic, each quality attributed to languishing femininity. Modern Shanghai aesthetics become doubly feminized when depicted as vanquished by imperial conquerors. The characterization of the colonial "other" as woman—personified in the seductive body of the Orient—doubly types the Chinese "modern girl" as a "femme fatale" who both stimulates the male fantasy and challenges masculine authority. Just as a postcolonial imagination lives on in the Western fascination with an exotic Orient that is accessible (subjugated) in Shanghai, the Chinese imagination of urban modernity identifies the figure of woman "with the exotic presence of Western civilization, reinforced by the fascination and anxiety with which the male (national) subject positions himself vis-à-vis the imperial West *and* the modern (native) woman."[33] The resulting excess of *yin* within Shanghai can be debilitating, as demonstrated by the opening lines of Mao Dun's classic novel *Ziye* (Midnight, 1933), where old Mr. Wu is overwhelmed by the sensory stimuli of the female body on the city streets.

It is one of life's little ironies that someone should be driving through the wide streets of Shanghai—that great city of the East with a population of three million—in such a modern conveyance as a motorcar, yet holding *The Supreme Scriptures* in his hands, his mind intent upon one text: "Of all the vices sexual indulgence is the cardinal; of all the virtues filial piety is the supreme."

Huei-fang cast a furtive glance at her father, then gazed out at all the fashionable women sitting in the cars all round them. Fu-fang giggled and took out her handkerchief to dab her lips. A whiff of perfume assailed the old fellow's nostrils, and it seemed to upset him. His heart fluttered, and his eyes fell instinctively upon Fu-fang and he saw now for the first time how she was decked out. Though it was still only May, the weather was unusually warm and she was already in the lightest of summer clothing. Her vital young body was sheathed in close-fitting light-blue chiffon, her full, firm breasts jutting out prominently, her snowy forearms bared. Old Mr. Wu felt his heart constricting with disgust and quickly averted his eyes, which, however, fell straight away upon a half-naked young woman sitting up in a rickshaw, fashionably dressed in a transparent, sleeveless voile blouse, displaying her bare legs and thighs. The old man thought for one horrible moment that she had nothing else on. But the worst was yet to come, for he quickly withdrew his gaze, only to find his youngest son Ah-hsuan gaping with avid admiration at the same half-naked young woman. The old man felt his heart pounding wildly as if it would burst and his throat burning as if choked with chilies.

The lights changed to green, and the car moved forward in a motley sea of traffic and humanity. On and on they went, while the din of the traffic, the stench of petrol-fumes, the women's perfume and the glare of neon signs pressed down like a nightmare on his frail spirit until his eyes blurred, his ears sang and his head swam; until his over-wrought nerves ached as if they would snap and his pounding heart could beat no faster.[34]

Mr. Wu intones the moral maxims contained in his *Supreme Scriptures* to no avail. As he becomes intoxicated by female flows in the modern city,

morality falls by the wayside, the colonized subject's incapacitation provoked further by his "feminine" hysteria ("over-wrought nerves," "frail
spirit," "pounding heart").

When victims of the city's intoxicating flows become further enervated
by the lucrative drug of the day, their fall is complete. In a city dominated
by commerce, the ready flow of addictive substances enhances the global
flows of capital in Shanghai. During the post-Reform Era (1990 onward),
as James Farrer points out in his research on Shanghai night life, the bar
scene in Shanghai transformed from a small service industry aimed at
foreign businessmen and tourists in the 1980s to a large industry sector
serving mostly local customers by the late 1990s.[35] China today has the
world's largest alcoholic drinks market, its share rising rapidly from 25
percent in 1997 to 30 percent in 2003, "the partying lifestyle [being] particularly attractive to the young and those in cosmopolitan cities like Shanghai who have the purchasing power to do so."[36] As turn-of-the-millennium
Shanghai bar culture has repackaged itself as a vibrant product for domestic consumers, the ubiquity of alcohol as the new global drug of choice
(although other drugs are readily circulated in Shanghai) means that liquor
flows have symbolically replaced the fortune, addiction, and decadence
connoted by opium flows in Old Shanghai.

Suzhou River (*Suzhou he*, 2000), written and directed by Lou Ye, exploits
the confluence of such local and global flows as allegories for querying the
city's future as it gentrifies and ostensibly "cleans up its act." The amalgam
of Shanghai's symbolic flows—its stagnant creek with its shady dealings, a
modern femme fatale mythically reborn from the water, and its debilitating
flows of alcohol—creates possible links between past and future. Even as
the film acknowledges the elimination of rooted ways of life, the postmodern narrative, while constantly undercutting itself, still courts the possibility that future urban identities can retain a sense of place and historical
consciousness. The film asks whether dreams can come true in a postmodern age, leaving the answer to the viewer.

Born in Shanghai, in 1965, Lou Ye graduated from the Beijing Film
Academy, in 1994. *Suzhou River*, his second feature, was filmed in Shanghai using 16 mm in the documentary style favored by many Sixth Generation directors. It was licensed for television but postproduction took place
in Germany, to avoid the censorship and time restraints of the domestic
film-licensure process. *Suzhou River* received the Grand Prize at the Paris
Film Festival, where Zhou Xun was named Best Actress (for her dual role

as Meimei and Mudan); Lou Ye received a Tiger Award (for first and second features) at the Rotterdam Film Festival, in recognition of his "experimentation in narrative forms and successful evocation of loss and wonder in the modern city."[37] The film readily borrows narrative elements from classic Hollywood cinema, particularly from Hitchcock's *Vertigo* and *Rear Window*, but, as the reviewer David Rooney rightly concludes, this is a far more interesting, inventive revisiting of Hitchcock than recent Hollywood retreads such as *Psycho* or *A Perfect Murder*. The quality of the film is enhanced by Karl Riedl's loose, jumpy editing, which enhances the material's edgy feel, and by the German composer Jorg Lemberg's score, which at times uncannily echoes Bernard Herrmann's *Vertigo* theme.[38]

The opening scenes of *Suzhou River* feature a lengthy montage of jump cuts, abrupt zooms, and dizzying pans of the people who live on Suzhou Creek and its banks, shot from the vantage point of a boat floating eastward toward the Huangpu River. Evocative music accompanies the voice of the narrator (performed by Lou Ye), who says that he often takes his camcorder to record Suzhou Creek, "where nearly a century of legends, stories, and memories have accumulated with the trash," because although filthy, "a lot of people are still here, depending on this river for their livelihood. . . . [I]f you watch for a long time this river will allow you to see everything: work, friendship, dads with kids, loneliness." The economy and culture of Shanghai and the prosperous Jiangnan region to the south of the Yangtze River have always been closely linked to the people who live on its waterways. Centuries before land or sea routes were developed out of the region, the Wusong River (the former name of Suzhou Creek) connected Jiangnan with the Grand Canal, which stretched north to Beijing. Beginning with the Tang dynasty (618–907) the Wusong provided flood control for the entire area and transported tea, silk, and porcelain from Nanjing and Yangzhou, which made it the main outlet for luxury exports produced inland and a key channel for early international trade. By the mid-thirteenth century, however, silt deposits were obstructing the passage of vessels, so the government widened the Huangpu River and gave the Wusong River, which became its tributary, its present-day name of Suzhou Creek. Most early immigrants to Shanghai arrived on its waters; when the Taiping Rebellion (1850–64) swept through Jiangsu Province, fleeing peasants caught sampans into the city. Migrant families continue to transport raw construction materials along the creek, as ships remain the preferred means of transport for the booming property developers in the region. As a result of gentrification, however, all shipping within city limits and all commercial barges on the lower reaches of the creek between Changshou Bridge and the Bund were scheduled to cease operations in May of 2007.[39]

Although opening shots in *Suzhou River* are reminiscent of the low shots of Suzhou Creek in the opening montage of *Malu tianshi* (Street angel, 1937), a classic Shanghai film which also features a marginalized urban class, Ban Wang points out crucial distinctions.

> In Lou Ye the montage is much more compelling in its vigorous, fast-paced searching for images of the common people living for generations on the river—in boats, in huts, on the riverbank—with blocks of half-demolished buildings and dilapidated housing. It hints at the normally slighted subculture of boat people, who are endowed with a history and past of their own, and confers on them serious attention, even dignity. This attention to a subculture of migrant laborers in Shanghai is evident through the striking absence of the glamorous icons of the city, the Bund and the Pudong development zone with the sky-scraping TV tower. These are consigned to the vague horizon while the fast-paced, ethnographic montage thrusts a dirty river block into the foreground.[40]

Indeed, as the "camera" drifts toward the Waibaidu Bridge it only briefly captures several indistinct shots of the Pearl of the Orient TV Tower and the hazy skyline of the financial district in Lujiazui. Instead of focusing on ultramodern Pudong, the camera abruptly turns back, with a brief pan up Broadway Mansions (Shanghai Daxia) before being enveloped in darkness under the bridge. The camera-eye deliberately eschews Shanghai's symbols of global modernity, intentionally recording its history as embedded in its culture of migrants, waterways, and former foreign concessions, where it locates its story.

The story is set in 1998, the year the Suzhou Creek Rehabilitation Project began, in a Suzhou Creek neighborhood near the (in)famous Waibaidu Bridge.[41] The videographer-narrator says, "Once I saw a baby born on a barge, I saw a girl jump from a bridge into Suzhou Creek, I saw the police haul the corpses of a young couple out of the river. As for love, I'd like to say I once saw a mermaid sitting on the riverbank combing her golden locks, but don't believe me, I'm lying." Although he "doesn't believe in mermaids," he meets a version of one in the Happy Tavern, whose owner hires him to film the tavern's underwater floorshow as a promotional gimmick. Eventually a complex relationship forms between the narrator and Meimei, who performs as a blond mermaid in an oversized fish tank, and a motorcy-

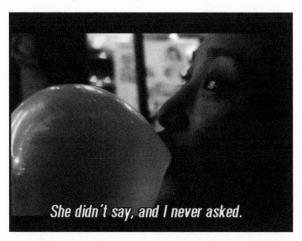

She didn't say, and I never asked.

Voyeuristic consumption of images: Meimei (Zhou Xun) performs for the videographer on Shanghai's kitschy Huanghe Street. Still from *Suzhou River.*

cle courier named Mada, who is pursuing his lost love, Mudan, a young girl with a striking resemblance to Meimei. The videographer, "enchanted by her appearance in the water," invites Meimei on a date, and she happily performs for his camcorder ("I liked looking at her, filming her, and she didn't mind"), both parties apparently more interested in surfaces than substance ("I didn't know anything about Meimei. She didn't say, and I never asked.") Soon they spend every day together, and he voyeuristically *consumes* her, leaving him *empty* when she's gone. "I can hardly stand it," he says, "because every time she leaves I fear she won't return. Every time she shuts the door I feel my life has stopped." Yet, instead of searching for her when she "disappears for several days on end, then suddenly reappears as if nothing has happened," he waits passively on his sundeck for her return, gazing down at the streets through the camcorder viewfinder until she reappears on the Waibaidu Bridge.

Meimei's newfound agency appears to be enabled by her identification with a love story more romantic than her own. Whenever she returns, tipsy, to her boyfriend, the videographer, she asks him if he is capable of true love, the kind that drives Mada, "a crazy guy who lives nearby who says he's searching for a girl he once loved." The narrator says he doesn't believe Mada's story ("There are too many love stories like that") and proceeds to spin his own. "Let's see," he says, "what was Mada doing before this? He's probably about twenty-six or twenty-seven . . . perhaps . . . before . . . after quitting school he hung out on the banks of the river with other lowlifes . . .

a friend came by with a stolen motorcycle . . . he thought he could ride it far away, strike it rich, return home in glory. But of course he just became a courier." Just as Wang Anyi represents the city's past through a "typical Shanghai girl" of the alley neighborhoods in *Changhen ge* (Song of everlasting sorrow, 1996), the narrator of *Suzhou River* imagines a "typical marginalized youth," who becomes caught up in the criminal underworld of Shanghai's wharf culture, as a means of interrogating the city's future.

Mada is charged with delivering Mudan to her aunt's house whenever her father, a liquor magnate who bootlegs whiskey from Eastern Europe, indulges in "his only two pursuits after his divorce—liquor and women." The motherless child soon falls in love with the handsome courier. But "maybe the story is not that romantic," the narrator suggests, "maybe something else is happening behind the scenes." After Mada's criminal overlords force him to kidnap Mudan and hold her for ransom, she leaps into the river off the Waibaidu Bridge to her apparent death, clutching his gift of the mermaid doll and vowing to return as a mermaid to haunt him. Years later, after hearing of reputed mermaid sightings by river folk, Mada returns to the riverside to search for Mudan, instead finding a look-alike in the grown-up Meimei. Although she disbelieves his story Meimei increasingly identifies with Mudan.

The first frame of the film, prior to the montage of Suzhou Creek, is entirely black; we hear a woman's voice ask, "If I left you someday would you pursue me? Would you pursue me forever?" This question, which we later learn is posed by Meimei to her boyfriend, permeates the entire narrative. A question of true romance, it is also a question of creating a smoothly edited, continuous historical narrative so that an emotional attachment from the past is carried forward into the future. If the recording and editing process is rough, with nauseating angles, disorienting cuts, narrative lacunas, and abrupt fades, it calls attention to the fact that the history is constructed, its story arbitrary. In the final scene the narrator says, "I could run after her, look for her like Mada . . . and then this love story of mine might go on. But I won't because nothing lasts forever. I'll just take another drink and close my eyes and wait for the next romance to come along." As he takes "another drink," the camera lurches nauseously; as he "closes his eyes," the film turns black.

In a chapter-length analysis of the film, Jerome Silbergeld interprets the ambiguous ending definitively. "There is only this much truth in the videographer's final, cynical self-presentation," Silbergeld insists.

This is the darkness with which the film mysteriously began and now abruptly ends, and into which Meimei has plunged in her leap of faith. In it lies the uncertainty and risk that such a leap requires. But preferring image to reality, the videographer is not prepared to go there; and so, he has now lost not only his girlfriend but the only model really worth shooting. This pitch-blackness may be the film's most important event, a withholding of that which can be named in truth or accurately shown, a suspension by which it challenges vicarious experience and questions image-making—even film, and even itself, that is to say—as an inherently credible medium.[42]

Silbergeld locates the film's optimism in the newly hopeful Meimei, in her renewed faith in the possibility of love in action, rather than as voyeuristically consumed object, which is in turn a denunciation of the inherent "lies" of simulated images. The film, implies Silbergeld, ultimately interrogates its own medium along the ethical lines invoked by Jean Baudrillard, who argues that images are immoral because they evoke a "brute fascination unencumbered by aesthetic, moral, social, or political judgments."[43]

What Silbergeld fails to account for in his reading of *Suzhou River* is what Baudrillard calls the "murderous capacity of images" to destroy identity.[44] By evoking such obsessive fascination that it can substitute for the "real," the creation of simulacra, says Baudrillard, instead acts as a "death sentence" for identity. When we are first introduced to Meimei, the "real" has already been substituted, her constructed identity already a given. "That's Meimei," says the narrator, "she's the mermaid." Constantly the center of voyeuristic attention, Meimei readily performs identity to maintain detachment from the other characters in the film. It is only after her identity becomes conflated with that of Mudan that Meimei becomes visibly dissatisfied with her objectification. "Sometimes she was inexplicably sad, I'm not sure why," says the narrator, filming a silent Meimei staring solemnly away from the camera during a rain shower, in contrast to their first date, when she performed for his camera on the kitschy, neon-lit streets of Huanghe Road, blowing bubbles and smoke to the classic jazz tune *Ye Shanghai* (Shanghai nights). By actively identifying with Mudan, however, Meimei traps herself in a new role, namely, the girl who must be found by the lover (who is made devoted by her absence), an identity that eventually consumes her.

Initially Meimei is not interested in Mada's quest, assuming he is just another drunk taken in by her mermaid show. Mada accepts that she is not

Mudan, but Meimei increasingly wishes she were, asking insistently, after sleeping with Mada, "Am I the girl you are looking for?" Taken up with the fairy tale, Meimei attempts to become the mermaid reincarnation that Mada is seeking, mistakenly assuming that by remaking herself like Mudan—for example, by applying rub-on tattoos to her thigh—she will become an object of genuine attachment. But Mada does not fall for the *appearance* of his lost love; instead he chooses to keep searching for the *real* Mudan, leaving Meimei to be consumed by yet another image, one merely designed to elicit a different response.

Mada eventually discovers Mudan selling liquor in a twenty-four-hour convenience store in the suburbs. They reunite by getting drunk on her father's bootlegged vodka, as they had done when they celebrated her birthday years before, but instead of riding the Harley along the dilapidated neighborhoods of Suzhou Creek, they now sit quietly, gazing across the Huangpu River at the sunrise over the Pudong skyline. The camera-eye, gazing fixedly at the shiny skyscrapers for the first time, foreshadows the death of the fairy-tale lovers, their sincerity incompatible with the artificiality of global modernity. The visual framing of the story, initiated by the camera-eye averting its gaze from Pudong, suggests that genuine romance can only be sustained along the byways of Suzhou Creek, the heart of Old Shanghai, which is rapidly becoming gentrified. Indeed, in the very next scene the narrator identifies the lovers' corpses while their mangled motorcycle is still being extracted from the creek. Momentarily jolted out of his cynical complacency, he exclaims: "I didn't believe it was true; I needed to see Meimei." Desperately in search of his muse, he scrambles past construction sites with yellow cranes (signifying the future) that are visually conflated with Meimei's yellow houseboat (connoting the past), the camera lurching wildly, replicating his sense of vertigo. Meimei follows him back to the accident site, shocked to discover something authentic ("Mada wasn't lying"!). In the next scene the narrator once again visits her houseboat, but she has disappeared, leaving behind the note, "come find me." In the final scene the drunken narrator floats aimlessly on a river skiff, the camera-eye (I) reeling as, he says, "I take another drink," then blacking out as he utters the film's final line: "and wait for the next romance to come along."

The question being posed here is not so much one of faith in true love as of access to the "real." Meimei is an overblown signifier for Shanghai, embodying its past, present, and future. The impossibility of such a blond-haired, sculpted image of perfection emerging unsoiled from the sordid creek dramatizes disjunctions within Shanghai's postsocialist develop-

The camera-eye casts a fleeting glance at Pudong's
shiny skyscrapers in the opening montage. It fixes the
skyline with a steady gaze only at the end of the film,
from the perspective of the doomed lovers, then gazes
at their faces before their untimely death. Stills
from *Suzhou River*.

ment. Cast as indifferent femme fatale and seductively packaged for a global consumer culture, she also embodies the southern penchant for fantastic tales. Unique (*xin*) yet manufactured, exotic (*qi*) yet homegrown, duplicitous (*huan*) yet sincere, Meimei attempts, whether as indigenous river goddess or globally commodified Disney mermaid, to seduce the poet to pursue her "to an underwater tryst: committing himself, in other words, forever."[45] Such a commitment is, by definition, fatal, and the narrator knows it. "The fatality," Baudrillard notes, "lies in this endless enwrapping of images (literally: without end, without destination) which leaves images no other destination than images."[46] Meimei's identity, rooted in images, creates a situation where there is "the equal impossibility of the real and of the imaginary."[47] Her inability to become either real (a subject rather than an object) or imaginary (the resurrected mermaid) traps her (as it trapped *The New Image of Shanghai Today*) in what Baudrillard terms "a gigantic simulacrum—not unreal, but a simulacrum, never again exchanging for what is real, but exchanging in itself, in an uninterrupted circuit without reference or circumference."[48]

Shanghai's future is left in question. The fairy tale in its purest form cannot coexist with globalization. But how will the narrator carry his story (history) into the future? Zhang Ailing's legacy as subversive allegorist and ethnographer of everyday life informs another interpretation of the film. Just as Zhang Ailing, in "Blockade," unmasks the Shanghai dream, gazing at the hypocrisy and monotony underlying this mythic epitome of Chinese urban modernity, Lou Ye focuses on the underbelly that sustains the shiny symbols of Shanghai global postmodernity. Like Zhang Ailing, Lou Ye exhibits the worldly Shanghai sensibility that locates the real in the every-day rather than in the mythic, the heroic, the revolutionary, or the mystic. It is this mundane sensibility that creates the sense of hope underlying these otherwise desolate (*cangliang*) narratives. Despite "its film noir elements of mean streets and cynicism, postmodern techniques, urban simulacra, and shop-worn sensibility of alienation and loneliness," most perceive *Suzhou River* (like Zhang Ailing's stories) to be "a delight to the eye, the ear, and the heart."[49] Ban Wang, for example, contrasts the film with the Sixth Genera-tion filmmaker Jia Zhangke's equally evocative *Xiao Wu* (Xiao Wu, 1997) in one aspect, "its ability to hope." He explains, "instead of recording an elusive, degraded reality, Lou Ye's film dares to tell a story, a 'love-story' with fairy-tale flavor, in a barren urban neighborhood threatened by forces of demolition and globalization."[50] Most interpret the film's ending optimisti-cally, although several critics, such as Vivian Lee, see Meimei's disappearance as evidence of a fallen myth, the relegation of the femme fatale to an existential wasteland revealing the other side of "Shanghai modern."[51]

To this viewer the film is neither "fallen myth," "fairy tale," nor "morality tale," but rather acknowledgment of the stories and dreams that sustain routine everyday life. Sharply attuned to the sense that "all that is solid melts into air," Shanghai characters such as the videographer cast a backward glance to the vanishing present of the riverbank culture in order to move into the future. Shanghai aesthetics have always been dominated by the need to recast identity amid disorienting change. The Jiangnan region, particularly Shanghai, is a historical breeding ground for hybrid cultural influences from north and south, East and West, tradition and modernity, leaving the individual to forge his identity in the mix. Shanghai urbanites, their "feminine" cultural character marked by nostalgia for a rapidly receding past and a ready adaptation to the future, maintain identity by embedding themselves in the real, the everyday, and the mundane. Exhibiting a "passive feminine response to the chaotic events of contemporary Chinese history," as C. T. Hsia puts it, they dare to dream dreams, bolstering their spirits by telling stories of the rumors spread in the lanes, byways, and waterways. Just as Zhang Ailing, in her era, acknowledged the cynical pragmatism sustaining the exotic Paris of the East, Lou Ye, in his era, reveals the simulacrum that feeds a globalizing Shanghai. Their quintessentially Shanghainese characters, such as Bai Liusu or the videographer, "flow" with their times, taking what comes, acknowledging contingencies, and allowing the momentary delights of the everyday (dreams, storytelling, "deep understanding") to sustain them "for a decade or so," or at least "until the next romance comes along."

"Finishing Off" Shanghai: Wang Anyi's *Song of Everlasting Sorrow*

Li Jing writes, "Just as Roland Barthes uses his semiotics discourse to interpret Japan in *Empire of Signs*, Wang Anyi uses her novelist discourse to interpret Shanghai. By abstracting Shanghai's spirit and flesh, she reendows every inch of its body with a refined soul."[52] Unlike *The New Image of Shanghai Today* or *Suzhou River*, Wang Anyi's monumental novel *Song of Everlasting Sorrow* (*Changhen ge*, 1996) does not merely attempt to portray one of modern Shanghai's imagined identities—its "successful men" (*chenggong renshi*), *xiaozi*, or femme fatales—but rather to epitomize its essence, a colossal task. The novel has accomplished just that in the eyes of many, including luminaries such as Leo Ou-fan Lee, who lauds it as "epic," and David Der-wei Wang, who, in his introduction to the Hong Kong edition, hailed it as the biggest breakthrough in Shanghai literature since the works of Zhang Ailing. The author's strong historical consciousness, particularly her attention to the often neglected socialist modernization of the 1950s and 1960s, further "sets Wang's work apart from the over-crowded field of marketing/consuming Shanghai."[53] The most acclaimed work by one of China's most eminent and prolific writers, *Song* won the coveted Mao Dun Literary Award in 2000, and was adapted to the stage in 2003 and to the cinema and television screen in 2005.[54] Despite Wang Anyi's manifest attempts not to "market" Shanghai, her work has single-handedly created a profitable cottage industry of spin-offs.

Later incarnations of the novel capitalize on the city's glamour and romance, whereas Wang Anyi's attempt to "finish off" Shanghai—to extract, refine, and perfect its essence—culls from the city its vitality in a process which, in the end, kills it off. Deadly serious in its ambitions, quite the opposite of Barthes's playful deconstruction of Japan, Wang Anyi's novel abstracts from the city its unique features until they become but empty signifiers in an "empire of signs." By ontologizing essential qualities from the body of the city, the organic aspect of urban identity so stressed by the architect Liang Sicheng is spirited away. In a narrative densely packed with metaphors for Shanghai, whose iterative details mirror the redundancy and triviality of its everyday life, there is no more breathing room, no more space to dream, no more whimsical desire, nowhere to go. The literary imagination bids a final adieu to the Shanghai dream, a dream not, as it is today, of the single-minded pursuit of material and financial supremacy, but the aspiration to a refined *lifestyle* that, while dependent on the commodity, was not consumed by it.

The novel traces the life of its principal protagonist, Wang Qiyao, a "typi-cal" product of the *longtang* (alley neighborhood), from her late teens in the 1940s to her death in the mid-1980s. The tripartite work, which corre-sponds to three significant historical periods in modern China, delineates Wang Qiyao's unpretentious life as a former Miss Shanghai and mistress to a prominent nationalist leader in the 1940s, her quotidian life as a "wid-owed" neighborhood nurse in the 1950s and early 1960s, and her spectral life as a single mother and empty nester in the early 1980s. The material details of everyday life displace the grand narratives of war, nation building, and revolution during these decades. So constructed, the protagonist's story becomes both a metonym for and a corrective to Shanghai's overdetermined representations. Where Republican Era Shanghai is typed as an exotic femme fatale, "Wang Qiyao" is a wholesome "Miss Third Place" and bored mistress; where socialist Shanghai is thought to be steeped in Maoist asceticism, "Wang Qiyao" is indulging in endless rounds of mahjong, dining, gossip, amorous liaisons; where Reform Era Shanghai proudly reclaims its cosmopolitan past, "Wang Qiyao" disparages post-Mao tastes as coarse imitations. Seemingly immune to the passage of time, she alone emanates that unique blend of elegance and banality that constitutes Shanghai's essence. Yet, almost overnight, she loses her grounding and poise, fades noticeably, and acts desperately, suffering a fateful death.

That *Song of Everlasting Sorrow* will chronicle a death is anticipated by its titular allusion. Like the famous narrative love poem for which it is named, the novel features a beauty who dies a shocking, premature death partly brought about by her excessive desire and desirability. Wang Der-wei (David Der-wei Wang) suggests that the novel mocks the sincere sentiments of the poet Bai Juyi's (772–846) original, the final lines of which recount the secret vow between the Tang emperor and his beloved concubine, Yang Guifei.[55]

> In the skies we shall be twin birds that fly together,
> On earth we shall be trees with branches intertwined.
> Heaven is enduring, earth long living, but they shall perish,
> The everlasting sorrow will never come to an end.[56]

In the novel the beauty is of the "girl next door" rather than the "empire destroying" variety, and the loves are unrequited. Yet the novel's sentiment of "everlasting sorrow" is, if less sublime, no less poignant. Both works describe the melancholic hearts of forlorn lovers, their joy disrupted by the exigencies of historical events. Unlike the historical personages referenced in the original poem, however, the metaphorical lover and beloved, as other narrative elements, are abstracted, and their relationship far more ambivalent, in the novel. Like Zhang Ailing, whose Shanghai love stories contrast the epic narratives of "loves that fell cities" with the mundane everyday sentiments of modernity, Wang Anyi characterizes Shanghai's pathos as something marginalized, trivial, and depoliticized. "This bottled-up pain is different from what the Tang Emperor felt at the death of Yang Guifei or the King of Chu felt for his beloved concubine," says the narrator. "It is not the kind of grand heroic suffering that moves heaven and earth; but base and lowly like pebbles and dirt, or the tentacles of ivy creeping stealthily out of bounds" (11; 12).[57]

In question here is the narrative voice. Is the narrator, as Wang Der-wei implies, deriding the plebian sentiments of nostalgia and regret that prevail in this metropolis? Many, including Wang Anyi's fellow Shanghai writer Chen Danyan, take her narrative voice to be satirical, resembling that of Marxist intellectuals of the 1930s, such as Xia Yan or Mao Dun, who critiqued the decadence of the bourgeois metropolis from an anti-urban bias.[58] Wang Anyi would likely agree, once asserting, "I can sum up *Song of Everlasting Sorrow* in one sentence; I wanted to write about an ineffectual [*cuirou*] capitalist class."[59] Yet reading the novel as a straightforward Maoist critique of the city as a breeding ground for capitalism and petit-bourgeois liberalism does not account for the *tristesse* that permeates the ironic narrative voice. This wistfulness is often construed as nostalgia for the glamour of "pre-liberation Shanghai," a position which is anathema to Wang Anyi.[60] A more convincing reading sees it as the generalized historical melancholy of a postmodern age, the culmination of a series of "tales of sorrow" that Wang Anyi wrote prior to the novel. In Xiaobing Tang's reading of Wang's earlier novellas he concludes that her "melancholy, in which the longing for a modern longing causes the deepest sorrow and ambivalence, gathers its historical content and relevance only in an age which deems itself 'post' and beyond all ideologies of the modern."[61] Xudong Zhang also reads *Song of Everlasting Sorrow* in this vein, more narrowly locating its melancholy in the unfulfilled dreams of China's bourgeois modernity and the lost collective ideals and life-forms of its socialist modernity.[62]

The abstracted "beloved" of the novel, then, may be "Chinese modernity" as manifest in three stages of Shanghai's twentieth-century development detailed in the novel: its Republican Era, its Socialist Era, and its Reform Era. Whether post-Reform policies "killed off" preceding forms of Shanghai modernity is a live question. Shanghai's boosters promote the idea that it has reclaimed its Republican Era cosmopolitanism, while others argue that the municipality retains too many socialist structures and practices.[63] But if a death *has* occurred, what, in Wang Anyi's literary vision, was shared in these three eras that no longer defines Shanghai today? Who is mourning this death, and why is the lover so ambivalent about the loss?

In addition to the melancholy induced by transnational postmodernism and the short-lived phases of Chinese modernity, the novel elegizes a local loss, in particular, the passing away of the unique ethos of Shanghai's alleyway courtyard neighborhoods. This dominant urban form, and the lifestyles it sustained, prevailed throughout decades of historical vicissitudes, including wartime and the Cultural Revolution, when all traditional or capitalist elements were supposed to be destroyed, only to be laid waste at the onslaught of global developmentalism. Writing in the mid-1990s, as Shanghai urban development was taking off with a vengeance, Wang Anyi mourns the intensely personal losses sustained by globalization, for, as many insist, Shanghai without its *longtang* is no longer Shanghai.[64] The ironic narrative voice thus undermines Shanghai's vaunted image as a glamorous global city rejecting the utilitarian values that caused its urban aesthetic to be destroyed. *Song of Everlasting Sorrow* is an instance of using disappearance to deal with disappearance, just as Walter Benjamin became fascinated with the Paris arcades at the moment their existence was threatened.

The narrative impulse to "kill off" Shanghai's essence can, in this sense, be read as historically accurate analogy. Ban Wang perceptively reads the novel as allegorizing Shanghai's modern history through the figure of the commodity, an analysis that can be expanded by relating the mournful narrative to the demise of a particular form of the commodity. The novel traces the commodity's evolution from the realm of exchange values (Wang Qiyao [Shanghai] up for purchase during the Republican Era), to the maximization of its use value via its auratic presence (ritualized consumption of Wang Qiyao's [Shanghai's] bourgeois past during the Maoist Era), to the rapid demise of its aura and obliteration of its exchange value and use value as it reenters the global market as simulacra. The mournful voice that frames this death, evocatively expressed in the first chapter of *Song of Everlasting Sorrow*, undermines the dominant cynical narrative that recounts the decline of "an ineffectual bourgeois capitalist class." The resulting composite conveys a complex mixture of grief and ambivalence over the eradication of an alluring—if trivialized by master narratives of history, the nation, and revolutionary politics—middle-class consumer lifestyle uniquely manifest in the everyday life of the Shanghai *longtang*. The narrative ambiguity toward the city derives from a simultaneous attraction to and rejection of the bourgeois commodity. Now that it is disappearing, the narrator is all the more ambivalent about its fatal attraction. For this form of middle-class consumerism could only exist in modern societies organized around the production and consumption of commodities; with the advent of a new social order organized around the play of images and signs, the commodity necessarily becomes devalued and its aura expires.[65]

The novel's pathos, "the everlasting sorrow of Wang Qiyao," is rooted in this loss of Shanghai's uniquely quotidian charms. The opening chapter grounds the novel in a familiar, domestic ambience through detailed descriptions of alleyways, rooftop pigeons, gossip, the boudoirs of young ladies, and the young ladies themselves, the "Wang Qiyaos" of Shanghai.

Although Wang Anyi disavows any aesthetic similarity to Zhang Ailing, in this chapter Wang adopts the celebrated technique of "uneven contrasts" (*cancha de duizhao*) that Zhang employed to illuminate the significance of "petty sentiments" and ground the "real." The novel opens by juxtaposing the glitter of the "city that never sleeps" against the voluminous dark recesses of its *longtang*.

> Looked down upon from the highest point in the city, Shanghai's *longtang*—her vast neighborhoods inside enclosed alleys—are a magnificent sight. The *longtang* are the backdrop of the city. Streets and buildings emerge around them in a series of dots and lines, like the subtle brushstrokes that bring life to the empty expanses of white paper in a traditional Chinese landscape painting. As day turns into night and the city lights up, these dots and lines begin to glimmer. However, underneath the glitter lies an immense blanket of darkness—these are the *longtang* of Shanghai.
>
> The darkness looks almost to be a series of furious waves that threaten to wash away the glowing dots and lines. It has volume, whereas all those lines and dots float on the surface—they are there only to differentiate the areas of this dark mass. . . . The darkness buoys up Shanghai's handful of illuminated lines and dots, supporting them decade after decade. Against this decades-old backdrop of darkness, the Paris of the Orient unfolds her splendor. (3–4; 3)

Shanghai's alley neighborhoods are naturalized—a raging wave of (plebian) mass(es) threatening "to wash away the glowing dots and lines" of splendor. "Gossip is the sediment that accumulates at the bottom," yet it is only within this shamefully base material that one can find a few things that are actually genuine (9; 10). Shanghai's modest *longtang*, gossip, vestal bedchambers, pigeons, and "Wang Qiyaos" appear as the naturally recurring elements of the city that embody its "authenticity" and "volume." In other words, they are signifiers that confer historical meaning on place.

Wang Anyi is not the first to present Shanghai's modern history as "natural." As Xudong Zhang points out, "It is against a corrupted history that the vitality of Shanghai was seen as *a force of nature,* whose explosive energy and transforming power were expected to forcibly yank China—or a particular group of Chinese—out of the vicious cycle of tradition."[66] Zhang's point is well taken; a recent study of Shanghai *lilong* housing repeatedly refers to it as a "natural" development: "It is important to understand that *lilong,* as a hybrid dwelling form, initially built by foreign developers and sold to local Chinese for profit, was *a product of natural processes* brought about by the 'market,' which met needs from both the supply and demand sides."[67] Wang Anyi, informed by Marxist thought, does not view Shanghai's modern history as a force of nature, but rather as shaped by the dialectic of natural history, a *fallen* nature worn down by historical progression.

Wang Anyi depicts this fallen nature in her abject descriptions of the *lilong*, her desire to rewrite the literary topography of the city evident in her displacement of its exotic qualities with the endless and repetitive details of everyday life. The cliché stereotypes of Old Shanghai—the Bund, jazz bars, coffee shops, Western restaurants, dance halls, music clubs, wild parties, beautiful women—appear in the novel as mere adornment to the urban core. Shanghai's lifeblood, Wang implies, does not flow in its magnificent colonial architecture and glamorous nightlife. Instead, it pulsates in the shadowed recesses of the city, those back alleys that "try hard to work their way into people's hearts" (8; 6). Here "the pavement is covered with a layer of cracks. Gutters overflow; floating in the discolored water are fish scales and rotten vegetable leaves, as well as the greasy lampblack from the stove. It is dirty and grimy, impure, here. Here the most private secrets are exposed, and not always in the most conventional fashion" (8–9; 6). This attention to the marrow of the city, the dank corners which expose secrets, is a corrective to the vaunted Shanghai scenes of urban beautification which "cleanse" the city but drain its vitality. Yet the urban core, like Suzhou Creek, has built up so many layers of residue that it, too, appears to have stagnated. Like Lou Ye, Wang Anyi resists focusing on shining postsocialist façades, instead attaching her gaze and sentiments to the materiality of its colonial and socialist periods.

Shanghai's *longtang* neighborhoods, a product of colonial culture, defined its residential life for over a century (1870s–1990s). *Shikumen lilong*, the formal architectural term for these rows of multistory residences, are urban modifications of Jiangnan-style compounds, with every two units sharing a common wall.[68] *Longtang*, or "alley as parlor" (*tang* is the front room of a house), is the local term for *lilong*, connoting the mix of public and private space in conditions of extreme urban density. *Lilong* housing was initially rented by foreign real estate speculators to Chinese living within the foreign concessions, but by the beginning of the twentieth century "new-style" *lilong* neighborhoods were constructed on a larger, more rational scale using Western building materials and technologies.[69] By the mid-twentieth century *lilong* housing accounted for three-quarters of the city's dwellings, mostly for middle and lower-middle classes. Chunlan

New construction looms over the *shikumen lilong*, its Shanghai alleyway life slated for destruction. Photo by author.

Zhao points out that as the first mass commodity housing to be produced and consumed in the dynamic of local-foreign interactions within a market mechanism, *lilong* dwelling played a transitional role in Chinese urban history by challenging values based in the traditional dwelling system. "The *lilong* housing neighborhood is a rich concept that refers not only to the materiality of this dwelling form but to the vivid social life within and around it."[70]

In *Song of Everlasting Sorrow* this urban life form appears as a relic of an already disappeared past, evocatively expressed in the opening chapter, which ends with an echo of Bai Juyi's poem: "Occasionally one finds in the Shanghai alleys a wall completely covered with a thick carpet of Boston ivy; the ivy, with its old, clinging tentacles, is emblematic of passions that have persisted through time. In persistence is inconsolable pain, on which are inscribed the records of time, the accumulated debris of time as it is pressed down and slowly suffocated. This is the everlasting sorrow of Wang Qiyao" (23; 26). The novelist elegizes the lost romance of the once vital commodity, a petrified artifact destined to be demolished or transformed into simulacra such as Xintiandi (New Heaven and Earth), a *shikumen lilong* renovated for commercial use.[71]

The first section of the novel explores the life of the commodity through the image of Shanghai as spectacle as it enters the realm of exchange value: Wang Qiyao as the object of the gaze in the film studio, on the cover of *Shanghai Life*, at the beauty pageant. The narrator mocks the subject's willing participation in its commodification: "[Shanghai was] a city of pleasure that found it difficult to get through the day unless it could find something to make it happy. When torrential floods hit Henan province and people all over China were donating to the disaster relief effort, Shanghai offered its passion and romance—holding a Miss Shanghai beauty pageant to raise money for the flood victims. . . . 'Shanghai' was already a virtual synonym for modernity, but 'Miss Shanghai' captured even better the modern cosmopolitanism of the city—after all, what could be more modern than a beauty queen?" (48; 55). In this passage the narrator indulges the superficial charms of the city while insinuating it is parasitic, a consumer of spectacle rather than a producer of labor (by, for example, building homes for the relocated flood victims). When Wang Qiyao models a simple white wedding gown during the finals of the 1946 "Miss Shanghai" contest, "Wang Qiyao felt truly herself; both she and the dress embodied the sentiment that this was going to be the last time. Along with this feeling came joy, sorrow, and a slight hint of being wronged" (64; 75) Wang Qiyao's premonition proved to be correct; she had offered herself up for display on stage, and in doing so had lost her "true self," becoming duly purchased as commodity. Wang Qiyao is more pragmatic than sentimental, admitting only to "minor regrets," which does not readily invite the reader's sympathy. Yet, as the narrator explains in the opening chapter, such regrets may be trivial in themselves, but they accumulate in the cramped neighborhood alleys, resulting in pathos of another order: "The *longtang* of Shanghai are incapable of holding the kind of grand pain that inspires legends. Its pain is broken up and evenly allocated throughout the city, so each person ends up with a small share" (11; 12).

The narrative ambivalence toward Wang Qiyao, and the city she represents, is in part because of the woman's (and the city's) historical dilemma. An ordinary girl from an average neighborhood, Wang Qiyao, once placed on display, has her features seen in a new light. Limited in her options, neither victim nor harlot, she is, not unlike Shanghai's partial "concession" to foreigners, neither fully compliant nor fully resistant. She is merely fatalistic, accepting the fruits of acquiescence while "regretting" her loss of self. She, like the city, is easily bought and sold, her image conforming to what its owners prescribe. This recalls one scholar's comments about Los Angeles (which, it may be argued, occupies a somewhat analogous position to Shanghai in the cultural economy of its own nation): "Los Angeles, it should be understood, is not a mere city. On the contrary, it is, and has been since 1888, a *commodity*; something to be advertised and sold . . . like automobiles, cigarettes and mouth wash."[72] For Shanghai, the development of its commodity culture is inexorably tied to its humiliation at the hands of foreigners. Wang Anyi's ambivalence toward Shanghai's urban culture is another example of the "element of self-hatred" that tends, according to Yang Dongping, to govern Shanghai pride.

The historical reality of a progressive loss of "self," shared by all Shanghai residents, explains the intense, timeless attraction Wang Qiyao retains for those in her orbit, including the narrator. Unlike Emma Bovary, who is denigrated by Gustave Flaubert's narrator for her ignorance, Wang Qiyao is depicted by Wang Anyi's narrator as a knowing flâneuse in the city, one who maintains a cynical distance even as she embodies its heart.[73] Wang Qiyao's cool self-consciousness enables her to win over men and women alike, invariably regaining their respect and admiration despite her station in life. Never merely the passive object of the gaze, she functions, as Chris Jenks once described the figure of the flâneur, as "an analytical form, a narrative device, and attitude towards knowledge and its social context."[74]

Wang Qiyao's quintessentially Shanghainese urbanity is rooted in her ability to appreciate the quotidian. Unlike her schoolmate Jiang Lili, who (unsuccessfully) strives to join the Communist Party, or her first suitor, Mr. Cheng, who is so attached to his idealized (failed) romance that he is unable to progress through later subsequent historical stages, Wang Qiyao readily adapts by immersing herself in the daily rituals of the *longtang* to which she moves after her lover dies in a plane crash. Through regular fraternizing with neighbors in afternoon teas, mahjong parties, dinners, and fireside chats, she helps create intimate, family-like bonds in an era which denounced such attachments and frivolous pursuits. Wang Anyi describes the Maoist period almost exclusively in terms of daily social gatherings in the alleys, highlighting the Shanghainese appreciation for commonplace pursuits, especially in contrast to the politicized activity that dominated the times. The Shanghai urbanite's apolitical lifestyle choice is justified as the most practical one. "The residents of Shanghai hewed to the little things of life, which left them stranded on the margins when it came to politics. If you told them that the Communist government belongs to the people, they would still keep their distance, due to modesty as well an overweening pride—deep down they still believed that they were the true masters of the city" (225; 242).[75] Ban Wang's reading of the second section of the novel, which details bourgeois practices in the *longtang* under socialism, is particularly illuminating. As a residual form of urban commercial culture, he explains, the socialist *longtang* is no longer a space of consumerism in the strictest sense, but "the presence of commodities opens a limited space for desire, enjoyment, and hence use value, even though this is vigilantly guarded against by the dominant ideology." He adds that "in the numerous scenarios of ritualized living and consumption in the *longtang*, the commodity in its downfall paradoxically rises to a more elevated status as an everyday cult around which the aura of a vanished life is imagined, savored, or even enacted."[76] Experience of the aura, as Walter Benjamin understood it, is "the unique phenomenon of a distance, however close it may be."[77]

Wang Qiyao as an auratic figure like "Old Shanghai" remains both elusive and accessible. She appears to transcend time (her age is regularly misjudged) and serves as an intermediary for those who cannot negotiate Shanghai's political and social upheavals. One of her paramours, Kang Mingxun, learns of her checkered past through the gossip networks, yet despite his need to protect his family reputation he cannot suppress his attraction to this marked woman: "*Who was this woman?* Kang Mingxun pined for the city's vanished glory, of which only the trolley bell remained, and it saddened him every time he heard it ring. Wang Qiyao was like a mysterious shadow of that feeling; like a phantom that came and went unsummoned, she haunted him. . . . This may have been a brand-new Wang Qiyao, but it was also a reincarnation of the old Wang Qiyao. He could barely recognize her, yet somehow seemed to know her only too well. He felt the joy and excitement of having something restored to him. *This is now an entirely different city*, he thought to himself, *the street names have changed, the buildings and streetlights are but the shell of their former selves, their core melted away and replaced.* . . . But Wang Qiyao was a true relic of the past: she would be able to help him steal his heart back from yesterday" (190–91; 204–5). Wang Qiyao's function, as a mediator between past and present, serves as a bridge for those unable to negotiate Shanghai's radical changes. "In the spell of aura," argues Ban Wang, "the commodity shifts from spectacle to use value. With this, the characters relate to the lost image of commodity as authentic experience, which finds its nurturing ground in daily rituals based not on traditional Chinese custom but on the memory of Republican Era commercial culture."[78]

After enjoying an obscure existence during the Maoist era, Wang Qiyao is "rediscovered" in the 1980s, when Shanghai enthusiastically reembraces the market, and its cultural and economic paucity obliges it to resurrect its romanticized consumer past. By the time of the novel's authorship, the initial excitement over market reforms and consumer culture had dampened considerably. The Shanghai cultural critic Wang Xiaoming explains the source of the dystopian sentiment of the mid-1990s: "Appeals for 'modernization' swept the nation in the mid-1980s [and] the logic that informed these appeals seemed rational to all, for there was a deep historical basis for the consensus they achieved. The twenty years of economic stagnation after the Great Leap Forward had indeed oppressed people far too long. . . . Who could have imagined that a decade later all of these rousing slogans would lose virtually all of their revolutionary charge, and become mere grandiloquent excuses for those in power to pillage society?"[79]

Put another way, the market, "endowed with a human face in nostalgic memory," as Ban Wang puts it, had engendered extreme forms of alienation. In a cultural climate adhering to the "end of history" thesis, where hegemonic market values pervaded all forms of social life, everything—healthcare, education, and even death—had entered the market as sheer commodity.[80] In a society premised on material prosperity for all, nostalgia for material culture had provided a livable space. Although the revival of the market appeared promising in the 1980s, under its neoliberal reconstitution the commodity became simulacrum, its aura lost. Baudrillard posits that such a condition arises due to "the end of transcendence" (a phrase borrowed from Herbert Marcuse), where individuals have become so immersed in the market, and so alienated as a result, that they can perceive neither their own true needs nor another way of life.[81]

In Marxist commodity theory, only when things are commodities, produced for exchange rather than direct consumption (exchange value), can they be said to also have use value. These two categories of value are comparable to the modes of art theorized by Benjamin: the auratic and the technologically reproducible. Just as the aura (in the novel, middle-class rituals) is an effect of the mass production that it seems to oppose (the commodified *lilong* lifestyle), so use value derives from the exchange value that it seems to contradict. Only in an age of technological reproducibility does one worry about the authenticity of objects ("Wang Qiyao" as type, the faceless masses); and only in an age of ubiquitous commodification does one question an object's usefulness (the indiscriminate destruction of the *longtang* a case in point).

To illustrate the absolute commercialization initiated during the Reform Era, the third part of *Song of Everlasting Sorrow* draws contrasts between the mode of production and utility that organized modern societies, and the mode of simulation that organizes postmodern societies devoid of historical consciousness. One passage describes the superficial atmosphere of the nightly parties in one of the new development zones (*xinqu*) that sprang up in the mid-1980s: "Under the sky of the new district, the joyful laughter coming from the thirteenth floor of this joint-venture construction suddenly dissipates and the music fades away. But how much does that bit of happiness really matter in this new district? . . . When you first arrive here, the place seems to lack a heart because it is so carefree—but that is because it hasn't had time to build up a reservoir of recollections; its mind is blank and has not begun to feel the need to call on its memory. Such is the spiritual state of the entire district. The laughter and gaiety coming from the thirteenth floor form but a drop in the ocean. The only one who seems a bit annoyed is the elevator attendant, as people come rushing in and out of the elevator, in couples or crowds, holding wine and flowers—mostly strangers, in all shapes, sizes, and colors" (330–31; 366–67). This meaningless circulation of deterritorialized signs of modernity—strangers, bouquets, wine—strikes Wang Qiyao as insincere and flat, completely lacking historical depth. From Wang Qiyao's perspective, the Shanghai of her daughter "Weiwei's era" is only a shadow of its former self.

> The electric trolleys that were the true heart of the city are now gone. . . . Along the Huangpu River, the stone walls on the Georgian buildings have all turned black, their windows masked by a layer of gray dirt. . . . And let's not even mention the Suzhou River, whose stench you can smell blocks away—scooped up, the water can probably be used directly for fertilizer. . . .
>
> The Shanghai *longtang* have grown gray . . . the gutters are clogged, and foul water trickles down the streets. Even the leaves of the sweet-scented oleanders are coated with grime. . . .
>
> But all this is secondary to the changes that have taken place in the heart of those dwellings. . . . Never touch the stair rail unless you want

several decades of accumulated dust on your hands . . . Should you peer into some of the dormer windows, you would see that the wood panels inside have been eaten away by termites. . . .

The streets are suddenly flooded with people spouting profanities and spitting everywhere. . . . All the elegance of old Shanghai seems to have been wiped out by a violent storm. Everything has become a challenge—taking a bus, going shopping, getting a shower, having one's hair cut—all involve doing battle with the crowds.

Food served in Western-style restaurants has also deteriorated. The plates and cups are all chipped, stained and crusted with bits of caked-on food, and seem not to have been washed in twenty years. The chef's apron, spattered with grease, likewise looks as if it has not been washed for at least twenty years . . . the old leather seats have been replaced by manmade material, and fresh flowers with plastic ones. . . .

Nothing could escape the prevailing crudeness and mediocrity in the general rush to produce instant results. Looking back, Wang Qiyao felt that people were much better off during the Cultural Revolution, when they had to wear the same blue cloth jackets rather than these outlandish outfits that did not fit them. At least back then they had the elegance of simplicity. (273–75; 299–302)

The bourgeois commodity is dusty and worn, its use value exhausted. Not even the most intense nostalgia can resurrect it in a crass, postrevolutionary culture which has lost all vestiges of its former refinement. Entrepreneurial attempts to capitalize on its exchange value are doomed. In the end, these incompatible approaches to the commodity bring about Wang Qiyao's demise.

As a signifier of old Shanghai, "Miss Shanghai" begins to accompany Wei-wei's friends to parties, although she remains out of the limelight, merely "whispering instructions to her partner" when it becomes clear he doesn't know the steps (297; 327). During a party in an exclusive high-rise apartment in the newly redeveloped Hongqiao District of the city, she meets Lao Kela (Old Color), who represents an emergent subculture of nostalgic youth fascinated with the Old Shanghai they never knew. Although initially disappointed to meet a faded, if attractive, middle-aged woman, Lao Kela, a twenty-six-year-old imitation of Mr. Cheng (who had met Wang Qiyao when she was that age), becomes her companion. The more he mingles with Wang Qiyao, the less her age troubles him, and he longs to merge fully with his nostalgic dream through sexual consummation. Although she derides his advances as delusional, Wang Qiyao's reconstituted identity rapidly destabilizes her. In a sudden reversal she succumbs to his dream world, assumes her misidentification, and begs Lao Kela to prostitute himself in exchange for some gold bars that she had been bequeathed. When he rejects her, Wang Qiyao experiences an emotional collapse, which foreshadows her physical one. Her life ends soon after Lao Kela's rejection, in a meaningless struggle over the box of gold with Changjiao, the boyfriend of Wei-wei's classmate; he strangles her frail body before sneaking out with the paltry goods. As she gasps for her last breath, she recalls a scene she had seen enacted in the movie studio decades earlier, and she realizes that the "dying" of the actress on the set anticipated her own. The simulated act prefigured the death of the "real," the "signified."

The novel's conclusion allegorizes the demise of the modern valuation of the commodity and the confusion over postmodern Shanghai identity. The manifest impossibility of "nostalgia" creating a lasting union with "Old Shanghai" dramatizes contradictions of Shanghai image-making, while the profit-motivated murder of "Old Shanghai" renders its history meaningless. Lao Kela's final rejection of Wang Qiyao articulates the political unconscious, its gnawing awareness of the historical crisis inherent in Shanghai's development as a global city. On the other hand, the narrative's portrayal of Changjiao's relationship with Wang Qiyao allegorizes an even more threatening confrontation between global image-making and everyday local culture. Changjiao is portrayed as an urban migrant on the make, an "outsider" (*waidiren*) who strains to assimilate into cosmopolitan Shanghai life by faking an identity as a "successful man" (*chenggong renshi*). Demographically, the majority of "new rich" in Shanghai are, in fact, new to the city, including a disproportionate number of entrepreneurial real estate developers who hail from the provinces.[82] In denigrating as inauthentic the social class typified by Changjiao, however, the novel ironically essentializes Shanghai along the same lines as its global image-makers. Further, by ontologizing Shanghai's alley life to such a point that it becomes ahistorical and self-contained, the novel effectively erases two expanding classes in the global city—the new rich and migrant laborers—precisely the hybrid mix represented by Changjiao's character. Changjiao is depicted as a narrow-minded individual who is unable to truly appreciate the "essence" of Shanghai (and who thus does not hesitate to kill her for a few gold bars). In this sense he functions as a scapegoat deflecting attention from the real reasons for Shanghai's transformation—its concentration of global capital.

The novel attributes the loss of the urban aura to its contamination by "inauthentic urbanites," former Maoists and provincial migrants characterized by a crass "rural" mentality. The primary reason for the bland character of Shanghai's "new development zones," however, is that global capital creates a new spatial logic, where "the space of flows" displaces the historically rooted spatial organization of common experience, "the space of places." Globalization exacts a heavy toll through the disappearance of place (both urban and rural) and, with it, history and memory (including architecture's own memory of itself). The urban sociologist Manuel Castells contends that the advent of this postmodern spatial logic means the end of any meaningful relationship between architecture and society.[83] With the attenuation of nation-state power and the rise of global cities and their regional economies, Shanghai and the Yangtze River Delta provide a "natural" context for urban and architectural design associated with globalization, just as the *lilong* were a "natural" development of colonial capitalism.

The problem with the "off-ground" architecture of globalization, argues Arif Dirlik, is not that it emerges in a vacuum, but that "it is a negation of the social as such," suggesting that "it may make sense under contemporary imbalances of power to let globalization have its spaces, as in Pudong and the many Pudongs of Global Capital, and rebuild architectures of sociability from spaces that have not completely lost memories of the social."[84] In 2003, in an attempt to achieve this, Shanghai designated twelve historical preservation areas, which together cover an area of twenty-seven square kilometers. The hope is that, before the city undergoes a total makeover, as Singapore did, it will retain pockets of social memory. However, as Ruan Yisan of Tongji University's Research Center for State Historical and Cultural Cities points out, Shanghai has listed only 652 individual buildings for preservation, compared to 4,000 in London and 1,200 in Paris, and, even worse, although 94 percent of London's heritage buildings can be classed as vernacular, none on Shanghai's list belongs to this category.[85]

Wang Anyi is equally pessimistic. The novelist construes a historical scenario whereby the commodity becomes fossilized, resulting in the eternal loss of visceral *longtang* life, where layers of residue can still penetrate the flesh. Her dismay is shared by Rem Koolhaas, who, despite being the quintessential architect of the global, nonetheless perceives it as a hegemonic architecture of disappearance. "The first time I went to Singapore, I was seven," he says, "and I arrived by boat. What I remember is the smell: equal parts rot and sweetness, the smell of the tropics. But when I went back two years ago that smell was gone. In fact, Singapore was gone, scrapped, its architecture a Petri dish of Chinese Stalinist modernism followed by Chinese postmodernism." He concludes, "We all inhabit conceptual Singapores."[86] If one understands global architecture as a commodity, the notion of it as the architecture of disappearance makes sense. Whereas modern societies are organized around the production and consumption of commodities, postmodern societies are organized around the play of images and signs, the organizing forms of a new social order where simulation rules. Commodities in such an era are no longer merely characterized by use value and exchange value, as in Marx's theory of the commodity, but by sign value. In addition to the commodity's exchange value and use value, the expression of style, prestige, luxury, and power through conspicuous consumption becomes an increasingly important function.

In the new development zones, the "droves of strangers" pouring "in and out of the elevators" with "bouquets and wine in hand" attest to a space of flows, the endless, faceless circulation of signs of prestige and luxury. Changjiao "plays" at being something he is not in a society of simulation, where identities are constructed by the appropriation of images which determine how individuals perceive themselves and relate to others. Baudrillard's understanding of the mid-twentieth-century transition from the earlier stage of competitive market capitalism to that of monopoly capitalism illuminates this reading. Because demand and consumption must now be artificially manufactured, he argues, economics, politics, social life, and culture are governed by the mode of simulation, whereby codes determine how goods are consumed and used, how politics unfold, how culture is produced and consumed, and how everyday life is lived.

Instead of a place of lived history, the Shanghai *longtang*, and its urban landscape more generally, are transformed into an artificial "New Heaven and Earth." The Shikumen Museum in Xintiandi sums up the contradictions inherent in Shanghai's contemporary image-making: "Xintiandi is a place that older people consider nostalgic, younger people consider trendy, foreigners consider Chinese, and Chinese consider foreign. It is a place where everybody finds something of his or her own. Xintiandi belongs not only to Shanghai, but to China and to the world." In other words, create your own meaning.

The Subject in the City

The Melancholic Urban Subject

Black Snow, Private Life, Breathing, and *Candy*

Art that features the city as subject has its counterpart in that which explores urban subjectivity. Two aspects of the subject in the city—the psychic subject and the moral subject—both figure prominently in postsocialist urban fiction. In this chapter I focus on the relationship of subjectivity to space, in particular, the dynamics between the city and ego formation, analyzing literature that portrays not the physical markers of the city, its layout, architecture, and landmarks, but the city as internalized in the consciousness of the individual. In other words, I explore the psychic rather than material space of the city.

Urban-design concepts, such as those in Kevin Lynch's seminal book, *The Image of the City* (1960), help illuminate how people perceive urban space from elements such as "paths," "nodes," and "edges." Also helpful are early psychoanalytical and social theories of subjectivity and space put forth by Sigmund Freud, Jacques Lacan, and Georg Simmel, as well as formulations by gender and cultural studies theorists such as Judith Butler, Elizabeth Grosz, and Douglas Crimp. Although Freud's theories have long been dismissed by many, their accuracy remains contested. Regardless of their scientific usefulness, they are relevant to discussions of twentieth-century Chinese fiction because Freud's works were read widely by young Chinese intellectuals, who were introduced to them during the "culture fever" (*wenhua re*) of the 1980s.[1] Highly influential during the postsocialist era, as they had been half a century earlier, Freud's psychoanalytic theories permeate constructions of modernist Chinese literature at various stages in its history. Jerome Silbergeld's point about contemporary Chinese film directors can be extended to authors: "They know both classical Freud and his Lacanian and post-Lacanian by-products."[2]

Through close readings of postsocialist novels, set in Shenzhen, Shanghai, and Beijing, that feature intensely interiorized experiences of these major metropolises, I examine dynamics between subjectivity and space. Liu Heng's *Hei de xue* (Black snow, 1988), one of the first post-Mao urban novels set in Beijing during the Reform Era, features a released ex-con attempting to negotiate the emerging market society. Chen Ran's *Siren shenghuo* (Private life, 1996) recounts a young woman's coming-of-age in the capital from the 1970s to the 1990s, her bildungsroman embedded in the city's transformation. Sun Ganlu's *Huxi* (Breathing, 1993) indulges the abstract ruminations of a playboy attempting to define his identity in the cramped physical and psychological conditions of Shanghai just prior to its urban redevelopment. Mian Mian's *Tang* (Candy, 2000) follows the psychological progression of "alternative" (*linglei*) youth seeking love in the decadent culture of postsocialist Shenzhen and Shanghai.

With the exception of *Black Snow*, each novel in question is ostensibly semiautobiographical (*ban zizhuan*), describing protagonists whose biographical details so closely parallel those of their authors that many readers conflate the two. While all fiction is somehow informed by authorial experience, the tendency to construct fictional narratives with transparently autobiographical details is especially prevalent in postsocialist urban fiction, as it was during the 1920s and 1930s. Urban fiction of the 1990s shares the same documentary drive as Sixth Generation films; both address the decade's postindustrial anxieties by blurring the lines between constructed and lived narrative. One should avoid interpreting these works as direct mimesis, yet it is clear that these accounts are continuous with common structures of everyday experience.

The young adults in these novels struggle with sexual obsessions, chemical dependency, and psychopathology, due in part to features of the urban space in question. Yet all four novels relegate physical descriptions of their urban settings to a bare minimum, instead detailing the contours of interior, psychic space. The claustrophobic interiority characterizing these narratives appears indifferent to the city, yet the city's background role in the texts speaks louder than words. The protagonists tend to be acted on rather than act, responding passively to cities perpetually in flux. The pressure exerted on the individual by the city is played out on the corporeal level, exacerbating identity confusion during a period of rapid urbanization and cultural transition. Given the flux of crowds, patterns of urban destruction and renewal, and new modes of transportation, communication, and socialization, attempts to define self and safeguard autonomy result in ill effects, both in real life and in fiction that elucidates contemporary experience.

Shifting urban configurations reshape Chinese conceptions of the self in several ways. First, protagonists often maintain a reserved public persona to mask a sense of repulsion and alienation from the city and its masses; in turn, their private lives are dominated by obsessive desire. Second, characters regularly construct their own private utopias in order to offset the exterior chaos of the metropolis and regain an integrated, autonomous sense of self. Third, this self-imposed isolation often results in psychopathic symptoms of melancholy, paranoia, and narcissism. While some literary critics have denounced these works as solipsistic, creative obsession with interiority is a common stratagem for addressing the universal problems of modernity as well as the strictures imposed by lingering socialist and Confucian norms that valorize collectivity. Liu Heng, Chen Ran, Sun Ganlu, and Mian Mian privilege the private, the local, the alternative, the homoerotic, and the feminine to reveal the hegemony of a public sphere represented by the state and its capitalist partners. As Tze-lan Sang argues in her analysis of Chen Ran's fiction, "Desire for seclusion must be read in terms of public residence, radical defiance of a state that has long encroached on private lives to the point of eliminating the private sphere."[3]

Subjectivity and Space: Ego Formation in the City

Georg Simmel's urban sociology is instructive in its notion that psychic and social manipulations of private space derive from efforts to preserve the autonomy of the subject in the city. He opens his well-known essay "The Metropolis and Mental Life" (1905) by saying, "The deepest problems of modern life derive from the claim of the individual to preserve the autonomy and individuality of his existence."[4] Simmel's essay has since been criticized on many counts, from Franco Moretti's denial that "shock" is the operative psychic mechanism in urban life to Janet Wolff's dismay that Simmel and other theorists of modernity mainly account for the experience of men rather than women.[5] However, Simmel indisputably broke new ground with his insights into the relationships between urban space and the psyche. He concludes that the continual stream of stimuli in the city engenders intellectualization and a blasé metropolitan attitude, stating that "the inner aspect of this outer reserve is not only indifference, but . . . a slight aversion, a mutual strangeness and repulsion," so that "what appears in the metropolitan style of life directly as dissociation is in reality only one of its elemental forms of socialization."[6]

The heightened desire for privacy so prevalent in postsocialist urban fiction thus conveys an essential element of urban socialization. In *Privacy, Intimacy, and Isolation* the philosopher Julie C. Inness conceptualizes privacy by identifying its functions, mechanisms, and values.[7] By *function*, Inness means the nature of the relationship between the agent and outside entities. Privacy might either separate areas of the agent's life from the public sphere, or provide her with control over them within the realm of the public sphere. The *mechanism* of privacy refers to the means by which it is safeguarded, and the *value* of privacy differs radically in various cultural contexts. In American culture, for example, privacy is considered of paramount importance, and its loss provokes talk of violation, harm, and loss of agency.[8] Privacy is also increasingly valued in urban China. In *China's Urban Transformation* the urban theorist John Friedmann devotes an entire chapter to expanding spaces of personal autonomy, identifying "the uses of disposable leisure time," "a home of one's own," "the new intimacy of life," "the reemergence of the private sphere," and "reshaping relations between state and self" as newly forming spaces for personal autonomy.[9]

Privacy can also be conceived as a condition to avoid, as it promotes isolation, deprivation, and separation. While privacy is positively valued in most modern liberal societies, Hannah Arendt points out the etymological connection between privacy and privation, stating that "in ancient feeling the privative trait of privacy, indicated in the word itself, was all important; it meant literally a state of being deprived of something, and even of the highest and most human of man's capacities."[10] The narrative ambivalence in these novels in part derives from the conflict between the modern liberal valuation of privacy as desirable and traditional valences of *si* as illicit and unhealthy.

Aside from their aversion to the crowd, retreat into private space, and display of psychological dissociation, the protagonists of these novels are indisputably melancholic. In Freud's classic formulation on the subject in his essay "Mourning and Melancholia" (1917), melancholia as a psychological fixation is related to disavowed loss that, if only acknowledged, would allow the disease to transmute into the more healthy process of mourning.[11] But what is it that these characters have lost, and what prevents them from identifying their losses? Are these losses related to the city, and if so, to what extent is the urban environment implicated in the formation of melancholic subjects? While one can hardly claim that city life singly engenders melancholy, it may be that conditions unique to the cities in question do, indeed, cause their subjects to experience losses which they themselves have difficulty identifying.

In his introduction to a collection of essays on melancholy in China, Wolfgang Kubin indicates that a collective Chinese sense of melancholy, or *youhuan yishi*, a term that implies "a concern for the imperilment" of the emperor, governor, and the state, can be traced back to the Song dynasty (960–1127). The infusion of Western existential ideas in the early twentieth century compounded this sense, resulting in central images of China as a "wasteland" and creating a sense of desolation and emptiness. Kubin concludes that, under socialism, "up until 1989 a ban on melancholy was implemented with the goal of remedying this mood."[12] In the postsocialist Chinese context it is clear that the urban space has become a topology for examining individual identity subsequent to the loss of collective, utopian, rural-based longings. Wang Xiaoming indicates that the "ban on melancholy" was reinstated after Deng Xiaoping's southern tour, when hype over market reforms blithely disavowed collective grief over the violent end, on June Fourth, to the liberal aspirations inspiring nationwide urban demonstrations.[13] Thus, melancholy also expresses the profound ambivalence that the writer, conscious of the approaching end of a century, sustains toward the course of twentieth-century Chinese history, given the rapid dissipation of revolutionary and Enlightenment ideals in a contemporary market society—losses that remain unacknowledged in mainstream culture.

Liu Heng's *Black Snow*: Anonymity as Annihilation

Liu Heng's *Black Snow* is one of the earliest post-Mao novels to express the kind of urban alienation theorized by Simmel. A third-person narrator reveals the intimate thoughts of Li Huiquan, who, in 1985, at the age of twenty-five, must negotiate the complexities of the emerging market economy in Beijing after being released from a labor-reform camp. Abandoned at birth and later bereaved by the death of his adoptive parents, Huiquan returns to his home, a hovel in the Yong'an District of East Beijing, where he is aided in his rehabilitation by his parole officer and the neighborhood-committee representative, Auntie Luo. He goes through the motions of transforming himself into a law-abiding modern citizen, peddling clothes as an entrepreneur (*getihu*, literally, "individual operator"), jogging to maintain his health, frequenting art museums and classical music concerts, and reading the daily papers to stay abreast of current events. The narrative is dominated, however, by a sense of Huiquan's utter alienation from the modern city and its masses. The few friends with whom he reestablishes contact show little concern for his well-being; they instead demonstrate the classic utilitarian traits of social relations in a market economy. He is especially repulsed by the estranging effects of the transforming cityscape. Emerging from his back lane to peruse the city, Huiquan experiences disaffection from the crowd milling along the "newly constructed, nearly identical matchbox apartments" that line the streets: "Did anyone out there give a damn? Up and down the street they strolled, men and women, not one of them so much as glancing at him. It was as though he didn't exist—no parents, no friends, just a pair of eyes and a beat-up old bicycle. He flitted around aimlessly, talking to no one. No one knew him, anyway. If they had known him, they'd probably have avoided him" (14; 14–15).[14] He "shuns human contact," and characterizes social relations in the city as utterly alienating.

> Something was going very wrong with his life, but he couldn't put his finger on it. . . . He felt as lost and as isolated as a leaf that has fallen from the tree. He knew there was precious little kindness to be drawn from the crowds passing before him. They didn't understand him, and he didn't understand them. Was anyone ever saddened by the pain of others? No. He was not moved by the sight of the blind street musician who had set up shop beside the bus stop; in fact, he assumed it was a sham, one of the oldest tricks in the world.
>
> The old lady who picked up trash on Spirit Run Street didn't earn his sympathy either. After spending all her waking hours buried in piles of garbage, she became little more than garbage in his eyes. No sympathy, no pity. Yet the absence of expression does express something—apathy. He got back the same as he gave. Was there a soul on earth who cared about the confusion in his mind when he awoke in the morning? Did anyone understand how his thoughts tormented him nightly? Surely not. If he were hit by a car tonight, he would be forgotten tomorrow. At most his mangled body would become a gory statistic and, briefly, a hot topic of conversation. People count for little in others' eyes. (241–43; 202–4)

As Huiquan wanders throughout the city, he is terrified by the apathy of the crowd, his own callousness, and the dire implications for a meaningful existence. Indeed, such morbid sentiments drive the novel toward its conclusion, where Huiquan appears destined to be extinguished in anonymity, stabbed by hoodlums to the point of death in an obscure alley. *Black Snow* closes with an abstract threat of further destruction: "The middle of the night. From the bowels of the city came the heavy thud of footsteps. Calmly he listened to them draw near" (313; 261).

Huiquan's fear of "anonymity" is one example of how new understandings of identity are forming in contemporary urban China. In her discussion of the concept, Ellen Hertz explains that traditional Chinese terms for anonymity are either *niming* (hidden or concealed name) or *wuming* (without a name; indefinable, indescribable). The former is more closely related to *si* (private, personal; secret, selfish, illicit), whereas the latter is associated with loneliness (*jimo, gudu, huangliang*), "but this is the loneliness associated with the solitude of the recluse, not the aloneness of the individual awash in the anonymous crowd. Chinese also has an extensive lexicon for describing anonymity from the point of view of those who are not anonymous—words, that is, for strangers or outsiders (*mosheng, xinlaizhe, shengke, wairen*). Thus, the notion of anonymity itself—which appears in the Western sociological tradition as a neutral term for the description of a certain brute experience of city life—presupposes a certain set of relations to the group, the self, and sacrifice that require untangling in the Chinese context."[15] Hertz concludes that the new Chinese experience of urban anonymity, or *facelessness*, is the experience of being part of a crowd in which one can neither have nor lose face because one's personal relation to the community is not at issue. Much of Huiquan's struggle is characterized by his lack of a defined community now that he is adrift in a "free market" without the prescribed relations of the socialist work unit.

One reason Huiquan isolates himself is to avoid further contact with the lonely individuals whose tortured lives he "reads" on a daily basis. To the extent that the crowd mirrors his own sense of loneliness, he attempts to shield himself from intimate interaction with others. Instead, his craving for intimacy is met through guarded mediation: by remembering warm moments with his deceased mother; by rereading a rare letter from a childhood friend still in reform camp "to extract what little warmth it contained" (76; 69). One of the functions of privacy is to protect the self not so much from surveillance, but from revealing vulnerable aspects of the self that may be disparaged by another. Perhaps an even greater fear is that, in exchanging meaningful information with another, one's suspicions about the emptiness of modern life may be confirmed. In this case, privacy is paradoxically devalued for the same reason it is prized. By separating areas of his life from the social sphere that would otherwise foster intimacy (compounding his anonymity [*niming*] through dour refusals to socialize), Huiquan withdraws into a state of isolation. A condition that safeguards intimate information, privacy simultaneously promotes the very breach in human contact that drives Huiquan to despair. In this sense, privacy becomes a trap, reinforcing his sense of futility and hampering his agency within the public sphere.

By withdrawing from meaningful social contact, Huiquan's life becomes dominated by obsessive desire. He resents intrusions into his private life, refusing to stop to chat with a childhood playmate, "begging off" when Auntie Luo invites him over to watch television and share New Year's Eve dinner with her family. Instead, alone in his refuge, "Huiquan's thoughts turned to lewd walls—toilet walls whose scars could not be whitewashed out of existence, battered walls about to topple under lustful assaults. Weird, obscene thoughts and excrement were in strange harmony there, forcing him to confront the filthy body he was trying to conceal. Huiquan knew there was no place he could hide. All alone on New Year's Eve, he added his own fantasies to those sordid walls. Rather than girls, maybe what had disgusted him all along was himself" (42–43; 39–40). As the novel progresses he becomes fixated on a bar singer, whom he escorts home nightly until she learns of his past incarceration. As his social and psychological disaffection increases, his obsession takes on violent dimensions; at one point, Huiquan envisions raping the girl in an alcove beneath the towering high-rises, and "his thoughts, obviously unhealthy and spooky, seemed those of a dispassionate observer" (133; 114).

In each of these instances, Huiquan demonstrates classic symptoms of melancholia as described by Freud. In addition to his exaggerated sense of social isolation, his obsessive ruminations on the meaninglessness of existence and his morbid fixations on the bar singer, he repeatedly engages in self-deprecation, one of the key Freudian distinctions between grief and melancholy.[16] In addition to passages divulging his sense of abjection, Huiquan states matter-of-factly that "nearly everyone is superior to him" and describes himself as "superfluous." He considers his admiration for the singer, in particular, to be "ridiculous and utterly worthless. His fantasies regarding women are nothing but emotional garbage" (134; 115). Importantly, his self-castigation is often linked to new estimations of worth in the money economy of the city. He thwarts Auntie Luo's attempts to match him with another girl, since "he did not enjoy trying to calculate his worth in the eyes of others. Worth-*less* was more like it" (264; 220). As he sells commodities to his customers, he claims that "he could no longer tell who was toying with whom. Like his merchandise, the people were absolutely devoid of value" (283; 237).

In *Black Snow* privacy masks repulsion toward the new market economy and the urban masses, even as the individual is himself implicated in these alienating practices. Some readers, such as Li Jiefei, interpret Huiquan's despondency as the generalized condition of a particular class of urbanites, "urban youth awaiting employment" (*chengshi daiye qingnian*). He points out that the problems of these "troubled youth" of the mid-1980s were exacerbated by their position straddling the change between a socialist and a semicapitalist urban economy, epitomized in their status as *getihu*. In the 1980s, when employment by state-sponsored work units prevailed, most *getihu* were independent peddlers from questionable backgrounds that prevented them from gaining proper employment, and they were thus considered social pariahs.[17] This is a case where China's transition from a socialist to market-based economy magnifies the sense of social alienation for a specific group of urbanites. However, the portrayal of privacy's function, value, and effects in *Black Snow* speaks, at the same time, to the broader phenomenon of modern alienation affecting a larger cross-section of China's urban citizenry, a fictional account that accords with Georg Simmel's sociology of the metropolis. Many of the themes in *Black Snow* are replicated in another Beijing novel, *Private Life*, which delineates different social, class, gender, and historical considerations while exhibiting remarkably similar effects in the relation of melancholic privacy to modern urban life.

Chen Ran's *Private Life*: Seclusion as Resistance

Chen Ran's controversial novel, *Private Life*, portrays life in Beijing through the interior monologue of the protagonist, Ni Niuniu. Niuniu engages in a form of self-diagnosis, retrospectively examining her coming-of-age after suffering a breakdown at the age of thirty, in the mid-1990s. The poetic chapter epithets and loosely recollected events of the novel convey a deep-seated pessimism toward life, in a narrative dominated by mistrust of men. Aside from her college boyfriend, Yin Nan, Niuniu's emotional attachments are exclusively to women, each of whom has been physically, emotionally, or sexually abused by men. Niuniu is close to her mother and has a mutually dependent emotional, sometimes sexual, relationship with Widow He, a neighbor ten years her senior. In contrast, Niuniu's emotionally distant father divorces her mother and abandons the family, and her teacher, Mr. T, humiliates her as a schoolgirl and seduces her as a teenager.

Like that of *Black Snow*, the narrative of *Private Life* is permeated with a sense of melancholy and impending doom (Niuniu reveals in the penultimate chapter that she has written her account to "get her affairs in order"), which some critics attribute to repressed anger at patriarchal culture. While *Private Life* is indisputably a feminist novel, a closer reading demonstrates that male dominance manifests in noxious urban spatial configurations, which compounds the narrative sense of angst and entrapment. The narrative's deliberations on mental breakdown identify sociospatial contributors to the protagonist's "disease," deconstructing its superficial diagnosis as the predictable outcome of female lack. However, Chen Ran uses the trope of melancholy to subvert stereotypes of the feminine *as* private, revealing the implicitly public aspects of the melancholic condition in the modern city. In this I agree with Wang Xiaoming, one of the few critics to identify Chen Ran's fiction as a quintessential response to the city—one of resistance.[18]

The publication of *Private Life* stoked critical debates over "female writing" (*nüxing xiezuo*) and "individualized writing" (*gerenhua xiezuo*). In a book chapter entitled "The Economics of Privacy: Publishing Women's Writing," Shuyu Kong details the ploys used to market "privacy literature" (*yinsi wenxue*) published by women in the wake of the 1995 International Women's Conference in Beijing.[19] A bestselling, sexually suggestive novel, *Private Life* attracted negative critical attention, ostensibly because of its autobiographical details and "immodest" flaunting of female sexual desire. Chen denounces these criticisms on all counts. She objects to inquisitive readers who naively equate her fiction with her personal life, protesting to her interviewer, Xiao Gang, "I do not agree when you call my works self-narratives [*zixushi*]. I like to write in the first-person voice, but that does not mean that my fiction is the autobiographical account of my personal life. . . . Certain details that you find in my fiction may be based on my real experience in the physical world, but, more commonly, they reflect only my psychological experience."[20] When I interviewed Chen Ran a year after the publication of *Private Life*, she insisted that it was attacked primarily because of its focus on an individual (*geren*), "which is disparaged by default since Chinese value writing about social issues. The first 'mistake,' according to Chinese cultural values, is to write about something private, something individual. But my perspective is exactly the opposite; I think the more individual something is, the more universal it is."[21] In a talk that Chen delivered to universities in England in 1994 and later published in the avant-garde literary journal *Zhongshan*, she insisted that her fiction was informed by a strong political consciousness (*zhengzhi secai, sixiang juewu*).[22] My reading of *Private Life* concurs with Chen's assessment; she privileges the private, the homoerotic, and the feminine in order to critique oppressive discourses and structures dominating the individual in Chinese society.

Niuniu's subjectivity manifests in nearly all of the forms described by Anthony Vidler, who discusses how metropolitan psychopathology became gendered as feminine over time. Its spatial characteristics were those "of necessary interiority, either mental or physical, or both; hence the ascription agora- or claustro-phobia. Its forms are those of stream of consciousness, of entrapment, of intolerable closure, of space without exit, of, finally, breakdown and often suicide."[23] Niuniu entertains the possibility of taking her own life at several junctures, and while she does not succumb to this provocation, she is eventually institutionalized, after a nervous breakdown. She emerges from the hospital only to seclude herself in her bathroom, which she decorates with flowers and mirrors, emulating the womb outside of which she has never quite located herself peaceably. Preoccupation with the womb dominates the text, and there is an unmistakably claustrophobic, narcissistic quality to Niuniu's world, a turning inward which is both a passive, fear-driven reaction and an active resistance.

In her analysis of the mutually defining relations between bodies and cities, Elizabeth Grosz argues that the city "orients and organizes family, sexual, and social relations insofar as the city divides cultural life into public and private domains . . . these spaces, divisions, and interconnections the roles and means by which bodies are individuated to become subjects."[24] Thus, the city, via the body, plays a vital role in the constitution of the subject through the delineation of public and private space. For Niuniu, however, ego formation is complicated by her perception that the relationship between public and private space in Beijing is permeable. Although she cloisters herself within her house in an attempt at self-preservation, the exterior space of the city constantly threatens to intrude: "The solemn and heavy breath of Beijing spreads through the house and fills my lungs. Like ashen, dirty time, it forever clings to the arms of all good people as it leads them silently away" (37; 30).[25] In this sense Niuniu's attempt to safeguard privacy seems dubious at best, suggesting a sense of powerlessness and lack of agency, as it did in *Black Snow*.

Niuniu's lack of autonomy is compounded by descriptions of the city as a male aggressor from which she must take refuge. She associates public space with male gender stereotypes of the dominant, blunt, insensitive, and time-bound, and private space with female tropes of the enigmatic, sensuous, perceptive, and eternal. She further imagines the "man-made" city to be encroaching on the organic female countryside, symbolized by the dominance of the countryside by the city.

> Because of all the noise and clamor, the city's heart is becoming every day emptier as its arms extend everywhere into the surrounding farms, covering the gentle fields of wheat and vegetables with hard asphalt roads, making them its own. It is getting harder and harder to find scenes of country life around the outskirts of this city, or smell the rich fragrance of the vegetables that grace our tables growing in the soil that nurtured them. All we can do is retreat to our balconies where we can symbolically "promote agriculture" to get a little feel of the farmer's life. As this city grows bigger and bigger, it is becoming more and more stupid and obtuse. (264; 209)

If the city, as Grosz suggests, divides life into public and private domains, "the space, divisions, and interconnections a means by which bodies become individuated to become subjects," Niuniu's subjectivity is dominated by resistance to the exterior, public domain—epitomized by city thoroughfares perceived as "male"—by which she is simultaneously repulsed and attracted. Niuniu at times goes out in public to mitigate her loneliness, only to find that her sense of repulsion is reinforced by the crowd. Niuniu's retreat to the streets almost always occurs after upsetting encounters with men in private spaces, whether the enclosed space of an office (after sexual molestation by Mr. T) or her home (after she "inadvertently" cuts up her father's woolen pants). When private space becomes sullied by male aggression, her valuation of public and private is reversed, and the streets become her "home" (*jiayuan*) (119; 96). The city streets can only be one's home in a limited sense, however. Michel de Certeau points out, "To walk is to lack a place. . . . [I]t is the indefinite process of being absent. . . . [T]he moving about that the city multiplies and concentrates makes the city itself an immense social experience of lacking a place."[26] Instead of laying claim to the city by walking through its main thoroughfares, Niuniu confines herself to the smaller, bordering streets.

Highly selective of which "paths" and "edges" (to use Lynch's city elements) define her particular experience of the city, she prefers wandering "uneven, irregular side streets" that are "free of people" in the "feminine" hues of early morning or rose-colored dusk, to strong, functional, ordered streets in broad daylight (47; 37–38). In this sense Niuniu's relationship to the city is similar to that of other fictional female characters, such as Clarissa Dalloway in Virginia Woolf's *Mrs Dalloway* (1925) or Rosemary in Ira Levin's *Rosemary's Baby* (1967), whose relationship to New York City is described as "one of oscillation and ambivalence. Rosemary oscillates between enjoyment and mistrust of the city and alternates physically between its public and private spaces. Her story expresses ambivalence towards the very possibility of women having a relationship with the city that does not threaten their autonomy and their privacy."[27]

Niuniu's hallucinations of the crowd dehumanize it, such as on one occasion, when, strolling down the streets, she imagines people morphing into grey, man-like wolves: "I was frightened because I had discovered that I could neither exist as an independent individual nor change myself into a female wolf" (46; 37). Like Lu Xun's madman, who feared being devoured by those around him as well his own implication in the man-eating practices of his cannibalistic society, Niuniu becomes overwhelmed by her lack of autonomy in the animalistic crowd. Rejecting the masses, she is nevertheless wed to them. Walter Benjamin characterizes Baudelaire's uneasy relationship to the crowd in similar terms: "As a *flaneur* [he] was made one of them, [yet] unable to rid himself of a sense of their essentially inhuman makeup . . . he becomes their accomplice, even as he dissociates himself from them."[28]

Although the novel's discourse on privacy casts it as an active, chosen condition, and one that is highly valued, narrative details exhibit fissures in this logic. The modern city remains a space that alienates individuals, especially women. The privileging of interiority and withdrawal into the self speaks more to a disenfranchisement and loss of agency than the seeming rational autonomy afforded by privacy. It is here that the narrative's intense preoccupation with privacy functions as social critique. Throughout the narrative it becomes clear that for Niuniu the function of privacy is protective, restricting access altogether, rather than controlling intimate aspects of life in the presence of others. This form of privacy necessarily creates a sense of social isolation. The private home and rooms within it, viewed principally as defensive fortresses, rather than as restorative realms, are encroached on by the chaotic intrusion of the city, by forced identification with its masses, and by its male design and signification.

After suffering a breakdown provoked by her boyfriend's forced exile and the traumatic deaths of her mother and Widow He in rapid succession, Niuniu is institutionalized for many months before receiving a clean bill of health. On returning home and pondering her illness, she decides her neurosis is anything but private: "I took a long walk along the streets between the Third and Fourth Ring Roads. As I looked around at this huge, crowded city, I thought back over the recent years of my life. . . . Maybe I really am sick, but certainly not 'agoraphobic' or 'mentally disordered' or whatever, as diagnosed by the doctors. My mind is as sharp as ever; I know myself. My problem is 'premature senility'—simple as that. And I'm convinced that there are a lot of other people suffering from the same thing. . . . It's going to be an epidemic by the end of the century" (264; 209).

Niuniu assesses her fin-de-siècle condition from the vantage point of Beijing's recently constructed Fourth Ring Road, built to provide yet another high-speed motorway around an ever-expanding city once confined by ancient walls. Her self-assessment is inextricably linked to the burgeoning city and the crowds among which she walks. Although she is diagnosed by psychologists as a self-isolating (*ziwo fengbi*) agoraphobic, Niuniu justifies isolation as her only means of maintaining viable subjectivity. To Niuniu, the city is an expanse without proper boundaries, one that threatens to invade both the internal domain of the individual and that of the outlying countryside.

> This is a city that lacks a sense of confinement [*queshao fengbigan de chengshi*]. . . . [T]he city's broad and long streets in no way separate the people spread throughout its every corner, allowing them space and psychological distance. . . . Endless rounds of information keep bursting like shells all around you. Row upon row of new buildings crowd together cheek by jowl. Windows like endless rows of eyes stare inquisitively into each other from every angle. Walls as thin as insects' wings. . . . [W]hether you're at home or on the street, your breathing, your muttering, your deepest inner thoughts are common knowledge among the crowds. (263–64; 208–9)[29]

What Chen Ran recounts is that postindustrial sense that time and space implode on the individual, an urban landscape where information "bursts like shells," and the "staring eye" windows and "insect-wing-thin" walls of congested high-rises threaten privacy. Stephen Kern's description of the perceived "compression of time and space" accompanying modern technological developments at the end of the nineteenth century occurs at warp speed in China at the end of the twentieth.[30]

As in *Black Snow*, the question of achieving rational autonomy in *Private Life* is further complicated by the hybrid state of China's postsocialist culture. While the ideals of socialism are ostensibly still operative in political discourse, the logic of the market prevails. Niuniu's tongue-in-cheek letter to the doctors after leaving the hospital reveals that she locates her ills in forced identification with the masses, an effect of both the political and spatial environments she has inhabited. Niuniu's letter mocks the outdated socialist discourse still prevalent in a corrupt capitalist environment. She writes, "You clarified my thinking, rectified my attitude, and reformed my over-all outlook, rekindling in me the same flame of enthusiasm for living and life that burns in the masses! . . . Sometimes I have a hankering to feel melancholy, but I just can't bring it off" (265–67; 210). Her political jabs gather force when she pens her response to a vegetable seller's query about how much money the mayor earns: "The mayor serves the people. He just doesn't think about things like that" (266; 211). Written at the height of then mayor Chen Xitong's fall from grace, for profiteering from the sale of prime Beijing real estate, Chen Ran's novel clearly addresses more than "private problems."

Niuniu further desecrates collective socialist norms by pouring her energy into decorating the most private of spaces, her bathroom, creating "another world" (269; 213). Obsession with interior design, especially of the bathroom, was a widespread phenomenon in Chinese cities in the mid-1990s. For example, Shanghai residents spent an average of ten thousand yuan ($1,230) modernizing their bathrooms in 1996. An article in *Shanghai huabao* (Shanghai pictorial) articulates the new fascination with bathrooms: "As the most private space in everyday life, bathrooms are where people can relax, examine and refresh themselves. We should create an elegant and pleasing atmosphere in a place in which a good mood begins."[31] Niuniu opts to sleep naked in her bathtub, surrounding herself with mirrors, her body itself becoming one of many decorations. In her dissociated state she imagines her bathtub as a coffin, contemplating suicide as she lies inside it. The private space of her bathroom is explicitly contrasted to the chaotic metropolitan streets: "The scene in the bathroom is very stylish, ordered and safe, whereas the outside scenery has deteriorated to a condition lacking order, form, and regulation, with everything in perpetual motion, constant clamor and turmoil. This world makes me unclear as to which is the dream—the interior, or the exterior" (270).[32]

Niuniu's paranoia seems to stem from the difficulty she has in distinguishing between interior and exterior worlds, a necessary differentiation in ego formation. She pours her energies into constructing her own private utopia in order to offset the exterior chaos of the metropolis and regain a sense of self. Just as Haussmann's Paris boulevards of the nineteenth century broke down the closed world of the old medieval enclaves, Beijing's old quarters are being overrun with major roadways, as commercial and residential developments destroy the secluded back-alley communities and their self-confined courtyard houses (*siheyuan*). Beijing's modern roads break down traditional barriers between public and private, and with the advent of late-capitalist technology, the spatial relations which order everyday life have experienced an even more extreme historical mutation, giving the impression that geographical space has shrunk. The socialist denunciation of privacy as decadent is compounded by a spatial implosion of private space due to neoliberal development. In this sense, Niuniu's redecoration of her bathroom can be understood as her response to the fragmentation she experiences within herself and outside in the city.

As estranged from her self as she is from others, unable to integrate herself into what she sees as the equally disjointed social space of the city, Niuniu describes herself as being in a perpetual state of "estrangement in familiarity" (*mosheng de shuren*) and plagued by an "uncanny" feeling of *Unheimlich* (63; 51). Niuniu's lack of cohesive presence manifests in a stage where she dubs herself "Ms. Zero." Her narcissism can be seen as a means of recuperating a lost sense of self, a condition that invites reanalysis of Freud's discussion of paranoia. Freud's highly contested hypothesis is that the paranoiac is warding off a homosexual wish-fantasy that manifests itself in the "return."[33] Chen Ran manipulates this assumption in narrating Niuniu's subconscious discomfort with same-sex desire, manifest in her dreams, where gender transmutes. Images of her sporadic sensual encounters with Widow He during her childhood and adolescence (54–57, 107–9; 44–46, 86–88) reoccur in dreams where anatomical parts of women and men blend and transform (156–59, 262–63; 125–27, 208). Her homoerotic desires often further mutate into narcissism, as she gazes at her body in the mirror while fondling her breasts or masturbating (183, 261–63; 146, 207–8). While Niuniu indulges in homoerotic visions, the critical voice of societal norms appears to invade these sensual scenes. On one occasion Niuniu dreams of dancing with Widow He, fantasizing that they slowly undress and gaze at each other as Niuniu shivers with narcissistic delight: "She was my mirror" (157; 126). Widow He kisses her, and Niuniu imagines growing a "third hand," her euphemism for a penis, in order to consummate her relationship with the older woman. As they sit panting, Widow He transforms into a man.

Taken aback, I said, What's happening?

He laughed slyly.

I said, I don't need you.

He said, Your lust needs me.

My face flushed red, and I said, In my heart I do not need you.

He said, You don't know yourself. Your real inner need is, in fact, me.

Feeling like I was the object of some joke, I looked anxiously everywhere for Widow He. I backed farther away from the man and shouted, I don't need you, I don't need you at all. . . . (158–59; 127)

In this dream sequence Niuniu's same-sex desire is thwarted as her female lover morphs into a man who insists that her true desire is in fact heterosexual, a point to which she halfheartedly acquiesces. She has, after all, acted on heterosexual desires, although these couplings leave her emotionally empty. Here, Freud's formulation of the paranoiac subject as one who suppresses homosexual desires is turned on its head. Instead, the subject's heterosexual desires impede her longed-for emotional, physical, and spiritual union with the same sex, subverting her goal of self-integration.

In her study of female same-sex desire in modern Chinese literature, Tze-lan Sang reads Chen Ran's *Private Life* alongside a corpus of works that reveal how lesbian desire is commonly trivialized or disavowed in China because of the pervasive belief, voiced recently by Ding Laixian, that "a woman's real happiness (including sexual pleasure in a real sense) . . . can result only from hand-in-hand cooperation with man."[34] Commenting on an explicit sex scene in *Private Life*, in which Widow He seduces Niuniu as a minor, Sang considers possible reasons why the passage was not banned, despite its depiction of child molestation. "Optimistically, one might argue that, by displacing adult eroticism onto a game between an adult and a child, Chen has succeeded in making the censors, who would otherwise have objected to a depiction of female homosexuality, tolerate the ambiguity and excitement of the same-sex encounter. More pessimistically, however, such tolerance might be construed as a sinister denial of the full sexual meaning of female-female contact," says Sang, adding that the Chinese penal code recognizes forced man-boy contact, but not forced woman-girl contact, as clearly sexual and abusive.[35] Because of the complicated history of lesbian desire and censorship in China, it is difficult to determine whether to interpret the novel's dream sequences as validation of heterosexual suppositions of normative behavior, or as the veiled critique of such assumptions.

What ultimately preoccupies Niuniu, however, is neither sex nor her sexual orientation, but her presence: her orientation in space and time. As she states, "Sexuality has never been a problem with me. My problem is different. I am a fragment in a fragmented age" (8; 7). Niuniu constantly assesses the relationship between her body, the city, and historical narrative. Yet she remains dissociated, unable to sustain identification with a holistic image rooted in time and space. Niuniu's childhood pet names for body parts underscore her degree of fragmentation. She calls her arms "Miss No" ("No, we won't get angry," she reminds herself, since she feels that her arms represent her mind), her legs "Miss Yes" (because her legs merely represent her limbs, not her will), and her fingers "Miss Chopsticks" (which she also instructs not to get angry, or they'll cause her to starve to death like the stubborn sparrow) (10–11; 8–10). From a young age she has thought of herself in Lacanian terms, experiencing the fantasy of the "body in bits and pieces," in which mind, limbs, and trunk can go their own separate ways. Niuniu thus regularly depicts herself as a "fragmentary person" who is physiologically and psychologically dismembered, leaving her unable to smoothly integrate the visual imago with the sensational ego.[36]

The implosion of the city compounds the subject's disjointed internal space and results in her breakdown, catalyzed by the sudden loss of the three loves in her life. Freud equates melancholia with the unconscious loss of a love object and the ensuing struggle between clinging to the object and facing reality.[37] Niuniu refuses to accept the fact that her loved ones are actually gone until she returns home from the psychiatric ward (244; 194). In the interim, she seems to follow the trajectory of the melancholic subject as traced by Freud, whereby her ego becomes identified with the abandoned object. For example, after Yin Nan's flight out of the country, Niuniu looks to the sky, thinking she spots an airplane flying toward her, which then mutates into Yin Nan, and finally into a vision of herself flying through the air: "There on the ground was the real me holding a kite string, controlling another self-same me up there in the blue" (223; 178). Her ego has clearly become identified with her lost love in yet another melancholic turn inward to regain a sense of self. Niuniu thus reorders her internal psychic space just as she reorganizes her exterior space, trying to regain autonomy by drawing sharp lines between ego and object, interior and exterior.

Judith Butler contends that the melancholic turn toward the ego to compensate for the lost object marks the partition between ego and object, and the internal and external worlds that they occupy. In her words, "If the melancholic turn is the mechanism by which the distinction between internal and external worlds is instituted, then melancholia initiates a variable boundary between the psychic and the social . . . that distributes and regulates the psychic sphere in relation to prevailing norms of social regulation."[38] What is "lost," in Butler's formulation, goes beyond specific individuals or items to a compilation of unavowable losses to which females and other "persons of lack" in society are always already subject as their egos are being formed.

In *Private Life* Niuniu, the melancholic subject, does indeed lay claim to loss which precedes speech, indicating "I left my mother's uneasy womb to enter a world I feared and was not ready for" (5; 4). Yet she attributes her apprehension not to gendered lack, but to her immersion in "the inexorable flow of time," in "the confusing clamor of the city," "the crowd," and "this modern life of indulgence and 'play,'" all features of the modern metropolis (2–8; 1–7). While I disagree with Butler that female lack necessitates an unfinished process of grieving central to the identifications that form the ego, elsewhere she suggests a less essentialist operation underlying melancholy, arguing that the melancholic subject is constituted in relation to forms of social power which regulate what losses will and will not be grieved, and that it is "in the social foreclosure of grief [that] we may find what fuels the internal violence of conscience."[39] Clearly Niuniu lacks a means of grieving her losses associated with the encroachment of modernity and the urban space. Instead, she is clinically labeled by the doctors as one stricken with "the housewife's disease," agoraphobia, while Niuniu sees herself as mercilessly beaten down by time's rapid passage in modern life, so much so that she believes herself to have contracted "early senility," presaging her impending death. With her prediction that many others will contract this disease, Niuniu's breakdown is revealed as a protest that moves beyond the private into the public sphere. The melancholic urban subject is one who is in revolt against the tyranny of the urgent inherent in modernity, angered at the transformation of the city into forms which subsume the individual, and threatened by the blurring of boundaries between public and private in postsocialist space.

Sun Ganlu's *Breathing*: The Impasse of Narcissism

Sun Ganlu's first novel, *Breathing*, is, in Chen Xiaoming's words, the avant-garde writer's "consummate description of 'urban interiority' [*chengshi neixin shenghuo*]."[40] Set in Shanghai in the early 1990s, the novel details a year in the life of Luo Ke, an angst-ridden playboy in his thirties who adopts a persona from a character in Saul Bellow's fiction—"I am a poet and I have a big dick" (12)—indulging in "liaisons with lovely flowers" in quintessentially Shanghai fashion.[41] A third-person narrator details Luo Ke's stream-of-consciousness musings, which shift through myriad memories in his attempt to define identity. Adrift in the metropolis, he appears to be cut off from ties to nation, family, lovers, and self. Scenes are described in an enigmatic style which avoids concrete imagery; rather, the language flows poetically with lush metaphors and random associations. What moves the narrative forward is not action, but progression toward philosophical and psychological resolution. As in *Private Life*, the materiality of the city is muted in *Breathing*, yet the subject's consciousness is both formed and informed by the city. The novel reflects on the boundaries of the nation, the preservation of autonomy in the city, and the homoerotic and narcissistic inclinations that incite paranoia. Like Niuniu, Luo Ke resists the city, resulting in an ambivalent sense of self and concomitant sense of dislocation as a public citizen.

Shanghai's spatial layout of the time, especially its deficient housing, severe pollution, and acute traffic congestion, contribute to the sense that Luo Ke is stagnant and immobilized in the city. To get to his current girl-friend's home, for example, Luo Ke must bike for fifteen miles, take a one-hour bus, and walk another twenty minutes, making frequent trysts thoroughly inconvenient. But if public space is intolerable, private space is at a minimum. The novel accurately reflects the spatial realities of Reform Era Shanghai, then the most densely populated city in China, where each household occupied less than five and a half square meters (fifty square feet) on average.[42] In the novel's opening scene, Luo Ke invites his girl-friend Xiang An to his home to have sex, as his father is away on a rare business trip. His tiny room is sparsely furnished with a desk and a narrow, uncomfortable bed. It is later revealed that Xiang An lives with her parents as well, but she must also share their bedroom. Another of Luo Ke's girl-friends, worried about his health, advises him to get out more, but the polluted public squares and parks hardly provide an attractive alternative. The idea that stifling interiors and crowded public spaces can alter one's psychological state is a common trope in literature. For example, Dostoevsky implies in *Crime and Punishment* that Raskolnikov's impulse to murder may have arisen while confined to a tiny, cramped room he rarely left, as he felt equally suffocated in the chaotic streets of nineteenth-century St Petersburg.[43]

In addition to arising from his claustrophobic living conditions, Luo Ke's melancholy stems from his disavowed losses. News of his lover Yi Mang's death, in Sydney, frames the novel in its opening and closing scenes, pervading the subsequent narrative with an unsettling tone, though the circumstances and confirmation of her death remain inconclusive until the novel's denouement. Yet Yi Mang's shrouded death is not the focus of Luo Ke's inquiry. Rather, the phone call triggers a series of memories, causing him to reassess his identity in light of his past relationships, his position in the city, and his place in the nation as a whole. After getting the news, Luo Ke hangs up the phone and mutters "I hate this room," offending Xiang An, who is in bed beside him. The narrator clarifies: "He knows that what he means to say is that he's disgusted with some other, larger concept of space" (3). The central problematic of the novel lies in identifying this abstract space, as questions of Luo Ke's sexual identity, urban positioning, and national boundaries are negotiated in relation to it. The novel is consumed by an overwhelming sense of *méconnaissance*, to use a Lacanian term, whereby Luo Ke cannot smoothly integrate his image of himself with the space that he occupies. It gradually becomes clear that traumatic events in Luo Ke's past—fighting in the Sino-Vietnam War as a teenager, the Tiananmen massacre, the emigration of loved ones, Yi Mang's death—have altered his perception of space, due to his psychic identification with these events. Paul Schilder's seminal essay, "Psycho-analysis of Space" (1935), provides insight into Sun Ganlu's highly abstract descriptions of interiority. Schilder indicates that "we live our lives in relation to love objects and our personal conflicts, and this is the space which is less systemized, in which the relations change, in which the emotions pull objects nearer and push them away."[44] In other words, we define private space according to our emotional attachments and traumas, in turn warping our perception of what is exterior to ourselves.

The city contributes to Luo Ke's depression by inciting in him a sense that he has been abandoned by friends and lovers who emigrated from Shanghai. Shanghainese have historically had the highest rates of departure from China, with Shanghainese women marrying foreign men at much higher rates than those from any other city. According to the *Beijing ribao* (Beijing daily) of 27 February 1992, over 1,700 Shanghai women married foreign men in 1991, with Beijing women, only 736 of whom married foreign men in that year, placing a distant second. Shanghainese were some of the first mainland Chinese to exit the country to study abroad in the early 1980s, and the single-minded pursuit of an exit visa only diminished a decade later, as the domestic economy began to provide more opportunities.[45] The rage to go abroad and the resulting disruption to personal relationships were desta-bilizing factors for individuals who remained behind, by choice or necessity. Although Luo Ke betrays little emotional attachment to Shanghai, he ac-knowledges that it has been his "home" for some thirty-odd years, and his disinterest in emigrating belies a tie to the city that he continually reas-sesses. Luo Ke's conversations with his overseas friends hardly whet his appetite to leave. Rather, his friends convey a sense of alienation in their new environs. His conversations with Yi Mang, for example, revealed she had lapsed into a life of drink and pornography, rivaling his own state of degener-ation (101). His friend in Sweden, Xu Bing, self-imposes chastity, fearing sexual disease after excessive indulgence in prostitutes (67). Liu Yazhi writes from Macau about barrenness, beatings by her former husband, her resolve to never remarry (79).

That these immigrants fail to find a sense of identity has a national as well as personal dimension. In a global era, in which demographic shifts include not only mobility from the countryside to the city, but exit from the nation-state altogether, one's identity becomes radically redefined. The foreigner becomes a mirror for self-identification, reminiscent of the alienated recog-nition the infant makes in Lacan's mirror stage. Similar to Su Tong and other avant-garde writers who subvert both the idealized rural imaginary and the vaunted urban modernity, Sun Ganlu deconstructs the cultural ap-peal of both the "domestic" and "foreign."[46] The avant-garde search for a new grounding for identity, a "larger concept of space," recalls Homi Bhabha's postcolonial theory of "Third Space," a space "which constitutes the discursive conditions of enunciation that ensure that the meaning and symbols of culture have no primordial unity or fixity; that even the same signs can be appropriated, translated, rehistoricized, and read anew."[47] Sun Ganlu differs from Chinese humanists such as Zhang Chengzhi who enact self-reinvention via recourse to "the other" (such as Zhang's identity as a Muslim Chinese).[48] Rather than posing the self-other dichotomy in the service of cultural renewal, Sun Ganlu presents a "foreign other" that func-tions spatially as a locus on which existential questions of meaning and iden-tity are infinitely projected but unresolved. Instead, Luo Ke's philosophical reflections are dominated by a drive to "elude the politics of polarity and emerge as the others of our selves."[49] Figuratively and literally situated in post-colonial space, living with his parents in a run-down foreign-style house (*yangfang*) in the former French Concession, Luo Ke is acutely aware of Shanghai's hybrid past as a semicolonial city as he seeks to reconfigure the di-chotomies between East and West, the Motherland and the imperialist Other.

Luo Ke's psychic ruminations on space ultimately converge on the body. The prominence afforded sex and gender in the novel disclose a relentless attempt to salvage corporeal identity from the wreckage of failed utopian values. Luo Ke spends his afternoons at the municipal library, systematically studying national and world histories. His musings on world events brings his personal history into focus, which is intertwined with his memories of developing sexual awareness. Recalling his adolescent years in Vietnam, his sexual associations become fused with memories of his toy planes, made from the scraps of American fighter planes, which he stored with his hoard of hundreds of Mao images (9). The boundaries of his body and those of nations, like so many motley toys in his collection, become inextricably linked in his subconscious. His cultural heritage is also sexually charged as he recalls that his "spiritual sustenance" in youth came from revolutionary novels like *Gao Yubao*, the popular autobiography of a People's Liberation Army revolutionary, whereas his "spiritual snacks" were titillating classics such as *The Golden Lotus* (*Jin Ping Mei*, a Ming novel banned as "pornographic") and the "Barefoot Doctor's Manual" (10).

As the weight of a failed collective identity and the trauma of unrealized socialist visions gathers on the body, Luo Ke attempts to evict the weight of history and fortify personal identity by exercising corporeal agency. The body, as Grosz submits, is the ultimate delimiter of public and private space in the city, yet given the extreme deficiency of both in Shanghai, the limitations of the body itself is suggested. Although he envisions himself as a womanizer, Luo Ke's sexual identity is repeatedly assaulted by homosexual advances, both real and imagined. One solicitation on a crowded bus leaves him feeling soiled and victimized, "yet the feeling is oddly familiar, a sense that permeates his everyday understanding of life in the city" (33–34). His ego boundaries are equally permeable with his older lover, Liu Yazhi, whom he figures as a "maze" in which he loses himself, a "womb" into which he is metaphorically drawn in a reversal of the birth process, and a "siren" with whom he is unable to control his actions. As a result he fears penetration, and his doubts about his sexual identity are heightened. After Yi Mang leaves him, he recoils at the fact he misses her so tremendously, "the way a woman misses her man" (102). Luo Ke suspects he is a latent homosexual, yet stymied by his inability to either love men or commit to heterosexual relationships, he concludes that only narcissistic love is possible (103). Like Niuniu, Luo Ke is unable to resist the modern city's assault on individual autonomy, and he fails to make the distinctions between internal and external that are necessary for ego formation. As a result, he repeatedly "fails" in love, ultimately determining that one has no hope of connecting with anyone but oneself (193).

Eventually, Luo Ke's paranoia in public urban space leads him, like Niuniu, to retreat into narcissism. He cloisters himself in his room, wary of further assaults on his gender identity risked by venturing into the city. Freud considered the defining characteristic of paranoia to stem from delusions which arise from warding off a homosexual wish-fantasy. Freud formulates these from various contradictions of the statement "I (a man) love him (a man)," the final form of which is a complete negation: "I do not love at all—I do not love anyone (i.e., I love myself)."[50] He locates the problem in a "fixation" which occurs during one of the normal stages of development, as the libido passes from autoeroticism, to narcissism, to homosexual object-choice, to heterosexual object-love. Lacan categorically denied that the element of homosexual repression was a cause of paranoia, yet both theorists locate the origin of paranoia in a preverbal, narcissistic stage; thus, paranoia can be seen as a symptom of fragmentation, decentering, and the loss of subject-object boundaries. Victor Burgin takes Lacan's analysis of narcissism one step further, drawing parallels between it and the postmodern urban condition, stating that as global citizens subject to multifarious images in the city, "we are left in a pre-Oedipal stage of fragmentation and disorganization."[51] It is via Burgin's understanding that I find Freudian categories useful for interpreting the prevalence of narcissism as a trope in postsocialist urban fiction. Luo Ke's experience of urban space is of being constantly bombarded by unwanted stimulation, resulting in a feeling of being "torn" and destabilized. Like Niuniu, Luo Ke embraces narcissism as a means of protecting a frail sense of self, preventing him from truly connecting with anyone *other* than himself (192–93).[52]

Mian Mian's *Candy*: Sugar-Coating the Urban Blues

Loosely basing her first novel, *Candy*, on her own experience, Mian Mian (pen name for Shen Wang, a.k.a. Kika) attained cult-like status among "alternative" youth for her hip, and sometimes poetic, descriptions of China's urban underground of promiscuity, crime, drugs, and rock music. Yet the most compelling aspect of her novel is its honest portrayal of the depression underlying relational and chemical dependencies, as when the protagonist, Hong, states during rehab: "First I'd spent all my energy trying to get love and alcohol, and then I'd laid my body down on the altar of heroin, and I had always known that this meant I was lonely and crazy"

(129).[53] Although honest about the source of her addictions, Hong chides excessive introspection: "Lately I've been playing that depressing game of 'What is the meaning of my life?' yet again" (171). During an interview, Mian Mian acknowledged that she addressed the subject of depression because she wanted people to understand that it was commonplace: "It's just like you've got a cold. I give people hope through my experience."[54] And yet *Shanghai Literature* dropped her first story, "Like a Prayer," from its planned publication, in 1987, because it depicted teenage suicide, which was considered too controversial a subject at the time. Similarly, *Candy* was banned by the authorities four months after publication, not for its portrayal of despondent youth, but for its depiction of drugs, crime, and illicit sex. In both instances her works were censored because they invited media exposure to pressing social problems which the party preferred to keep under wraps.

Candy details the life of Hong, a girl who drops out of a "key" high school amid Shanghai's staid culture of the 1980s, intending to "find herself" in the enterprising boomtown of Shenzhen, a Special Economic Zone (SEZ) across the border from Hong Kong. In 1980, Shenzhen was appointed the first of five SEZs nationwide, and a futuristic city emerged from the rice paddies of the one-time fishing village. The SEZs were integral to Deng's economic reforms in the 1980s, as state controls were relaxed in these zones to provide incentives for foreign direct investment and to enable experiments with privatization. Andrea Lingenfelter describes the cultural ethos during its first decade of development: "The relative freedom soon created a frontier mentality, and many forms of vice and corruption came to flourish alongside more legitimate private enterprise. Prostitution, drugs, and organized crime, which had been suppressed to a remarkable degree in post-1949 China, thrived in laissez-faire Shenzhen. At the same time, the influx of investment from Hong Kong, Taiwan, and the West was accompanied by a flood of cultural influences."[55] Mian Mian's own experience of Shenzhen, a place with no history, family, or community ties, left her cold: "A lot of lost people came to Shenzhen from elsewhere. They all dreamed of using money to save their life. It is such a cruel city. It has no heart. There is no such thing as friendship there."[56] In her novel, on the other hand, friendship is all-important. Consequently the urban anomie in *Candy*, unlike that described in *Black Snow*, *Private Life*, and *Breathing*, where the protagonists become isolated in the city, is mitigated by Hong's more resilient ties to friends and family, especially in Shanghai.

Hong comes of age with the city as she makes her way on its mean streets. After forming an unrequited attraction to a noncommittal rock musician and acquiring alcohol and heroin addictions in Shenzhen, she returns to Shanghai, in the mid-1990s, for rehab. The second half of the novel describes her attempts to fend off bouts of suicidal depression while participating in the "confectionary" lifestyle of the Shanghai "bobo" (*bourgeois bohémien*) emerging in Shanghai in the late 1990s. Despite staying clean and gaining focus through writing, Hong recognizes that Shanghai offers little more than "candy" to satisfy her cravings. Shanghai had transformed during Hong's time in Shenzhen, and she finds its ongoing makeover "more beautiful and more hollow all the time" (158). Shenzhen does not come off any better: "I swore I would never come back to this town in the South ever again. This weird, plastic, bullshit Special Economic Zone, with all that pain and sadness, and the face of love, and the whole totally fucked-up world of heroin, and the late-1980s gold rush mentality, and all that pop music from Taiwan and Hong Kong. This place had all of the best and all of the worst. It had become my eternal nightmare" (128).

Despite such malaise, Hong deeply identifies with urban life, unlike Huiquan, Ni Niuniu, and Luo Ke. Before leaving Shenzhen, Hong ponders how her neighborhood has affected the development of her subjectivity.

> It was just a city street. But in the days that followed, I couldn't stop thinking about that street. And while those memories tormented me, that street was still where I had grown up. In the old days, the street was populated with prostitutes, pimps, johns, drug dealers, young girls selling flowers, beggars, and shish kebab vendors. Later on, the police descended on the place, a lot of police, and you didn't see all those people anymore. My street was gone; those warm but terrifying sounds were gone. The stores also disappeared, and new high-rises went up on either side of the road. Their dark eye sockets came to occupy a place in my life, their lights going on, their lights going off. They were always there, in my gray times, in my brightest hours, and there was nothing that could separate me from this secret. Sometimes I suspected that this secret had robbed me of the strength to wait for the future. (123–24)

As terrifying as urban life may be, it also defines her, is an integral part of her psyche; she resonates with its pulses, and, like it or not, can no longer "wait for the future" (124). Unlike Niuniu, whose uneasy immersion in Beijing's "fast forward to the future" leaves her feeling "prematurely senile," Hong is acclimated to this urban temporality.

While not immune from the toxic effects of city life, Hong survives them, in part by embodying stereotypically Shanghainese qualities of superficial-ity and artifice. Hong's narrative is framed by two deaths, the teenage suicide of Lingzi, her best friend in high school, and the apparent suicide of Apple, a gay high school classmate who reintroduces her to the "new Shang-hai" of the mid-1990s. In Shenzhen she mingles with prostitutes, pimps, bouncers, drug addicts, and rock musicians, who are mostly in desperate, often lethal, situations. In Shanghai she is twice forcibly institutionalized with mentally ill murderers before emerging from rehab to reunite with former classmates plagued by drug addictions and fears of AIDS. Although she lives for years in a chemically dependent haze, attempting suicide on a number of occasions, her life force eventually wins out. In fact, her melan-cholic lover, Saining, derides her gloom as feigned: "You say you want to die. You'll never die. . . . Apple died, but you, who have tried to kill yourself more times than I can count, you won't die. . . . You're a first-rate actress. You like anything that's fake" (264–65). Hong ruminates, in response, "I felt re-morseful and afraid. Perhaps all we have is our innocence and confusion, and to lose these would be to lose everything. What the hell had we been up to all those years? That night, I obliterated all of the good that we had shared in the past. I destroyed it all" (265).

In this sense *Candy* poses a challenge to the uniformly dismal portrayal of the melancholic urban subject who devolves into narcissism or (self-) annihilation. Confronted by her melancholic partner, Hong finally "avows" her casualties, to use Freud's term. Recognizing that she had been mourn-ing an adolescent confusion that was no more, she cuts her losses and moves on. Despite her ostensible artifice, an accusation levied by critics against the novel's author as well, Hong's theatricality is a conscious de-fense against the city's harsher realities. For example, after repeatedly sub-jecting herself to stories by naïve-looking mental hospital patients who recount, expressionless, their murder of innocent children and spouses ("my old man was so tiny—just one squeeze and he was dead"), Hong swears off such "honesty." "I swore I would never again ask another patient why she was in this clinic" (137). Subsequently, Hong justifies her new attention to image (versus substance) as a forced attempt to blend in with the city she had deserted in her youth: "I always put a lot of care and effort into picking out whatever clothing, jewelry, and makeup colors I am going to wear, and I need to walk around in a cloud of perfume and to have many secrets . . . I'm just trying to blend in. I need to. It's my way of falling in love with this city, because the truth of the matter is, I never stop thinking about leaving. I've always felt it wasn't right for me, but where else can I go?"

(167). Despite her ambivalence, Hong recuperates agency by replicating the hyped global images that characterize Shanghai, particularly that of its women.

Megan Ferry situates this novel, along with Mian Mian's persona more generally, in the long tradition of the self-fashioning of the woman writer in modern China. "Not only do Wei Hui [the author of *Shanghai Babe*] and Mian Mian join in with other women writers to blur the line between the authorial and fictional self," she argues, "they manipulate the line in a very sophisticated fashion . . . showing that the author, too, is a fictional creation with social, political, and economic performative functions."[57] Stephan Feuchtwang analyzes this newfound agency along similar lines.

> A heightened version of narcissistic *si* is the breaking of taboos of privacy to create scandal that can be commercially exploited, a fiction of sexual life that is apparently also autobiography. There are four agencies of this process. Two of them reside in the writer. One is the narrator of the fiction, who is a sympathetic public commentator on intimacy and narcissism. The other is the writer as self-exhibitionist and aspirant to celebrity. They collude with a third agent: the commercial publisher. The fourth is, of course, the purchaser positioned as sympathizer, confirmed in the goodness of intimacy and narcissism, or as voyeur, admirer or skeptic, open to the claims of rivals to be more authentic exhibitionists of what is secret, painful and vulnerable.[58]

What both Ferry and Feuchtwang suggest is that the writer (especially the female writer) of Chinese urban fiction that features privacy, intimacy, and narcissism is complicit with the social and commercial forces that define her, and therefore any presumption of autonomy and agency is delusional. As evidence of this conundrum, Ferry quotes one of Mian Mian's earlier stories, "La La La," wherein the protagonist says, "When writing I hoped to find rationality, but now the only thing I can confirm is that this time, writing made me into an industrious woman. Damn. Are we really out of control for the sake of freedom or is our freedom itself uncontrollable?"[59]

A writer such as Mian Mian, and her various fictional characters, may be not so much a poser as a fish in waters deemed unsavory by traditional ethical norms. Commercial incentives and market logic have brought literary production more into line with popular culture, provoking fears that Chinese literature is suffering the "loss of its humanistic spirit." Critics such as Meng Fanhua and Ben Xu argue that Chinese intellectuals, by retreating into cultural conservatism, have failed in their mission to impact society.[60] Megan Ferry concurs, concluding that Mian Mian and Wei Hui "not only . . . run the risk of identifying with the commercialism that surrounds their writings, but their 'subversive' project overlooks a pervasive cultural conservatism that does not seek to change reality."[61] Yet one could also argue, as does Shuyu Kong, that the expansion of venues for publishing since the 1990s has "opened up space for greater diversity in public discourse and for a kind of cultural pluralism, thereby freeing literature from the recent decades of political and social moralism."[62] The most innovative artists continually seek new ways of engaging the public, regardless of their material success. That they use new cultural technologies and global media platforms to do so does not detract from their potential to effect change or create new ways of viewing and experiencing the world.

By reading a novel such as *Candy* against a larger body of dystopian city tales, one entertains the possibility of the historical transformation of the melancholic urban subject in China. The four novels under consideration, published between 1988 and 1999, demonstrate the meaning and effects of privacy in the city with a remarkable coherence. In each novel, autonomy is valued as a means of recuperating losses inherent in China's urbanization: loss of meaning, intimacy, self-respect, community, boundaries, space, and ethical norms. While many of the works give credence to the value of privacy as an end in itself (i.e., the respect afforded to rational, autonomous individuals), in practice, the consequent autonomy results in forms of psychological rupture that elucidate particularities of China's cultural context. First, the defensive posture maintained by fictional characters who stubbornly expose idiosyncratic experiences may be due in part to the after-effects of Maoist prohibitions against subjectivity, from the 1940s to the end of the 1970s. Rejection of metaphors of the nation-state or collective, the main literary strategy from the May Fourth period through the 1980s, is one of the key distinctions of postsocialist urban fiction.[63] Second, although large-scale demolition is a regular feature of any metropolis in the world, China's urban modernization is historically unparalleled in terms of its scale and rapidity, and its cultural experience of modernity is accelerated by global flows of information. The privileging of privacy and interiority for these fictional characters is necessarily set in sharp relief against urban landscapes perpetually in flux. Further, the melancholy inherent in city narratives addresses the discontinuity between socialist norms and utilitarian market realities. For most of the protagonists in these novels, the rapid dissipation of idealistic passion in a modern postrevolutionary world devoid of collective ethical standards marks a traumatic instance of confusion and loss. Authors also valorize marginalized cultural values to critique those oppressive discourses and structures that continue to dominate the individual in Chinese society. Just as China's postsocialist avant-garde artists began to capitalize on consumer culture to accomplish their own purposes, the "alternative fiction" examined here avows cultural loss, a psychologically necessary step toward flourishing in the city through alternate modes of empowerment.

6

Postsocialist Urban Ethics

Modernity and the Morality of Everyday Life

If a story seems moral, do not believe it.

Tim O'Brien, *The Things They Carried*

We address ourselves, not to their humanity, but to their self-love, and never talk to them of our necessities but of their advantages.

Adam Smith, *The Wealth of Nations*

The moral philosopher Ross Poole introduces his book *Morality and Modernity* by categorizing the modern dilemma of ethical positioning: "The modern world calls into existence certain conceptions of morality, but also destroys the grounds for taking them seriously."[1] The characterization of modern society as "commercial" or "market" society, given its canonical formulation by Adam Smith in the eighteenth century, continues to dominate mainstream economic thought and conceptions of modern morality. Smith's maxim of self-interest serving the social good, whereby "private vices" are recast as "public benefits," undermined the long-standing premise of virtue ethics that the motivation for an act be continuous with its effects. Once concern with the self is reckoned to be the most effective source of social flourishing, the resulting ethical dilemma, according to Poole, is that the "knight of virtue" must either adopt the quixotic stance of clinging to the moral principle whatever the consequences, or move toward a more utilitarian evaluation of human acts.

Individuals acting according to Smith's reasoning ultimately create an identity independent of their property holdings, work, and social relationships. Whereas in Confucian and Aristotelian virtue ethics these social forms define the place from which choices are made, under the logic of the market they become not sources of identity but roles which one might assume better to achieve one's purposes. Poole traces the ethical dilemma of modernity from the classical political economy of "the market," through the Marxist analysis of capital accumulation, to the Weberian account of modernity as "rationality," and finally to nihilist, liberal, feminist, nationalist, and communitarian detractors of "instrumental reason." He concludes that the moral identity constructed in each of these formulations of modernity—where "reason and morality come apart"— remains a vulnerable one: "We do not have reason to act as morality requires; nor do we have reason to consider the claims of morality to be true." The solution, he suggests, is to go "beyond modernity itself" by creating ways of life which challenge the rationalized structures of mainstream social life, providing for "convergence between our individual well-being and the conditions necessary to sustain the way of life as a whole."[2]

Poole's analysis in *Morality and Modernity* underscores how the concept of the market and its operative moral logic, the fundamental achievement of eighteenth-century classical political economy, still holds today for many in the mainstream of modern commercial societies. Poole's account of modernity is largely informed by Anglo-European sources, yet he details conceptions which have also been formulated, reformulated, or rejected by Chinese intellectuals during China's past century of urban development. Several novels set in urban China in the 1990s depict characters who must negotiate the shifting ethical terrain of the postsocialist city. Qiu Huadong, Zhu Wen, and He Dun write novels dominated by one of the key questions debated by ethical philosophers—the relationship between individual action and the greater good. Narrative ethics have particular salience in contemporary China, as the postsocialist era has seen China's strong tradition of literature as moral discourse threatened by a market-driven popular culture often unmindful of moral mission. By exploring intersections of the narrative and the normative in literature, one can interrogate the shifting relations among text, ethics, and everyday life in late-twentieth-century China, uncovering correlatives between fiction and the ethical issues which arise in conjunction with urban commercial life.

While I do not subscribe to a univalent understanding of modernity, I use the term in two distinct senses here. First, I refer to a mode of life in which an individual's rational faculties reign in lieu of arbitrary, external authorities. The subtle demise of the *danwei*, or socialist "work unit," is a key contributor to the new cultural logic of China's urban space, as urbanites are increasingly free to make their own decisions about livelihood and lifestyle. The *danwei* system, first initiated with the advent of industrialization in the early twentieth century, provided its occupants with a place to work, sleep, eat, and receive all life essentials without leaving the walled enclave that marked the boundaries of their "unit." The *danwei* defined urban culture to such a degree that some analysts have gone so far as to equate the two cultures during the Maoist era. During that time, life in the city was not so much an experience of "the crowd," "night life," "material desire," "alienation," "risk," "stimulation," and the like, as it was a constant negotiation of the confines of an administrative community situated within the larger urban environment. However, as Chinese citizens divorce themselves from government institutions in increasing numbers, becoming employed by foreign-owned companies or establishing themselves as entrepreneurs, founding research institutes and consulting firms, or operating as independent writers, filmmakers, and artists, a new cultural logic is becoming operative.

The hybrid space of contemporary Chinese urban culture is a postrevolutionary society permeated by market values. Nonetheless, cultural theorists such as Dai Jinhua and Luo Gang have pointed out the fallacy of prematurely assigning the Western implications of citizenry to contemporary Chinese society. Dai Jinhua argues that in the 1990s cultural *discourse*, rather than material conditions themselves, actively worked to construct and validate the values of a Chinese middle class, thereby negating decades of socialist striving for a classless society by unambiguously endorsing class-based status. Similarly, Xin Yang characterizes *xiaozi* (petit bourgeois) culture as a fantasy, attributing its prominence to media constructions rather than to the lived realities of a political class. Luo Gang also decries the fact that theorists are far too eager to make ready connections between a "market society" (*shichang shehui*) and the independence from the state that results in an active "public sphere" (*gonggong changhe*). He agrees with Dai that *middle class* has become a misleading term in cultural discourse, becoming code for China's imminent emergence as a new modern state girded by a "civil society." Luo argues instead that the public sphere in China will follow a unique trajectory that differs from the progression theorized by Habermas in relation to the former Eastern Soviet bloc.[3]

In addition to the historical argument of rationality, where the rise of a semi-civil society in China is affording increased autonomy from the state,

I also refer to a more concrete notion of modernity: the individual and collective experience of the modern world, particularly as it is embodied in ideas which represent a reaction to the social and economic processes of modernization. Among many contemporary urban Chinese there is a consciousness about being modern, a taken-for-granted feature of life embedded in everyday thinking and behavior. While urban fiction of the 1990s has been critiqued for its forthright, thus "unimaginative," depictions of everyday life, what is fascinating about this stylistic turn away from the avant-garde and historical fiction of the 1980s is precisely its emphasis on the everyday and the relationship of such a move to historical shifts in modernity.[4]

From the perspective of urban aesthetics in other settings, it is quite remarkable the way in which various cultures pioneered new art forms that, despite the separation of centuries, exhibit a common thread celebrating ordinariness. In his discussion of "Dutch-led mercantile modernity, British-led industrial modernity, and American-led consumer modernity," for example, Peter Taylor details how in the midst of the "High Tradition" dominating seventeenth-century Europe and its culture of absolutism, the Dutch developed a counter-baroque style of "realism" based on scenes from the world in which they lived.[5] Dutch genre painters drew directly on their own experiences to mirror life as they saw it, and rather than relying on commissions, they sold their works, thereby creating the first art market. The English novel of the eighteenth century relied on depictions of comfortable middle-class life to appeal to a mass market. By the mid-twentieth century, Hollywood films had turned from portraying the glamorous life to depicting more secure, cozy, and domestic scenes of everyday American life. The same bourgeois domesticity is evident in all of these genres—ordinary people living comfortable lives. During the thriving economy that fostered Song dynasty urbanization a similar phenomenon occurred in the transition from the tradition of court painters to the emergence of professional artists who sold their works to urban citizens, often depicting scenes from everyday life, such as that in the early-twelfth-century silk painting *Qing-ming shanghe tu* (Spring festival on the river). Each of these aesthetic developments demonstrates a relationship between depictions of everyday life and a market economy. Likewise, postsocialist Chinese urban fiction portrays the comforts of the Chinese middle class, yet this mode of existence is immediately put into question. The characters in new urban fiction rarely revel in their well-to-do status without deliberation, and they often make radical lifestyle changes.

The increased possibilities for autonomy that have emerged in China's contemporary urban culture have caused the average citizen to reexamine her values in conjunction with lifestyle choices, an especially difficult task given the new stratification of society due to privatization and market forces. By the late twentieth century, both the traditional Confucian mores demeaning merchants and the modern socialist values condemning capitalists had been largely undermined. According to the literary critic Li Jiefei, in the late 1980s Chinese urbanites began to openly flaunt their wealth without concern for appearing unethical, and "[by the early 1990s] nearly everyone became willing to openly state that the reason they worked so hard was for financial gain, no longer considering it immoral to do so."[6] Further, new technologies of transportation, communication, and socialization have intensified domestic and global flows of population, commodities, and information. Hence, the urgency with which ethical questions are explored in the urban fiction of the 1990s derives in part from the fact that a broader sector of society is impacted by the logic of the marketplace than during previous periods of urbanization in China.

It is in this context that new ethical dilemmas arise for urban Chinese citizens. Under the logic of the market, altruism, or the aspiration to a "higher" ideal than pure self-interest, is considered irrational behavior. Yet while the persistent rhetoric of loyalty to the state above self rings hollow to the average Chinese citizen, shadows of both socialist and Confucian ethics remain. How, then, does one live in a society in which the kind of identity presupposed by the market is that of an individual whose well-being may best be achieved in ways which detract from the overall social well-being? Morality in the modern world, including in contemporary urban China, is often asserted nostalgically as a bygone, inaccessible entity.

Of course there are ethicists who dispute the notion that modernity is unable to sustain a moral grounding. Charles Taylor, for example, has provided an elaborate framework for reclaiming what he terms the "ideal of authenticity" which underlies, but has been misconstrued by, the culture of individualism and moral relativism operative in contemporary Western societies.[7] Jürgen Habermas, in his comprehensive theorizing of modernity, amends Max Weber's exclusive emphasis on instrumental rationality by introducing the notion of communicative interaction and its salutary ramifications for the public sphere.[8] While their projects differ in approach, both Taylor and Habermas attempt to negotiate the gap between self and other, subject and society. In other words, they try to bring together the two questions which dominate ethical inquiry yet suggest sharply incommensurable points of view: the ethical question addressing the public sphere, "How ought one live?"; and that determining individual morality and the constitution of the self, "What ought I to do?" Rejecting a Nietzschean genealogy of morals, and subsequent deconstructionist discourse which concludes that acts and motives are contingent, overdetermined, invariably self-interested products of prevailing ideologies, these critics argue that ethical principle is still relevant to public life.

Since the 1980s Chinese intellectuals have deliberated the relevance of various formulations of modernity, including Habermas's neoliberalism and Taylor's communitarian philosophy, to contemporary China.[9] With the rise in the late 1990s of what Xudong Zhang has termed postnationalism, scholarship by Chinese liberals began promoting more classical Anglo-Saxon traditions of liberalism, offering Chen Yinke and Gu Zhun as pioneers of this line of thought in early-twentieth-century China. The Shanghai philosopher Zhu Xueqin's seminal essay on liberalism (1998), for example, argued that private property, a free-market economy, and a negative conception of political liberty were essential to progress in China.[10] The literary critic Wang Xiaoming, initially influenced by the rising tide of *guoxue* (Chinese learning) which emphasized scholastic research on Chinese social, cultural, and intellectual history, conducted regular seminars for young scholars in Shanghai, introducing them to the works of leading Chinese thinkers on the ethics of modernity, including the philosopher Wang Guowei and the cultural historian Chen Yinke.[11] Despite these more measured attempts to historicize the liberal discourse of public ethics, the Leftist scholar Wang Hui rightly concludes that the dominant "ethics" in post-Reform China is neoclassical economics, which, "understood in its most rigidly liberal acceptation, has acquired the force of an ethics in China. Laissez-faire axioms form a code of conduct, as rules of the commodity which no agent may violate. So currently economics is not just a technical discipline, any more than its predecessors [sociology in the late Qing; the natural sciences during May Fourth]: it too is an imperative world view."[12]

The Narrative Ethics of Postsocialist Urban Fiction

Chinese literary theory has traditionally promoted narrative, which serves as the "example," to illustrate the moral choice, which is, by necessity, the ultimate end of ethical inquiry. Yet, while literary theory remained embedded in ethical paradigms throughout much of the twentieth century, the intensely commodified post-Mao popular culture has challenged literary culture's ability to suggest a distinct moral mission. Many of the cultural debates in China in the 1990s centered on morality and the relationship between individual action and social good, particularly in the absence of restraints on human behavior that prevailed under socialist modes of production. A nationwide debate over the loss of "humanist spirit" (*renwen jingshen*) was launched, in 1993, by liberal cultural intellectuals in Shanghai who criticized the effects of market reforms, which resulted in the increasing irrelevance of the humanities as the commodity came to monopolize the public sphere. They lamented the vulgarization of society, maintaining that Chinese society had "lost" its moral sensibilities, especially its knowledge of "ultimate concerns" (*zhongji guanhuai*).[13] Not unlike Robert Bellah, who decried the threat that utilitarianism and expressive individualism pose for public life, these scholars sought to recover a language of commitment to a greater purpose.[14]

On the other hand, those critics who disagreed with such a dour assessment of contemporary culture instead celebrated the "postmodern sensibilities" exhibited by the very works criticized by *renwen jingshen* advocates. Notably, two of the most prominent targets of the *renwen jingshen* debates, Wang Shuo's fiction and Jia Pingwa's *Feidu* (City in ruins, 1993), also represented breakthroughs in urban fiction. Subsequent urban fiction written in the 1990s was referred to by various epithets, including "new urbanite fiction" (*xin shimin xiaoshuo*), "new generation" (*xin shengdai*), "belated generation" (*wansheng dai*), and "new state of affairs" (*xin zhuangtai*), the latter term resulting from intense discussion between the Nanjing-based journal *Zhongshan* and the Beijing-based *Wenyi zhengming*, as they attempted to characterize the urban fiction of Liu Xinwu, Wang Meng, He Dun, Han Dong, Zhang Min, Zhu Wen, Lin Bai, Chen Ran, Qiu Huadong, Wang Anyi, and others.[15] Postmodern critics celebrated the absence of "interiority" in these "unreflective" works, which directly represented the raw, vulgar reality of contemporary urban culture. Chen Xiaoming, for example, saw in these city narratives a desire to "capture the external shape of contemporary life, to plunge into this life on its own terms, so as to be freed, in the process, from the Enlightenment nightmare long bedeviling literature."[16] He claimed, "Life in this age already has no interiority. People are obsessed with elevating themselves from poverty, and are continually incited by the prospect of instant riches. Writers of the 'belated generation' have a firm grasp on such tendencies of our time. Without any polishing or ornamentation, they put in front of us the chaotic and vibrant conditions of such a life, presenting a swift, indiscriminate flux of phenomena. Their method of directly representing the appearances of life serves to highlight the rawness of a coarse and vulgar reality."[17]

Chen and other "post- critics" have devoted many writings to the cause of rejecting what they believe to be the elitist and moralistic tradition of modern Chinese literary discourse.[18] The anti-ethical bias that dominated Western literary theory during much of the latter half of the twentieth century permeated critical circles in China as well. The Peking University professors Chen Xiaoming, Dai Jinhua, Han Yuhai, and Zhang Yiwu, the Tsinghua University professor Wang Ning, the writer and former minister of culture Wang Meng, and the Nanjing editor Wang Gan are well read in the critical schools that arose or redefined themselves during what Geoffrey Galt Harpham terms "the Theoretical Era" (1968–87). Harpham points out that each of the most prominent schools, including semiotics, deconstruction, feminism, Marxism, and psychoanalysis, took as their founding premise the radical inadequacy of such Enlightenment concepts such as "the universal subject," "the subject of humanism," or the "traditional concept of the self."[19] Ethics for many was but a cover for power, hypocrisy, and unreality, and became heavily implicated in the assessment of crimes committed by or on behalf of the Enlightenment subject.

For many "post" and "New Left" Chinese literary theorists, the collective investment by Chinese academics in the 1980s in so-called Marxist humanism and other thinly veiled Enlightenment projects, followed by the "Chinese learning" of self-styled liberals in the 1990s, merely perpetuated the intellectual elitism and paternalism that has traditionally inhibited popular participation and a vital public sphere in China. Xudong Zhang, for example, claims that "despite its posing as quasi-political dissent, the new scholastic discourse operated within the safe parameters of academic professionalization and through the marketing of knowledge, both of which are along the official lines of 'socialism with Chinese characteristics.' "[20] Neo-Marxists such as Zhang decry the extent to which the complex interactions between the postsocialist state and global capital are neglected by neoliberals who simply pit the total state against the universal civil society. He claims that neoliberal Chinese scholarship tends to perpetuate binary oppositions, whereas New Left intellectuals, who regularly participate in critical-theoretical discourses in Western academia, question both socialist and capitalist assumptions of universal modernity. While some New Left critics, such as Wang Ning, have a tendency to merely repackage previously formulated theories, others, such as Gan Yang, Cui Zhiyuan, and Wang Hui, have engaged in genuinely innovative approaches to theorizing modernity from a postsocialist context.[21] Similarly hybrid theories are forming in the newly emerging and open-ended discourse of ethical criticism in the Western academy; thinkers such as J. Hillis Miller, Stanley Cavell, Simon Critchley, Ewa Ziarek, Robert Eaglestone, Geoffrey Galt Harpham, and Martin Halliwell have sought to reconsider the moral implications of what Miller calls the "act" of reading by fusing the poststucturalist insights of continental theory with the more analytical impulses of Anglo-American criticism.[22]

From the perspective of more substantive formulations of narrative ethics, the debates in China between those advocating a return to Enlightenment values and those promoting postmodernism seem simply to confuse moralizing with morality. Perhaps because the new urban fiction was written neither as national or cultural allegories, as were the avant-garde works of the 1980s, nor as the thinly veiled didacticism which has dominated so much Chinese literature, these tales of everyday life were assessed either as decadent deviations from literature's true purpose or as refreshing departures from the plague of authorial judgment.[23] Yet Chen Xiaoming's laudatory claim that the new urban fiction lacks "interiority" is not supported in close readings of the fiction which he commends. There is no mistaking this fiction's blunt verisimilitude; yet one cannot consider it "unreflective." China's late-twentieth-century urban tales, far from being perfunctory narratives, are permeated with questions of individual morality and "ultimate concerns." Unlike renwen jingshen advocates, I do not primarily think about narrative ethics in relation to the beneficial or harmful effects of stories. By this I do not mean to suggest that "mature" readers are somehow immune to the effects others may suffer. Even now when I read Yu Hua's 1987 story "Xianshi yizhong" (One kind of reality), for example, I tend to gloss over his surrealistic descriptions of violence given the shock I experienced in my first reading. Does this mean Yu Hua's fiction is "bad" for me? Am I masochistic to expose myself to the violence of his text over and over again? It is a valid question, but one which is impossible to answer, partially because, as Wayne Booth points out, "the minds we use in judging stories have been constituted in part by the stories we judge. Thus there is no 'control group' consisting of untouched souls who have lived lifetimes without narrative so that they might study unscathed the effects on others."[24] More important, the minds we use to judge stories are constituted by our unique subjectivities, the particular lives we live, our individual experiences and sensitivities.

Yet unlike neo-Aristotelians such as Wayne Booth or Martha Nussbaum, neither do I consider literature to enable a heuristic working out of ethical difficulties. Instead of approaching literature as a kind of rehearsal of life that scholars such as Nussbaum set in opposition to "theory" (both by moral philosophers and by literary critics), Geoffrey Harpham believes that "within ethical theory, narrative serves as the necessary 'example,' with all the possibilities of servility, deflection, deformation and insubordination that role implies."[25] The ethics of narrative, Harpham insists, is inherent in the formal characteristics of its plot.

> The most general and adequate conception of a narrative plot is that it moves from an unstable inaugural condition, a condition that *is* but *ought not*—through a process of sifting and exploration in search of an unknown but retrospectively inevitable condition that *is* and truly *ought-to-be*. Narrative cannot posit a static *is*; this function is allocated to "description," which inhabits narrative like a cyst. Nor can it prescribe an unresisted *ought*: this is the business of sermons. What it can—indeed what it must—do is to figure a process of rejecting disjunction in favor of ultimate union. Narrative plot thus provides what philosophy cannot, a principle of formal necessity immanent in recognizable worldly and contingent events that governs a movement toward the eventual identity of *is* and *ought*.[26]

Harpham's account of narrative ethics is compelling, particularly because his formulation of ethical criticism is consistently informed by Emmanuel Levinas's maxim that ethics is defined by engagement with the other. Harpham's account of the formal necessities of plot of as a representational structure that negotiates the relation, cultivated by ethical philosophers since Hume, of *is* and *ought*, is viable. However, the teleological prescription that plot *must* result in the ultimate union of the two appears inadequate. Can one conclude, for example, that what "is" at the conclusion of Yu Hua's "One Kind of Reality"—the penis of the victimizer-victim's dissected body is grafted onto another patient—is what "ought" to happen? Perhaps, if one defines narrative closure as Harpham does, as achieving a moral order that is "other" to that which preceded it, an "other" to whatever it is in the narrative that *is* but *ought not to be*, such as the foiling of an attempt to thwart the propagation of progeny.

Theorists such as Richard Kearney argue that "storytelling is never neutral" in that "there is no narrated action that does not involve some response of approval or disapproval relative to some scale of goodness or justice—though it is always up to us readers to choose for ourselves from the various value options proposed by the narrative. The very notion of cathartic pity and fear, linked as it is to unmerited misfortune, for example, would collapse if our aesthetic responses were to be totally divorced from any empathy or antipathy toward the character's ethical quality."[27] The problem is that some fiction fails to adhere to such strictly Aristotelian notions of narrative. Postmodern narratives such as D. M. Thomas's *The White Hotel* or Yu Hua's post–Cultural Revolution short stories do not deliver the requisite value options that Kearney guarantees for narrative. Consider, for example, Andrew Jones's apt description of Yu Hua's postmodern short stories: "In Yu Hua's fiction violence is presented in the absence of any of the familiar interpretative codes with which we might assuage the queasiness and visceral disgust that his work often provokes."[28] Marsha Wagner concurs that Yu Hua's early fiction "avoids all moralizing, value judgment, class analysis, and other kinds of didactic language. On the surface of Yu Hua's work there is no message, no positive model, no moral lesson. He presents non-heroic characters who have lost their will power and are driven by inner and outer forces beyond their control."[29] Kearney admits that narratives of trauma do challenge his theory, citing Lawrence Langer's account of Holocaust narratives as "the most convincing argument I have come across to date *against* the ethical character of narratives."[30]

The inadequacy of the foregoing accounts of narrative ethics derives from the fact that they focus almost exclusively on plot, while failing to attend to language itself, which is the basis of the Chinese hermeneutic tradition. A helpful corrective is offered by Levinas, and by scholars such as Simon Critchley and Robert Eaglestone, who have related his philosophy to literary criticism. For Levinas the ethical relation is one in which I am related to the face of the other whom I cannot evade, and an ethical reading is one in which one reads against what is *said* in the text in order to remain faithful to what the text *says*. This understanding of literary ethics goes some way toward resolving the fundamental tension between Aristotelian and classical Chinese poetics: in the former, the ethical moment is found in the relationship between the constitutive parts of narration; in the latter, language itself is moral. The canonical declaration in Chinese poetics that *shi yan zhi* (the poem articulates what is on the mind and heart intently) becomes a way of verbalizing a pre-ontological condition, a said that reveals the saying, to use Levinas's terms. This differs from an Aristotelian understanding of mimesis, because in the Chinese formulation poetry is not subject to analysis as an object distinct from its maker. Whereas a poem is something made (*poiema*, "a poem," from *poein*, "to make"), a *shi* already exists; it can only be refined and crafted. To quote Stephen Owen, "The *shi* is not the 'object' of its writer, it *is* the writer—the outside of an inside."[31]

To complicate matters, the Taoist tradition of narrative ethics recognizes, as does Levinas, the limitations of language in conveying ethical truth. The Laozi begins with the famous line "The Way that can be told is not the constant Way," and Zhuangzi reiterates this idea: "The Great Way is not named, Great Discriminations are not spoken. If the Way is made clear, it is not the way. If discriminations are put into words, they do not suffice."[32] Like Zhuangzi, Levinas qualifies the usefulness of words because "the said, the appearing, arises in the saying. Essence then has its hour and its time. Clarity occurs, and thought aims at themes. But all that is in function of a prior signification proper to saying, which is not ontological. Our task is to establish its articulation antecedent to ontology."[33] For Levinas, as for Zhuangzi, the saying is all too easily transformed into *doxa*, to such an extent that it is "forgotten" in the said.

Another challenge posed by the Chinese tradition to Aristotelian narrative ethics is the stark fact that Chinese moral narrative was dominated by history, whereas fictional narratives, or *xiaoshuo*, literally "minor accounts," initially modeled on the oral tales of Buddhist storytellers, were traditionally considered, as Lu Xun writes in his history of Chinese *xiaoshuo*, "chit-chat of no great consequence."[34] Timothy Wong points out that "the dependency on orality, and oral storytelling's propensity to wander easily from *shi* to *xu*—from what is actual to what is made up—are what fundamentally kept *xiaoshuo* '*xiao*' or 'minor' in a narrative tradition which, quite opposite to Aristotle's, favored deliberate literate accounts of what *did* happen over spontaneous oral accounts of what *could* happen."[35] Liang Qichao and his successors, especially Lu Xun, attempted to change the social and moral status of Chinese fiction, and many literary critics in China today are inheritors of the May Fourth tradition that affords fiction the ethical powers once restricted to history and especially poetry, the purpose of which, according to the Great Preface to the *Book of Songs*, is to influence the world, to teach and transform man. Theories of narrative ethics require an awareness of the complex ways in which literature in various traditions has, and has not, signified as moral discourse. Understandings of narrative informed by Levinas's Judaic ethics, a Taoist understanding of language, and a Chinese poetics which accounts for the immediacy, subjectivity, and contingency of the creative act provide a more full-bodied account of the relationship of narrative to ethics than Aristotelian poetics alone. By accepting such insights, one can understand even narratives of trauma as ethical narrative, not because they function heuristically, allegorically, or teleologically, resolving the tension between what *is* and what *ought-to-be*, but because they stand as bleak witnesses to inhumanity.

Qiu Huadong's *Fly Eyes* and the Dilemma of Quotidian Existence

Ethical questions permeate the novel *Yingyan* (Fly eyes, 1998). Qiu Huadong recounts, in five stories, the lives of professional youth in Beijing and, consciously modeling himself on Dos Passos, he provides a pastiche of individual lives that inform the complexity of the city. The characters in his novel acknowledge that they are "two-dimensional people" (*pingmian ren*) who resist delving into existential questions. Yet, while they indulge in hedonistic urban pleasures, they also admit they are "bored" and "disgusted" with such a lifestyle. What distinguishes Qiu's depiction of this generation is his characters' uneasy self-consciousness about their superficiality. As in most postsocialist urban novels, in *Fly Eyes* each of Qiu's characters make abrupt lifestyle changes in the early 1990s, often from being idealist artists, poets, or scholars to being businesspersons in every conceivable line of work. But as they recollect the idealism of their pasts, those satiated with the get-rich materialistic lifestyle of the 1990s attempt to return to a slower, more holistic, simpler way of living. It soon becomes obvious, however, that the "thinkers" and "closet idealists" in Qiu's stories are unable to survive in the new logic of the metropolis. Those characters who attempt to find a deeper sense of meaning and value in the city perish in the attempt, whereas the "survivors" are those who opt to live prosaic, middle-class lives.

The first of the five stories features Yuan Jingsong, a twenty-something fashion-magazine photographer whose daily routines are particularly poignant demonstrations of urban decadence. Jingsong's habits include spying on his newlywed neighbors through the zoom lens of his Nikon camera from his high-rise apartment on the Third Ring Road, obsessively watching Sharon Stone films, and stalking women along Beijing's thoroughfares. There are multiple textual indications that his obsessions arise from his sense of modern isolation in the crowd, as demonstrated by his observation of passengers on the Beijing subway, where "everyone sitting there was thinking their own thoughts, some even using the newspaper to hide their faces as they read, and others still wearing their sunglasses . . . with no one willing to make eye contact with anyone else" (2).[36] As Georg Simmel theorized about turn-of-the-century Berlin, the modern metropolis is governed by the need of its inhabitants to distance themselves from other individuals in the crowd, the "fear of contact, a spatial fear stemming from the too rapid oscillation between closeness and distance in modern life," a familiar urban (non)response to the saying, as theorized by Levinas, that "passivity to which the ego is reduced in proximity."[37] Zhang Ailing described the same tendency in cosmopolitan Shanghai, in her short story "Fengsuo" (Blockade, 1943), where the passengers in a stopped tram furiously read everything at their disposal to avoid making eye contact with others.[38] Such mental distancing becomes essential to maintaining one's identity in the crowd, but repeated failure to acknowledge the other inevitably creates a sense of isolation alien to human nature.

In *Fly Eyes*, Jingsong's desire to reverse the isolationist aspects of the modern metropolis and create meaningful connections with others motivates him to enact extreme measures. He quits his job and attempts to live as a "nature man" within the city. Camping out by the moat which had surrounded the former city wall, the foul Hucheng River now encircling Beijing's Second Ring Road, Jingsong's organic form of contact with the crowd dispels his loneliness, and he regains a sense of social connection and intimacy by sending handwritten letters to his friends, instead of using computers or fax machines. After fortuitously photographing a murder, he infuses his life with meaning through an obsessive pursuit to single-handedly crack the case. He does apprehend the murderers, but is unable to defend himself, and they easily dispose of him. Jingsong had already tipped off the cops, who arrive in time to arrest the criminals, but find Jingsong, whom they label an "anonymous bystander," shot to death at the scene. The story concludes bluntly with the evening paper's account of Jingsong's death: "At the scene there was also an anonymous man who got caught in crossfire while crossing the road. The police are investigating his identity" (69). The irony is obvious: the attempts of this would-be hero to counter the alienating effects of the city by enacting virtue are quixotic. Yuan Jingsong dies in the city as an inconsequential, unknown entity, the very fear which grips the alienated Beijing protagonist of Liu Heng's *Hei de xue* (Black snow, 1988), one of the first post-Mao urban novels. Such narratives castigate the operative logic of the market economy in the 1990s. To quote Allan Bloom, a well-known critic of the moral mediocrity bred by modernity, "There is nothing particularly noble about [modern life]. Survivalism has taken the place of heroism as the admired quality."[39]

Qiu follows this first story with another tale of a quixotic attempt to find significance within the strictures of the urban marketplace. "Wild Nights," part 2 of *Fly Eyes*, recounts how four of Yuan Jingsong's former classmates try to dispel the boredom of their daily routines in the city by playing madly at "night games." The opening scene, in which they lie alongside the tracks of an oncoming train in a game of "Who dies?," exemplifies the extremes to which they go to seek their thrills. Each manifests troubling signs of maladjustment to city life. Zuo Yan is obsessed with videogames, isolating himself from his friends and even venturing out to the tracks to "play" the game alone; Qin Jie, a former poet who owns a sports-car dealership, gets high on the "speed" of fast cars and fast women; Yu Lei is ousted by his "wife," whom he had pragmatically married in order to register for an apartment; and He Xiao gambles away his earnings in the stock market ignoring his home life altogether. Bored by their "night games," He Xiao persuades the others to get pilot licenses, so they can do "air art" for kicks. One day the friends enter forbidden airspace above Beijing's commercial district, where the police threaten to shoot them down if they don't halt. The others turn back but He Xiao keeps flying into the commercial district above the Third Ring Road. " 'He's crazy,' Qin Jie said. 'He's completely insane!' But He Xiao was perfectly sober. His flying skill was excellent, yet he knew he was out of fuel so had no choice. Blinded by the sunshine glaring off the glass walls of a shopping center, he closed his eyes and crashed into it. From a distance, the vestiges of He Xiao's helicopter looked like a tree branch jutting from that seventy-floor building" (111). Qiu Huadong's repeatedly use of such disjunctive nature metaphors to describe gruesome urban scenes foregrounds the alienating artificiality of the city. In what has now, post–September 11, become a particularly poignant image, the pilot crashing his plane into a seventy-floor skyscraper in Beijing's commercial district highlights the impassivity of the shiny modern symbol of progress, which mocks any attempts by these urban novelty-seekers to alter the capitalist forces shaping the modern metropolis. Global capitalism gives rise to a Chinese urban cultural aesthetics where hegemonic images proliferate, replete with both imagined and historical referents.

While two of the friends, shaken by He Xiao's death, leave their ranks in the newly emergent middle class by being airlifted to the wilderness to live as *yeren* (savages), cut off from civilization, Zuo Yan, an Internet addict, remains in the city. The final scene features Zuo Yan in a cozy apartment, making love to his new bride, whom he has met over the Internet, and dreaming of one "savage" cannibalizing another in a barren northeastern forest (152). Again, this urban fable foregrounds the modern ethical dilemma. Those characters who strive to find meaning perish in the attempt, whereas the survivors live prosaic, middle-class lives. Zuo Yan "survives" by reinvesting himself in the very scripts which dominate modern urban life, where ordinary life itself becomes a central moral value, and work and family are affirmed in place of the allegedly more transcendent values of, say, philosophic contemplation, religious devotion, or revolutionary zeal. Here, as in many of Qiu's stories, "idealists" are unable to flourish in the city, yet their omnipresent specter haunts his depictions of urban middle-class life. Zuo Yan's postcoital dreams of the noble savage betray his sense of unease in the city: "The savage in the forest was all alone; perhaps he had relied on his partner's flesh to survive. The sun peeked through the depths of the forest and seeing it the savage was suddenly aroused. Knife in hand, he let out a sharp whistle as he ran wildly toward the sun. The tone resonated in all four directions, a lonely yet glorious sound. Zuo Yan rolled over and this dream vanished. Now in his dreams he was fleeing through the city in his car, with another black Nissan in hot pursuit. Unable to unwind, he drove madly through the city streets" (152–53).

Qiu Huadong's tales of bourgeois life emphasize the terror inherent in the claustrophobic predictability of middle-class life. This dread is aptly illustrated in the paintings of fellow Beijing resident Zeng Hao, who, like Qiu Huadong, subverts middle-class representation by introducing anxiety into his images of interiority and domesticity. In paintings such as *5 p.m. in the Afternoon* (1996), a miniaturization of a couple in their modern apartment, a sense of angst arises from a skewed spatial relationship within an overwhelmingly empty environment. The insecurity within the interior space derives from its "collectivity," since everything in it represents knowledge shared by society at large. The space has no set boundaries, only stereotypical images. Zeng's paintings of these miniaturized lives, like Qiu Huadong's urban tales, disembody middle-class representations by foregrounding their reproducibility. The miniature, as Susan Stewart explains, is something that does not attach itself to lived historical time. Unlike the metonymic world of realism, which attempts to erase the break between the time of everyday life and the time of narrative by mapping one perfectly on the other, the metaphoric world of the miniature makes everyday life absolutely anterior and exterior to itself. The reduction in scale that the miniature presents skews the time-and-space relations of everyday life, and as an object consumed, the miniature finds its use value transformed into the infinite time of reverie.[40] The titles of Zeng's paintings—for example, *December 31st, Thursday Afternoon, Yesterday, Friday 5:00 p.m., 17:05, July 11th*—

Zeng Hao, *4:06, May 9, 1998,* oil on canvas, 175 x 200 cm. Courtesy Zeng Hao.

further illustrate the illusion of modernity, which like the miniature narrowly focuses on the infinite present by indicating a quotidian moment, rather than a significant date in history. This "flattening" or self-conscious "forgetting" of the past is also one of the hallmarks of urban fiction in the 1990s, which results in a sense of distorted reality by conveying a sense of perpetual present.

Another story from *Fly Eyes* features a heroic figure whose death appears more tragic than quixotic. "Two-Dimensional People" juxtaposes the lifestyle choices of two brothers. As the story opens, the younger brother has changed his career from philosophy student to night-club disc jockey, much to his elder brother's dismay. At large in the wee hours of the night, often frequenting other clubs after getting off work, the DJ winds up in a context of heightened danger, as organized crime in the city operates on much the same hours. Unaware of these perils, he declares himself a "two-dimensional man" who "belongs to the night," and soon hooks up with He Ling, an alluring "woman in red" who shares his values. The elder brother's job is hazardous by choice—he is a beat cop responsible for busting

Zeng Hao, *October 27, 2004*, oil on canvas, 150 x 130 cm. Courtesy Zeng Hao.

organized crime rings in Beijing. Predictably, He Ling, helplessly caught in a tangled web of crime and unable to "escape the city," where "bullets fly and people die," implicates the DJ. The elder brother later dies while defending the couple from a notorious mobster (268). Once again, the "hero" perishes, while the "petty man" (or self-styled "two-dimensional man") survives and "gets the girl."

Disgusted by the city's evil excesses and the superficiality of contemporary urban practices, the couple concedes they are nevertheless already wed to it: "We'd want to return [to Beijing] the moment we left it, because this is our stage, it is the place which nourishes dreams, and we depend on it for our very breath" (250). Despite their repulsion, they recognize their reflection in the faces in the crowd as desperate individuals lacking character. To reverse the hollowing experience wrought by modern urban life, the couple self-consciously adopts the prevalent mindset of the middle class, namely, the belief that one must organize one's activities and identities around certain goals—that without these goals life would be pointless. They vow to renounce their nightlife and instead embrace a mainstream lifestyle of "substance." But

Zeng Hao, *Midnight June 11, 2005*, oil on canvas. Courtesy Zeng Hao.

their affirmation of middle-class values brims with tongue-in-cheek cynicism. "Suddenly He Ling and I realized we should bid our nightlife adieu, dismiss our two-dimensional lifestyle, and start engaging in the daytime. Precisely! From this day on we will engage in the daytime and go about 'adding,' vigorously pursuing that reliable, substantive part of life. We'll work hard, earn money, buy a house, buy a car, buy a television, have a kid, respect our parents, take on the most tiring and banal responsibilities of life. Forge ahead! Charge into life and be a person of substance. We smelled the fresh morning air, the air which would sustain our breathing for the next half of our life. Forge ahead!" (293). Such sarcasm about the predictability of modern every-day life, rather than leading to a radical redesign of society, actually bolsters the status quo. The mock revolutionary zeal with which the couple adopts bourgeois values contrasts sharply with their awareness of the superficiality of consumer culture, which they had once castigated. Yet their strategy of self-consciously distancing themselves from the social arrangements to which they are party provides a sense of satisfaction that is incompatible with a desire for change.

Indeed, the bourgeois reinforcement of the status quo is one of the primary manifestations of modernity in the urban marketplace. Meng Fanhua accurately characterizes the "new cultural conservatism" that prevails among China's urban elite: "First, it rejects radical criticism and opts for moderate and steady discursive practice. Second, it gives up anxious concern about and questioning of the collective, focusing on the personal; third, it declines quests for ultimate values, goals, or faith, and is instead concerned with solutions to local problems."[41] In Qiu Huadong's city narratives the characters that successfully negotiate the city space exhibit precisely these characteristics, whereas those who seek ultimate values, radical lifestyle choices, and contribution to the collective good perish. By ludicrously underscoring the logic which informs social conservatism among the Chinese middle class, Qiu Huadong's narrative also implicates the self-satisfied scholasticism of intellectuals. Predictably, the new professionalism among Chinese academics has given rise to a series of attacks by critics. Ben Xu, for example, has launched an extensive argument against the new social conservatism among Chinese middle-class intellectuals, claiming they have capitulated to the state agenda of renewed nationalism in the 1990s.[42] Xudong Zhang claims that the symbolic capital of high academic discourse (largely modeled on American academic practices) "has reinforced a social ego taking part in the heightened social division of labor and a new middle-class ideology."[43] Wang Xiaoming interprets China's enthusiastic post-reform embrace of a new ideology of consumption and excessive individualism as an overreaction to the traumatic memory of revolution and collective deprivation.[44]

The ironic truth that Qiu Huadong's narratives present is that despite the media hype over China's ostensible "liberalization" and emerging "individualism," Chinese urbanites subject to the constraints of commercial culture experience the same limitations as their counterparts elsewhere. There is no doubt that market capitalism has increased social productivity, but at the cost of dissociating this from a certain degree of human happiness. It has achieved not satisfaction, but frustration; not creativity and repose, but endless repetition, punctuated with occasional satiation. And it is an achievement of capitalism that it has succeeded in identifying this state of affairs with a concept of rationality. Ultimately, the ethical dilemma played out in Qiu Huadong's narratives of "free" individuals is well summarized by John Stuart Mill, who delineated contradictions between the Enlightenment principles of autonomy and the lived reality of conformity, which is a denial in practice of this very individuality. In *On Liberty* Mill states,

Society has now fairly got the better of individuality, and the danger which threatens human nature is not the excess but the deficiency of personal impulses and preferences. I do not mean that they choose what is customary in preference to what suits their own inclination. It does not occur to them to have any inclination, except what is customary. Thus the mind itself is bowed to the yoke: even in what people do for pleasure, conformity is the first thing thought of; they like in crowds; they exercise choice only among things commonly done; peculiarity of taste, eccentricity of conduct, are shunned equally with crimes; until by dint of not following their own nature they have no nature to follow: their human capacities are withered and starved.[45]

The problem with indulging desires in consumer society, according to Mill, is that it merely replicates earlier forms of repression by propagating the lowest common denominator of the masses, rather than providing avenues for individual expression and identity. In modern market societies one's identity is no longer given by the culture of the *polis*, the *danwei*, the commune, or the neighborhood. Property, housing, work, and even social relationships become exchangeable items with the same external relationship to their owners as any other commodity. Because the tremendous creativity unleashed by capitalism also entails immense destructiveness, modernity enacts a contradiction between the actuality of power and the equally inescapable experience of passivity. To quote Marshall Berman, "To be modern is to find ourselves in an environment that promises us adventure, power, joy, growth, transformation of ourselves and the world—and at the same time, threatens to destroy everything we have, everything we know, everything we are."[46]

Seeking "The Good" in Zhu Wen's *What's Trash, What's Love?*

Whereas Qiu Huadong's stories in *Fly Eyes* read rather transparently as morality tales, Zhu Wen's novel *Shenme shi laji, shenme shi ai* (What's trash, what's love?, 1998) explores ethical questions with far more subtlety.[47] Zhu Wen's comic novella *Wo ai meiyuan* (I love dollars, 1995) shook the literary establishment with the carefree manner in which the young male protagonist, a Nanjing author in his early twenties, has casual sex with prostitutes and even arranges for his father to join him in his escapades. This attempt to turn the sexual conservatism of the 1980s on its head (while adding a twist to the notion of filial piety) is one of the hallmarks of the urban literature of the 1990s—a celebration of individuality and social freedom often expressed in sexual licentiousness.[48] While retaining the witty tone of his earlier work, Zhu Wen's *What's Trash, What's Love?* engages themes raised in *I Love Dollars* in far more depth. Zhu Wen depicts the angst and confusion plaguing Xiao Ding, a floundering Nanjing writer in his late twenties, and his circle of friends, which is not easily remedied by lucrative jobs, free love, drugs, or even sacrificial volunteer work. Rather than writing about social aimlessness in a didactic, moralizing manner, Zhu Wen meticulously recounts his protagonist's thoughts and actions, leaving the reader to draw his or her own conclusions. Xiao Ding is a conflicted character who obstinately refuses to assist a friend's search for his daughter (who had been kidnapped and gang-raped, an increasingly common occurrence in the Chinese metropolis), but then actively seeks to do volunteer work in an attempt to find purpose. The novel ends as it opens, with the protagonist alone in a crowded bar, his mouth gaping wide in a ludicrous silent scream, an appropriate coda for a work that depicts modern urban life as cyclical and meaningless.

As Xiao Ding is one of a growing number of freelance artists, there is no work unit to monitor his comings and goings. His days are not governed by any organizing principle—they blend together just as his frequent naps fuse his waking and sleeping hours. Like many characters in urban fiction of the 1990s, Xiao Ding appears to be controlled strictly by desires for sex, nourishment, sleep, and autonomy. Although he initially maintains a modicum of social interaction, he becomes increasingly cranky and withdrawn, especially after contracting venereal disease. Toward the end of the novel he rarely makes contact with others, preferring to isolate himself within his apartment. On the one hand, he ostensibly values his privacy and prevents others from encroaching it, apparently so that they will respect his autonomy. He is only willing to help others on his own terms and views any attempt to force his hand as a violation of his agency. Yet as the novel progresses, it dawns on him that something is amiss in such an autonomous lifestyle, and he begins a fruitless search to make what he refers to as "real contact" with others.

One of the novel's most humorous incidents conspicuously underscores the prevalence of alienating norms in urban culture. Bored by his bohemian lifestyle, Xiao Ding seeks out a charitable agency to do volunteer work. When the director of the Love and Virtue Foundation interviews him, however, she is utterly incapable of comprehending that he would be willing to do "something for nothing," and becomes obsessed with discovering his ulterior motive for volunteering. Xiao Ding's altruistic aspirations are thwarted, as Love and Virtue remains firmly wed to the logic of the marketplace. This ludicrous illustration of the utilitarian ethic dominating consumer society demonstrates that it becomes "common sense" to assume that self-interest is the only real motivation for behavior. Xiao Ding's "voluntarism" fiasco deals his laissez-faire approach to life a severe setback. His encounter with the strictly utilitarian logic operative in society slowly alerts him to his moral incapacitation and insignificance. Where he had once indulged in sex at whim, he has painfully experienced the consequences in his diseased body, and where he had once felt no qualms about living his life strictly based on his own desires, a low-grade anxiety now plagues him.

While the narrative resists interdiegetic introspection, it invites the reader to engage in a series of extradiegetic questions, to use Gerard Genette's terminology. What is an individual conceived by utilitarianism if not a passive subject, subject *to* rather than the subject *of* his wants? If in one sense such an individual is at the center of social life, given that the market aims at the gratification of his desires, does he not drop out of consideration in another sense? Is not such an individual little more than the place of origin of these desires and the equally empty place of return? Zhu Wen's novel illustrates how the ceaseless activity of the market obscures the circularity of the path between desire and gratification, and how one of its main functions is to conceal the emptiness of the ends pursued. In his essay on the novel Huang Fayou also relates Xiao Ding's aborted attempts to engage in society through charitable work to the supremacy of exchange value in a market economy: "The tide of turning people into commodities is the real cultural root cause miring Xiao Ding in the bog of alienated freedom. In this age when the principle of exchange becomes the highest norm and the snares of mutual exploitation are all around, if a single frail individual does not want to turn himself into a thing, then it seems the only choice is to find freedom in the fragmentary."[49]

In a final scene Xiao Ding tries to explain to a former girlfriend his quest for "real contact" with life. She naively concludes that "sexual contact" is what he is really after; much to Xiao Ding's chagrin, even *this* idea now repulses him. He senses for the first time that he is, in fact, in search of something more substantial than the superficial life he has been living. It seems that the protagonist has been unconsciously attempting to answer the question implied by the novel's title: is there in fact a "greater good" such as "love" to be achieved in this life? Or is it all, in the final analysis, simply trash? The novel pursues this question through the protagonist's repeated engagement with the immanence of "face": how does one respond to the presence of the other? In the absence of the regulation provided by the state-owned work unit, the individual is afforded so much autonomy he is almost at a loss. Not only must he regulate his daily routines and coordinate his social activity, with the deterioration of ethical norms inherent in socialism it also becomes incumbent on him to develop an entirely new value system. The ethical saying, to return to Levinas, requires that before the face one not merely contemplate it, but acknowledge it. While the text of Zhu Wen's novel, the said, portrays a character woefully incapable of responding to others, the dominant motif, or "saying behind the said," of the entire novel is the ethical "putting into question of my spontaneity by the presence of the other." Zhu Wen's novel functions ethically by repeatedly demonstrating the pervasiveness of what Levinas calls the "exposedness to the other where no slipping away is possible."[50]

The final image of the novel, Xiao Ding sitting alone in a bar with his mouth agape, calls to mind classic motifs of urban alienation such as that encapsulated in Edvard Munch's *The Scream* (1893), where the subject's angst is inextricably tied to the presence of nameless "others" who highlight his sense of aloneness. Zhu Wen's portrayal of Xiao Ding's foiled attempt to do good, and his new self-awareness in the wake of sexual disease, seems to corroborate Nietzsche's claims that the alleged good of altruism is parasitic on egoism and that sickness is necessary for self-knowledge. Xiao Ding exhibits what Nietzsche termed passive nihilism; he is one who takes a last desperate stand on behalf of morality in the belief that morality and meaning are lost but *ought* to exist, rather than being an active nihilist who not only accepts the loss of morality but celebrates it. As if corroborating this worldview, Zhu Wen and other Nanjing writers indicated, in an interview in 1997, that their writing demands a degree of courage which few in society can muster, for their work impels them to "gaze directly upon the purposelessness of modern life."[51]

Indeed, the perception of a lack of "ultimate concerns" in postsocialist culture was the very crisis that launched the "humanist spirit" (*renwen jingshen*) debates. In them the Shanghai literary critic Wang Hongsheng acknowledged the excruciating condition whereby "the historical facts of the twentieth century have shattered everything ever believed in by humanity" without shattering the *need* to believe.[52] In his study of Zhu Wen's fiction Jason McGrath, drawing on analyses by Song Mingwei and Wang Hongsheng, argues that Xiao Ding's nihilism is instead the very foundation of his freedom.[53] He compares Xiao Ding to the figure of Benjamin's flâneur, where "the protagonist's lack of material motivation or ideological direction [is] accompanied by a genuine autonomy of both mental and physical movement. . . . [T]he very precondition of the individual's new freedom is the disappearance of stable social institutions as anchors for the individual subjectivity."[54] Detachment from external loci of control requires the subject to create his own meaning.

He Dun's Fatalistic City Narratives

He Dun differs from Zhu Wen and Qiu Huadong in that his morality tales lack their sardonic edge. Instead, He Dun delineates in a matter-of-fact way the moral fallout accompanying urban business success stories. He Dun graduated from art school in the 1980s and taught art in a Changsha middle school for a number of years before quitting his job to do business in interior design. His lifestyle change, from idealistic academic to practical businessman, followed the pattern of many in the early 1990s who chose to "take the plunge" (*xiahai*) into business. With his changed lifestyle came an evolution of his values and worldview, so he wrote to describe attitudinal shifts that accompanied the "new state of affairs" of the 1990s, where individual choices abounded and personal ethics were redefined and reexamined. He first gained critical acclaim for his realistic accounts of Changsha, in his novellas *Didi ni hao* (Hello, younger brother, 1993), *Shenghuo wuzui* (Life is not a crime, 1993), and *Wo bu xiangshi* (I don't care, 1993).[55]

Hello, Younger Brother features a young man, Deng Heping, who is disillusioned after failing to get into Peking University and unmotivated by his subsequent job as an elementary school teacher. He eventually quits his job and joins a classmate selling cigarettes on the open market. Through this pursuit, he meets and falls in love with his classmate's wife, Dandan, whose contacts get him a job managing a nightclub. After his classmate is executed for dealing heroin, and Heping's own marriage to a singer-turned-movie star sours, he marries Dandan, and the couple starts an extremely successful business supplying decorating materials. But the story ends on a shocking note: just as Heping has established himself in a profitable job with a lovely wife, both his wife and unborn child are killed in a motorcycle accident. In *Hello, Younger Brother* the value of material success in the 1990s is shown to be as ephemeral as political or academic success proved to be in the 1980s.

Throughout his works, He Dun provides detailed descriptions of how conspicuous consumption functions pragmatically in the market. Xiaobing

Tang points out that "Heping first signals his rise in status by smoking an American brand of cigarette, and his footwear progresses from generic 'pointy and shiny black shoes' to 'Italian-made crocodile skin shoes,' which he is quick to put up on a table as a means of convincing his friends of his ambition. When the business of his Hongtai Decoration Materials store flourishes, bringing in a net profit of 700,000 yuan (equivalent to U.S. $85,900), he rewards himself by upgrading his Chinese-made Nanfang motorcycle to a Royal Honda."[56] The sign value of objects reinforces a logic of differentiation and establishes a distinctive hierarchy of taste, status, and identity through participation in what Baudrillard terms a "social discourse of objects" that contributes to a "general mechanism of discrimination and prestige."[57] According to Dai Jinhua in her perceptive article on the politics of Chinese pop culture, the Chinese media greatly contributed to this logic of differentiation by defining their targets in terms of middle-class taste and consumption levels. Discussing an article, in a 1995 issue of *Jingpin gouwu zhinan* (Best buys), that provides detailed instruction about what merchandise to buy to live up to a given income level, and a housing ad that states, "For those who have high status," Dai concludes that commercial culture has entered Chinese public discourse as unambiguously class biased.[58] He Dun's narratives illustrate Dai's point. Heping has already "read" the "political economy of the sign," to borrow Baudrillard's terminology, and is well aware of the utilitarian function served by his consumption. By flaunting his material success, Heping is able to attract more business, simultaneously enticing friends and lovers.

Yet He Dun destabilizes such capitalist power dynamics in his fiction by recalling their radical divergence from the ethics of an earlier age governed by ideals of social equality and socialist mottoes of "to each according to his or her need." The opening and closing scenes of *Hello, Younger Brother* provide an ethical framing to an otherwise fairly straightforward narrative. The novella opens with a description of Heping's revolutionary father, who was appointed assistant county head at the age of twenty-six after leading a brigade of communist guerrillas in ousting his own landlord father from his estate. His progress toward a bright future, however, is arrested by subsequent political upheavals and his father's legacy as a landlord, so he fails to advance beyond his initial position. Similarly, Heping's success starts when he is twenty-six, and by the time he is thirty he truly seems, in the words of Confucius, to have "established himself." In relating Heping's rise and fall to his father's, He Dun also links Heping's tragedy to the historical transformation of the political *guangchang*, or "square," and all it signified to the father's generation, into the commercial *guangchang*, or "shopping plaza," of the postsocialist era. Ultimately consumer culture, like revolutionary politics, fails to ensure stability.

Recognizing the contingent nature of success in the market economy, most characters in He Dun's fiction adopt a fatalistic worldview. In the closing scene the narrator recounts Heping's agony over the tragic fate of his wife and unborn child, via a series of "what ifs": "if" Dandan hadn't insisted on going to the department store on Shaoshan Road to buy an artificial flower arrangement for the living room of their newly decorated apartment, "if" Heping's motorcycle had been repaired on time, then his wife's last, primal scream would not eternally haunt Heping. Early in the story, Heping's encounter with Dandan is also credited to fate.

> That morning, as Didi [Heping] rode his motorcycle to Double Swallow Wonton Shop, he bumped into Dandan, who was just leaving the shop. How lucky! If he was still at home talking with his wife, if he had given the "Mainland Girl" film script a serious read, he wouldn't have run into Dandan today, and probably wouldn't have run into her in a lifetime. Dandan's uncle had just arranged a job for her in an office on Hainan Island. If that morning Didi had, as usual, spent five mao at that dumpling stand to buy two *baozi* [steamed buns], he wouldn't have run into Dandan. It just so happened that for the past few days that man from Hubei only put a tiny amount of filling in his *baozi*, infuriating Didi every time. Yesterday he bitterly censured the peddler, "Your *baozi* are getting worse and worse! They're not even worth biting into!" Today he didn't even glance at him as he rode past. Of course, Didi could have gone to another stand or to a noodle shop to eat breakfast, but it was probably providence that he passed the Double Swallow Wonton Shop, not even thinking about wontons, but fifty or so meters past the shop he suddenly realized he wanted them. (333)

A similar litany of coincidences concludes the story, framing Heping's greatest "success" in life as circumstance. While the notion of *yuanfen*, or "destiny," is the bedrock of traditional Chinese popular belief, He Dun's recurrent references to fate strike the reader with renewed force in the wake of twentieth-century campaigns to eradicate "superstitious ideas" in mainland China.

In fact many directly relate the resurrection of superstitious practices in the 1990s to the market economy. He Dun elaborates on this in one of his more ideologically explicit novels, *Ximalaya shan* (The Himalayas, 1998).

As the teacher-turned-businessman protagonist puts it, "Few Chinese businessmen in the 1990s adhere to faith or ideology, they rarely mention beliefs, politics or ideas, and they definitely don't discuss movies or art; what they talk about is superstition. That's the entirety of their belief system!" (358).[59] He proceeds to enumerate the ways in which superstition rules Chinese business practices, from calling on diviners to determine auspicious dates for groundbreaking or buying a car, to choosing lucky names for the business. While such reliance on fortune might seem to detract from entrepreneurial initiative in a burgeoning commercial society, the notion of fate also relieves the individual of a demoralizing sense of personal responsibility for failure. A fatalistic mindset provides comfort to an underdog or loser, such as the struggling teacher in *Life Is Not a Crime*, while allowing for self-congratulation when one becomes successful, as when the teacher finally succeeds in business.

Whereas He Dun's earlier works present bleak, minimalist vignettes of the tumultuous rise and fall of fortunes, his later novels, such as *Women xiang kuihua* (We are like sunflowers, 1995) and *The Himalayas*, introduce introspective protagonists actively searching for ideals in a decadent urban environment only to find that their seeking fails to provide any spiritual grounding. In *The Himalayas*, as in Qiu Huadong's stories, the market logic of the metropolis resists morality; holistic forms of identity are sought instead in small towns and the pristine Tibetan mountain range. The novel recounts the life of an attractive, artistic couple, Huang Jiangli and Luo Ding, who teach in a Changsha middle school. Jiangli's struggles with Principal Peng, who refuses to promote her, and Ding's gradual rise to prominence in the Grand Cultural Development Company, where he has relocated, creates tension between the couple as their values come into conflict. Disillusioned with her dead-end job, Jiangli makes up excuses to spend more time with her parents in Whitewater, the small county seat of her youth. She reunites with high-school classmates who still reside there and spends her time socializing, gossiping, and dancing with them. She soaks in the fresh air and regains her small-town "heroine" status, admired by the townspeople for her beauty and musical abilities. Luo Ding feels suffocated by small-town life; as disgusted as he is with Changsha's pollution, he finds himself longing to return to his home there: "No matter how good a county seat may be, it's always twenty years behind the provincial capital" (86), he declares to his wife, whom he denigrates for being so "countrified" (362). Luo Ding also seeks to escape the pressures of the urban grind, but for him this takes the form of dreaming of travel to the Himalayas, which figures symbolically as the ultimate utopia.

Though Luo Ding senses money will not satisfy his deepest longings, he feels pressured by his in-laws to raise his menial social status as a teacher. Consequently, after he is promoted to company manager and supplied with a pager, cell phone, motorcycle, and expense account, he shows off his new belongings and revels in his status during a visit with Principal Peng, who has terrorized their lives in the school *danwei* with his petty autocracy. Luo Ding is ecstatic when, as he is in the middle of lambasting Principal Peng, blowing smoke in his face from his expensive American-brand cigarettes, his pager and cell phone sound simultaneously, "fucking ringing off the hook!" (364). As in He Dun's earlier novellas, commodities conspicuously serve as power brokers, immediately raising an individual's social "worth." The perks of Luo Ding's new job not only boost his social standing, but also alter his perception of the world. Whereas he had previously spurned the propositions of a divorced female colleague, Yuanyuan—attracted instead to "gentle, virginal" women like Jiangli, not women with a "strong sex drive"—it is precisely at this juncture of the novel that he begins to find Yuanyuan attractive (95). Taking her up on a "business invitation" to tour Shenzhen, he allows "thoroughly modern Yuanyuan" to "remake" him, leading him to dance disco, purchase fashionable clothes, and truly experience a "real city," where he dazedly counts the stories on the shiny skyscrapers. In the end, however, Luo Ding is inconsolable when Jiangli leaves him for a new job in Whitewater, and he never fully adapts to his new lifestyle in business.

The novel is rife with pathos and nostalgia for a sense of goodness that seems irretrievably lost in the modern world. Stereotypically, the ills of the city are conveyed via its "fallen women." The "virginal" Jiangli must return to more rural abodes to regain her pristine innocence, while worldly Yuanyuan epitomizes the attractions and vices of "Babylon." Similarly, Luo Ding bemoans the inevitable decline of his secretary, who has taken to drinking and swearing "with the boys": "Even the good girls like Xiao Liu change in such a society" (377). Sensing that the only possibility of regaining his moral integrity is either to retreat into a backward town, as his wife had, or to leave civilization altogether, Luo Ding opts for the latter. Yuanyuan travels with him to the Himalayas, but returns alone, reporting that he perished in an avalanche. The novel closes with Xiao Liu recalling Luo Ding's abrupt departure for the mountains: "I remember how Luo Ding . . . threw his motorcycle key, his cell phone, and his pager on Manager Yang's desk and said, 'Manager Yang, I'm returning this stuff, I'm leaving.' Then he turned to look at me and said gently, 'I'm leaving, Xiao Liu.' I was stunned that he said 'leaving' because he should have said 'see you later.' Was this some sort of sign?" (408).

The novel is unquestionably melodramatic, yet the protagonist's desire to "leave it all behind" is indicative of a growing sentiment among urban professionals. As for so many modern professionals worldwide, Tibet functions as an oasis in the popular imagination for an increasing number of Chinese urbanites who, according to media coverage, see the isolated region of snowcapped mountains as a simpler, untainted alternative to the pressures of modern life. In 2002 more than 720,000 Chinese tourists visited Tibet, up nearly 30 percent from the previous year. A growing number, like our novel's protagonist, have no intention of returning to their previous urban existence. A article in *The Washington Post* in 2003 reported that some—like Fei Tiere, a fifty-six-year-old former Shanghai electrician, or "Nyima Tsering," a thirty-three-year-old former Beijing software engineer—have quit their jobs and, "determined to leave behind their old life and everything it represented," even adopted Tibetan names. Fei's journey to Tibet, like that of so many, was motivated by the sentiment that urban life has become a matter of "keeping up with the Joneses": "In Beijing, in Shanghai, it's all about materialism. Your neighbor buys a car, and then you have to buy a better one. Life is so stressful. But here, it's different."[60]

In postsocialist urban aesthetics, long-standing cultural norms of moderation, the socialist legacy of equality, and the search for more sustainable lifestyles call into question the rising income gaps and rampant corruption of capitalist modernity. Many artists follow a trajectory similar to that of He Dun, in which earlier ambivalent or cynical attitudes toward consumer culture become more explicitly critical of urban corruption at the beginning of the twenty-first century. For example, Zhu Wen's second film, *South of the Clouds* (Yun de nanfang, 2004), counters the ills of consumer modernity by taking solace in traditional values and rejecting the modern city for a pristine, rural existence. Similarly, the notoriously cynical filmmaker Feng Xiaogang levels serious critiques of decadence and corruption in his commercial hits, *Cell Phone* (Shouji, 2004) and *A World without Thieves* (Tianxia wuzei, 2005). In these films Feng departs from his more straightforward irony (associated with Wang Shuo's fiction) of "mocking everything" (*tiaokan yiqie*), instead creating films which, while still entertaining, deliver a more transparent "moral." In each of these twenty-first-century narratives ethical issues of neoliberal capitalism are critiqued through nostalgic recourse to traditional, yet increasingly inaccessible, rural values, expressing deepening collective anxieties about modernization.

The Paradox of Ethics

As a renewed emphasis on Leftist ethics emerged in the latter half of the 1990s, Chen Xiaoming's initially laudatory assessments of the urban fiction of that decade turned more critical. In 1999, in a book on contemporary urban fiction, he argued that "the majority of 'belated generation' authors overemphasize the superficial and emotional aspects of contemporary life while rarely detailing the contradictions arising from rapid accumulation of capital. The 'belated generation' is full of vitality but lacks profundity."[61] Ironically, in 2000, in a book on postsocialist urban culture, Wang Xiaoming, who (against Chen Xiaoming) had disparaged most earlier urban fiction, praises narratives of the late 1990s, such as Zhu Wen's *What's Trash, What's Love?*, for exposing "an extremely great spiritual problem," which is, to his mind, the only topic worthy of literary inquiry.[62] Similarly, in 1999, in his book on urban fiction, Li Jiefei praises the proliferation of urban "narratives of desire" (*yuwanghua xushu*) because to his mind such works evidence sensitive engagement with recurrent real-life dilemmas, rather than shallow responses to market demands by lowering literary standards to create bestsellers.[63]

In a brief rejoinder to the many critics who have accused urban writers of moral decadence, Qiu Huadong acknowledges the challenge of writing ethical narratives. In his essay "Who Is the Enforcer of Morality?," he criticizes those who indiscriminately confuse an author's moral code with that conveyed in his fiction: "During a period in which the economy is rapidly developing without the control of a cultural and ethical system, it is necessary to be vigilant about spiritual values. Who, however, acts as the enforcer of that morality? Who is authorized to be the judge? Unfortunately it seems that the possibility of establishing space for ideological pluralism remains in the very distant future."[64] Qiu Huadong's wariness recalls Mu Shiying's tone in "Preface to *Public Cemetery*" when he defended the Shanghai modernists of the 1930s against attacks of "urban decadence" from both the Left and the Right. The defensive tone of both rebuttals calls attention to the fact that despite several decades of decline in "public ethics," ethical ideas lie deep in Chinese culture, where notions of "being a good person" and "behaving properly" remain embedded in the grammar of everyday Chinese language. Further, it demonstrates the tenacity of a prevalent mode of criticism that interprets fiction at the level of plot and thematic content rather than by examining the *saying* behind the *said*. Such critical approaches overlook the powerfully ethical dimension to these narratives, which is their most defining feature.

A sensitive reading of postsocialist urban fiction reveals that it underscores the ethical issues that emerged as the crumbling ideologies of the 1980s were supplanted by the logic of the market, leaving individuals with the burden of creating new belief systems. The fictional characters analyzed in this chapter respond to the ethical dilemmas posed by consumer modernity in a variety of ways. In *Fly Eyes* Qiu Huadong's characters attempt exaggerated heroics, hermit-like retreat, and mock allegiance to prosaic middle-class values as a means of instilling their lives with purpose. Zhu Wen's protagonist is a passive nihilist, self-aware but unable to enact a meaningful modern existence. He Dun's characters take solace in traditional values, countering the ills of consumer modernity by resigning themselves to fate or by rejecting the city for a pristine, rural existence. In all three novels the protagonists seem incapable of establishing a moral basis for modern urban life. Once they become self-conscious they resort to extreme measures to extricate themselves from the ethical dilemma of engaging in mundane, everyday modern life, with its apparent lack of idealism and purpose. The characters eventually reflect on their actions with the recognition that something is amiss in their modern urban lifestyles. In most cases these authors conclude their narratives in an open-ended fashion, which results in moral ambiguity. They may not achieve satisfactory answers to their attempts to transform what *is* into what *ought-to-be*, yet these authors unquestionably probe ethical issues arising in relation to their urban reality. Postsocialist urban narratives suggest an ongoing inquiry into the relationship between individual authenticity and public ethics by grappling with pressing ethical questions that arise in conjunction with modern commercial life. The real paradox of ethics is that a discourse that seems to promise answers is so obsessed with questions.

Conclusion

Sustainable Chinese Aesthetics

Several years ago at an academic conference a colleague declared that our research interests are born of trauma. Despite an affinity for Jungian introspection, I dismissed this idea out of hand. The process of writing this book made me reconsider. Did my adolescent experience of uprooting from my urban neighborhood community to a sterile new suburban development beg for expression? Perhaps my renewed sense of community while teaching in a Nanning work unit awakened an earlier sense of loss. Did my intense identification with the hopes and anguishes of the 1989 demonstrations speak to something in the collective unconscious? Yet there was more. This study was also galvanized by everyday, but equally significant, experience: my "humanities-deficient" engineering education, for example, and my brief career in the automobile industry. I began to perceive, however inchoately, flaws in *Roger and Me* trickle-down economics and in bloated corporate business interests. I observed colleagues at computers gleefully tuned in to news reports, delighting in "Operation Desert Storm," the first major conflict involving the United States since Vietnam. I sensed a parochial nationalism and faith in pseudorationalism that eluded more pressing historical, cultural, and environmental questions. Observing similar trends in Chinese society led to my central research question: how is capitalist urban development changing Chinese culture? What seemed key to answering this question was the study of aesthetics, an area of inquiry seriously undervalued during the Deng and Reagan eras, when science, technology, and economics reigned supreme. I believed, perhaps naively, that the time and effort expended in answering various dimensions of this question would be well spent, and would resonate beyond a Chinese audience.

Today my scholarly interests swing back to the scientific pole. When I first embarked on field research on Chinese urban aesthetics, I left behind a part-time job at the NASA Goddard Institute for Space Studies, where my office was adjacent to that of James Hansen, the scientist who in 1988 presented his now famous climate forecast before Congress, at the invitation of Senator Al Gore. At the time, my dual identities as "cloud studies data-input clerk" and "Chinese literature doctoral student" seemed light years apart. No longer. In the twenty-first century, China's exponential urbanization poses hazards to far more than its cultural identity; its development threatens the very survival of the planet. On the other hand, its development could also save it. Some of the most creative solutions to sustainability are inherent in the Chinese aesthetic tradition, evidenced by the increasing international prominence of architects, designers, and artists who integrate classical Chinese aesthetics into modern technologies. Chinese aesthetics in painting, poetry, architecture, and garden and urban design prefigure one of the essential concerns of sustainability, harmony between humans and nature (*tianren heyi*). The renewal among a growing number of artists and practitioners of the spiritual and social principles inherent in classical aesthetics, disparaged under Maoist socialism and postsocialist neoliberalism, may guide the just and sustainable application of science, technology, and economic development.

Environmental issues are notably absent in this volume, but can be extracted from its conclusions. One of these conclusions is that Weberian specialization of knowledge may threaten the survival of the species, despite having yielded stunning technological advances. That the conceit of limitless technological prowess appears in ancient wisdom literature, such as the Hebrew tale of the Tower of Babel, underscores that while such presumptions are nothing new, they demand vigilance. Prioritization of one realm of human knowledge (e.g., "the sciences") over another (e.g., "the humanities") presumes a divide that is artificial at best and, if taken to extremes, detrimental. When Mao reversed these priorities during the Great Leap Forward, prioritizing human voluntarism over scientific rationality, tragedy ensued. What is necessary now, as the move toward urban cultural studies in China suggests, are more holistic forms of intellectual inquiry that make explicit the dynamics between scientific and economic theories and the ethical, social, and environmental resources that sustain them.

This bourgeoning of urban cultural studies is a significant manifestation of new urban aesthetics in China. Inspired by critiques of capitalist urban mass culture pioneered by the Frankfurt School for Social Research, Althusser's and Gramsci's Marxism, and the Centre for Contemporary Cultural Studies of Birmingham University, Chinese intellectuals are targeting uses of scientific rationality and ideology that annihilate human freedoms and natural environs. Just as mass-society theorists viewed industrialization as atomizing urbanites both socially and morally, Shanghai intellectuals view the decline of mediating social organizations resulting from postindustrial urbanization as giving rise to a spurious and ineffectual moral order. Similarly, the emergence of the idea of "Thatcherism" by members of the Centre for Contemporary Cultural Studies has inspired new understandings of the positioning of urban intellectuals given the hegemony of neoliberal development.

A second conclusion I draw from this study is similar in kind; that is, it is not so much a finding as a confirmation of the wisdom of traditional poetics. I have drawn on Aristotelian assumptions about art, seeing the poet as an imitator *and* creator disclosing the *telos*, or "ultimate form" of actions, through peculiar forms of *mimesis*. These aesthetics dovetail with the seminal Confucian statement on art in the Shujing (Book of Documents) that the *zhi*, the "preoccupation" of the artist, what is "on the mind intently," becomes a *shi* (poem) when properly articulated. As the seers of culture, as those who closely observe natural and social phenomenon, artists give word, tone, and form to operative principles and their potential outcomes. The urban aesthetics of Fang Fang, Liu Heng, Zhang Huan, and Jia Zhangke thus expose the historical, social, and environmental underbelly of municipal development practices, as a corrective to official dogma. Artists such as Cai Guo Qiang, Zeng Hao, Chen Ran, and Qiu Huadong reveal the apocalypse imminent in everyday urban middle-class life. Mian Mian, Lou Ye, Shi Yong, and the Gao Brothers seriously play off popular culture, these deeply cynical, deeply idealistic "truth-tellers" denouncing the very artifice they fixate and capitalize on. Artists are not above the ills of society, but in extracting and articulating its principles and obsessions they reveal truths and attend to cherished, if obscured, human values. Relations between the "artist," the "artifact," and the "world," according to the Chinese hermeneutic tradition, assert necessary connections between the internal and external, between manifestations of culture and the (ethical) obsessions of its creators.

Many Chinese artists, not discussed in this book due to its limited scope and focus on urban art, powerfully express the ethical, environmental, and social fallout from indiscriminate capitalist development and antihumanist strains of culture. Li Yang's mordant critique of utilitarian market ethics in his film *Mang jing* (Blind shaft, 2003) features barren, strip-mined hills, which mirror corrupt practices in the coal industry, where workers' lives, easily expendable, are worth no more than cheap funeral payoffs. More than a critique of capitalism, Li's film is a trenchant, "Lu Xun–esque" exposé of abiding inhumanities in Chinese culture, not unlike the concepts underlying Zhang Dali's *Man and Beast* bronze series. Jia Zhangke first features the devalued worker in his film *Shijie* (The world, 2004), and even more poignantly in his award-winning film *Sanxia haoren* (Still life, 2006) and his documentary *Dong* (Dong, 2006). In each of Jia's films to date, the downtrodden, unkempt environment, whether urban or rural, discloses devalued humanity in postsocialist China, a failure to care for others and the earth. Lu Chuan's *Kekexili* (Mountain patrol, 2004), based on the true story of a journalist who joins a mountain patrol in search of Tibetan antelope poachers, is set in the harsh, deforested Qinghai-Tibetan plateau. This celebrated film not only brought global attention to the plight of this endangered species, but, shot as cinéma vérité, made manifest the harsh aridity of the landscape, which is attributable to the fact that global warming is melting the plateau's glaciers, China's primary water source, at 7 percent annually. In communicating the environmental and ethical repercussions of neoliberal development, China's filmmakers, visual artists, and authors have the potential to move the global political, economic, and technological imagination, which draws on more than data.

In addition to profiling Chinese aesthetics that critique utilitarian development, I have detailed ways in which urban aesthetics manifest changing Chinese conceptions of autonomy, ethics, and citizenry. China's rapid construction and deconstruction of disparate epistemological frameworks —from traditional humanistic and religious ethics, to Enlightenment rationality and Marxist revolution, to end-of-history neoliberalism—has forged a unique cultural memory and ethical lacuna. These histories, their memory still fresh for some artists, may prevent their more perilous tendencies from being repeated in the future. Artists such as Chen Ran, Sheng Qi, and Song Dong have made forceful political statements on rights to privacy and autonomy, the right to choose one's lifestyle and live with dignity in the city, and the right to be valued for being human rather than for contributing to political glory or collective orchestration. Others, such as Qiu Huadong, Zhu Wen, Liu Heng, Sun Ganlu, He Dun, and Zeng Hao, express the anomie and privation inherent in new urban forms of socialization, particularly after Confucian or socialist ethics have been deconstructed and market ethics are but an oxymoron. Younger generations of artists, born in the 1970s and 1980s, such as Mian Mian, Wei Hui, Chun Shu, and Han Han, reveal an ongoing search for ethical grounding even as they fully embrace the urban experience.

This book does not predict the future of Chinese urban aesthetics, but rather recounts trends. It suggests that despite the immense destruction to the ecology and cultural heritage wrought by neoliberal urban development, postsocialist urban aesthetics has also fostered new realms of agency by provoking creative solutions to urban development, new forms of critical engagement, and a nascent civic society. The conundrums wrought by capitalist urban modernity—using or being used by the establishment; manipulating or selling out to global capital; atrophying in narcissistic privation or revitalizing private and public spheres—are thorny. In the main, however, China's artists and intellectuals have not been undermined by capital or popular culture, but continue to pursue ideals of truth and beauty and explore strategies for meaningful political and social engagement. Artists and editors such as Zhang Dali, Huang Rui, and Jiang Jun are optimistic about the potential for urban modernization to expand opportunities for discourse and activism in the public sphere. Intellectuals such as Wang Hui, Wen Tiejun, Lu Xueyi, and Wang Xiaoming have reengaged in class and cultural criticism, even as their research is financed by the very economic and political interests they ostensibly critique.

The phenomenon of public-minded artists and intellectuals enacting social critique via commercial venues itself constitutes a new urban cultural aesthetics and emergent forms of civic governance. The legacy of socialist egalitarianism on popular thought, coupled with the increasing influence of market-embedded activism, has the potential to stem the indiscriminate ecological and heritage destruction characterizing postsocialist urban development. Further, as urban development dominates questions of global sustainability, Chinese critical inquiry now extends beyond the historical modern dilemma of "whither China?" The significance of this new historical development cannot be underestimated. Despite the fact that the U.S. government and media continue to analyze China according to imperialist and Cold War epistemologies, China's global acts, like those of other international powers, are increasingly more strategic and pragmatic than ideological. A growing number of China's officials and urban intellectuals, regularly engaged in international exchanges and "the marketplace of ideas," are moving beyond a parochial nationalism to embrace cosmopolitan worldviews. If one adopts a Gramscian view of popular urban culture, then this emergent civil sphere remains suspect as a source of political agency, as the dominant class is seen to maintain hegemony by reinforcing its ideology through cultural structures. If one adopts the views prevalent in the Shanghai Center for Cultural Studies, then the emergent middle class (as opposed to the working class) is identified as harboring the most potential for social change, and is to be targeted for reeducation and reconstruction of dominant elite class ideologies.

As the term *reconstruction* suggests, one positive trajectory in postsocialist urban aesthetics is the recent move beyond the censure of human failing to the fostering of human flourishing. The Beijing-based artist Zhu Ming, whose philosophical attachments are to Taoist philosophy, articulated such global aesthetic aims in a recent interview. When I asked his primary motivation for doing performance art in remote, natural environments, he answered, "I hope that through my art I can convey the relationship between man and nature, that is to say, to explore ideal conditions for an individual to flourish on this planet. . . . As an artist I can only try my best to communicate, but have no way of ensuring society will listen. But of course my aim is for each individual, Chinese and foreigner, to flourish."[1] Another example is the sustainable design of Yeo Kangshua's and Li Xiaodong's award-winning Yuhu Elementary School and Community Center located in the UNESCO World Heritage Site of Lijiang, Yunnan. Charged with "using unprocessed local materials to produce a contemporary visual effect," they used limestone, cobblestone, and wood to create an affordable modern structure that blends naturally with its surroundings.[2] As practicing Buddhists, dedicated educators, and practitioners of principles in China's rich architectural heritage, Yeo and Li regularly theorize how to apply traditional Chinese spatial conceptions, architectural, and landscape aesthetics to contemporary urban design.[3]

Some harbor great hopes that such Chinese intellectuals will draw on the collective wisdom of China's impressive civilization and traumatic history to forge sustainable development models for the future. Such suppositions go beyond the conclusions of this study, which are far more modest. What my research indicates is that both designers of Chinese cities and producers of Chinese urban art have been on a steep learning curve during the past three decades. The speed with which urban design and architecture practices are changing, and with which urban artists are entering into dialogue with policy makers and designers, suggests a trend with the potential to stem the current rate of environmental and heritage destruction both domestically and globally. The growing number of Chinese architects, designers, and artists who integrate modern technologies with a traditional aesthetics of harmony between human and nature may bode well for China and the planet, if their practices become dominant.

Above all, China's new urban aesthetics manifests in the immanent sociability that *is* the city. The rise in civic activism by intellectuals, artists, and citizens is starting to counter historic patterns in spatial design and administration of Chinese cities—uniformity, regularity, hierarchy, cellularity, ritual symbolism—all of which support governmental control of society. New urban forms such as the *xiaoqu* (community) are replacing that of the earlier *danwei* (work unit). The Chinese characters for both terms prioritize the spatial over the social, yet *xiaoqu* members are starting to advocate for their individual and communal rights in new ways. Although modern planning practices did not account for community and property concerns in adopting market-based strategies, such concerns pushed Chinese planning to evolve dialectically, each act of conflict resolution resulting in a redefinition of the urban. The regime's "unintended outcome" of "popular resistance to urban expansion and redevelopment" is now pitted against their "intended outcome" of "sustainable growth."[4] This urban aesthetics of sociability attempts to govern the city for its good; it embodies an emerging form of urban governance with the potential to foster radically new forms of urban vitality in China.

Notes

Introduction

1 Jim Yardley, "Farmers Being Moved aside by China's Real Estate Boom," *New York Times*, 8 December 2004.

2 See, for example, the essays in Gulden, *Farewell to Peasant China* and *What's a Peasant to Do?* According to the fifth national population census of 2000, China's urbanization rose from 12 percent in 1952 to 17 percent in 1978, 30 percent in 1996, and 36 percent in 2000 (quoted in Li Zhang, *China's Limited Urbanization*, 4). In 2004 the World Bank calculated China's urban population to be 39 percent of its total population.

3 Chan, "Urbanization and Rural-Urban Migration since 1982," 273.

4 Yan, *Private Life under Socialism*. See especially chapter 5, "Domestic Space and the Quest for Privacy."

5 Zhu, *The Transition of China's Urban Development*, 30.

6 Li Zhang argues that even during the postsocialist period China's systematic characteristics, particularly its state-biased development, continues to constrain urbanization. While Kam Wing Chan's analyses demonstrate that China's urbanization rate under socialism averaged 4.3 percent annual urban growth, on a par with other developing nations, Zhang and others maintain this level constitutes "limited urbanization" in the sense that China's industrial output during that period exceeded urbanization rates typically associated with those levels. By comparing China's urbanization in 2000 to that in other socialist countries, developing countries, and all countries, Zhang concludes that even in 2000 China remained under-urbanized by 14–16 percent relative to these three categories. See Chan and Xu, "Urban Population Growth and Urbanization in China since 1949";

Chan, "Urbanization and Rural-Urban Migration since 1982" and *Cities with Invisible Walls*; and Zhang, *China's Limited Urbanization*, esp. 5, 11.

7 Xudong Zhang, *Whither China?*, 8. See also Francis's conclusions in "Reproduction of Danwei Institutional Features in the Context of China's Market Economy."

8 The New Housing Movement was established, in 1999, to develop creative strategies for municipal development, culminating with published proceedings from an international conference that took place in Shanghai in June 2000 (Dan and Zhu, *Zouxiang xin zhuzhai* [Toward new housing]).

9 See Li Gan, Xiong, and Cai, *Zhongguo dangdai wenxue shi* (History of contemporary Chinese literature).

10 Some of the most significant of these studies include Sit, *Beijing*; Davis et al., *Urban Spaces in Contemporary China*; Yusuf and Wu, *The Dynamics of Urban Growth in Three Chinese Cities*; Zhu, *The Transition of China's Urban Development*; Davis, *The Consumer Revolution in Urban China*; Tang and Parish, *Chinese Urban Life under Reform*; Chen et al., *China Urban*; Lü, Rowe, and Zhang, *Modern Urban Housing in China, 1840–2000*; Rowe and Kuan, *Architectural Encounters with Essence and Form in Modern China*; Logan, *The New Chinese City* and *Urban China in Transition*; Chen, Liu, and Zhang, *Urban Transformation in China*; Broudehoux, *The Making and Selling of Post-Mao Beijing*; Friedmann, *China's Urban Transition*; Bray, *Social Space and Governance in Urban China*; Wu's edited volumes *Restructuring the Chinese City*, *Globalization and the Chinese City*, and *China's Emerging Cities*; Wu, Xu, and Yeh, *Urban Development in Post-Reform China*; and Campanella, *Concrete Dragon*.

11 Yang Dongping's bestselling *Chengshi jifeng* (Urban vicissitudes), for example, discusses media, film, and literature in the context of urban cultural change. Li Jiefei wrote an excellent study of 1990s urban literature, *Chengshi xiangkuang* (City frame). Li Tiangang's informative cultural history, *Renwen Shanghai* (Cultural Shanghai), details the formation of civil society in Shanghai. Lü Xinyu's acclaimed *Jilu Zhongguo* (Documentary China) is the first book-length work on the subject. An increasing number of books criticize urban-design practices from a humanist and social-planning perspective, including Yu Kongzhi and Li Dihua's *Chengshi jingguan zhilu* (A path for urban landscape).

12 See, for example, Hockx and Strauss, *Culture in the Contemporary PRC*; Laughlin, *Contested Modernities*; Zhang, *The Urban Generation*; Lu, *Chinese Modernity and Gobal Biopolitics*; Lu, *China's Literary and Cultural Scenes at the Turn of the Twenty-first Century*; McGrath, *Postsocialist Modernity*.

13 The most significant of these studies include Wang, *High Culture Fever*; Ben Xu, *Disenchanted Democracy*; Tong, *The Dialectics of Modernization*; Xudong Zhang, *Chinese Modernism in the Era of Reforms, Postsocialism and Cultural Politics*, and *Whither China?*; Davies, *Voicing Concerns*; Wang, *One China, Many Paths*; Gu and Goldman, *Chinese Intellectuals between State and Market*.

14 Quoted in Wakin, "Pilgrim with an Oboe, Citizen of the World," *New York Times*, 8 April 2007.

15 Li, *Chengshi xiangkuang* (City frame), 2.

16 Qiu, *Yingyan* (Fly eyes), 250.

17 Zhang Yiwu was one of the first to theorize this in relation to literature. See his "Hou xin shiqi wenxue" (Post–New Era literature), 184.

18 Fei, *Xiangtu Zhongguo* (Rural China); translated as *From the Soil: The Foundations of Chinese Society*.

19 Mote, "The Transformation of Nanking, 1350–1400," 105.

20 Ibid., 103.

21 Zhang, *The City in Modern Chinese Literature and Film*, 5.

22 Fei Xiaotong conveys a prevalent Leftist line in his diatribe that the treaty ports are essentially communities of "dependent consumers and parasites" which gain their wealth from exploitative relationships with the country, (serving as) gateways to the Occident rather than the vast, underdeveloped hinterland. See Hsiao-tung Fei [Fei Xiaotong], *China's Gentry*, 98–108.

23 Murphey, *The Fading of the Maoist Vision*, 28.

24 Quoted in Li, *Renwen Shanghai* (Cultural Shanghai), 50.

25 Shen Honglei and Wu Xinyi, "Pudong Takes Six Steps as the World Takes One," *China Today*, April 2003, emphasis added.

26 Chow, *The Protestant Ethnic and the Spirit of Capitalism*, chap. 1.

27 Bergère, " 'The Other China.' " See also Sheng, "Lun 'haipai' wenhua."

28 Li, *Renwen Shanghai*, 10. Similarly, Linda Cooke Johnson argues, in *Shanghai: From Market Town to Treaty Port, 1074–1858*, that China's urban-rural continuum persisted throughout Shanghai's development, and that the interdependence between Shanghai and the provinces was never substantively altered during its development from an important commercial port during the Song, a cotton-production center serving the entire empire during the Ming, and a commercial port city affecting the lower Yangzi economy during the Qing.

29 Quoted in Kinkley, *The Odyssey of Shen Congwen*, 158.

30 Shen, *Shen Congwen wenji* 12:158–59.

31 Fei, "Peasantry and Gentry," 14.

32 Zhang, *The City in Modern Chinese Literature and Film*, 13.

33 Ibid., 124.

34 Gaubatz, *Beyond the Great Wall*, 253.

35 Strand, " 'A High Place Is No Better Than a Low Place,' " 108.

36 Leng Wangu, "Beijing cheng wanbuke chai" (Beijing's walls must not be torn down), *Aiguo bao* (The nationalist), 8 September 1912, 1, quoted in Strand, " 'A High Place Is No Better Than a Low Place,' " 115.

37 Quoted in Zhu, *The Transition of China's Urban Development*, 15.

38 Yusuf and Wu, *The Dynamics of Urban Growth in Three Chinese Cities*, 48.

39 Zhu, *The Transition of China's Urban Development*, 17.

40 Ibid., 26.

41 Mao, "Zai Yan'an wenyi zuotan huishang de jianghua" (Talks at the Yan'an conference on the arts).

42 See Leaf, "Urban Planning and Urban Reality under Chinese Economic Reforms," and Lü Junhua's four-part series on Beijing's old and dilapidated housing renewal.

43 Quoted in Zha, *China Pop*, 55.

44 Cheng, "Urban Image and Urban Aesthetics." A revised version of this lecture was published as "Urban Image and Urban Aesthetics: Urban Aesthetics in Cross-cultural Perspective," *Edebiyat Fakültesi Dergisi* (Journal of Faculty of Letters) 25, no. 2 (2009): 59–71.

45 Lu, "Danwei."

46 The *hukou* system, first set up in cities in 1951 and extended to rural areas in 1955, was officially promoted as a measure to designate one's legal residence, but one of its major functions was migration control and management. While there is not yet a national policy to abolish the nonagricultural and agricultural *hukou* categorization, some provinces, such as Jiangxi, have announced a cancellation of dual-status classification. See Li Zhang's description of *hukou* reform from 1979 to 2000, in *China's Limited Urbanization*, 57–96.

47 Taylor, *Modernities*, 33; and Li Jiefei, *Chengshi xiangkuang* (City frame), 39–40.

48 Cited in Fraser, "Inventing Oasis," 33.

49 See Cai, *Shensheng huiyi* (Sacred memories); and Wang Xiaoming, "A Manifesto for Cultural Studies."

50 Influential scholarship on class analysis by historians and social scientists includes Lu *Dangdai Zhongguo shehui liudong* (Social mobility in contemporary China); Sun, *Zhuanxing yu duanlie* (Transformation and rupture); Lu, *Dangdai Zhongguo shehui jieceng yanjiu baogao* (Report on social classes in contemporary China); Li, "Shichang zhuanxing yu Zhongguo zhongjian jieceng de daiji gengti" (Market changes and the generational replacement of the Chinese middle class); Sun, "Zhongguo shehui jiegou zhuanxing de zhongjinqi qushi yu yinhuan" (Recent trends and latent dangers in the transformation of China's social structure); Li, *Zhongguo xinshiqi jieji jieceng baogao* (Report on social classes in China in the New Era).

51 Wang, *Illuminations from the Past*, 251–52.

1. Designing the Postsocialist City

Passages from this chapter previously appeared in "Review of *Remaking Beijing: Tiananmen Square and the Creation of a Political Space*," *Modern Chinese Literature and Culture* (2007), http://mclc.osu.edu/rc/reviews.htm; and in "Diagnosing Beijing 2020: Mapping the Ungovernable City," *Footprint: Delft School of Design Journal* 1, no. 2 (2008): 15–29.

1 See Taylor, "Havens and Cages," 548.

2 Abramson, review of *The Making and Selling of Post-Mao Beijing*, by Anne-Marie Broudehoux.

3 Neville Mars and Martijn de Waal, "Beijing and Beyond," 15 October 2004, website of Dynamic City Foundation (printouts on file with author). Jacques Feiner cites an increase in urban population of 0.7 to 1 billion by 2030 ("Regional Planning in the Kunming-Zurich Partnership," 114).

4 "Twenty New Cities to Be Set Up in China Every Year," *People's Daily Online*, 14 August 2000.

5   Qiu, "China's Urbanization and Urban Planning."

6   See chap. 7 in Bray, *Social Space and Governance in Urban China*.

7   See, for example, Wang, *Brand New China*; Latham, Thompson, and Klein, *Consuming China*; Gerth, *China Made*.

8   Lu, *Remaking Chinese Urban Form*, 163.

9   Selected examples include Jacobs, *Meiguo dachengshi de si yu sheng* (The death and life of great American cities); Koetter, *Bingtie chengshi* (Collage city); Lynch, *Chengshi xingtai* (Good city form). See Bao, "Jianzhuxue fanyi chuyi" (A modest proposal for translations of architectural theory), for a discussion of continued weaknesses in architectural practices in China due to limited translations and for a full list of related translations through 2005.

10 Fingerhuth, "Urban Design for Kunming," 53. The essays in *The Kunming Project*, the source volume for Fingerhuth's piece, are presented bilingually in English and Chinese.

11 Lin Shu, *Jianzhushi Liang Sicheng* (Architect Liang Sicheng), quoted in Wang Jun, *Chengji* (City records), 335–36.

12 The term "late capitalism" was popularized the same year by its use in Marxist economist Ernest Mandel's dissertation, which characterized late-stage capitalism as being dominated by the fluidities of financial capital.

13 Calvino, *Invisible Cities*, 69.

14 Ibid.

15 H. S. Becker, "Italo Calvino as Urbanologist," 25 November 2006, website of H. S. Becker (printouts on file with author).

16 Lefebvre, "The Urban Illusion," 163–64.

17 See Lash and Urry, *Economies of Signs and Space*; Castells, *The Informational City* and "The Space of Flows."

18 Lefebvre, "The Urban Illusion," 164.

19 Koolhaas, introduction to *Great Leap Forward*, 2.

20 Ma and Wu elaborate on these processes in "Restructuring the Chinese City," 3.

21 Hart-Landsberg and Burkett argue that "once the path of pro-market reforms was embarked upon, each subsequent step in the reform process was largely driven by tensions and contradictions generated by the reforms themselves" (*China and Socialism*, 16).

22 Leitner et al., "Contesting Urban Futures," 4.

23 Yang Xifeng, vice director of the Shanghai Lingang New City Administrative Committee Land and Planning Department, interview by the author, Lingang, Shanghai, 5 November 2006.

24 The municipal population of Quanzhou in 1997, for example, was 6.5 million, although its registered nonagricultural population, "an alternative way of thinking about 'urban,'" was only 850,000, with many living in built-up areas not continuous with the Old City district of Licheng and its adjacent suburbs, which in 1994 had a population of 185,000 (300,000 if one included rural migrants). See Abramson, Leaf, and Ying, "Social Research and the Localization of Chinese Urban Planning Practice," 170.

25 See Friedmann, *China's Urban Transition*, 35, 54–5; and Zhu, *New Paths to Urbanization*.

26 Abramson, review of *The Making and Selling of Post-Mao Beijing*, by Anne-Marie Broudehoux.

27 Wu, *Remaking Beijing*, 7.

28 Sit, *Beijing*, 215.

29 Wu, "Lun Zhongguo chengshi huanjing de xin yu jiu" (On the old and the new in Chinese urban environments).

30 Abramson, review of *The Making and Selling of Post-Mao Beijing*, by Anne-Marie Broudehoux.

31 Fang, *Children of the Bitter River* (a translation of *Fengjing*), 129.

32 CCTV International, *Urban Housing Documentary Series*, part 1 of 10: "Siheyuan" (Quadrangles), aired 26 July 2004.

33 CCTV International, *Urban Housing Documentary Series*, part 2 of 10: "Pengzi" (Shantytowns), aired 27 July 2004.

34 Wu, "The Birth of Ruins." Broudehoux discusses the relocation process of the Central Academy of Fine Arts in *The Making and Selling of Post-Mao Beijing*, 127–28.

35 Abbas, *Hong Kong.*

36 In *The Poetics of Space*, Gaston Bachelard theorizes universal attachments to the childhood home. In *Xiangtu Zhongguo* (Rural China, 1947), Fei Xiaotong relates Chinese attachment to the village home and soil to its land-bound, agrarian roots of culture.

37 Joe Carter, interview by author, Beijing, 11 May 2005 (tape on file with author). Similarly, my Shanghainese relatives moved, in 1990, from their alley housing in Puxi to new construction in Pudong and cannot understand why I would choose to would live in a 1930s apartment building in the former French Concession, where it is "dirty, noisy, and crowded."

38 Jonathan Watts, "Eviction Orders: Elderly Are Evicted as Leafy Old Beijing Is Bulldozed in Build-up to 2008 Olympics," *Guardian*, 6 September 2003, 19.

39 Louisa Lim, "Evictions, the Dark Side of Shanghai Growth," 13 December 2006, in the series *Shanghai Builds for the Future*, 11–15 December 2006, website of NPR (printouts and sound clips on file with author). Peter Hibbard, an architect and Shanghai resident, provides architectural and historical details based on archival research on the Capitol Building in his guide *The Bund Shanghai: China Faces West*. For example, a group of Italian marines stormed the Capitol Theatre in January 1929, during a screening of Frank Borzage's *Street Angel* (1928); because Mussolini took offense at the film, he ordered his marines to confiscate and burn the celluloid reel. Renamed under Japanese occupation, the "Culture News Theatre" screened Japanese propagandist newsreels and documentaries between 1943 and 1945.

40 Louisa Lim told me she later learned details about the holdouts from other residents and the developer. Louisa Lim, interview by author, Shanghai, 19 December 2006 (field notes on file with author).

41 Phone conversation with Ms. Wang, a former resident of Capitol Building, Shanghai, 2 January 2007.

42 Abramson, "Urban Planning in China," 14.

43 Public remarks by Shu Haolun after a screening of *Nostalgia*, Museum of Contemporary Art, Shanghai, 7 February 2007.

44 For example, a banner hung in the Yong Ye Li neighborhood in Shanghai, demolished in 2002 to build upscale residential high-rises, read, "The new round of 'old town reconstruction' needs the residents' support and cooperation" (*Xin yilun jiuqu gaizao jincheng, xuyao guangda jumin de zhichi yu peihe*).

45 Li, "Residential Mobility and Urban Change in China," 177–78.

46 In 2006 over 30 percent of the population of Jing An District in Shanghai were over the age of 59, and 30 percent of the city as a whole is predicted to be over the age of 60 by 2020. See Howard French, "As China Ages, a Shortage of Cheap Labor Looms," *New York Times*, 30 June 2006.

47 This migrant family previously operated their hair salon, for seven years, out of larger quarters in Luwan District. They rented from a state-owned work unit whose leader pocketed the rent without reporting it to the state, in turn allowing the migrants to avoid paying taxes. The family moved to Xuhui District only when their neighborhood was sold to developers. Interview by author, Shanghai, 23 October 2006 (field notes on file with author).

48 See, for example, Li Zhang, "Migrant Enclaves and Impacts of Redevelopment Policy in Chinese Cities."

49 Jordan, "Collective Memory and Locality in Global Cities," 46.

50 In "The Work Unit" Yi Zhongtian traces the etymology of *liu* to the expression "wander about without a home" (*liuli shisuo*) (Dutton, *Streetlife China*, 58–61). Wang Shan ("Leuninger") voices the stereotype that "floating" leads to criminality in his bestselling *A Third Eye on China* (1994): "In the move to the city, the peasants not only lose their social connections, but also lose any restraints upon their actions" (qtd. in Dutton, *Streetlife China*, 89).

51 Pan, "Historical Memory, Community-Building and Place-Making in Neighborhood Shanghai," 132–33.

52 The best introduction to this phenomenon is Zhou and Ma, "Economic Restructuring and Suburbanization in China."

53 See, for example, Giroir, "A Globalized Golden Ghetto in a Chinese Garden," and Li Zhang, "Migrant Enclaves and Impacts of Redevelopment Policy in Chinese Cities."

54 Finnane, "The Origins of Prejudice," 232, cited in Sun, "Anhui Baomu in Shanghai," 181.

55 Gaitano, "Filial Daughters, Modern Women," 72.

56 Zheng, "From Peasant Women to Bar Hostesses: Gender and Modernity in Post-Mao Dalian," 106.

57 For details on the "Together with Migrants" project, see Zhan, *Rural Labour Migration in China*.

58 Zhu Shanjie, interview by author, Shanghai, 20 January 2007. See also Zhu Shanjie's "Hechu shi jiayuan? Shanghai nongmingong zidi xuexiao zhi yipie" (Where is home? A glance at Shanghai schools for the children of rural migrant workers), which is based on research he conducted in migrant schools in Baoshan District, Shanghai, June–July 2006, unpublished report provided to the author on 20 January 2007.

59 See "Shanghai ming gong zidi xuexiao bei guanbi yinfa chongtu" (Closing of migrant schools incites conflict), BBC Chinese.com, 9 January 2007; and Howard French, "China Strains to Fit Migrants into Mainstream Classrooms," *New York Times*, 25 January 2007.

60 Wu, "Transplanting Cityscapes," 192.

61 Giroir, "A Globalized Golden Ghetto in a Chinese Garden," 222.

62 Liu, *Wo yanzhong de jianzhu yu huanjing* (My view of architecture and its environment), 5.

63 Giroir, "A Globalized Golden Ghetto in a Chinese Garden," 223.

64 Similarly, new-urbanism communities in Chapel Hill, North Carolina, are named Southern Village and Meadowmont to conjure up quaint rural qualities, although they are not situated in villages, meadows, or mountains.

65 Wu, "Transplanting Cityscapes: The Production of Townhouse and Gated Community in Urban China," presented at the Second Annual China Planning Network Conference, Boston, 17–18 March 2005; revised for publication as "Transplanting Cityscapes: Townhouse and Gated Community in Globalization and Housing Commodification."

66 Li Yu, "Cardiff and China," 18 December 2006, website of the Urban China Research Center of Cardiff University (printouts on file with author).

67 Qiu, "China's Urbanization and Urban Planning."

68 Abramson, "Urban Planning in China," 7.

69 Yan, *Zhongguo chengshi fazhan wenti baogao* (Report on issues in China's urban development), 112–13.

70 Feng Jicai, "Gu yu hu" (Drumming and shouting), *Wenhui Bao*, 18 January 2001, quoted in Yan, *Zhongguo chengshi fazhan wenti baogao* (Report on issues in China's urban development), 103.

71 John Barber, "Instant Modernity," *Globe News and Mail*, 23 December 2004.

72 Rowe and Kuan, *Architectural Encounters with Essence and Form in Modern China*, 171.

73 Neville Mars, former associate of Rem Koolhaas at the Office for Metropolitan Architecture (OMA) and director of Dynamic City Foundation, expressed this sentiment to me in conversation, Beijing, 14 May 2005); Ivana Benda, partner of Allied Architects International, acknowledged this mentality prevails among foreign architects (Ivana Benda, interview by author, Shanghai, 15 April 2005 [tape on file with author]).

74 Hsing, "Global Capital and Local Land in China's Urban Real Estate Development," 183.

75 Rowe and Kuan, *Architectural Encounters with Essence and Form in Modern China*, 187.

76 Abramson, review of *The Making and Selling of Post-Mao Beijing*, by Anne-Marie Broudehoux.

77 Dirlik, "Architectures of Global Modernity, Colonialism, and Places," 37.

78 Private conversation with an architect at Skidmore, Owens, and Merrill, Shanghai, 3 November 2006 (field notes on file with author).

79 Goldberger, "Shanghai Surprise," 144.

80 Gaubatz, "From Shanghai to Xining, Isomorphism, Urban Image, and Urban Design in China's Interior Cities."

81 Yan et al., "The Development of the Chinese Metropolis in the Period of Transition," 54.

82 Yan, "Urban Spatial Planning and Infrastructure in Beijing."

83 Wu, *Rehabilitating the Old City of Beijing*, 41–42.

84 Ivana Benda, "Organized Chaos and Design of Large Architectural and Urban Complexes," unpublished report provided to the author on 8 February 2007.

85 Wu, *Remaking Beijing*, 94–95.

86 Abramson, "Urban Planning in China," 5.

87 Broudehoux, *The Making and Selling of Post-Mao Beijing*, 33, 35.

88 Ibid., 5.

89 Bray, *Social Space and Governance in Urban China*, 176.

90 One of the best discussions of the role of public parks in Republican Era China is in Dong, *Republican Beijing*.

91 Abramson, Leaf, and Ying, "Social Research and the Localization of Chinese Urban Planning Practice," 168.

92 Zhang, "Zongxu" (General introduction), 1–5.

93 Ibid., 3.

94 Ivana Benda, "Organized Chaos and Design of Large Architectural and Urban Complexes," unpublished report provided to the author on 8 February 2007.

95 Dubai's World Islands are a particularly utopian project for the super rich. Arranged according to a world map, each of the three hundred islands ("countries") "will be sold to selected private developers with pricing beginning at AED 25 million (US$ 6.85 million). The only means of transportation between the islands will be by marine or air." See the website for Dubai World Islands (printouts on file with author).

96 "World Beaters—Some of the Most Ambitious Construction Projects in South East Asia Are up for Grabs," 2 May 2004, press release posted on the website of Burchill VDM, an engineering firm, after it was awarded the contract with Tongji University for planning Yangshan New City (printouts on file with author).

97 Zhang Rui, "Shanghai's Lingang New City Open for Investment," http://www.China.org.cn, 31 March 2006; "Port City Emerges in Shanghai," *China Daily Online*, 18 April 2006.

98 Wu, "Beyond Gradualism," 9.

99 Site visit to Lingang New City and Yangshan Deepwater Port, 5 November 2006 (field notes on file with author).

100 See "Eleven Satellite Cities Planned for Beijing," *Shenzhen Daily*, 4 January 2006; "Beijing to Build Eleven Cities," 3 January 2006, website of the Embassy of the People's Republic of China in the United States (printouts on file with author); and "Official Announcement of Beijing's Eleven New Towns Plan" (Beijing shiyige xincheng guihua zhengshi fabu), 8 November 2007, website of the Beijing Municipal Government (printouts on file with author).

101 "Eleven Satellite Cities Planned for Beijing," *Shenzhen Daily*, 4 January 2006.

102 Abramson, Leaf, and Ying, "Social Research and the Localization of Chinese Urban Planning Practice," 175.

103 Wang Shuangming, interview by author, Quanzhou, Fujian, 27 November 2006 (tape on file with author).

104 Ibid.

105 Liu and Zhou, "Kunming shidian xiangmu de huigu" (How Kunming became a pilot project), 14.

106 Wehrlin, "Urban Design within the Greater Kunming Region," 106.

107 Zeng Hao, interview by author, Shanghai, 22 December 2006 (tape on file with author).

108 Nearly every foreign urban-design expert I interviewed attested to this trend.

109 Yan Song, Ding, and Knapp, "Envisioning Beijing 2020 through Sketches of Urban Scenarios."

110 Alex Pasternack, "Beijing's Olympic-Sized Traffic Problem," http://www.chinadialogue.net, 2 January 2007.

111 Ibid.

112 China Planning Network, *China Planning Network Report*, 2006 (printout on file with author).

113 Websites for English-language collaborative forums on urban China include the China Planning Network website, http://chinaplanningnetwork.org; FAR China website, http://www.sinocities.net; People's Architecture website, http://www.peoplesarchitecture.org; Dynamic City Foundation website, http://www.dynamiccity.org; and Urban China Research Network website, http://mumford.albany.edu/chinanet/index.asp.

114 See, for example, Abramson, "The Dialectics of Urban Planning in China."

115 After being promoted to deputy director of Shanghai Urban Planning and Administration Bureau, Wu Jiang created twelve conservation areas and doubled the number of municipally preserved buildings, but intimated to Markus Berg, a former classmate in Germany and planner in Shanghai, that at times his hands are tied with regard to enforcing policy (conversation with Markus Berg, October 2006, Shanghai). Huang Yan, deputy director of the BMCUP who led the planning and construction side of China's Olympic bid, has alluded to similar political restrictions. Zhou Lan integrates legacies from China's rich cultural heritage into Nanjing's contemporary urban design, but she was appointed urban planning bureau chief in 2003, after considerable damage had already been wreaked on the city's cultural heritage and favorable *fengshui*. See Zhou Lan, "Quanqiuhua beijingxia Zhongguo kuaisu chengshihua jieduan de difang kongjian tese suzao."

116 Huang Yan, quoted in "China Pulls Up the Drawbridge," *New York Times*, 19 September 2004.

117 Hou and Obrist, eds., *Cities on the Move*, n.p. "Cities on the Move"—a combination of installations, performances, multimedia, architectural projects, videos, and films by more than one hundred artists and architects from China, Indonesia, Japan, Korea, Malaysia, Philippines, Singapore, Thailand, and Europe—traveled from 13 May 1997 to 27 June 1999, from Vienna (Secession

Museum), to Bordeaux (CAPC Centre of Contemporary Art), New York (PS1), Copenhagen (Louisiana Museum), London (Hayward Gallery), and Bangkok (Rama IX Art Museum).

118 Karen Smith, "Rong Rong: Records of the Observer" (1998). unpublished manuscript, cited in Wu, *Transience*, 107.

119 "Xingwei yishu yinfa guansi" (Performance art incites lawsuit), 1 July 2003, http://sina.com.cn (printout on file with author).

120 Anonymous official (from the Nanning City Planning Administration Bureau), interview by author, Nanning, Guangxi, 30 September 2004 (tape on file with author).

121 Alex Pasternack, "Beijing's Olympic-Sized Traffic Problem," http://www.chinadialogue.net, 2 January 2007.

122 See "China's Unpaid Migrant Workers Vent Anger as New Year Approaches," European Intelligence Wire, 28 January 2003; and "Migrant Worker in Shenzhen Sets Himself on Fire in Pay Dispute," Xinhua New Agency, 21 November 2007.

123 Goldberg, *Performance*, 60.

124 Qiu, *Yingyan* (Fly eyes), 111.

125 Sassen, "Reading the City in a Global Digital Age," 25.

126 David Barboza, "China Drafts Law to Boost Unions and End Abuse," *New York Times*, 13 October 2006.

127 See, for example, Ren, "Globalization and Grassroots Practices." Jennifer Hsu was less optimistic in "Defining Boundaries of the Relationship."

128 Huang Rui, interview by author, Shanghai, 11 November 2006 (tape on file with author).

129 Ibid.

130 Ibid.

131 Private communication with Zheng Xuewu, founder of Beijing International Arts Camp.

132 Zhang Xian, address presented at the Symposium on Shanghai First Fringe. Chen Liangyu, former Communist Party secretary of Shanghai, was deposed for corruption on 25 September 2006, becoming the highest level Communist Party member fired since the Beijing mayor Chen Xitong was jailed for corruption in 1998.

133 Jiang Jun, editor-in-chief of *Urban China*, interview by author, Shanghai, 26 January 2007 (tape on file with author).

134 "China Apologizes for Abolishing Beijing's Architecture," *Royal Institution of Chartered Surveyors* 26 (2006).

135 Jiang Jun, editor-in-chief of *Urban China*, interview by author, Shanghai, 26 January 2007 (tape on file with author).

136 Tuan, "Rootedness versus Sense of Place," 270–71.

137 Rowe and Kuan, *Architectural Encounters with Essence and Form in Modern China*, 208.

138 Zhang, *Pingchang jianzhu* (For a basic architecture), 69.

2. Theorizing the Postsocialist City

1 Duggan, *The Twilight of Equality?*, 68. The relevance of the Seattle protests to worldwide "campaigns against corporate rapacity" is detailed in Cockburn, St. Clair, and Sekula, *Five Days That Shook the World*, 7.

2 Wang, "The 1989 Social Movement and the Historical Roots of China's Neoliberalism," 64. An earlier version of the essay appeared in *Taiwan shehui yanjiu jikan* (Taiwan: A radical quarterly in social studies) in late 2001, and an abbreviated version appeared as Wang Hui, "La défaite du movement social de Tiananmen: Aux origins du néolibéralisme en China," *Le Monde Diplomatique* (April 2002), 20–21.

3 Harvey, *A Brief History of Neoliberalism*, 200–201.

4 Ibid., 198–99.

5 Wang, "The 1989 Social Movement and the Historical Roots of China's Neoliberalism," 45.

6 Duggan, *The Twilight of Equality?*, xiii.

7 Some of the more prominent discussions on China include Wang Hui, "The 1989 Social Movement and the Historical Roots of China's Neoliberalism"; Siming Li and Tang, *China's Regions, Polity and Economy*; Hart-Landsberg and Burkett, *China and Socialism*; Harvey, *A Brief History of Neoliberalism*, esp. "Neoliberalism with Chinese Characteristics"; and Sargeson, "Full Circle?"

8 Conversation with Wang Xiaoming, director of the Center for Contemporary Cultural Studies at Shanghai University, October 2006 (field notes on file with author). Edward Gu positions the category of "cultural affairs" as "more favorable to market-oriented reforms" and "less politically sensitive" than the category of "literature and arts" (Edward Gu and Goldman, *Chinese Intellectuals between State and Market*, 34, fig. 1.1).

9 Huters, Introduction, 4.

10 Wang Xiaoming, "A Manifesto for Cultural Studies," 281. A longer version of this essay was published as "China, on the Brink of a 'Momentous Era.' "

11 Wang, "A Manifesto for Cultural Studies," 281.

12 Ibid., 282.

13 Harvey, *A Brief History of Neoliberalism*, 192.

14 Hart-Landsberg and Burkett, *China and Socialism*, 16.

15 Davies, "Self-Made Maps of Chinese Intellectuality," 32.

16 There is a huge literature on these debates. Some of the best English-language overviews are included in Barmé, *In the Red* and "The Revolution of Resistance"; Davies, *Voicing Concerns*; Xudong Zhang, ed., *Whither China?*; Wang, *One China, Many Paths*; and Gu and Goldman, *Chinese Intellectuals between State and Market*.

17 Davies, *Voicing Concerns*, 15.

18 "The practical critiques and social movements aimed at neoliberalism have included a number of key elements that are mutually contradictory—some radical, some moderate, and some conservative. In my opinion, the principal task of the progressive forces in contemporary China is to prevent these cri-

tiques from developing in a conservative direction (which would include attempts to move back to the old system), and also to push strongly to urge the transformation of these elements into a driving force seeking broader democracy and freedom in both China and the world." Wang, "The 1989 Social Movement and the Historical Roots of China's Neoliberalism," 45.

19 J. Kahn and J. Yardley, "Amid China's Boom, No Helping Hand for Young Qingming," *New York Times*, 1 August 2004.

20 See Wen Jiabao's "Report on the Work of the Government," delivered to the National People's Congress on 5 March 2005, published in *China Daily*, 15 March 2005; Joseph Kahn, "China Worries about Economic Surge that Skips the Poor," *New York Times*, 4 March 2005; Jim Yardley, "China Plans to Cut School Fees for Its Poorest Rural Students," *New York Times*, 13 March 2005; Stephen Green, "China's 'New Socialist Countryside,'" *Business Week*, 9 March 2006.

21 Harvey, *A Brief History of Neoliberalism*, 5.

22 Robin Wright and Ellen Knickmeyer, "U.S. Lowers Sights on What Can Be Achieved in Iraq," *Washington Post*, 14 August 2005.

23 A. Juhasz, "Ambitions of Empire," quoted in Harvey, *A Brief History of Neoliberalism*, 6.

24 Renato Ruggiero, "Charting the Trade Routes of the Future: Towards a Borderless Economy," an address to the International Industrial Conference, San Francisco, 29 September 1997, available at the website of the World Trade Organization (printouts on file with author).

25 Cline, "Doha Can Achieve Much More than Skeptics Expect," 22, quoted in Hart-Landsberg, "Neoliberalism: Myths and Reality," 1.

26 United Nations Development Program, *Human Development Report, 1999*, 3, cited in Harvey, *A Brief History of Neoliberalism*, 19.

27 Echo Shan, "One in Seven Chinese Living on under US$1 Daily," *China Daily*, 15 May 2006.

28 Hart-Landsberg and Burkett, *China and Socialism*, 67. In 2006 *China Daily* reported the Gini coefficient as 0.4, but acknowledged that the World Bank estimates it at 0.45. See "Urban Rich-Poor Gap at Alarming Levels," *China Daily*, 6 February 2006. For a detailed report on the accelerating income gap in China, see the series "China's Great Divide," *New York Times*, 31 December 2004.

29 Even intellectuals with liberal leanings, such as the economist He Qinglian, acknowledge this. In 2000 He wrote, "What we can be sure of is that China's entry into the WTO will accelerate its rapid social polarization" ("A Listing Social Structure," 187). He's piece was originally published as "Dangqian Zhongguo shehui jiegou yanbian de zongti xing fenxi," *Shuwu* (Books) (March 2000): 3–16. An earlier English translation was first published as "China's Listing Social Structure," *New Left Review* 5 (2000): 69–99.

30 Hart-Landsberg, "Neoliberalism," 2.

31 Kipnis, "Neo-leftists versus Neo-liberals," 246. The economist Qin Hui argues that Marx never equated primitive accumulation with the early "stages"

of capitalism: "Describing primitive accumulation as a necessary historical stage is a misreading" ("Shehui gongzheng yu xueshu liangxin" [Social justice and the scholarly conscious], 18).

32 Wang, "The 1989 Social Movement and the Historical Roots of China's Neoliberalism," 44.

33 Tong, *The Dialectics of Modernization*.

34 Huters, Introduction, 6.

35 Wang, "The 1989 Social Movement and China's Neoliberalism," 65.

36 Qin, "Dividing the Big Family Assets," 158–59.

37 Wang, *One China, Many Paths*, 31.

38 Gu and Goldman, Introduction, 6.

39 Karabel, "Toward a Theory of Intellectuals and Politics," 208.

40 Bourdieu, *In Other Words*, 145, quoted in Gu and Goldman, Introduction, 5.

41 Eyerman, Svensson, and Soderqvist, *Intellectuals, Universities, and the State in Western Modern Societies*, 2.

42 Brint, *In an Age of Experts*.

43 Wang, *Zi xuan ji* (Selected works), 1; cited by Davies, "Self-Made Maps of Chinese Intellectuality," 27.

44 Davies, "Self-Made Maps of Chinese Intellectuality," 38.

45 Wang, "Duobi chonggao" (Avoiding the sublime).

46 The minutes of these round-table discussions are published in *Dushu* (Reading) 3, 4, 5, 6, 7 (1993), and major essays from the ensuing debates are collected in Wang, *Renwen jingshen xunsi lu* (Thoughts on the humanist spirit).

47 Wang et al., "Kuangye shang de feixu," 1–2.

48 Arnold, *Culture and Anarchy*, 33.

49 Barmé, *In the Red*, 284.

50 Wen, "Guanyu renwen jingshen taolun zongshu" (A summary of the humanist spirit discussions). Ben Xu also summarizes Wen's article in " 'From Modernity to Chineseness.' "

51 Xu Jilin, "The Fate of an Enlightenment," 196. An abridged version of this essay, titled "Qimengde mingyun: Ershi nian laide Zhongguo sixiangjie," was published in *Ershiyi shiji* (1998), 12.

52 Wang Chaohua, *One China, Many Paths*, 21.

53 Ye Zhaoyan, interview by author, Nanjing, 8 April 1997 (tape on file with author).

54 Mao Shi'an, interview by author, Shanghai, 30 July 1997 (tape on file with author).

55 Urban fiction written in the 1990s was referred to by various epithets, including "new urbanite fiction" (*xin shimin xiaoshuo*), "new generation" (*xin shengdai*), "belated generation" (*wansheng dai*), and "new state of affairs" (*xin zhuangtai*), the last term resulting from intense discussion by the Nanjing-based journal *Zhongshan* and Beijing-based *Wenyi zhengming* attempting to characterize urban fiction by Liu Xinwu, Wang Meng, He Dun, Han Dong, Zhang Min, Zhu Wen, Lin Bai, Chen Ran, Qiu Huadong, Wang Anyi, and others. See Lin Xinwu and Zhang, *Liu Xinwu Zhang Yiwu duihua lu* (Record of conversa-

tions between Liu Xinwu and Zhang Yiwu), 222. Jia Pingwa's sensational novel, *Feidu*, was not yet translated into English at time of writing, but Yiyan Wang translates the title as *Defunct Capital* in *Narrating China*, and others translate it as *City in Ruins* and *Abandoned Capital*.

56 Wang et al., "Kuangye shang de feixu," 3.

57 Ibid., 4–5.

58 Ibid., 6–7.

59 Bai, Wang, Wu, and Yang, "Xuanze de ziyou yu wenhua taishi" (Freedom of choice and cultural trends), 86–88. This essay originally appeared in *Shanghai wenxue* (Shanghai literature) 199: 4 (1994): 68–76.

60 Chen, "Guanyu 'renwen jingshen' taolun de liang feng xin" (Two letters on the "humanist spirit" discussions), 143–44.

61 Assessments of intellectual strategies in the 1980s relative to the state continue to date. A recent publication of retrospectives on the decade by leading intellectuals is Zha, *Bashi niandai fantan lu* (Interviews on the 1980s).

62 Ben Xu elaborates on various schools of "cultural conservatism," including cultural traditionalists engaged in new national studies (*xin guoxue*), younger post intellectuals (*hou zhishifenzi*) for whom "realistic" thinking transforms Western-born "postmodern" and "postcolonial" theories, and an older generation of scholars who reversed their 1980s pro-Enlightenment positions in favor of an evolutionist view of change (such as Chen Lai, Li Zehou, and Liu Zaifu). See Xu, "Contesting Memory for Intellectual Self-Positioning."

63 Meng, "Wenhua bengkui shidai de taowang yu guiyi" (Escape and support in an age of cultural collapse), 53.

64 Xu, "Contesting Memory for Intellectual Self-Positioning," 158.

65 Zhang, "Houxinshiqi wenxue" (Post–New Era literature), 184. The "New Era," in distinction from that dominated by Maoism, is a political-cultural designation for the period of modernizing reforms instated by Deng Xiaoping in 1979.

66 Zhang, " 'Fenlie' yu 'zhuanyi' " ("Disruption" and "change"), 8–9. Xie Mian and Zhang Yiwu outline several characteristics of "post-allegorical" writing in the "post–New Era" (*Da zhuanxing* (The great transition), 29–45.

67 Zhang Yiwu identifies a wide variety of *xin zhuangtai* writers, including Qiu Huadong, Liu Xinwu, Wang Anyi, He Dun, Han Dong, Zhang Min, Diao Dou, Shu Ping, Chen Ran, and Lin Bai. Drawing from the *Xiandai hanyu cidian* (Modern Chinese dictionary) (Shangwu yinshuguan, 1996), he defines *zhuangtai* as "the form in which people or objects are expressed." See Zhang, "Postmodernism and Chinese Novels of the 1990s."

68 Liu and Zhang, *Liu Xinwu Zhang Yiwu duihualu*, 202, 204.

69 Sontag, "Notes on 'Camp,'" 288.

70 See McDougall and Hansson, *Chinese Concepts of Privacy*; Yunxiang Yan, *Private Life under Socialism*; Farquhar, *Appetites: Food and Sex in Postsocialist China*; and Friedmann, *China's Urban Transformation*.

71 See "Introduction" on the website of East Asian Regional Conference in Alternative Geography (printouts on file with author).

72 See "About IACS" on the website of the Inter-Asia Cultural Studies Society (printouts on file with author).

73 See "Announcement" for 2007 IACS Shanghai Conference, on the website of the Inter-Asia Cultural Studies Society (printouts on file with author).

74 Zhang, "The Making of the Post-Tiananmen Intellectual Field," 33.

75 Zhang and Song, "China Can Say No to America," 55.

76 Zhang, "The Making of the Post-Tiananmen Intellectual Field," 34.

77 Zhang and Song, "China Can Say No to America," 55.

78 According to media watchdogs, "When Chinese officials disputed the U.S. account, protesting that the attack could not have been a mistake, establishment journalists immediately took sides in this debate. The *New York Times* diplomatic correspondent Jane Perlez (10 May 1999) referred to 'the accidental bombing, portrayed in China as deliberate.' A *Washington Post* editorial (May 17, 1999) that discussed China's reaction to 'NATO's unintentional bombing of China's embassy' was indignant that the official Chinese press was 'milking the bombing for propaganda value' by reporting that the missile strike had been intentional. *USA Today* continues to refer to the 'accidental bombing' of the embassy (October 20, 1999)." See "U.S. Media Overlook Exposé on Chinese Embassy Bombing," *Fairness and Accuracy in Reporting*, 22 October 1999.

79 Zhang, "The Making of the Post-Tiananmen Intellectual Field," 36–37.

80 Kipnis, "Neo-leftists versus Neo-liberals: PRC Intellectual Debates in the 1990s."

81 Wang Xiaoming, "A Manifesto for Cultural Studies," 287. Having said this, Wang's rhetoric does at times slip back into using Cultural Revolution binary oppositions, such as *po* (to destroy) and *li* (to build up). See my discussion on this at the end of this chapter.

82 Qin Hui, "Liberalism, Social Democracy, and the Questions of Contemporary China," cited in Zhang, "The Making of the Post-Tiananmen Intellectual Field," 28.

83 Wang, "A Manifesto for Cultural Studies," 275.

84 Zhang, "The Making of the Post-Tiananmen Intellectual Field," 1.

85 Davies, "Self-Made Maps of Chinese Intellectuality," 25–26.

86 Wang, "The Teaching and Institutionalization of Cultural Studies."

87 Wang Xiaoming discussed the real estate market case studies in "The Secret of the New Rich in Contemporary China."

88 Zhang, "The Making of the Post-Tiananmen Intellectual Field," 6.

89 Wang, "A Manifesto for Cultural Studies," 290–91.

90 Ibid.

91 Ibid., 289.

92 Barmé and Davies, "Have We Been Noticed Yet?"

93 See Wang, *Refeng shuxi* (Hot air book series) and "The Teaching and Institutionalization of Cultural Studies."

94 Zhu Shanjie, conversation with the author, Shanghai, 26 September 2006.

95 Wang, "The Teaching and Institutionalization of Cultural Studies."

96 Quoted in Duggan, *The Twilight of Equality?*, 34

97   Ang, "Shui xuyao wenhua yanjiu?" (Who needs cultural studies?), cited in Xu, "Where Has the Aura Gone?"

98   Alisa Solomon, "Sexual Smokescreen," *Village Voice*, 25 November 1997, 56, cited in Duggan, *The Twilight of Equality?*, 34.

99   Ibid., 31.

100 During, Introduction, 14–15. See Xu, "Where Has the Aura Gone?," 20–21.

101 Xu, "Where Has the Aura Gone?," 25–26.

102 Wang, "The Teaching and Institutionalization of Cultural Studies."

103 Ibid.

104 Zhao, "Underdogs, Lapdogs and Watchdogs," 55.

105 Xu Hui, "Morality Discourse in the Marketplace."

106 Zhao, "Underdogs, Lapdogs and Watchdogs," 56.

107 "Writer Tie Ning to become First Woman to Chair Chinese Writer's Association," 6 November 2006, website of China Media Project (printouts on file with author).

3.   Performing the Postsocialist City

Passages from this chapter previously appeared in "Review of *Remaking Beijing: Tiananmen Square and the Creation of a Political Space*," *Modern Chinese Literature and Culture* (2007), http://mclc.osu.edu/rc/reviews.htm; "Diagnosing Beijing 2020: Mapping the Ungovernable City," *Footprint: Delft School of Design Journal* 1.2 (2008); and "Spaces of Disappearance: Aesthetic Responses to Contemporary Beijing City Planning" *Contemporary China* 13.39 (2004).

1   Anthony M. Tung, quoted in Mariana Torres, "The Clash of Tradition and Modernity in Amazing Beijing," website of Vermont Critic (printouts on file with author); Celestino Soddu, "Beijing Identity in Progress: Generated Architectures to Increase the Identity of Beijing: Images Before and After the Increasing Identity," designed by Celestino Soddu with his Virtual Office Argenìa, website of Argenìa (printouts on file with author).

2   Yang, *Chengshi jifeng* (Urban vicissitudes), 2d edn, back cover.

3   Ibid., 1st edn, 7.

4   Shen Yue, "Zichan jieji quanli ying yi wei shimin quanli" ("Bourgeois rights" should be translated as "townspeople's rights"), *Tianjin shehui kexue* (Tianjin social science), 4 (1986), cited in Guobin Yang, "Civil Society in China," 1.

5   The first scholar to use the term *public sphere* in relation to China was Craig Calhoun, who focuses on how the movement transformed Tiananmen Square from an official ceremonial space into a public sphere of critical discourse, and on how cultural debates and mass-media discourse had an impact on the movement. See his "Tiananmen, Television and the Public Sphere." Six articles representing various views on civil society in China, presented at the 1993 UCLA symposium, are published in *Modern China* 19 (1993).

6   Guobin Yang, "Civil Society in China." The seven books Yang surveys are Deborah S. Davis et al., *Urban Spaces in Contemporary China*; Deborah S. Davis, *The Consumer Revolution in Urban China*; Kluver and Powers, *Civic*

Discourse, Civil Society, and Chinese Communities; Brook and Frolic, Civil Society in China; Madsen, China's Catholics; White, Howell, and Shang, In Search of Civil Society; Perry and Selden, Chinese Society.

7   One of the most notable accounts of the cultural effects of urban demolition (especially in Paris, Petersburg, and New York) in the nineteenth century and the twentieth is Marshall Berman's All That Is Solid Melts into Air.

8   Lin, Chengnan jiushi and Memories of Peking.

9   Liu, Zhonggulou (Bell and drum tower).

10 Yang Dongping discusses Wang Shuo's legal battles in Chengshi jifeng, 550.

11 Cited in Kong, Consuming Literature, 23.

12 Ibid., 22.

13 Yao, "The Elite Class Background of Wang Shuo and His Hooligan Characters," 436.

14 Wang, Wo shi Wang Shuo (I am Wang Shuo), 34.

15 Yao, "The Elite Class Background of Wang Shuo and His Hooligan Characters," 439.

16 Cultural T-shirts emblazoned with favorite Wang Shuo expressions such as mei jinr (depleted) were popular in many of China's cities before they were banned in late 1992.

17 Kong, Consuming Literature, 26.

18 Yao, "The Elite Class Background of Wang Shuo and His Hooligan Characters," 432.

19 The first publication run of the novel (over 200,000 copies), in December 2003, sold out within the month, and a second run of over 200,000 was immediately issued, in January 2004. While there is no precise definition for "bestseller," in the United States a soft-cover book that sells over 200,000 copies is considered a bestseller. In China popular titles can sell several hundred thousand or even millions of copies, yet some presses, such as Zuojia chubanshe (Writer's Press), count books with sales of over 30,000 copies (which accounted for almost 40 percent of their annual output value in 2001) as bestsellers. See Feng Jing, "Age of Bestsellers."

20 According to the journalist Yu Kai, "The publication of the novel became a literary event at that time, but mostly due to the unbelievable efforts on the author's part: even many critics admitted they had not tried to read the novel" ("New Chapter for Realist Literature," China Daily, 29 December 2003.

21 Kong, Consuming Literature, 34.

22 Zhu Linyong, "Larger than Life," China Daily, 24 April 2007.

23 Yang Dongping, interview by author, Shanghai, 14 May 2007 (tape on file with author).

24 Helen Walters, "OMA's Race to Construct in China," http://www.businessweek.com, 9 November 2006.

25 Strand, Rickshaw Beijing, 6.

26 The location debate was broadly represented by two proposals: the old-center plan of Zhu Zhaoxue and Zhao Dongri and the west-suburb plan of Liang Sicheng and Chen Zhanxiang. Those in favor of the Old City argued that

because it was the historical capital and the founding ceremony of the PRC had been held in Tiananmen Square, it should be the seat of the new government. Wu Liangyong comments, "There was little mention of the significance of the Old City or the historic architecture it contained. The idea underpinning this proposal was that making way for a new world required destroying the old." *Rehabilitating the Old City of Beijing*, 17. The west-suburb proposal, on the other hand, considered the need for aesthetic and historical continuity. Its authors wrote, "Introducing modern high-rise buildings to the central heritage area would alter the street patterns and damage townscape, which would be contradictory to our principles concerning the protection of cultural relics." Quoted in Wu, *Rehabilitating the Old City of Beijing*, 17.

27 Wu Hung, *Remaking Beijing*, 8–9.

28 See Zhu and Kwok, "Beijing." In the 1950s a large metropolitan region of 16,800 square kilometers was demarcated for Beijing, yet by the mid-1990s the built-up area was only about 1,370 square kilometers, or 8 percent of the total. See Liangyong Wu, *Rehabilitating the Old City of Beijing*, 28. The comprehensive urban plan for Beijing in 2020, however, as displayed in 2007 in the Beijing Urban Planning Exhibition Hall, is to fully develop the 16,800-square-kilometer metropolitan area for urban residential and commercial use.

29 Yan et al., "The Development of the Chinese Metropolis in the Period of Transition," 42.

30 The Beijing muncipal government has officially renamed Fourth Ring Road as Olympic Boulevard, as it is "the principal expressway connecting the majority of the Olympic venues located in the west, northwest and north parts of the city . . . designed to have eight-lanes with 147 flyovers to connect with the major streets of the city" (website of the 2008 Beijing Olympics [printouts on file with author]).

31 "Beijing shiyige xincheng guihua zhengshi fabu" (Official announcement of Beijing's eleven new towns plan), *Beijing ribao* (Beijing daily), 8 November 2007.

32 Costa et al., *Urbanization in Asia*, 75.

33 Surveys conducted in 1994 and 1998 both estimated the floating population in Beijing to be 3.2 million, or 30 percent of the total population. Cited in Gu and Liu, "Social Polarization and Segregation in Beijing," 201.

34 David Eimer, "China Races to Olympic Glory While 20m of Its Children Are Denied School," *Daily Telegraph*, 3 April 2007. China's official population statistics place Beijing's rise from 13.67 million in 2000 to 15.38 million in 2005. See "Annual Net Population Growth in Beijing Should Not Exceed 200,000," *Peoples Daily Online*, 14 September 2006.

35 Because the housing-reform program created excessively high prices, most developers urged original residents to move out so that more units could be sold at market prices. Another reason residents moved was that unclear lines of responsibility between various levels of government and the development agencies kept infrastructure improvement chronically lagging behind housing development. See Wu, *Rehabilitating the Old City of Beijing*, 54–55.

36 Statistics cited in Sit, *Beijing*, 215–24. Between 1982 and 1990, the actual population growth of Beijing's urban center, near suburbs, and far suburbs was 3.38 percent, 40.45 percent, and 13.12 percent, respectively. Cited in Yan et al., "The Development of the Chinese Metropolis in the Period of Transition," 41.

37 Sit, *Beijing*, 215.

38 In Kim et al., *Culture and the City in East Asia*, 147.

39 See Wu, *Remaking Beijing*, esp. chap. 5.

40 Ibid., *Remaking Beijing*, 139.

41 For example, a group of innovative architects were excluded from the public exhibition of the Association of Chinese Architects in the Conference of World Architects in 1999. See Wu, *Exhibiting Experimental Art in China*, 184–86. There are indications, however, that such architects are not only attracting broader public notice, but also starting to win contracts. Several of the designs featured in an alternative exhibition, "An Exhibition of Experimental Works by Young Chinese Architects," which took place at the Beijing International Convention Center on 22 June 1999, were scheduled for construction. Essays on experimental architecture and photos from this exhibition are featured in *Jinri xianfeng* (Avant-garde today) 8 (2000).

42 See, for example, Yan et al., "The Development of the Chinese Metropolis in the Period of Transition"; Fu, "The State, Capital, and Urban Restructuring in Post-Reform Shanghai"; Zhou and Logan, "Market Transition and the Commodification of Housing in Urban China"; Wu, "Real Estate Development and the Transformation of Urban Space in China's Transitional Economy, with Special Reference to Shanghai"; and Gu and Liu, "Social Polarization and Segregation in Beijing." See also Lu, *Dangdai Zhongguo shehui jieceng yanjiu baogao* (Report on social classes in contemporary China).

43 Wu Hung discusses the Central Academy of Arts demolition experience and artistic reaction, in *Transience*, 109–13.

44 Wu, *Rehabilitating the Old City of Beijing*, xx–xxi.

45 Zhou and Logan, "Market Transition and Commodification of Housing in Urban China," 142.

46 Li Jiefei elaborates on the differences between Beijing fiction by Liu Heng, Wang Shuo, and Qiu Huadong, in *Chengshi xiangkuang* (City frame), 160–87.

47 Lu, "Rewriting Beijing," 332.

48 Qiu, *Chengshi zhanche* (City tank), 59, 1.

49 Ibid., 1–2.

50 Yokomitsu, *Shanhai*, 309–10, translated in Lippit, "Topographies of Empire."

51 Qiu Huadong, *Chengshi zhanche* (City tank), 11.

52 Ibid., 45.

53 Liu, "Is There an Alternative to (Capitalist) Globalization?," 178.

54 Zhang, "Hou xin shiqi wenxue" (Post–New Era literature), 184.

55 Zhang, "'Fenlie' yu 'zhuanyi'" ("Disruption" and "change"), 8–9. Xie Mian and Zhang Yiwu outline several characteristics of "post-allegorical" writing in the post–New Era, in *Da zhuanxing* (The great transition), 29–45.

56 Quoted in Wu, *Exhibiting Experimental Art in China*, 136. Lu Peng critiques the cultural debates of the 1990s and their deleterious effects on contemporary artistic production, in the introduction to his *Zhongguo dangdai yishu shi, 1990–1999* (History of Chinese contemporary art, 1990–1999).

57 Vine, "Report from Shanghai," 30.

58 Barthes, *Image, Music, Text*, 34.

59 Zhao, Zheng, and Sheng, *Guannian Yishu 21* (Concept 21).

60 Sheng Qi, interview by author, Anfang (Darkroom) Studio, 798, Beijing, 12 May 2007 (tape on file with author). He indicated that other groups also performed in China during these years, including artists in Hangzhou and Xiamen, but due to limited communications they were unaware of each other's existence. After the June Fourth massacre, in 1989, all five members of Concept 21 went into self-exile overseas, where some still reside.

61 See, for example, Wu Wenguang's internationally released documentary *Bumming in Beijing* (1991), which follows five resident artists in 1988–89, and Zhao Liang's documentary *Farewell Yuanmingyuan* (2007), which presents the police crackdown on the village in 1994–95, when Zhao resided there. Thomas Berghuis discusses harsh conditions in both villages, in *Performance Art in China*. Xu Zhiwei shot hundreds of black-and-white photographs of happenings and performances in Yuanmingyuan Artist's Village (provided to me in May 2007). Shu Yang, curator of "Photography of Chinese Performance Art" (Beijing, May 2007), provided me with an introduction to the exhibition.

62 Zhu, "Illusory Bubble,"13.

63 Gao, "From Elite to Small Man," 164.

64 Tragically, Jia's angst-ridden roles in both films hit close to home. Despite successfully completing a drug rehabilitation program in the early 1990s (detailed in Zhang Yang's film, *Quitting* [Zuotian], 2001, for which Jia won a Silver Screen Award for Best Actor at the 2002 Singapore International Film Festival), he is believed to have relapsed and committed suicide; however, there is no public information on the actor's fate.

65 Qiu, *Yingyan* (Fly eyes), 250.

66 Qiu, "*Post-Sense Sensibility.*"

67 In her essay "One Place after Another," Miwon Kwon discusses a similar shift from "concepts" to "effects" in late-twentieth-century European and American installation art in terms that echo Qiu Zhijie's concerns.

68 Wu, *Transience*, 111.

69 From Wu Hung's interview with Sui Jianguo, quoted in Wu, "The Birth of Ruins."

70 Del Lago et al., "Space and Public," 84.

71 Photos of Zhang Dali's and Wang Jingsong's works appear in *Jinri xianfeng* (Avant-garde today) 9 (2000), 7–8. Zhang Nian's video was featured at a special exhibition of Chinese video art, Tsinghua University Art Department, 23 June 2001. Chinese video art has made great gains as a formally sanctioned discipline in art departments in the past few years, partially because the authorities link it with modern technology (i.e., "progress") and thus fail to

monitor it as closely as other potentially subversive art forms, such as performance and installation art.

72 Del Lago et al., "Space and Public," 76.

73 Owen, *Readings in Chinese Literary Thought*, 232.

74 Li and Yeo, *Rationale of the Intangible*, 29.

75 Knight, *The Heart of Time*, 223.

76 Song Dong, interview by author, Beijing Gongshe (Beijing commune), 798, Beijing, 7 May 2007 (tape on file with author).

77 Ibid.

78 Song Dong, interview by author, at his home in Xisi, Beijing, 22 June 2001 (tape on file with author).

79 Wu Hung discusses works by Song Dong and Yin Xiuzhen, in *Transience*, 120–26.

80 Zhu Ming, interview by author, at his home in Tongzhou, Beijing, 12 May 2007 (tape on file with author).

81 Wu, "Yishujia xianchang" (Artist scene), 172.

82 Ibid., 180.

83 Zhang Dali, interview by author, in Yishu Dongqu (Art east district), Beijing, 9 May 2007 (tape on file with author).

84 Leng Lin, *Shi wo* (It's me), 168, translated and cited in Wu, "Zhang Dali's *Dialogue*," 750.

85 See Wu, "Zhang Dali's *Dialogue*."

86 Jonathan Watts, "Once Hated, Now Feted—Chinese Artists Come Out from behind the Wall," *Guardian*, 11 April 2007.

87 Leng Lin's preface, appearing in both English and Chinese, overlaid a huge computer-generated image of the curator himself, which foregrounded the logistics of exhibition. Quoted in Wu, *Exhibiting Experimental Art in China*, 106.

88 Western descriptions of Chinese experimental art often exoticize these works. For example, RoseLee Goldberg describes Cai Guo Qiang's "explosions of gunpowder in landscape" performances as "bring[ing] to the West a deeply spiritual sensibility that is as mysterious as it is curiously recognizable" by conveying "a Chinese view of human beings as a microcosm of the universe" (*Performance*, 60). Yet Cai's performances, formally titled *The Century with Mushroom Clouds: Project for Twentieth Century* (1996) and enacted against the Manhattan skyline and at the Nevada Nuclear Test Site, signify American economic and military hegemony and are in fact far more transgressive than such characterizations imply.

89 Wu Hung traces the function of the Imperial Ancestral Temple from its traditional use, through its instantiation as the Workers' Cultural Palace under Mao, to its promotion as a commercial site used to stage, among other events, a Pierre Cardin fashion show and a performance of *Turandot* in 1998. See *Exhibiting Experimental Art in China*, 94–98.

90 Discussed in ibid., 181–83.

91 "Wildlife" is well documented in its extensive catalog, *Yesheng* (Wildlife). Wu

Hung also discusses "Wildlife" and "Departing from China," in *Exhibiting Experimental Art in China*, 181, 142–44, respectively.

92 The curator Zhang Zhaohui discusses the "Food as Art" show in "Jinri chujing" (Today's context). The art critic Feng Boyi discusses "Persistent Deviation," "Post-Sense Sensiblity," and "It's Me" in "Jiushiniandai dangdai yishu de jiben xingtai he geju" (The fundamental form and structure of 1990s contemporary art).

93 Wu, *Exhibiting Experimental Art in China*, 133.

94 Zhang Dali, interview by author, in Yishu Dongqu (Art east district), Beijing, 9 May 2007 (tape on file with author).

95 Ibid.

96 *Man and Beast*, Zhang Dali's solo show, presented as part of the exhibition "Three Unities," curated by Mathieu Borysevicz and Yan Yang, ddmwarehouse, Shanghai, 26 May–24 June 2007.

97 Zhang Dali, interview by author, in Yishu Dongqu (Art east district), Beijing, 9 May 2007 (tape on file with author).

98 The Gao Brothers exhibition "Zhua xiaojie" (Arresting prostitutes), held at Beijing New Art Projects, Second Space, Dashanzi Art District, Beijing, opened on 28 April 2007.

99 Gao, "From Elite to Small Man," 164.

4.   **Consuming the Postsocialist City**

1 Pieterse, *Globalization and Culture*, 78–79.

2 Fei, "Peasantry and Gentry," 14.

3 Scholars prepared a "roster of world cities" through compiling data into scoring systems in which alpha world cities included London, Paris, New York, and Tokyo, which each scored twelve, and Chicago, Frankfurt, Hong Kong, Los Angeles, Milan, and Singapore, which each scored ten. Beta world cities scoring more than six but less than ten included San Francisco, Sydney, and Moscow. Gammas scored less than seven but more than three. Beaverstock, Smith, and Taylor, "A Roster of World Cities," cited in Byrne, *Understanding the Urban*.

4 Wasserstrom, "Is Global Shanghai 'Good to Think'?"

5 Zhang, "Shanghai Nostalgia," 360.

6 Zhong, "Shanghai Literature and Beyond," 101.

7 Yang, *Chengshi jifeng* (Urban vicissitudes), 352–55, 332–37, 316.

8 Ibid., 1.

9 Ibid., 121.

10 Xudong Zhang, "Shanghai Nostalgia," 360.

11 Zhong, "Shanghai Literature and Beyond," 101.

12 Zhou, "Shanghai qi" (Shanghai spirit), 62. Originally published in *Yusi* (Spinners of words) 112 (1 January 1927).

13 Dai, "Imagined Nostalgia," 158.

14 See Saul, *The Collapse of Globalism and the Reinvention of the World*. Wang

Xiaoming discusses Shanghai catchphrases in "Cong 'Huaihai Lu' dao 'Meijia Qiao'" (From "Huaihai Road" to "Meijia Bridge"), 314. Originally published in *Wenxue Pinglun* (Literary review) 3 (2002): 5–20.

15 See Yang, "Cyber Writing as Urban Fashion: The Case of Anni Baobei," *Southeast Review of Asian Studies* (2006).

16 Shi Yong, interview by author, Shanghai, 26 May 2005 (tape on file with author).

17 Ibid.

18 Shi Yong's explanation for participants of *The New Image of Shanghai Today* (on file with the author).

19 Shi Yong, interview by author, Shanghai, 26 May 2005 (tape on file with author).

20 Shi Yong's explanation of *Adding One Concept on Top of Another* (on file with the author).

21 Bhabha, "Of Mimicry and Man," 86.

22 The text and graphics for Zhou Tiehai's *B Shares* is reproduced in Hou and Obrist, *Cities on the Move*.

23 "Abstraction today is no longer that of the map, the double, the mirror or the concept. Simulation is no longer that of a territory, a referential being or a substance. It is the generation by models of a real without origin or reality: a hyperreal. The territory no longer precedes the map, nor survives it. Henceforth, it is the map that precedes the territory—precession of simulacra—it is the map that engenders the territory." Baudrillard, *Selected Writings*, 166.

24 Shi Yong, interview by author, Shanghai, 26 May 2005, emphasis added (tape on file with author).

25 Ibid.

26 Zhang, "Shanghai Nostalgia," 349–50.

27 Seagoing vessels docked on the Huangpu River, with Suzhou Creek docking barges plying wares along the inland waterways. After the Treaty of Nanjing, signed in 1842, Suzhou Creek divided the British Concession on the southern bank from the American settlement on its northern bank, until they merged in 1863 into the International Settlement. When the Japanese invaded Shanghai in 1937, the creek formed the boundary between the International Settlement (south) and the Japanese Concession (north).

28 "Suzhou Creek Rehabilitation," 1998, website of the Asian Development Bank (printouts on file with author).

29 I do not take issue with rehabilitation per se. The creek's black color and foul smell, first reported in 1920, rendered portions of the city nearly uninhabitable; prior to rehabilitation people living near the river had to barricade themselves inside to avoid noxious fumes. Yet the multibillion-dollar gentrification process has been rife with corruption, cramming real estate developments along the banks in violation of setback regulations.

30 Yang, *Jingpai yu haipai bijiao yanjiu* (A comparative study of the Beijing and Shanghai Schools), 178.

31 Xiao and Wang, "Nanfang de xiezuo" (Southern writing), 117.

32 Hsia, *History of Modern Chinese Fiction*, 165.

33 Lee, "The City as Seductress," 135.

34 Mao, *Midnight*, 7–10.

35 Farrer, "Bars in Reform-Era Shanghai."

36 Anne Nugent, "Alcoholic Drinks: Propping Up the Global Bar," 26 March 2004, available at the website of Euromonitor International (printout on file with author).

37 Silbergeld, *Hitchcock with a Chinese Face*, 117n1.

38 Rooney, review of *Suzhou River*.

39 Brandon Zatt, "The Horns of the Creek," http://www.cityweekend.com.cn, 4 December 2006. Interestingly, Yuan dynasty waterworks, intended to dredge Wusong River silt, were discovered in Shanghai in May 2001. See "Ancient River Control Works Discovered in Shanghai," *People's Daily Online*, 20 October 2002.

40 Wang, *Illuminations from the Past*, 254.

41 "February 1, 1998" appears in the film, on police tape that cordons off the Happy Tavern after it is closed. The elegant steel Waibaidu Bridge, built by an Englishman in 1907 at the confluence of Suzhou Creek and the Huangpu River, is a symbol of colonial humiliation. Its name initially referred to its positioning as the outermost (*wai*) ferry crossing, but later played on an alternate meaning of *wai*, which is exemplified in the saying "foreigners [*wai*] cross for free [*baidu*]"; from 1937 to 1941, Japanese soldiers would stop Chinese, humiliate them, and punish them if they hadn't shown proper respect, while foreigners were allowed to "pass freely."

42 Silbergeld, *Hitchcock with a Chinese Face*, 43.

43 Baudrillard, *The Evil Demon of Images*, 28.

44 Baudrillard, *Simulations*, 10.

45 Jerome Silbergeld explicates the motif of the river goddess in classical Chinese literature, particularly in Cao Zhi's third-century poem "Luoshen Fu" (Rhapsody on the Goddess of the Luo River), in *Hitchcock with a Chinese Face*, 26.

46 Baudrillard, *The Evil Demon of Images*, 29.

47 Ibid.

48 Ibid.

49 From the DVD cover of *Suzhou River*.

50 Ban Wang, *Illuminations from the Past*, 255.

51 Lee, "The City as Seductress," 156.

52 Li, "Bu maoxian de lucheng" (A risk-free path), 351. Originally published in *Dangdai zuojia pinglun* (Contemporary author criticism) 1 (2003): 25–39.

53 Zhang, *Shanghai Nostalgia*, 370.

54 Zhao Yaomin, of the Shanghai Dramatic Arts Center, wrote the stage adaptation of *Song of Everlasting Sorrow*, which debuted in April 2003, was directed by Su Leci, and starred Zhang Lu as Wang Qiyao. The Hong Kong actress Maggie Cheung Ho Yee (Zhang Keyi) plays the lead in the mainland television series *Song of Everlasting Sorrow* (2005). Stanley Kwan's film *Everlasting Regret* (2005), starring the Taiwanese pop diva Sammi Cheng and the Hong Kong Star Tony

Leung, won the Open Prize Award at the Venice Film Festival in 2005 and the Film of Merit Award at the Hong Kong Film Critics Society Awards in 2006, where Leung won Best Actor.

55 Wang, *Ruci fanhua* (Urban splendor), 119.

56 Bai, "The Everlasting Sorrow," 211.

57 Parenthetical pages in text refer, respectively, to Wang, *Chang hen ge* (Song of everlasting sorrow), and to the English translation by Michael Berry and Egan, *Song of Everlasting Regret*.

58 Chen, "Shanghai Writers on Shanghai Writing."

59 Wang Anyi, interview by author, Shanghai, 20 May 1997 (tape on file with author).

60 Wang Anyi insisted, "I didn't write it for nostalgic reasons. Everyone mentions nostalgia, but I don't really see it being about nostalgia at all. Wang Qiyao is a product of the old society (*jiu renwu*). To write the story of this character you *have* to write about the past and the memory of the past. It is dictated by the nature of the story" (ibid.).

61 Tang, "Melancholy against the Grain," 339. In this chapter Tang discusses *My Uncle's Story* (Shushu de gushi, 1990), *Sadness for the Pacific* (Shangxin Taipingyang, 1993), and *Records and Fiction* (Jishi yu xugou, 1993).

62 Xudong Zhang, *Shanghai Nostalgia*, 383.

63 Jeffrey Wasserstrom explores differing positions on this question, in "Is Global Shanghai 'Good to Think'?"

64 Wasserstrom notes "the often-made claim (which seems believable, if hard to test) made about Shanghai in the 1990s: that, at certain moments, between one-quarter and one-half of all the world's cranes were in operation [there]" ("Is Global Shanghai 'Good to Think'?," 212). Chunlan Zhao refers to the generalization that Shanghai without its *longtang* is no longer Shanghai, in "From *Shikumen* to New-Style," 73.

65 Wang Anyi's literary intuition about the devaluation of the neoliberal commodity is verified by quantitative analysis. See, for example, ul Haque, "Commodities under Neoliberalism."

66 Zhang, "Shanghai Nostalgia," 367. Emphasis added.

67 Zhao, "From *Shikumen* to New-Style," 72. Emphasis added.

68 *Shikumen* means stone archway; *li* means neighborhood; *long* (or *nong*, in Shanghai dialect) means alley.

69 Foreigners initiated a business model of mass production for quick profit, where the buildings were constructed by their compradors and local builders. The earliest *lilong* compound resembled the *lifang* residential ward in imperial capitals, but instead of being enclosed by solid walls in the manner of the *lifang*, the *lilong* was enclosed by shops open to surrounding streets. The latter's commercial character expanded into the residential *lilong*, where the main living space of a house, usually on the second floor, looked out through large windows to the alley (*longtang*) beyond the small courtyard. This spatial feature reversed the introverted pattern of the traditional courtyard house, as

the *lilong* became a milieu of mixed residential and commercial activities. See Liang, "The Meeting of Courtyard and Street."

70   See Zhao, "From *Shikumen* to New-Style," 50–51.

71   Albert Wing Tai Wai discusses how Shanghai has been "museumized" to conjure up "Old Shanghai," in "Place Promotion and Iconography in Shanghai's Xintiandi."

72   Mayo, *Los Angeles*, 319, quoted in Mike Davis, *City of Quartz*, 17.

73   For example, Flaubert writes that Emma "set out towards La Huchette, unaware that she was hastening to offer what had so angered her a while ago, not in the least conscious of her prostitution" (*Madame Bovary*, 244).

74   Jenks, "Watching Your Step," 148.

75   Censorship in the PRC is alive and well. This passage, among others, was censored in the 2004 edition of the novel, published by People's Press (Renmin chubanshe) for the Mao Dun Award Series.

76   Wang, *Illuminations from the Past*, 230.

77   Benjamin, "The Work of Art in an Age of Mechanical Reproduction," 222.

78   Wang, *Illuminations from the Past*, 230.

79   Wang, "A Manifesto for Cultural Studies" ("Binlin 'da shidai' de Zhongguo"), 278.

80   *Mangjing* (Blind shaft, 2003), Li Yang's film on coalminers whose deaths are recompensed through payoffs, and *Xu Sanguan maixue ji* (Chronicle of a blood merchant, 1995), Yu Hua's novel on the blood-infusion market, are poignant critiques of the neoliberal phenomenon of commodifying bodies and corpses. Ellen Moodie documents similar neoliberal trends in El Salvador, in "Microbus Crashes and Coco-cola Cash."

81   Baudrillard, *The Consumer Society*.

82   A lament often heard among long-term residents of Shanghai is that they have been displaced to its cheaper suburbs, its downtown now being occupied primarily by migrant entrepreneurs, who comprise the majority of the city's new rich and service classes.

83   Castells, *The Castells Reader on Cities and Social Theory*, 350.

84   Dirlik, "Architectures of Global Modernity, Colonialism, and Places," 55.

85   Ruan, "The Conservation of Shanghai's Historical and Cultural Heritage against the Background of Market Economy," 236.

86   Koolhaas, "Architecture and Globalization," 239, cited in Dirlik, "Architectures of Global Modernity, Colonialism, and Places," 52.

5.   **The Melancholic Urban Subject**

Portions of this chapter appeared in an earlier form in "Privacy and Its Ill Effects in Post-Mao Fiction," in *Chinese Concepts of Privacy*, edited by Bonnie McDougall and Anders Hansson (Boston: Brill, 2002).

1   For a detailed discussion of the intellectual trends of the 1980s, see Jing Wang, *High Culture Fever*.

2 Silbergeld, *Hitchcock with a Chinese Face*, 3.

3 Sang, *The Emerging Lesbian*, 221.

4 Simmel, "The Metropolis and Mental Life," 409.

5 For critiques of Simmel, see Moretti, "Homo Palpitans"; Wolff, "The Invisible Flaneuse."

6 Simmel, "The Metropolis and Mental Life," 415–16.

7 See Inness, *Privacy, Intimacy and Isolation*.

8 A joint survey conducted in 1999 by the *Wall Street Journal* and the National Broadcasting Corporation (NBC) suggested, for example, that privacy was the issue that concerned U.S. citizens most about the twenty-first century, ahead of overpopulation, racial tensions, and global warming (cited in Lester, "The Reinvention of Privacy," 27). The terrorist attacks of September 11, however, have provoked new public debate in the United States, wherein the value of individual-privacy rights are being reevaluated relative to national-security concerns.

9 Friedmann, "Expanding Spaces of Personal Autonomy."

10 Arendt, *The Human Condition*, 38.

11 Freud, "Mourning and Melancholia."

12 Kubin, Introduction, 14, 10.

13 Wang Xiaoming states, "Even after the terrible, bloody shock of June 1989, as soon as the top leaders proclaimed that economic reform would continue, people quickly recovered from their depression, as if nothing much had happened; at worst a slight detour. The tune of 'modernization' struck up again, and the rhythm of 'reform' beat even faster, as if China had more hope than ever. I can clearly remember how loud the clamor for modernization was in 1992, when the slogan was launched once again, drowning out all other sounds, filling everyone's ears with one ringing call: 'This is modernization—hurry up and hop on the bandwagon or you'll miss it!'" ("A Manifesto for Cultural Studies," 281).

14 Parenthetical pages in text refer, respectively, to Liu Heng, *Hei de xue*, and to Howard Goldblatt's English translation, *Black Snow*.

15 See Hertz, "Face in the Crowd," 280.

16 "In grief the world becomes poor and empty; in melancholia it is the ego itself. The patient represents his ego to us as worthless, incapable of any effort and morally despicable; he reproaches himself, vilifies himself and expects to be cast out and chastised" (Freud, "Mourning and Melancholia," 167).

17 Li Jiefei, *Chengshi xiangkuang* (City frame), 50.

18 Wang Xiaoming, interview by author, Shanghai, March 1997. Many prominent literary critics—including Chen Sihe, of Fudan University, and Chen Xiaoming, of Peking University (formerly of the Chinese Academy of Social Sciences)—interpret *Private Life* as solipsistic. Chen Sihe, interview by author, Shanghai, 28 July 1997; and Chen Xiaoming, interview by author, Beijing, 7 June 1997. In "Chen Ran," Dai Jinhua, of Peking University, analyzes Chen Ran's works in relationship to Freudian concepts of *lianmu* (love for the mother) and *lianfu* (love for the father), which constitutes a straightforward

autobiographical reading of Chen's work: Chen's parents divorced during her childhood; her father abandoned the family; her relationship with her mother is especially close.

19 Kong, *Consuming Literature*.

20 Chen Ran, "Ling yishan kaiqi de men" (Another open door), an interview by Xiao Gang, quoted in Sang, *The Emerging Lesbian*, 221.

21 Chen Ran, interview by author, Beijing, July 1997 (tape on file with author).

22 Chen Ran, "Chaoxingbie yishi yu wode chuangzuo" (Gender-transcendent consciousness and my creative writing).

23 Vidler, "Bodies in Space/Subjects in the City," 45.

24 Grosz, "Bodies-Cities," 250. Emphasis added.

25 Parenthetical pages in text refer, respectively, to Chen Ran, *Siren shenghuo* (Private life), and to John Howard-Gibbon's English translation, *A Private Life*. This passage is my own translation.

26 De Certeau, *The Practice of Everyday Life*, 103.

27 Marcus, "Placing *Rosemary's Baby*," 122.

28 Benjamin, "On Some Motifs in Baudelaire," 171.

29 I emend the first two sentences of Howard-Gibbon's translation to highlight psychological connotations in the original.

30 See Kern, *The Culture of Time and Space, 1880–1918*.

31 Quoted in Tang, "Decorating Culture," 309. The bathroom so symbolizes the growing importance of privacy in China that a popular play, *Cesuo* (Toilet, 2004), details the radical transformation of postsocialist urban culture via the evolution of public bathrooms.

32 My rather literal translation of this passage emphasizes Chen's focus on interiority and exteriority.

33 See Freud, "On the Mechanism of Paranoia."

34 Ding Laixian, "Nüxing wenxue ji qita" (Female literature and other things), *Zhonghua dushu bao*, 20 December 1995, quoted in Sang, *The Emerging Lesbian*, 177.

35 Sang, *The Emerging Lesbian*, 209.

36 In her discussion of Lacan's mirror stage Kaja Silverman defines "presence": "When [the imago] seems unified with [the ego], the subject experiences that mode of 'altogetherness' generally synonymous with 'presence'" ("The Bodily Ego," 17).

37 Freud, "Mourning and Melancholia," 166–70.

38 Butler, "Psychic Inceptions: Melancholy, Ambivalence, Rage," 171.

39 Ibid., 183.

40 Chen, "Sun Ganlu: Chengshi mengyouzhe" (Sun Ganlu: City sleepwalker), 183.

41 Parenthetical pages in text refer to Sun Ganlu, *Huxi* (Breathing).

42 This statistic is based on a 1985 study cited in Yang, *Chengshi jifeng* (Urban vicissitudes), 220. In an interview, Ge Fei, an acclaimed avant-garde writer who moved to Shanghai, in the 1980s, to attend college, acknowledged that his hardest adjustment was to the cramped living quarters: "In the coun-

tryside we had a large, spacious house, but in Shanghai I had to share a room with seven others, and I'd never had to live with so many people in such close quarters before. Nothing you did was private—everything was public knowledge. There wasn't space to think. There was no such thing as private secrets. Lack of space was the hardest adjustment" (interview by author, Shanghai, 17 April 1997 [tape on file with author]).

43 Raskolnikov's family worries about how his "coffin-like" room has altered his thinking, as is evident from his sister Rodya's remark that "one's surroundings have a great deal to do with crime, I can assure you" (Dostoevsky, *Crime and Punishment*, 282, 309).

44 Schilder, "Psycho-analysis of Space," 278.

45 Negative portrayals of emigration emerged in popular culture at this same time. Plays, books, television shows, and films featured the disillusionment of those who went abroad, including, for example, the wildly popular television miniseries *Beijingren zai Niuyue* (A Beijingen in New York) from 1993 and a novel by the Shanghai writer Tang Ying, *Meiguo laide qizi* (A wife from America), which was later adapted by her husband, Zhang Xian, as a (well-received) play about a Shanghai native who married an American and lived miserably in the United States before returning to marry a Shanghainese man.

46 See Visser, "Displacement of the Urban-Rural Confrontation in Su Tong's Fiction."

47 Bhabha's Third Space, in the context of postcolonial theory, is constructed as that space through which the interpretation in the communicative act between self and other is worked out. See Bhabha, *The Location of Culture*, 37.

48 See, for example, Zhang Chengzhi's article "My God Does Not Reside Overseas," and Xinmin Liu's discussion in "A Marginal Return?"

49 Bhabha, *The Location of Culture*, 38.

50 See Freud, "On the Mechanism of Paranoia."

51 Burgin, *In/Different Spaces*, 120.

52 "In China homosexuality is considered abnormal, but because Shanghai is an international city with a tradition of accepting Western ideas, it is more accepting of unconventional behavior. But this isn't a story about homosexuality, although Luo Ke has some latent homosexual tendencies. Actually, everyone is a potential homosexual, just like narcissism. It's not a question of loving or not—it's a question of the object of that love" (Sun Ganlu, interview by author, Shanghai, 27 June 1997 [tape on file with author]).

53 Parenthetical pages in text refer, respectively, to Mian Mian, *Tang* (Beijing: Zhongguo xiju chubanshe, 2000) and to Andrea Lingenfelter's English translation, *Candy*.

54 "Author Mian Mian Challenges China," 7 March 2005, http://news.bbc.co.uk.

55 Lingenfelter, "Translator's Note," vii–viii.

56 Mian, "A Conversation with the Author of *Candy*," 284.

57 Ferry, "Marketing Chinese Women Writers in the 1990s," 672.

58 Feuchtwang, "Reflections on Privacy in China," 227.

59 Ferry, "Marketing Chinese Women Writers in the 1990s," 668.

60 See Meng, "Wenhua bengkui shidai de taowang yu guiyi" (Escape and support in an age of cultural collapse); and Xu, "Contesting Memory for Intellectual Self-Positioning."

61 Ferry, "Marketing Chinese Women Writers in the 1990s," 674.

62 Kong, *Consuming Literature*, 1.

63 See Zhang, "Hou xin shiqi wenxue" (Post–New Era literature), 184.

6. Postsocialist Urban Ethics

Portions of this chapter were published as "Urban Ethics: Modernity and the Morality of Everyday Life," in *Contested Modernities in Chinese Literature*, edited by Charles Laughlin (New York: Palgrave, 2005).

1 Poole, *Morality and Modernity*, ix.

2 Ibid., 158, 151.

3 See Dai, "Invisible Writing"; Yang, "Cyber Writing as Urban Fashion"; and Luo, "Shei zhi gonggong xing?" (Whose public characteristics?). Xudong Zhang states categorically that "the post-Mao Chinese 'public sphere' is a sham whose only existence is in the realm of ideology and fantasy" ("The Making of the Post-Tiananmen Intellectual Field," 22).

4 Li Tuo, a critic who popularized the works of avant-garde writers of the late 1980s both in China and abroad, was the most virulent of several who decried the style of new urban literature at a conference sponsored by *Beijing wenxue* (Beijing literature) in Beijing in June 1997, which was attended by both "avant-garde" and "new urbanite" writers.

5 Taylor, *Modernities*, 30.

6 Li, *Chengshi xiangkuang* (City frame), 39–40.

7 See Taylor, *The Ethics of Authenticity*.

8 Habermas's arguments in *Theorie des kommunikativen Handelns* are summarized by many theorists, including in Poole, *Morality and Modernity*, 78–85, and in Taylor, *Sources of the Self: The Making of the Modern Identity*, 509–10.

9 See Tong, *The Dialectics of Modernization*. Although Habermas had "commanded enormous philosophical and moral authority among Chinese intellectuals since the 1980s," he was "dismissed overnight as a shameless apologist for war" when he supported the 1999 war in Kosovo, which incited widespread Chinese nationalism after the Chinese embassy in Belgrade was hit by American cruise missiles on 9 May 1999. See Zhang's discussion of Habermas's "fall from grace," in *Whither China?*, 36–37.

10 See Zhu Xueqin, "1998: Ziyouzhuyi de xueli yanshuo" (1998: Liberal discourse), part 1, *Nanfang Zhoumo* (Southern weekend), 25 December 1998; part 2, *Zhongguo tushu shangbao* (China book business report), 5 January 1999.

11 Xudong Zhang denounces the "self-glorifying and self-pitying tone in the Chen Yinke literature" as "indicative of the Chinese 'liberal' scholars' search for a moral and psychological anchor as well as symbolic power in a time of socioeconomic differentiation" (*Whither China?*, 20). Yet Wang Xiaoming's biweekly seminars, which I attended in the spring of 1997, while keen to

uncover historical precedents to the Chinese problem of modernity, generated passionate, politically committed discussions, rather than serving as mere philological exercises in arcane scholarship.

12 Wang, "The New Criticism," 77–78.

13 The *renwen jingshen* debates were sparked by responses to a series of round-table discussions sponsored by the journal *Dushu* (Reading). The minutes of these discussions are published in *Dushu* 3, 4, 5, 6, 7 (1993). Follow-up articles are collected in Wang Xiaoming, *Renwen jingshen xunsi lu* (Thoughts on the humanist spirit). Wen Liping summarizes the discussions in "Guanyu renwen jingshen taolun zongshu" (A summary of the humanist spirit discussions). Ben Xu, in turn, summarizes Wen's article, in "'From Modernity to Chineseness.'"

14 Bellah, *Habits of the Heart*, 131–33.

15 See Liu and Zhang, *Liu Xinwu Zhang Yiwu duihua lu: "Hou shiji" de wenhua liaowang* (Record of conversations between Liu Xinwu and Zhang Yiwu: Gazing at "post-era" culture), 222.

16 Chen, "Jianyao pingjie" (Brief commentary [on He Dun's "Life is not a crime"]), 304

17 Chen, "Wanshengdai yu jiushi niandai wenxue liuxiang" (The belated generation and the literary trends in the 1990s), 6.

18 The term "post critic" was coined by the then London-based scholar Yiheng Zhao in his controversial essay "Post-isms and Chinese New Conservatism," in which he argued that the various "post" theories advocated by scholars such as Zhang Yiwu and Chen Xiaoming were aligned with the bureaucratic encouragement of intellectual conformism

19 Harpham, *Shadows of Ethics*, 18.

20 Zhang, *Whither China?*, 21.

21 For example, Cui Zhiyuan has argued, in "Institutional Innovation and a Second Liberation of Thought," that China must eliminate its fixation on market ideology and the "institutional fetishism" of imitating capitalist models from the West and instead innovate by incorporating what was valuable from its socialist experience. Wang Hui's scholarship also historicizes received notions of modernity in China's past two centuries of development, while challenging Cui's economic assessments, such as Cui's lauding of Town-Village Enterprises (TVES) as original forms of collective but not state ownership that have proved economically very dynamic. Wang instead sees the success of TVES as a temporary function of the dual price structures that came into force with the early reforms, which enabled the TVES to buy raw materials at state prices and sell outputs at market prices.

22 See Miller, *The Ethics of Reading*; Cavell, *This New Yet Unapproachable America*; Critchley, *The Ethics of Deconstruction*; Ziarek, *The Rhetoric of Failure*; Eaglestone, *Ethical Criticism*; Harpham, *Shadow of Ethics*; Halliwell, *Modernism and Morality*.

23 Some consider the rejection of metaphors of the nation-state, the main literary strategy from the May Fourth period until the 1980s, to be one of the key

distinctions of urban fiction of the 1990s. See Zhang, "Hou xin shiqi wenxue" (Post–New Era literature), 184.

24 Booth, *The Company We Keep*, 40.

25 Harpham, *Shadows of Ethics*, 33.

26 Ibid., 36.

27 Kearney, *On Stories*, 155.

28 Jones, "The Violence of the Text," 39.

29 Wagner, "The Subversive Fiction of Yu Hua," 236.

30 Kearney, *On Stories*, 153, referring to Langer, *Holocaust Testimonies*, 183. See also Geddes, *Evil after Postmodernism: Histories, Narratives, Ethics*, especially Shattuck, "Narrating Evil."

31 Owen, *Readings in Chinese Literary Thought*, 41.

32 Watson, *Zhuangzi*, 39–40.

33 Levinas, *Otherwise than Being*, 37.

34 Lu Xun, *A Brief History of Chinese Fiction* (*Zhongguo xiaoshuo shilue*), 1.

35 Wong, presentation at the international conference "Literary Studies in the Age of Globalization."

36 Parenthetical pages in text refer to Qiu, *Yingyan* (Fly eyes).

37 Simmel, *The Philosophy of Money*, 474; Levinas, *Otherwise than Being*, 92.

38 Zhang, "Fengsuo."

39 Bloom, *The Closing of the American Mind*, 84.

40 Stewart, *On Longing*, 65.

41 Meng, "Wenhua bengkui shidai de taowang yu guiyi" (Escape and support in an age of cultural collapse), 53.

42 Xu, "Contesting Memory for Intellectual Self-Positioning," 159.

43 Zhang, *Whither China?*, 20.

44 See Wang, *Zai xin yishi xingtai de longzhao xia* (Under the shroud of the new ideology), especially 238–42.

45 Mill, *On Liberty*, 190.

46 Berman, *All That Is Solid Melts into Air*, 15.

47 Zhu Wen, *Shenme shi laji, shenme shi ai* (What's trash, what's love?).

48 Zhu Wen's decadent depiction of sexuality is perhaps one of the major reasons critics have not been fully appreciative of his fiction. Li Jiefei is an exception, and makes the astute point that narration of corporal desire is one of the defining features of urban fiction in the 1990s, unlike the idealization of romantic love which defined most writing in the 1980s. He agrees that using sex as an easy means of "approaching another" debases its meaning; however, he points out that it is a fundamental characteristic of a commercialized urban society. See Li, *Chengshi xiangkuang* (City frame), chap. 2, "Quti de yuwang" (Corporal desire).

49 Huang Fayou, "Zai youdangzhong qiu kun" (Trapped in idleness), 78, translated and cited in McGrath, *Postsocialist Modernity*, 86.

50 Levinas, *Otherwise than Being*, 40.

51 Zhu Wen, Han Dong, Lu Yang, Wu Chenjun, and other Nanjing writers and artists, interview by author, Nanjing, 1 August 1997.

52 Wang et al., "Xiandai renwen jingshen de shengcheng" (The generation of modernist humanist spirit), 231, also cited in McGrath, *Postsocialist Modernity*, 87.

53 See McGrath, *Postsocialist Modernity*, 81–88; Song, "Piaoliu de fangzi he xuwang de lutu" (Floating houses and fabricated journeys); and Wang et al., "Xiandai renwen jingshen de shengcheng" (The generation of modernist humanist spirit).

54 McGrath, *Postsocialist Modernity*, 81.

55 Subsequent in-text page references to all three novellas are from He Dun, *Shenghuo wuzui*.

56 Tang, "Decorating Culture," 534.

57 Baudrillard, *For a Critique of the Political Economy of the Sign*, 30, quoted in Tang, "Decorating Culture," 535.

58 Dai, "Invisible Writing," 44.

59 Parenthetical pages in text refer to He Dun, *Ximalaya Shan* (The Himalayas).

60 "China's Hippies Find their Berkeley," *China Daily*, 22 September 2003.

61 Chen, *Fangzhen de niandai* (Age of imitation), 187.

62 Wang, *Zai xin yishi xingtai de longzhao xia* (Under the shroud of the new ideology), 205.

63 Li Jiefei, *Chengshi xiangkuang* (City frame), 79.

64 Qiu Huadong, "Shei shi daode zhifaren?" (Who is the enforcer of morality?), *Nanfang zhoumo* (Southern weekend), 25 April 1997, 5.

Conclusion

1 Zhu Ming, interview by author, at his home in Tongzhou, Beijing, 12 May 2007 (tape on file with author).

2 Li Xiaodong, quoted in Moffat, "Yuhu Elementary School and Community Center," 11. See also Gregory, "Elementary Education"; and Martin, "Li Xiaodong."

3 Li Xiaodong, interview by author, Beijing, April 2005 (tape on file with author). See also Li and Yeo, *Rationale of the Intangible*.

4 See Abramson, "The Dialectics of Urban Planning in China," 74, fig. 4.1, "Dialectical logic of changing urban planning practice in China."

Bibliography

Abbas, Ackbar. *Hong Kong: Culture and the Politics of Disappearance*. Minneapolis: University of Minnesota Press, 1997.

Abramson, Daniel B. "The Dialectics of Urban Planning in China." *China's Emerging Cities: The Making of New Urbanism*, ed. Fulong Wu, 66–86. London: Routledge, 2007.

——. Review of *The Making and Selling of Post-Mao Beijing*, by Anne-Marie Broudehoux. Modern Chinese Literature and Culture Resource Center Publication, February 2005.

——. "Urban Planning in China: Continuity and Change." *Journal of the American Planning Association* 72, no. 2 (spring 2006): 197–216.

Abramson, Daniel B., Michael Leaf, and Tan Ying. "Social Research and the Localization of Chinese Urban Planning Practice: Some Ideas from Quanzhou, Fujian." *The New Chinese City: Globalization and Market Reform*, ed. John Logan, 167–80. Oxford, Mass.: Blackwell, 2002.

Ang, Ien. "Shui xuyao wenhua yanjiu?" (Who needs cultural studies?). *Wenhua yanjiu* (Cultural studies) 1 (2000): 55–63.

Arendt, Hannah. *The Human Condition*. Chicago: University of Chicago Press, 1958.

Arnold, Matthew. *Culture and Anarchy*. New Haven, Conn.: Yale University Press, 1994.

Bachelard, Gaston. *The Poetics of Space*. Boston: Beacon, 1992.

Bai Juyi. "The Everlasting Sorrow." *The White Pony: An Anthology of Chinese Poetry from the Earliest Times to the Present Day*, ed. Robert Payne, 257–63. New York: J. Day, 1947.

Bai Ye, Wang Shuo, Wu Bin, and Yang Zhengguang.

"Xuanze de ziyou yu wenhua taishi" (Freedom of choice and cultural trends). *Renwen jingshen xunsi lu* (Thoughts on the humanist spirit), ed. Wang Xiaoming, 84–99. Shanghai: Wenhui chubanshe, 1996.

Bao Zhiyu. "Jianzhuxue fanyi chuyi" (A modest proposal for translations of architectural theory). *Jianzhu shi* (Architect) 2 (2005): 75–85.

Barmé, Geremie. *In the Red: On Contemporary Chinese Culture.* New York: Columbia University Press, 1999.

——. "The Revolution of Resistance." *Chinese Society: Change, Conflict, and Resistance,* ed. Elizabeth J. Perry and Mark Selden, 198–220. London: Routledge, 2000.

Barmé, Geremie, and Gloria Davies. "Have We Been Noticed Yet? Intellectual Contestation and the Chinese Web." *Chinese Intellectuals between State and Market,* ed. Edward Gu and Merle Goldman, 75–108. London: RoutledgeCurzon, 2004.

Barthes, Roland. *Image, Music, Text.* Translated by Stephen Heath. New York: Hill and Wang, 1977.

Baudrillard, Jean. *The Consumer Society: Myths and Structures.* London: Sage, 1998.

——. *The Evil Demon of Images.* Sydney: Power Institute of Fine Arts, 1987.

——. *For a Critique of the Political Economy of the Sign.* Translated by Charles Levin. St. Louis: Telos, 1981.

——. *Selected Writings.* Edited by Mark Poster. Stanford, Calif.: Stanford University Press, 1988.

——. *Simulations.* New York: Semiotext(e), 1983.

Beaverstock, Jonathan V., Richard G. Smith, and Peter J. Taylor. "A Roster of World Cities." *Cities* 16 (1999): 445–58.

Bellah, Robert. *Habits of the Heart.* Berkeley: University of California Press, 1985.

Benjamin, Walter. "On Some Motifs in Baudelaire." *Illuminations: Essays and Reflections,* 155–200. Edited by Hannah Arendt. New York: Schocken, 1969.

——. "The Work of Art in an Age of Mechanical Reproduction." *Illuminations: Essays and Reflections,* 217–52. Edited by Hannah Arendt. New York: Schocken, 1969.

Bergère, Marie-Claire. " 'The Other China': Shanghai from 1919 to 1949." *Shanghai: Revolution and Development in an Asian Metropolis,* ed. Christopher Howe, 1–34. Cambridge: Cambridge University Press, 1981.

Berghuis, Thomas. *Performance Art in China.* Beijing: Timezone 8, 2007.

Berman, Marshall. *All That Is Solid Melts into Air: The Experience of Modernity.* London: Verso, 1983.

Bhabha, Homi K. *The Location of Culture.* New York: Routledge, 1994.

——. "Of Mimicry and Man: The Ambivalence of Colonial Disourse." *The Location of Culture,* 85–92. New York: Routledge, 1994.

Bloom, Allan. *The Closing of the American Mind.* New York: Simon and Schuster, 1987.

Booth, Wayne C. *The Company We Keep: An Ethics of Fiction.* Berkeley: University of California Press, 1988.

Bourdieu, Pierre. *In Other Words: Essays towards a Reflective Sociology.* Stanford, Calif.: Stanford University Press, 1990.

Bray, David. *Social Space and Governance in Urban China: The Danwei System from Origins to Reform.* Stanford, Calif.: Stanford University Press, 2005.

Brint, Steven. *In an Age of Experts: The Changing Role of Professionals in Politics and Public Life.* Princeton, N.J.: Princeton University Press, 1994.

Brook, Timothy, and B. Michael Frolic, eds. *Civil Society in China.* Armonk, N.Y.: M. E. Sharpe, 1997.

Broudehoux, Anne-Marie. *The Making and Selling of Post-Mao Beijing.* London: Routledge, 2004.

Burgin, Victor. *In/Different Spaces.* Berkeley: University of California Press, 1996.

Butler, Judith. "Psychic Inceptions: Melancholy, Ambivalence, Rage." *The Psychic Life of Power: Theories in Subjection,* 167–98. Stanford, Calif.: Stanford University Press, 1997.

Byrne, David. *Understanding the Urban.* New York: Palgrave, 2001.

Cai Xiang. *Shensheng huiyi* (Sacred memories). Shanghai: Dongfang chuban zhongxin, 1998.

Calhoun, Craig. "Tiananmen, Television and the Public Sphere: Internationalization of Culture and the Beijing Spring of 1989." *Public Culture* 2, no. 1 (1989): 54–71.

Calvino, Italo. *Invisible Cities (Le città invisibili).* Translated by William Weaver. New York: Harcourt, 1974.

Campanella, Thomas. *Concrete Dragon: China's Urban Revolution and What It Means for the World.* New York: Princeton Architectural, 2008.

Cartier, Carolyn. *Globalizing South China.* Malden, Mass.: Blackwell, 2001.

Castells, Manuel. *The Castells Reader on Cities and Social Theory.* Edited by Ida Susser. Oxford: Blackwell, 2002.

———. *The Informational City.* Oxford: Blackwell, 1989.

———. "The Space of Flows." *The Rise of the Network Society,* 407–59. Oxford: Blackwell, 1996.

Cavell, Stanley. *This New Yet Unapproachable America: Lectures after Emerson after Wittgenstein.* Albuquerque, N.M.: Living Batch, 1989.

Chan, Kam Wing. *Cities with Invisible Walls: Reinterpreting Urbanization in Post-1949 China.* Hong Kong: Oxford University Press, 1994.

———. "Urbanization and Rural-Urban Migration since 1982: A New Baseline." *Modern China* 20, no. 3 (1994): 243–81.

Chan, Kam Wing, and Xu Xueqiang. "Urban Population Growth and Urbanization in China since 1949: Reconstructing a Baseline." *China Quarterly* 104 (1985): 583–613.

Chang, Eileen. *Love in a Fallen City.* Translated by Karen Kingsbury. New York: New York Review of Books, 2007.

Chen, Aimin, Gordon G. Liu, and Kevin H. Zhang, eds. *Urban Transformation in China.* Chinese Economy Series. Burlington, Vt.: Ashgate, 2004.

Chen Danyan. "Shanghai Writers on Shanghai Writing." Presented at the Shanghai International Literary Festival, 19 March 2007.

Chen, Nancy, Constance D. Clark, Suzanne Z. Gottschang, and Lyn Jeffery, eds. *China Urban: Ethnographies of Contemporary Culture.* Durham, N.C.: Duke University Press, 2001.

Chen Ran. "Chaoxingbie yishi yu wode chuangzuo" (Gender-transcendent consciousness and my creative writing). *Zhongshan* (Purple mountain) no. 93 (1994): 105–7.

——. *Siren shenghuo* (Private life). Yangzhou: Jiangsu wenyi chubanshe, 1996. Translated by John Howard-Gibbon as *A Private Life*. New York: Columbia University Press, 2004.

Chen Sihe. "Guanyu 'renwen jingshen' taolun de liang feng xin" (Two letters on the "humanist spirit" discussions). 15 November 1994. Reprinted in *Renwen jingshen xunsi lu* (Thoughts on the humanist spirit), ed. Wang Xiaoming, 142–48. Shanghai: Wenhui chubanshe, 1996.

Chen Xiaoming. *Fangzhen de niandai: Chao xianshi wenxue liubian yu wenhua xiangxiang* (Age of imitation: Surrealist literary developments and cultural imaginations). Taiyuan: Shanxi jiaoyu chubanshe, 1999.

——. "Jianyao pingjie" (Brief commentary [on He Dun's "Life is not a crime"]). *Zhongguo chengshi xiaoshuo jingxuan* (Anthology of Chinese urban fiction), ed. Chen Xiaoming, 226–27. Lanzhou: Gansu renmin chubanshe, 1994.

——. "Sun Ganlu: Chengshi mengyouzhe" (Sun Ganlu: City sleepwalker). *Chen Xiaoming xiaoshuo shiping* (Chen Xiaoming critiques fiction), 182–86. Kaifeng: Henan Daxue chubanshe, 2002.

——. "Wanshengdai yu jiushi niandai wenxue liuxiang" (The belated generation and the literary trends in the 1990s). Preface to *Shenghuo wuzui* (Life is not a crime), by He Dun, 1–9. Beijing: Huayi chubanshe, 1995.

——, ed. *Zhongguo chengshi xiaoshuo jingxuan* (Anthology of Chinese urban fiction). Lanzhou: Gansu renmin chubanshe, 1994.

Cheng Xiangzhan. "Urban Image and Urban Aesthetics." Lecture presented to the College of Design, Architecture, Art, and Planning, University of Cincinnati, 21 February 2007.

Chow, Rey. *The Protestant Ethnic and the Spirit of Capitalism*. New York: Columbia University Press, 2002.

Chung, Chuihua Judy, ed. *Great Leap Forward: Harvard Design School Project on the City*. Cambridge, Mass.: Harvard Design School, 2001.

Cline, William. "Doha Can Achieve Much More than Skeptics Expect." *Finance and Development* 42, no. 1 (March 2005): 22–24.

Cockburn, Alexander, Jeffrey St. Clair, and Allan Sekula. *Five Days that Shook the World: The Battle for Seattle and Beyond*. New York: Verso, 2001.

Costa, Frank J., Ashok K. Dutt, Laurence J. C. Ma, and Allen G. Noble, eds. *Urbanization in Asia: Spatial Dimensions and Policy Issues*. Honolulu: University of Hawaii Press, 1989.

Critchley, Simon. *The Ethics of Deconstruction: Derrida and Levinas*. Oxford: Basil Blackwell, 1992.

Cui Zhiyuan. "Institutional Innovation and a Second Liberation of Thought." *Twenty-first Century* (August 1994): 5–16.

Dai Jinhua. "Chen Ran: Geren he nüxing de shuxie" (Chen Ran: Writing the individual and the feminine). Afterword to *Siren Shenghuo* (Private life), by Chen Ran, 272–94. Yangzhou: Jiangsu wenyi chubanshe, 1996.

——. "Imagined Nostalgia." Translated by Judy T. H. Chen. *boundary 2* 24, no. 3 (fall 1997): 143–61.

——. "Invisible Writing: The Politics of Chinese Mass Culture in the 1990s." *Modern Chinese Literature and Culture* 11, no. 1 (spring 1999): 43–44.

Dan Xiaohai and Zhu Chengjun, ed. *Zouxiang xin zhuzhai: Mingtian women zhu zai nali?* (Toward new housing: Where will we live tomorrow?). Beijing: Zhongguo jianshe gongye chubanshe, 2001.

Davies, Gloria. "Self-Made Maps of Chinese Intellectuality." *Voicing Concerns: Contemporary Chinese Critical Inquiry*, ed. Gloria Davies, 17–46. Lanham, Md.: Rowman and Littlefield, 2001.

——, ed. *Voicing Concerns: Contemporary Chinese Critical Inquiry.* Lanham, Md.: Rowman and Littlefield, 2001.

Davis, Deborah S., ed. *The Consumer Revolution in Urban China.* Berkeley: University of California Press, 2000.

Davis, Deborah S., Richard Kraus, Barry Naughton, and Elizabeth J. Perry, eds. *Urban Spaces in Contemporary China: The Potential for Autonomy and Community in Post-Mao China.* Cambridge: Cambridge University Press, 1995.

Davis, Mike. *City of Quartz: Excavating the Future in Los Angeles.* 1990. Reprint, New York: Vintage, 1992.

de Certeau, Michel. *The Practice of Everyday Life.* Translated by Steven Rendell. Berkeley: University of California Press, 1984.

Del Lago, Francesca, Song Dong, Zhang Dali, Zhan Wang, and Wang Jianwei. "Space and Public: Specificity in Beijing." *Art Journal* 59 (2000): 75–87.

Dirlik, Arif. "Architectures of Global Modernity, Colonialism, and Places." *Modern Chinese Literature and Culture* 17, no. 1 (spring 2005): 33–61.

Dong, Madeline Yue. *Republican Beijing: The City and Its Histories, 1917–1937.* Berkeley: University of California Press, 2003.

Dostoevsky, Fyodor. *Crime and Punishment.* Translated by David McDuff. New York: Viking, 1991.

Duggan, Lisa. *The Twilight of Equality? Neoliberalism, Cultural Politics, and the Attack on Democracy.* Boston: Beacon, 2003.

During, Simon. Introduction to *The Cultural Studies Reader*, ed. Simon During, 1–30. London: Routledge, 1993.

Dutton, Michael. *Streetlife China.* Cambridge: Cambridge University Press, 1998.

Eaglestone, Robert. *Ethical Criticism: Reading after Levinas.* Edinburgh: Edinburgh University Press, 1997.

Eyerman, R., L. G. Svensson, and T. Soderqvist, eds. *Intellectuals, Universities, and the State in Western Modern Societies.* Berkeley: University of California Press, 1987.

Fang Fang. *Children of the Bitter River: A Novel.* Translated by Herbert Batt. Norwalk, Conn.: EastBridge, 2006.

Farquhar, Judith. *Appetites: Food and Sex in Postsocialist China.* Durham, N.C.: Duke University Press, 2002.

Farrer, James. "Bars in Reform-Era Shanghai." Presentation at the Asian Studies Conference Japan, Tokyo, 20 June 2004.

Fei, Hsiao-tung. *China's Gentry: Essays on Urban-Rural Relations*. Chicago: University of Chicago Press, 1953.

———. "Peasantry and Gentry: An Interpretation of Chinese Social Structure and Its Changes." *American Journal of Sociology* 52 (July 1946): 1–17.

Fei Xiaotong. *Xiangtu Zhongguo* (Rural China). 1947. Reprint, Beijing: Xinhua chubanshe, 1985. Translated by Gary Hamilton and Wang Zheng as *From the Soil: The Foundations of Chinese Society*. Berkeley: University of California Press, 1992.

Feiner, Jacques. "Regional Planning in the Kunming-Zurich Partnership." *The Kunming Project: Urban Development in China: A Dialogue*, ed. Carl Fingerhuth and Ernst Joos, 113–30. Basel: Birkhäuser, 2002.

Feng Boyi. "Jiushiniandai dangdai yishu de jiben xingtai he geju: Cong qunian shiyiyuefen Beijing sange zhanlan tanqi" (The fundamental form and structure of 1990s contemporary art: A discussion of three Beijing exhibitions since last November). *Yishujia* (Artist) 1 (2000): 48–51.

Feng Jing. "Age of Bestsellers." *Beijing Review* no. 13 (2001), http://www.bjreview.com.cn. Printout on file with author.

Ferry, Megan M. "Marketing Chinese Women Writers in the 1990s, or the Politics of Self-Fashioning." *Contemporary China* 12, no. 37 (2003): 655–76.

Feuchtwang, Stephan. "Reflections on Privacy in China." *Chinese Concepts of Privacy*, ed. Bonnie McDougall and Anders Hansson, 211–30. Leiden: Brill, 2002.

Fingerhuth, Carl. "Urban Design for Kunming." *The Kunming Project: Urban Development in China: A Dialogue*, ed. Carl Fingerhuth and Ernst Joos, 47–60. Basel: Birkhäuser, 2002.

Fingerhuth, Carl, and Ernst Joos, eds. *The Kunming Project: Urban Development in China: A Dialogue*. Basel: Birkhäuser, 2002.

Finnane, Antonia. "The Origins of Prejudice: The Malintegration of Subei in Late Imperial China." *Comparative Studies in Society and History* 35, no. 2 (1993): 211–38.

Flaubert, Gustave. *Madame Bovary*. Eited by Margaret Cohen. Translated by Eleanor Marx Aveling, revised by Paul de Man. New York: W. W. Norton, 2005.

Francis, Corinna-Barbara. "Reproduction of Danwei Institutional Features in the Context of China's Market Economy: The Case of Haidian District's High-Tech Sector." *China Quarterly* 147 (1996): 839–59.

Fraser, David. "Inventing Oasis: Luxury Housing Advertisements and Reconfiguring Domestic Space in Shanghai." *The Consumer Revolution in Urban China*, ed. Deborah S. Davis, 25–53. Berkeley: University of California Press, 2000.

Freud, Sigmund. "Mourning and Melancholia." *General Psychological Theory: Papers on Metapsychology*, 164–84. New York: Touchstone, 1997.

———. "On the Mechanism of Paranoia." 1911. Reprinted in *General Psychological Theory: Papers on Metapsychology*, 29–35. New York: Simon and Schuster, 1997.

Friedmann, John. *China's Urban Transition*. Minneapolis: University of Minnesota Press, 2005.

——. "Expanding Spaces of Personal Autonomy." *China's Urban Transition*, 77–93. Minneapolis: University of Minnesota Press, 2005.

Fu, Zhengji. "The State, Capital, and Urban Restructuring in Post-Reform Shanghai." *The New Chinese City: Globalization and Market Reform*, ed. John Logan, 106–20. Oxford: Blackwell, 2002.

Gaitano, Arianne M. "Filial Daughters, Modern Women: Migrant Domestic Workers in Post-Mao Beijing." *On the Move: Women and Rural-to-Urban Migration in Contemporary China*, ed. Arianne M. Gaitano and Tamara Jacka, 41–79. New York: Columbia University Press, 2004.

Gao Minglu. "From Elite to Small Man: The Many Faces of a Transitional Avant-Garde in Mainland China." *Inside Out: New Chinese Art*, ed. Gao Minglu, 149–66. Berkeley: University of California Press, 1998.

Gaubatz, Piper Rae. *Beyond the Great Wall: Urban Form and Transformation on the Chinese Frontiers*. Stanford, Calif.: Stanford University Press, 1996.

——. "From Shanghai to Xining, Isomorphism, Urban Image, and Urban Design in China's Interior Cities." Presentation at Fudan University International Urban Forum, Shanghai, 3 November 2006.

Geddes, Jennifer, ed. *Evil after Postmodernism: Histories, Narratives, Ethics*. London: Routledge, 2001.

Gerth, Karl. *China Made: Consumer Culture and the Creation of the Nation*. Cambridge, Mass.: Harvard University Asia Center, 2003.

Giroir, Girard. "A Globalized Golden Ghetto in a Chinese Garden: The Fontainebleau Villas in Shanghai." *Globalization and the Chinese City*, ed. Fulong Wu, 208–25. London: Routledge, 2006.

Goldberg, RoseLee. *Performance: Live Art since 1960*. New York: Harry Abrams, 1998.

Goldberger, Paul. "Shanghai Surprise: The Radical Quaintness of Xintiandi." *New Yorker*, 26 December 2005, 144–45.

Gregory, Rob. "Elementary Education." *Architectural Review* 218 (2005): 52–55.

Grosz, Elizabeth. "Bodies-Cities." *Sexuality and Space*, ed. Beatriz Colomina, 241–54. New York: Princeton Architectural, 1992.

Gu, Chaolin, and Haiyong Liu. "Social Polarization and Segregation in Beijing." *The New Chinese City: Globalization and Market Reform*, ed. John Logan, 198–211. Oxford: Blackwell, 2002.

Gu, Edward, and Merle Goldman. "Introduction: The Transformation of the Relationship between Chinese Intellectuals and the State." *Chinese Intellectuals between State and Market*, ed. Edward Gu and Merle Goldman, 1–20. RoutledgeCurzon Studies on China in Transition. London: RoutledgeCurzon, 2004.

——, eds. *Chinese Intellectuals between State and Market*. RoutledgeCurzon Studies on China in Transition. London: RoutledgeCurzon, 2004.

Gulden, Gregory Eliyu. *What's a Peasant to Do? Village Becoming Town in Southern China*. Boulder, Colo.: Westview, 2001.

——, ed. *Farewell to Peasant China: Rural Urbanization and Social Change in the Late Twentieth Century*. Armonk, N.Y.: M. E. Sharpe, 1997.

Habermas, Jürgen. *Theorie des kommunikativen Handelns*. 2 vols. Frankfurt: Suhrkamp, 1981.

Halliwell, Martin. *Modernism and Morality: Ethical Devices in European and American Fiction*. New York: Palgrave, 2001.

Harpham, Geoffrey Galt. *Shadows of Ethics: Criticism and the Just Society*. Durham, N.C.: Duke University Press, 1999.

Hart-Landsberg, Martin. "Neoliberalism: Myths and Reality." *Monthly Review* (April 2006): 1–2.

Hart-Landsberg, Martin, and Paul Burkett. *China and Socialism: Market Reforms and Class Struggle*. New York: Monthly Review Press, 2005.

Harvey, David. *A Brief History of Neoliberalism*. Oxford: Oxford University Press, 2005.

He Dun. *Shenghuo wuzui* (Life is not a crime). Beijing: Huayi chubanshe, 1995.

———. *Ximalaya Shan* (The Himalayas). Nanjing: Jiangsu wenyi chubanshe, 1998.

He Qinglian. "A Listing Social Structure." *One China, Many Paths*, ed. Chaohua Wang, 163–88. London: Verso, 2003.

Hertz, Ellen. "Face in the Crowd: The Cultural Construction of Anonymity in Urban China." *China Urban: Ethnographies of Contemporary Culture*, ed. Nancy N. Chen, Constance D. Clark, Suzanne Z. Gottschang, and Lyn Jeffery, 274–93. Durham, N.C.: Duke University Press, 2001.

Hibbard, Peter. *The Bund Shanghai: China Faces West*. Hong Kong: Odyssey, 2007.

Hockx, Michael, and Julia Strauss, eds. *Culture in the Contemporary PRC*. Cambridge: Cambridge University Press, 2005.

Hou, Hanru, and Hans Obrist, eds. *Cities on the Move*. Exhibition catalog for Secession: Vienna. Ostfildern-Ruit: Verlag Gerd Hatje, 1997.

Hsia, C. T. *History of Modern Chinese Fiction*. New York: Columbia University Press, 1979.

Hsing, You-tien. "Global Capital and Local Land in China's Urban Real Estate Development in Shanghai." *Globalization and the Chinese City*, ed. Fulong Wu, 167–89. London: Routledge, 2006.

Hsu, Jennifer. "Defining Boundaries of the Relationship: Beijing Migrant Civil Society Organizations and the Government." Paper presented at Fudan University International Urban Forum, Shanghai, 4 November 2006.

Huang Fayou. "Zai youdangzhong qiu kun: Zhu Wen he *Shenme shi laji shenme shi ai*" (Trapped in idleness: Zhu Wen and *What's Trash, What's Love?*). *Wenyi zhengming* (Literature and arts contention) no. 1 (2002): 75–80.

Huang, Yan. "Urban Spatial Planning and Infrastructure in Beijing." *Land Lines* 16, no. 4 (October 2004): 1–5.

Huters, Theodore. Introduction to *China's New Order: Society, Politics, and Economy in Transition*, by Wang Hui, ed. and trans. Theodore Huters, trans. Rebecca E. Karl, 1–40. Cambridge, Mass.: Harvard University Press, 2003.

Inness, Julie C. *Privacy, Intimacy and Isolation*. New York: Oxford University Press, 1992.

Jacobs, Jane. *Meiguo dachengshi de si yu sheng* (The death and life of great American cities). Beijing: Fanyi chubanshe, 2006.

Jenks, Chris. "Watching Your Step: The History and Practice of the Flâneur." *Visual Culture*, ed. Chris Jenks, 142–60. New York: Routledge, 1995.

Johnson, Linda Cooke. *Shanghai: From Market Town to Treaty Port, 1074–1858*. Stanford, Calif.: Stanford University Press, 1995.

Jones, Andrew F. "The Violence of the Text: Reading Yu Hua's Experimental Fiction." Master's thesis, University of California, Berkeley, 1993.

Jordan, Jennifer. "Collective Memory and Locality in Global Cities." *Global Cities: Cinema, Architecture, and Urbanism in a Digital Age*, ed. Linda Krause and Patrice Petro, 31–48. New Brunswick, N.J.: Rutgers University Press, 2003.

Juhasz, Antonia. "Ambitions of Empire: The Bush Administration Economic Plan for Iraq (and Beyond)." *Left Turn* 12 (February–March 2004): 27–32.

Karabel, Jerome. "Toward a Theory of Intellectuals and Politics." *Theory and Society* 25 (1996): 205–33.

Kearney, Richard. *On Stories*. London: Routledge, 2002.

Kern, Stephen. *The Culture of Time and Space, 1880–1918*. Cambridge, Mass.: Harvard University Press, 1983.

Kim, Won Bae, Clyde Michael Douglass, Sang-Chuel Choe, and Kong Chong Ho, eds. *Culture and the City in East Asia*. Oxford: Clarendon, 1997.

Kinkley, Jeffrey. *The Odyssey of Shen Congwen*. Stanford, Calif.: Stanford University Press, 1987.

Kipnis, Andrew. "Neo-leftists versus Neo-liberals: PRC Intellectual Debates in the 1990s." *Intercultural Studies* 24, no. 3 (2003): 239–51.

Kluver, Randy, and John H. Powers. *Civic Discourse, Civil Society, and Chinese Communities*. Stamford, Conn.: Ablex, 1999.

Knight, Sabina. *The Heart of Time: Moral Agency in Twentieth-Century Chinese Fiction*. Cambridge, Mass.: Harvard University Asia Center, 2006.

Koetter, Fred. *Bingtie chengshi* (Collage city). Beijing: Zhongguo jianzhu gongye chubanshe, 2003.

Kong, Shuyu. *Consuming Literature: Best Sellers and the Commercialization of Literary Production in Contemporary China*. Stanford, Calif.: Stanford University Press, 2005.

Koolhaas, Rem. "Architecture and Globalization." *Reflections on Architectural Practices in the 1990s*, ed. William S. Saunders, 232–39. New York: Princeton Architectural, 1996.

———. "Introduction: City of Exacerbated Difference." *Great Leap Forward: Harvard Design School Project on the City*, ed. Judy Chung, 27–28. Cambridge, Mass.: Harvard Design School, 2001.

Kubin, Wolfgang. Introduction to *Symbols of Anguish: In Search of Melancholy in China*, ed. Wolfgang Kubin, 7–16. Bern: Peter Lang, 2001.

Kwon, Miwon. "One Place after Another: Notes on Site Specificity." *Space, Site, Intervention: Situating Installation Art*, ed. Erika Suderburg, 38–63. Minneapolis: University of Minnesota Press, 2000.

Langer, Lawrence. *Holocaust Testimonies: The Ruins of Memory*. New Haven, Conn.: Yale University Press, 1991.

Lash, Scott, and John Urry. *Economies of Signs and Space*. London: Sage, 1994.

Latham, Kevin, Stuart Thompson, and Jakob Klein, eds. *Consuming China: Approaches to Cultural Change in Contemporary China*. London: Routledge, 2006.

Laughlin, Charles, ed. *Contested Modernities in Chinese Literature*. New York: Palgrave, 2005.

Leaf, Michael. "Urban Planning and Urban Reality under Chinese Economic Reforms." *Planning Education and Research* 18 (1998): 145–53.

Lee, Vivian P. Y. "The City as Seductress: Reimagining Shanghai in Contemporary Chinese Film and Fiction." *Modern Chinese Literature and Culture* 17, no. 2 (2005): 133–66.

Lefebvre, Henri. "The Urban Illusion." *The Urban Revolution*, 151–64. Translated by Robert Bononno. Minneapolis: University of Minnesota Press, 2003.

Leitner, Helga, Eric Sheppard, Kristin Sziarto, and Anant Maringanti. "Contesting Urban Futures: Decentering Neoliberalism." *Contesting Neoliberalism: Urban Frontiers*, ed. Helga Leitner, Jamie Peck, and Eric S. Sheppard, 1–25. New York: Guilford, 2006.

Leng Lin. *Shi wo* (It's me). Beijing: Zhongguo wenlian chubanshe, 2000.

Lester, Toby. "The Reinvention of Privacy." *Atlantic Monthly*, March 2001, 27–39.

Levinas, Emmanuel. *Otherwise than Being, or Beyond Essence*. Pittsburgh: Duquesne University Press, 1998.

Li Gan, Xiong Jialiang, and Cai Shuxian, eds. *Zhongguo dangdai wenxueshi* (History of contemporary Chinese literature). Beijing: Kexue chubanshe, 2004.

Li Jiefei. *Chengshi xiangkuang* (City frame). Taiyuan: Shanxi jiaoyu chubanshe, 1999.

Li Jing. "Bu maoxian de lucheng: Lun Wang Anyi de xiezuo kunjing" (A risk-free path: On Wang Anyi's writing predicament). *Wang Anyi yanjiu ziliao* (Wang Anyi research material), ed. Wu Yiqin, 340–62. Jinan: Shandong chubanshe, 2006.

Li Peilin, ed. *Zhongguo xinshiqi jieji jieceng baogao* (Report on social classes in China in the New Era). Liaoning: Renmin chubanshe, 1995.

Li Qiang. "Shichang zhuanxing yu Zhongguo zhongjian jieceng de daiji gengti" (Market changes and the generational replacement of the Chinese middle class). *Zhanlüe yu guanli* (Strategy and management) 3 (1999): 35–44.

Li, Si-ming. "Residential Mobility and Urban Change in China: What Have We Learned So Far?" *Restructuring the Chinese City: Changing Society, Economy, and Space*, ed. Fulong Wu, 175–91. London: Routledge, 2005.

Li, Si-ming, and Wing-Shing Tang. *China's Regions, Polity and Economy*. Hong Kong: Chinese University Press, 2000.

Li Tiangang. *Renwen Shanghai: Shimin de kongjian* (Cultural Shanghai: A space for urban citizens). Shanghai: Shanghai jiaoyu chubanshe, 2004.

Li Xiaodong and Yeo Kangshua. *Rationale of the Intangible: A Theoretical Framework towards the Understanding of Chinese Spatial Conception*. Singapore: National University of Singapore Centre for Advanced Studies in Architecture, 2005.

Liang, Samuel Xunxiang. "The Meeting of Courtyard and Street: Mapping Residential and Commercial Spaces in the *Lilong*, Shanghai, 1870–1896."

Presentation at the Association of Asian Studies Annual Meeting, Chicago, 1 April 2005.

Lin Haiyin. *Chengnan jiushi* (My memories of old Beijing). Taipei: Taiwan Chuwen chubanshe, 1969. Translated by Nancy Ing and Chi Pang-yuan as *Memories of Peking: South Side Stories*. Hong Kong: Chinese University Press, 1992.

Lin Shu. *Jianzhushi Liang Sicheng* (Architect Liang Sicheng). Tianjin: Scientific Technology Press, 1996.

Lingenfelter, Andrea. "Translator's Note." *Candy*, vii–ix. Boston: Little, Brown, 2003.

Lippit, Seiji Mizuta. "Topographies of Empire: Yokomitsu Riichi's Shanghai." *Topographies of Japanese Modernism*, 73–116. New York: Columbia University Press, 2002.

Liu Heng. *Hei de xue*. Beijing: Gongren chubanshe, 1988. Translated by Howard Goldblatt as *Black Snow*. New York: Grove, 1993.

Liu Kang. "Is There an Alternative to (Capitalist) Globalization? The Debate about Modernity in China." *The Cultures of Globalization*, ed. Fredric Jameson and Masao Miyoshi, 164–90. Durham, N.C.: Duke University Press, 1998.

Liu, Xinmin. "A Marginal Return? The Problematic in Zhang Chengzhi's Reinvention of Ethnic Identity." *Contemporary China* 6, no. 16 (1997): 567–80.

Liu Xinwu. *Wo yanzhong de jianzhu yu huanjing* (My view of architecture and its environment). Beijing: Zhongguo jianzhu gongye chuabanshe, 1998.

——. *Zhonggulou* (Bell and drum tower). Beijing: Renmin wenxue chubanshe, 1985.

Liu Xinwu and Zhang Yiwu. *Liu Xinwu Zhang Yiwu duihua lu: "Hou shiji" de wenhua liaowang* (Record of conversations between Liu Xinwu and Zhang Yiwu: Gazing at "post-era" culture). Guilin: Lijiang chubanshe, 1996.

Liu Xue and Zhou Jie. "Kunming shidian xiangmu de huigu" (How Kunming became a pilot project). *The Kunming Project: Urban Development in China: A Dialogue*, ed. Carl Fingerhuth and Ernst Joos, 13–17. Basel: Birkhäuser, 2002.

Logan, John, ed. *The New Chinese City: Globalization and Market Reform*. Oxford: Blackwell, 2002.

——. *Urban China in Transition*. Malden, Mass.: Blackwell, 2008.

Lu, Duanfang. *Remaking Chinese Urban Form: Modernity, Scarcity and Space, 1949–2005*. London: Routledge, 2006.

Lu Feng. "Danwei." *Social Sciences in China* (fall 1989): 53–58.

Lu, Jie. "Rewriting Beijing: A Spectacular City in Qiu Huadong's Urban Fiction." *Contemporary China* 13, no. 39 (2004): 323–38.

——, ed. *China's Literary and Cultural Scenes at the Turn of the Twenty-first Century*. London: Routledge, 2008.

Lü Junhua. "Beijing's Old and Dilapidated Housing Renewal (Part 1)." *China City Planning Review* 9, no. 3 (1993): 27–35.

——. "Beijing's Old and Dilapidated Housing Renewal (Part 2)." *China City Planning Review* 9, no. 4 (1993): 28–40.

——. "Beijing's Old and Dilapidated Housing Renewal (Part 3)." *China City Planning Review* 10, no. 1 (1994), 42–54.

——. "Beijing's Old and Dilapidated Housing Renewal (Part 4)." *China City Planning Review* 10, no. 2 (1994), 34–46.

Lü Junhua, Peter G. Rowe, and Zhang Jie, eds. *Modern Urban Housing in China, 1840–2000.* Munich: Prestel, 2001.

Lu Peng. *Zhongguo dangdai yishu shi, 1990–1999* (History of Chinese contemporary art, 1990–1999). Changsha: Hunan meishu chubanshe, 2000.

Lu, Sheldon Xiao-peng. *Chinese Modernity and Global Biopolitics: Studies in Literature and Visual Culture.* Honolulu: University of Hawaii Press, 2007.

Lü Xinyu. *Jilu Zhongguo: Dangdai Zhongguo xin jilu yundong* (Documentary China: The new documentary movement in contemporary China). Beijing: Shenghuo, dushu, xinzhi sanlian shudian, 2003.

Lu Xueyi, ed. *Dangdai Zhongguo shehui liudong* (Social mobility in contemporary China). Beijing: Shehui kexue wenxian chubanshe, 2004.

——, ed. *Dangdai Zhongguo shehui jieceng yanjiu baogao* (Report on social classes in contemporary China). Beijing: Shehui kexue wenxian chubanshe, 2002.

Lu Xun. *A Brief History of Chinese Fiction* (*Zhongguo xiaoshuo shilue*). Translated by Gladys Yang and Yang Hsien-yi. Beijing: Foreign Languages Press, 1964.

Luo Gang. "Shei zhi gonggong xing?" (Whose public characteristics?). *Shanghai wenxue* (Shanghai literature) 5 (1999): 76–78.

Lynch, Kevin. *Chengshi xingtai* (Good city form). Beijing: Huaxia chubanshe, 2001.

Ma, Laurence J. C., and Fulong Wu. "Restructuring the Chinese City: Diverse Processes and Reconstituted Spaces." *Restructuring the Chinese City: Changing Society, Economy and Space*, ed. Laurence J. C. Ma and Fulong Wu, 1–20. New York: Routledge, 2005.

Madsen, Richard. *China's Catholics: Tragedy and Hope in an Emerging Civil Society.* Berkeley: University of California Press, 1998.

Mao Dun. *Midnight.* Translated by Hsu Meng-hsiun and A. C. Barnes. Peking: Foreign Languages Press, 1955.

Mao Zedong. "Zai Yan'an wenyi zuotan huishang de jianghua" (Talks at the Yan'an conference on the arts). 1942. Reprinted in *Mao Zedong lun wenyi* (Mao Zedong discusses the arts), 34–68. Beijing: Renmin chubanshe, 1992.

Marcus, Sharon. "Placing *Rosemary's Baby.*" *differences* 5, no. 3 (1993): 121–54.

Martin, Jean-Marie. "Li Xiaodong: Scuola Elementare Yuhu, Lijiang, Cina." *Casabella* 71, no. 1 (2006–2007): 92–99.

McDougall, Bonnie, and Anders Hansson, eds. *Chinese Concepts of Privacy.* Leiden: Brill, 2002.

McGrath, Jason. *Postsocialist Modernity: Chinese Cinema, Literature, and Criticism in the Market Age.* Stanford, Calif.: Stanford University Press, 2008.

Meng Fanhua. "Wenhua bengkui shidai de taowang yu guiyi: Jiushi niandai wenhua de xinbaoshouzhuyi jingshen" (Escape and support in an age of cultural collapse: The neoconservative spirit of 1990s culture). *Zhongguo wenhua* (Chinese culture) 4 (1994): 52–54.

Mian Mian. "A Conversation with the Author of *Candy*: Mian Mian talks with Jonathan Napack of the *International Herald Tribune.*" 2001. Reprinted in *Candy* (*Tang*), by Mian Mian, 283–86. Translated by Andrea Lingenfelter. Boston: Little, Brown, 2003.

———. *Tang*. Beijing: Zhongguo xiju chubanshe, 2000. Translated by Andrea Lingenfelter as *Candy*. Boston: Little, Brown, 2003.

Mill, John Stuart. *On Liberty*. London: Dent, 1964.

Miller, Hillis. *The Ethics of Reading*. New York: Columbia University Press, 1987.

Moffat, David. "Yuhu Elementary School and Community Center: Lijiang, China." *Places* 16, no. 3 (fall 2004): 10–13.

Moodie, Ellen. "Microbus Crashes and Coco-cola Cash: The Value of Death in 'Free-Market' El Salvador." *American Ethnologist* 33, no. 1 (February 2006): 63–80.

Moretti, Franco. "Homo Palpitans: Balzac's Novels and Urban Personality." *Signs Taken for Wonders*, 109–29. New York: Verso, 1983.

Morrow, Mayo. *Los Angeles*. New York: A. A. Knopf, 1933.

Mote, F. W. "The Transformation of Nanking, 1350–1400." *The City in Late Imperial China*, ed. G. William Skinner, 101–54. Stanford, Calif.: Stanford University Press, 1977.

Murphey, Rhoads. *The Fading of the Maoist Vision*. Agincourt, Ontario: Methuen, 1980.

Owen, Stephen. *Readings in Chinese Literary Thought*. Cambridge, Mass.: Council on East Asian Studies, Harvard University, 1992.

Pan, Tianshu. "Historical Memory, Community-Building and Place-Making in Neighborhood Shanghai." *Restructuring the Chinese City: Changing Society, Economy, and Space*, ed. Fulong Wu, 122–37. London: Routledge, 2005.

Perry, Elizabeth J., and Mark Selden, eds. *Chinese Society: Change, Conflict, Resistance*. London: Routledge, 2000.

Pieterse, Jan Nederveen. *Globalization and Culture: Global Mélange*. Lanham, Md.: Rowman and Littlefield, 2004.

Poole, Ross. *Morality and Modernity*. London: Routledge, 1991.

Qin Hui. "Dividing the Big Family Assets." *One China, Many Paths*, ed. Chaohua Wang, 128–59. London: Verso, 2003.

———. "Shehui gongzheng yu xueshu liangxin" (Social justice and the scholarly conscious). *Zhongguo de Xianjing* (China's pitfalls: Primary capital accumulation in contemporary China), ed. He Qinglian, 15–28. Hong Kong: Mingjing chubanshe, 1997.

Qiu Baoxing. "China's Urbanization and Urban Planning." Keynote address presented at Fudan University International Urban Forum, Shanghai, 3 November 2006.

Qiu Huadong. *Chengshi zhanche* (City tank). Beijing: Zuojia chubanshe, 1997.

———. *Yingyan* (Fly eyes). Changchun: Changchun chubanshe, 1998.

Qiu Zhijie. "*Post-Sense Sensibility*: A Memorandum." *Exhibiting Experimental Art in China*, Wu Hung, 167–71. Chicago: Smart Museum of Art, 2000.

Ren Yuan. "Globalization and Grassroots Practices: Community Development in Contemporary Urban China." *Globalization and the Chinese City*, ed. Fulong Wu, 292–309. London: Routledge, 2006.

Rodan, Garry, and Kevin Hewison, ed. *Neoliberalism and Conflict in Asia after 9/11*. London: Routledge, 2006.

Rooney, David. Review of *Suzhou River*. *Variety*, 14 February 2000, 42.

Rowe, Peter G., and Seng Kuan. *Architectural Encounters with Essence and Form in Modern China*. Cambridge, Mass: MIT Press, 2002.

Ruan Yisan. "The Conservation of Shanghai's Historical and Cultural Heritage against the Background of Market Economy." *The Proceedings of Shanghai International Symposium on Conservation of Historical Architecture and Historical Areas* (10 October 2004). Shanghai: Shanghai Urban Planning Administration Bureau.

Ruggiero, Renato. "Charting the Trade Routes of the Future: Towards a Borderless Economy." Address to the International Industrial Conference, San Francisco, 29 September 1997.

Sang, Tze-lan. *The Emerging Lesbian: Female Same-Sex Desire in Modern China*. Chicago: University of Chicago Press, 2003.

Sargeson, Sally. "Full Circle? Rural Land Reforms in Globalizing China." *Neoliberalism and Conflict in Asia after 9/11*, ed. Garry Rodan and Kevin Hewison, 141–60. London: Routledge, 2006.

Sassen, Saskia. "Reading the City in a Global Digital Age: Between Topographic Representation and Spatialized Power Projects." *Global Cities: Cinema, Architecture, and Urbanism in a Digital Age*, ed. Linda Krause and Patrice Petro, 15–30. New Brunswick, N.J.: Rutgers University Press, 2003.

Saul, John Ralston. *The Collapse of Globalism and the Reinvention of the World*. Woodstock, N.Y.: Overland, 2005.

Schilder, Paul. "Psycho-analysis of Space." *International Journal of Psychology* 16 (1935): 274–95.

Shattuck, Roger. "Narrating Evil: Great Faults and 'Splendidly Wicked People.' " *Evil after Postmodernism: Histories, Narratives, Ethics*, ed. Jennifer Geddes, 45–55. London: Routledge, 2001.

Shen Congwen. *Shen Congwen wenji* (Shen Congwen's collected works). 12 vols. Guangzhou: Huacheng chubanshe, 1982.

Sheng Feng. "Lun 'haipai' wenhua de 'bianyuan' wenhua tezheng jiqi lishi zuoyong" (On the "marginal culture" characteristics and historical function of "Shanghai style" culture) *Shehui Kexue* (Social science), no. 1 (1986): 20–23.

Shu Haowen. Public remarks after a screening of *Nostalgia*, Museum of Contemporary Art, Shanghai, 7 February 2007.

Silbergeld, Jerome. *Hitchcock with a Chinese Face: Cinematic Doubles, Oedipal Triangles, and China's Moral Voice*. Seattle: University of Washington Press, 2004.

Silverman, Kaja. "The Bodily Ego." *The Threshold of the Visible World*, 9–38. New York: Routledge, 1996.

Simmel, Georg. "The Metropolis and Mental Life." *The Sociology of Georg Simmel*, 409–24. Edited by Kurt H. Wolff. New York: Free Press, 1950.

——. *The Philosophy of Money*. Translated by T. Bottomore and D. Frisby. London: Routledge, 1978.

Sit, Victor F. S. *Beijing: The Nature and Planning of a Chinese Capital City*. World City Series. New York: John Wiley, 1995.

Song Mingwei. "Piaoliu de fangzi he xuwang de lutu: Lijie Zhu Wen" (Floating houses and fabricated journeys: Understanding Zhu Wen). *Shanghai wenxue* (Shanghai literature) (September 1997): 66–71.

Song, Yan, Chengri Ding, and Gerritt Knapp. "Envisioning Beijing 2020 through Sketches of Urban Scenarios." *Habitat International* 30 (2006): 1018–34.

Sontag, Susan. "Notes on 'Camp.'" *Against Interpretation, and Other Essays*, 275–92. New York: Dell, 1966.

Stewart, Susan. *On Longing: Narratives of the Miniature, the Gigantic, the Souvenir, the Collection*. Durham, N.C.: Duke University Press, 1993.

Strand, David. "'A High Place Is No Better Than a Low Place': The City in the Making of Modern China." *Becoming Chinese: Passages to Modernity and Beyond*, ed. Wen-hsin Yeh, 98–136. Berkeley: University of California Press, 2000.

——. *Rickshaw Beijing: City People and Politics in the 1920s*. Berkeley: University of California Press, 1989.

Sun Ganlu. *Huxi* (Breathing). Guangzhou: Huacheng chubanshe, 1993.

Sun Liping. *Zhuanxing yu duanlie: Gaige yilai Zhongguo shehui jiegou de bianqian* (Transformation and rupture: Changes in China's social structure under reform). Beijing: Qinghua Daxue chubanshe, 2004.

Sun Liping, Li Qiang, and Shen Yuan. "Zhongguo shehui jiegou zhuanxing de zhongjinqi qushi yu yinhuan" (Recent trends and latent dangers in the transformation of China's social structure). *Zhanlüe yu guanli* (Strategy and management) 5 (1998): 1–17.

Sun, Wanning. "Anhui Baomu in Shanghai: Gender, Class, and a Sense of Place." *Locating China: Space, Place, and Popular Culture*, ed. Jing Wang, 171–89. New York: Routledge, 2005.

Tang, Wenfang, and William L. Parish. *Chinese Urban Life under Reform: The Changing Social Contract*. Cambridge: Cambridge University Press, 2000.

Tang, Xiaobing. "Decorating Culture: Notes on Interior Design, Interiority, and Interiorization." *Chinese Modern: The Heroic and the Quotidian*, 295–315. Durham, N.C.: Duke University Press, 2000.

——. "Melancholy against the Grain: Approaching Postmodernity in Wang Anyi's Tales of Sorrow." *Chinese Modern: The Heroic and the Quotidian*, 316–40. Durham, N.C.: Duke University Press, 2000.

Tang Ying. *Meiguo laide qizi* (A wife from America). Shanghai: Shanghai yuandong chubanshe, 1995.

Taylor, Charles. *The Ethics of Authenticity*. Cambridge, Mass.: Harvard University Press, 1992.

——. *Sources of the Self: The Making of the Modern Identity*. Cambridge, Mass: Harvard University Press, 1989.

Taylor, Peter J. "Havens and Cages: Reinventing States and Households in the Modern World-System." *World-Systems Research* 6, no. 2 (summer–fall 2000): 544–62.

——. *Modernities: A Geohistorical Interpretation*. Cambridge: Polity, 1999.

Tong, Shijun. *The Dialectics of Modernization: Habermas and the Chinese Discourse of Modernization*. Sydney: Wild Peony, 2000.

Tuan, Yi-Fu. "Rootedness Versus Sense of Place." 1980. Reprinted in *Cultural Geography: Critical Concepts in the Social Sciences*, ed. Nigel Thrift and Sarah Whatmore, 1:270–71. London: Routledge, 2004.

ul Haque, Irfan. "Commodities under Neoliberalism: The Case of Cocoa." United Nations Conference on Trade and Development G-24 Discussion Paper Series, No. 25, January 2004. New York: United Nations, 2004.

United Nations Development Program. *Human Development Report, 1999*. New York: Oxford University Press, 1999.

Vidler, Anthony. "Bodies in Space/Subjects in the City: Psychopathologies of Modern Urbanism." *Difference* 5, no. 3 (1993): 31–51.

Vine, Richard. "Report from Shanghai: After Exoticism." *Art in America*, July 2001, 30–35.

Visser, Robin. "Displacement of the Urban-Rural Confrontation in Su Tong's Fiction." *Modern Chinese Literature* 9, no. 1 (1995): 113–38.

Wagner, Marsha. "The Subversive Fiction of Yu Hua," CHINOPERL *Papers* nos. 20–22 (1999): 219–43.

Wai, Albert Wing Tai. "Place Promotion and Iconography in Shanghai's Xintiandi." *Habitat International* 30 (2006): 245–60.

Wang Anyi. *Chang hen ge* (Song of everlasting sorrow). Beijing: Zuojia chubanshe, 1996. Translated by Michael Berry and Susan Chan Egan as *The Song of Everlasting Sorrow*. New York: Columbia University Press, 2008.

Wang, Ban. *Illuminations from the Past: Trauma, Memory, and History in Modern China*. Palo Alto, Calif.: Stanford University Press, 2004.

Wang, Chaohua, ed. *One China, Many Paths*. London: Verso, 2003.

Wang Der-wei. *Ruci fanhua* (Urban splendor). Shanghai: Shanghai shudian chubanshe, 2006.

Wang Hongsheng, Geng Zhanchun, He Xiangyang, Zeng Fan, and Qu Chunjing. "Xiandai renwen jingshen de shengcheng" (The generation of modernist humanist spirit). *Renwen jingshen xunsi lu* (Thoughts on the humanist spirit), ed. Wang Xiaoming, 222–38. Shanghai: Wenhui chubanshe, 1996.

Wang Hui. *China's New Order: Society, Politics, and Economy in Transition*. Edited and translated by Theodore Huters. Translated by Rebecca E. Karl. Cambridge, Mass.: Harvard University Press, 2003.

——. "The New Criticism." *One China, Many Paths*, ed. Chaohua Wang, 55–86. London: Verso, 2003.

——. "The 1989 Social Movement and the Historical Roots of China's Neoliberalism." *China's New Order: Society, Politics, and Economy in Transition*, ed. Theodore Huters, 46–77. Cambridge, Mass.: Harvard University Press, 2003.

——. *Zi xuan ji* (Selected works). Guilin: Guangxi shifan daxue chubanshe, 1997.

Wang, Jing. *Brand New China: Advertising, Media, Commercial Culture*. Cambridge, Mass.: Harvard University Press, 2008.

——. *High Culture Fever: Politics, Aesthetics, and Ideology in Deng's China*. Durham, N.C.: Duke University Press, 1996.

Wang Jun. *Chengji* (City records). Beijing: Xinhua shudian, 2003.

Wang Meng. "Duobi chonggao" (Avoiding the sublime). *Dushu* (Reading) (January 1993): 10–16.

Wang Shuo. *Wo shi Wang Shuo* (I am Wang Shuo). Beijing: Beijing International Cultural Press, 1992.

Wang Xiaoming. "China, on the Brink of a 'Momentous Era'" (Binlin "da shidai" de Zhongguo). Translated by Robin Visser. *positions* 11, no. 3 (winter 2003): 585–611.

———. "Cong 'Huaihai Lu' dao 'Meijia Qiao': Cong Wang Anyi xiaoshuo chuangzuo de zhuanbian tanqi" (From "Huaihai Road" to "Meijia Bridge": On the metamorphosis of Wang Anyi's fiction writing). *Wang Anyi Yanjiu Ziliao* (Research materials on Wang Anyi), ed. Wu Yiqin, 306–29. Jinan: Shandong wenxue chubanshe, 2006.

———. "A Manifesto for Cultural Studies" (trans. of unpublished MS, "Binlin 'da shidai' de Zhongguo," 1999). Translated by Robin Visser. *One China, Many Paths*, ed. Chaohua Wang, 274–91. London: Verso, 2003.

———. "The Secret of the New Rich in Contemporary China." Presentation at the Association of Asian Studies Annual Meeting, Chicago, 1 April 2005.

———. "The Teaching and Institutionalization of Cultural Studies: The Case of the Department of Cultural Studies at Shanghai University." Presentation at the IACS Teaching Cultural Studies Workshop Chungli, Taiwan, 13 January 2006.

———, ed. *Refeng shuxi* (Hot air book series). Shanghai: Shanghai shudian chubanshe, 2007.

———, ed. *Renwen jingshen xunsi lu* (Thoughts on the humanist spirit). Haishang feng xilie (Shanghai culture series). Shanghai: Wenhui chubanshe, 1996.

———, ed. *Zai xin yishi xingtai de longzhao xia: Jiushiniandai de wenhua he wenxue fenxi* (Under the shroud of the new ideology: Culture and literary analysis of the 1990s). Nanjing: Jiangsu renmin chubanshe, 2000.

Wang Xiaoming, Zhang Hong, Xu Lin, Zhang Ning, and Cui Yiming. "Kuangye shang de feixu: Wenxue he renwen jingshen de weiji" (Ruins in the wilderness: The crisis of literature and humanist spirit). *Shanghai wenxue* (Shanghai literature) 189, no. 6 (1993): 63–70.

Wang, Yiyan. *Narrating China: Jia Pingwa and His Fictional World*. London: Routledge, 2006.

Wasserstrom, Jeffrey. "Is Global Shanghai 'Good to Think'? Thoughts on Comparative History and Postsocialist Cities." *World History* 18, no. 2 (2007): 199–234.

Watson, Burton, trans. *Zhuangzi: Basic Writings*. New York: Columbia University Press, 2003.

Wehrlin, Matthias. "Urban Design within the Greater Kunming Region." *The Kunming Project: Urban Development in China: A Dialogue*, ed. Carl Fingerhuth and Ernst Joos, 97–112. Basel: Birkhäuser, 2002.

Wen Liping. "Guanyu renwen jingshen taolun zongshu" (A summary of the humanist spirit discussions). *Wenyi lilun yu piping* (Literary theory and criticism) 3 (1995): 119–34; 4 (1995): 123–38.

White, Gordon, Jude A. Howell, and Shang Xiaoyuan, eds. *In Search of Civil*

Society: Market Reform and Social Change in Contemporary China. Oxford: Clarendon, 1996.

Wolff, Janet. "The Invisible Flâneuse: Women and the Literature of Modernity." *Theory, Culture and Society* 2, no. 3 (1985): 37–46.

Wong, Timothy. Presentation at the international conference "Literary Studies in the Age of Globalization," Beijing Normal University, 27–29 June 2004.

Wu, Fulong. "Beyond Gradualism: China's Urban Revolution and Emerging Cities." *China's Emerging Cities: The Making of New Urbanism,* 3–25. London: Routledge, 2007.

———. "Real Estate Development and the Transformation of Urban Space in China's Transitional Economy, with Special Reference to Shanghai." *The New Chinese City: Globalization and Market Reform,* ed. John Logan, 153–66. Oxford: Blackwell, 2002.

———. "Transplanting Cityscapes: Townhouse and Gated Community in Globalization and Housing Commodification." *Globalization and the Chinese City,* ed. Fulong Wu, 190–207. London: Routledge, 2006.

———, ed. *China's Emerging Cities: The Making of a New Urbanism.* London: Routledge, 2007.

———, ed. *Globalization and the Chinese City.* London: Routledge, 2006.

———, ed. *Restructuring the Chinese City: Changing Society, Economy, and Space.* London: Routledge, 2005.

Wu, Fulong, Jiang Xu, and Anthony Gar-On Yeh. *Urban Development in Post-Reform China: State, Market, Space.* London: Routledge, 2007.

Wu Huanjia. "Lun Zhongguo chengshi huanjing de xin yu jiu: Yi Beijing wei li" (On the old and the new in Chinese urban environments: The case of Beijing). *Jianzhu xuebao* (Architectural studies) 6 (1988): 33–37.

Wu Hung. "The Birth of Ruins: Inventing a Modern Visual Culture." Lecture presented at the "Global Perspectives on Contemporary Chinese Art" symposium, University of Chicago, 17 April 1999.

———. *Exhibiting Experimental Art in China.* Chicago: Smart Museum of Art, 2000.

———. *Remaking Beijing: Tiananmen Square and the Creation of a Political Space.* Chicago: University of Chicago Press, 2005.

———. *Transience: Chinese Experimental Art at the End of the Twentieth Century.* Smart Museum of Art: University of Chicago, 1999.

———. "Zhang Dali's *Dialogue: Conversation with a City.*" *Public Culture* 12, no. 3 (2000): 749–68. Reprinted in *Cosmopolitanism,* ed. Carol A. Breckenridge, Sheldon Pollack, and Homi Bhabha, 189–208. Durham, N.C.: Duke University Press, 2002.

Wu Liangyong. *Rehabilitating the Old City of Beijing: A Project in the Ju'er Hutong Neighborhood.* Vancouver: University of British Columbia Press, 1999.

Wu Wenguang. "Yishujia xianchang: Fangwen Zhang Dali" (Artist scene: Interview with Zhang Dali). *Jinri xianfeng* (Avant-garde today) 9 (2000): 166–86.

Xiao Hua and Wang Zheng. "Nanfang de xiezuo" (Southern writing). *Dushu* (Reading) 8 (1995): 113–18.

Xie Mian and Zhang Yiwu. *Da zhuanxing: Hou xinshiqi wenhua yanjiu* (The great transition: Studies in the culture of the post–New Era). Harbin: Heilongjiang jiaoyu chubanshe, 1995.

Xu, Ben. "Contesting Memory for Intellectual Self-Positioning: The 1990s' New Cultural Conservatism in China." *Modern Chinese Literature and Culture* 11, no. 1 (spring 1999): 157–92.

———. *Disenchanted Democracy: Chinese Cultural Criticism after 1989.* Ann Arbor: University of Michigan Press, 1999.

———. "From Modernity to 'Chineseness': The Rise of Nativist Cultural Theory in Post-1989 China." *positions* 6, no. 1 (1998): 227–28.

Xu, Gang Gary. "Where Has the Aura Gone? Reflections on Cultural Studies, Neoliberalism, and Literature as the Auratic Event." *Concentric* 31, no. 2 (2005): 15–39.

Xu Hui. "Morality Discourse in the Marketplace: Narratives in the Chinese Television News Magazine *Oriental Horizon*." *Journalism Studies* 1, no. 4 (2000): 637–49.

Xu Jilin. "The Fate of an Enlightenment: Twenty Years in the Chinese Intellectual Sphere (1978–98)." Translated by Geremie R. Barmé and Gloria Davies. *Chinese Intellectuals between State and Market*, ed. Edward Gu and Merle Goldman, 183–203. London: RoutledgeCurzon, 2004.

Yan Xiaopei, Li Jia, Jianping Li, and Jizhuan Weng. "The Development of the Chinese Metropolis in the Period of Transition." *The New Chinese City: Globalization and Market Reform*, ed. John Logan, 37–55. Oxford: Blackwell, 2002.

Yan, Yunxiang. *Private Life under Socialism: Love, Intimacy and Family Change in a Chinese Village, 1949–1999.* Stanford, Calif.: Stanford University Press, 2004.

Yan Zheng, ed. *Zhongguo chengshi fazhan wenti baogao* (Report on issues in China's urban development). Beijing: Zhongguo fazhan chubanshe, 2004.

Yang Dongping. *Chengshi jifeng: Beijing he Shanghai de wenhua jingshen* (Urban vicissitudes: The cultural spirit of Beijing and Shanghai). 1st edn., Beijing: Dongfang chubanshe, 1994; 2d edn., Beijing: Xinxing chubanshe, 2006.

Yang, Guobin. "Civil Society in China: A Dynamic Field of Study." *China Review International* 9, no. 1 (2002): 1–16.

Yang, Xin. "Cyber Writing as Urban Fashion: The Case of Anni Baobei." *Southeast Review of Asian Studies* 28 (2006): 1–8.

Yang Yi. *Jingpai yu haipai bijiao yanjiu* (A comparative study of the Beijing and Shanghai Schools). Xian: Taibo wenyi chubanshe, 1994.

Yao, Yusheng. "The Elite Class Background of Wang Shuo and His Hooligan Characters." *Modern China* 30, no. 4 (October 2004): 431–69.

Yesheng: 1997 nian jingzhe shi (Wildlife: Commencing Jingzhe Day, 1997). Exhibition catalog. Beijing: Xiandai yishu zhongxin, 1998.

Yi Zhongtian. "The Work Unit: 'Face' and Place." *Streetlife China*, ed. Michael Dutton, 58–61. Cambridge: Cambridge University Press, 1998.

Yokomitsu, Riichi. *Shanghai.* Tokyo: Kaizosha, 1932.

Yu Kongzhi and Li Dihua. *Chengshi jingguan zhilu* (A path for urban landscape). Beijing: Zhongguo jianshe gongye chubanshe, 2003.

Yusuf, Shahid, and Weiping Wu. *The Dynamics of Urban Growth in Three Chinese Cities*. New York: Oxford University Press, 1997.

Zha Jianying. *Bashi niandai fantan lu* (Interviews on the 1980s). Beijing: Sanlian chubanshe, 2006.

———. *China Pop: How Soap Operas, Tabloids, and Bestsellers Are Transforming a Culture*. New York: New York Press, 1995.

Zhan, Shaohua. *Rural Labour Migration in China: Challenges for Policies*. MOST Policy Papers 10, New Series MOST-2. Paris: UNESCO/MOST (Management of Social Transformations) Programme, 2005.

Zhang Ailing. "Fengsuo" (Blockade). *Zhang Ailing wenji* (Collected works of Eileen Chang), 99–111. Vol. 1. Hefei: Anhui wenyi chubanshe, 1992.

Zhang Chengzhi. "My God Does Not Reside Overseas." *The Heroes' Paths in Wilderness*, 253–64. Shanghai: Zhishi, 1994.

Zhang Hongyan. "Zongxu: Zhongguo chengshi shehui de lailin" (General introduction: The arrival of Chinese urban society). *Dushi wenhua yu dushi jingshen: Zhong wai chengshi wenhua bijiao* (Urban culture and urban spirit: A comparison of Chinese and foreign city culture), ed. Lixun Chen, 1–5. Nanjing: Dongnan daxue chubanshe, 2002.

Zhang, Li (1955–). *China's Limited Urbanization: Under Socialism and Beyond*. New York: Nova Science, 2004.

Zhang, Li (1965–). "Migrant Enclaves and Impacts of Redevelopment Policy in Chinese Cities." *Restructuring the Chinese City: Changing Society, Economy, and Space*, ed. Fulong Wu, 243–59. London: Routledge, 2005.

Zhang Xian. Address presented at the Symposium on Shanghai First Fringe. Shanghai, 11 November 2006.

Zhang Xiaobo and Song Qiang. "China Can Say No to America." *New Perspectives Quarterly* 13, no. 4 (1996): 55–56.

Zhang, Xudong. *Chinese Modernism in the Era of Reforms: Cultural Fever, Avant-Garde Fiction, and the New Chinese Cinema*. Durham, N.C.: Duke University Press, 1997.

———. "The Making of the Post-Tiananmen Intellectual Field: A Critical Overview." *Whither China? Intellectual Politics in Contemporary China*, ed. Xudong Zhang, 1–78. Durham, N.C.: Duke University Press, 2001.

———. *Postsocialism and Cultural Politics: China in the Last Decade of the Twentieth Century*. Durham, N.C.: Duke University Press, 2008.

———. "Shanghai Nostalgia: Postrevolutionary Allegories in Wang Anyi's Literary Production in the 1990s." *positions* 8, no. 2 (2000): 249–87.

———, ed. *Whither China? Intellectual Politics in Contemporary China*. Durham, N.C.: Duke University Press, 2001.

Zhang, Yingjin. *The City in Modern Chinese Literature and Film: Configurations of Space, Time, and Gender*. Stanford, Calif.: Stanford University Press, 1995.

Zhang Yiwu. " 'Fenlie' yu 'zhuanyi': Zhongguo 'hou xin shiqi' wenhua zhuanxing de xianshi tujing" ("Disruption" and "change": Realistic prospects for China's "post-New Era" cultural transition). *Dongfang* (Orient) 2 (1994): 8–11.

——. "Hou xin shiqi wenxue: Xin de wenhua kongjian" (Post–New Era literature: A new cultural space). *Wenyi zhengming* (Literary contention) 6 (1992): 9–10.

——. "Postmodernism and Chinese Novels of the 1990s." Translated by Michael Berry. *boundary 2* 24, no. 3 (1997): 247–59.

Zhang Yonghe. *Pingchang jianzhu* (For a basic architecture). Beijing: Zhongguo jianzhu gongye chubanshe, 2002.

Zhang Zhaohui. "Jinri chujing: Guanyu 'yishu dacan' " (Today's context: On the "Food as Art" project). *Meishu jie* (Arts circle) 147, no. 2 (2000): 12–13.

Zhang Zhen, ed. *The Urban Generation: Chinese Cinema and Society at the Turn of the Twenty-first Century*. Durham, N.C.: Duke University Press, 2007.

Zhao, Chunlan. "From *Shikumen* to New-Style: A Rereading of *Lilong* Housing in Modern Shanghai." *Architecture* 9, no. 1 (2004): 49–76.

Zhao Jianhai, Zheng Yuke, and Sheng Qi. *Guannian Yishu 21: Zhongguo zuizao de xingwei yishu guanti* (Concept 21: China's first performance artists group). Beijing: Concept 21, 2007.

Zhao, Yiheng. "Post-isms and Chinese New Conservatism." *Ershiyi shiji* (Twenty-first century) (February 1995): 4–15.

Zhao, Yuezhi. "Underdogs, Lapdogs and Watchdogs: Journalists and the Public Sphere Problematic in China." *Chinese Intellectuals between State and Market*, ed. Edward Gu and Merle Goldman, 43–74. London: RoutledgeCurzon, 2004.

Zheng, Tiantian. "From Peasant Women to Bar Hostesses: Gender and Modernity in Post-Mao Dalian." *On the Move: Women and Rural-to-Urban Migration in Contemporary China*, ed. Arianne M. Gaitano and Tamara Jacka, 80–109. New York: Columbia University Press, 2004.

Zhong, Xueping. "Shanghai Literature and Beyond: An Interview with Li Ziyun." *Modern Chinese Literature* 9, no. 1 (1995): 101–12.

Zhou Lan. "Quanqiuhua beijingxia Zhongguo kuaisu chengshihua jieduan de difang kongjian tese suzao: Nanjing de tansuo he shijian" (Inheriting urban culture during China's period of rapid urbanization in the context of globalization using Nanjing as an example). Keynote address delivered at Fudan University International Urban Forum, Shanghai, 3 November 2006.

Zhou, Min, and John Logan. "Market Transition and the Commodification of Housing in Urban China." *The New Chinese City: Globalization and Market Reform*, ed. John Logan, 137–52. Oxford: Blackwell, 2002.

Zhou, Yixing, and Laurence J. C. Ma. "Economic Restructuring and Suburbanization in China." *Urban Geography* 23, no. 3 (2000): 205–36.

Zhou Zuoren. "Shanghai qi" (Shanghai spirit). *Shanghai: Jiyi yu xiangxiang* (Shanghai: Memory and imagination), ed. Ma Fengyang, 61–64. Shanghai: Wenya chubanshe, 1996.

Zhu, Jieming. *The Transition of China's Urban Development: From Plan-Controlled to Market-Led*. Westport, Conn.: Praeger, 1999.

Zhu Ming. "Illusory Bubble: Dialogue between Zhu Ming and Li Xianting." *Zhu Ming: 1994–2006 Art Works*, 12–19. Beijing: Chinese Contemporary, 2007.

Zhu Shanjie. "Hechu shi jiayuan? Shanghai nongmingong zidi xuexiao zhi yipie"

(Where is home? A glance at Shanghai schools for the children of rural migrant workers). Unpublished paper, 2006 (copy on file with the author).

Zhu Wen. *Shenme shi laji, shenme shi ai* (What's trash, what's love?). Nanjing: Jiangsu wenyi chubanshe, 1998.

Zhu, Yu. *New Paths to Urbanization in China: Seeking More Balanced Patterns.* Commack, N.Y.: Nova Science, 1999.

Zhu, Zixuan, and Reginald Yin-Wang Kwok. "Beijing: The Expression of National Political Ideology." *Culture and the City in East Asia*, ed. Won Bae Kim, Clyde Michael Douglass, Sang-Chuel Choe, and Kong Chong Ho, 125–50. Oxford: Clarendon, 1997.

Ziarek, Ewa Ponowska. *The Rhetoric of Failure: Deconstruction of Skepticism, Reinvention of Modernism.* New York: State University of New York Press, 1996.

Index

Hitchcock, Alfred, 197

Hoggart, Richard, 120

home, 30, 38–40, 42, 58, 80, 228, 236–37

Homeland, Flour, and Flower (*Guxiang, mian, he huaduo*; Liu Zhenyun), 138–39

Hong Hao, 168

"hooligan literature" (*wanzhu wenxue*), 100, 109, 137, 139

Hou, Hanru, 68, 79

household registration system (*hukou*), 18, 150, 166

Hsia, C. T., 92, 193–94, 205

Huang, Yan, 57, 67

Huang Fayou, 277

Huang Rui, 77–78, 291

Huang Zhuan, 151–52

humanist spirit (*renwen jingshen*) debates, 13, 21, 100–106, 109–10, 119, 126, 261, 278; Wang Shuo as catalyst for, 134, 136–37

"Human Series, The" (*Ren xilei*; Concept 21), 153

Huntington, Samuel, 85, 111

Huters, Theodore, 97

hutong (Beijing alley) culture, 36, 40, 134, 135–36, 240

I Don't Care (*Wo bu xiangshi*; He Dun), 279

I Love Dollars (*Wo ai meiyuan*; Zhu Wen), 275–76

Image of the City, The (Lynch), 225

inequality, 87, 93, 95

infrastructure, 15, 19, 42, 70, 144

Inness, Julie C., 228

intellectuals, 21, 86, 88, 91–92, 98–103, 110, 127–28; co-optation of, 106–7, 118–24

interiority, 226–27, 235–39, 243–45, 253, 261–63, 270

Internet literature (*wangluo wenxue*), 6, 110, 120, 179

In the Heat of the Sun (*Yangguang canglan de rizi*; Jiang Wen), 136, 157

Invisible Cities (Calvino), 27, 30–31

"It's Me," 166–69

Jacobs, Jane, 79

Jameson, Fredric, 102, 107, 151

Jenks, Chris, 214

Jia Hongsheng, 154–55

Jiang Jun, 79–80, 291

Jiang Wen, 136, 157

Jiang Yikui, 57

Jia Pingwa, 105, 107, 109, 147, 261

Jia Zhangke, 37, 76, 204, 289, 290

jingpai (Beijing style), 13, 16, 131–32, 133, 178

jingwei (Beijing flavor), 131–32, 135–36. See also *xin jingwei*

Jones, Andrew, 265

Jordan, Jennifer, 46

June Fourth massacre (1989), 67, 91, 100, 107, 111–12, 180; artistic responses to, 73, 172–74; market reforms continued after, 89, 186, 229

Kang Mu, 153

Karabel, Jerome, 98–99

Kearney, Richard, 264–65

Keep the Height by All Means (Shi Yong), 189, 191

Kern, Stephen, 238

Kipnis, Andrew, 91, 96, 114–15

Knight, Sabina, 163

Knox, Paul, 6

Kong, Shuyu, 137, 234, 253

Koolhaas, Rem, 15, 31, 55, 79, 140, 220–21

Kosuth, Joseph, 183

Kuan, Seng, 54–56

Kubin, Wolfgang, 229

Kunming, 29, 64–65

Kwok, Reginald Yin-Wang, 144–45

Lacan, Jacques, 225–26, 242, 245, 246, 248

"La La La," 252

Landscape (*Fengjing*; Chen Shaoxiong), 73, 75

UNESCO, 36, 48, 64–65, 292

urban aesthetics, 4–7, 10, 20–24, 76, 152, 258, 284, 288–93

Urban China (*Chengshi Zhongguo*), 67, 78–80

urbanization, 1–4, 33–34, 132, 253; artistic responses to, 38, 133, 158–68; rates of, 28–29, 59, 142

urban planning, 14–16, 34–35, 53–63, 66, 84; in Beijing, 140–46; in Kunming, 29–30, 64–65; in Nanning, 70–71; in Shanghai, 56, 67, 192–93, 197–98, 220

urban-rural relations, 1–4, 10–11, 14–15, 141

urban subjectivity, 6, 21–22, 225–27, 235–38, 250

Urban Vicissitudes (*Chengshi jifeng*; Yang Dongping), 131–32

Urry, John, 31

Vidler, Anthony, 235

Virilio, Paul, 20, 38

"Volcker Shock," 92

von Hayek, Friedrich, 92–93

Wagner, Martha, 265

Wang, Ban, 19, 198, 204, 209, 215–16

Wang, Chaohua, 91, 97–98, 102

Wang, David Der-wei, 206–7

Wang Anyi, 6, 192, 261; *Song of Everlasting Sorrow*, 12, 22, 180, 200, 205–21

Wang Gan, 106, 262

Wang Guowei, 260

Wang Hongsheng, 278

Wang Hui, 89–92, 99, 114–15, 121, 127, 260, 262, 291; controversial award to, 119; on neoliberalism, 86–87, 96–97

Wang Jingsong, 160

Wang Jun, 35, 76, 80, 140

Wang Meng, 100, 102, 110, 261, 262

Wang Ning, 262

Wang Shuangming, 64

Wang Shuo, 147, 157, 284; in humanist spirit debates, 100–2, 105–10, 261; as "phenomenon," 21, 134–39

Wang Xiaobo, 21, 135, 139, 157

Wang Xiaoming, 19, 216, 229, 260, 274; in cultural studies, 114–22, 124–25, 291; on globalization, 87, 89–91, 97, 179; in humanist spirit debates, 100–101, 105; on urban literature, 127, 234, 285

Wang Xiaoshuai, 165; *Frozen*, 21, 154–58

Washington Consensus, 93, 97

Wasserstrom, Jeffrey, 176

watchdog journalism, 125–26

We Are Like Sunflowers (*Women xiang kuihua*; He Dun), 282

Weber, Max, 21, 256, 259, 288

Wei Hui, 252–53, 291

Welcome to China Southern Airlines (Xu Tan), 71–72

Wen Liping, 102

Wen Tiejun, 86–87, 115, 127, 291

What's Trash, What's Love? (*Shenme shi laji, shenme shi ai?*; Zhu Wen), 275–79, 285–86

"Whither China?" 7, 23, 92, 111, 114, 291

"Who Is the Enforcer of Morality?" (Qiu Huadong), 285

"Wildlife: An Experimental Art Project," 169

Williams, Raymond, 120

Wolff, Janet, 227

Wong, Timothy, 266

Woods, Benjamin, 56

Woolf, Virginia, 237

"Work of Art in the Age of Mechanical Reproduction, The" (Benjamin), 109

work unit (*danwei*), 33, 231, 257, 278; decline of, 7, 18, 275; influence of, 29, 58, 293

World, The (*Shije*; Jia Zhangke), 290

World Trade Organization (WTO), 86, 95–96

Robin Visser is an associate professor of Chinese at the University of
North Carolina, Chapel Hill.

Library of Congress Cataloging-in-Publication Data

Visser, Robin, 1962–
Cities surround the countryside : urban aesthetics in
post-socialist China / Robin Visser.
p. cm.
Includes bibliographical references and index.
ISBN 978-0-8223-4709-5 (cloth : alk. paper)
ISBN 978-0-8223-4728-6 (pbk. : alk. paper)
1. Cities and towns—China—History—21st century.
2. City and town life—China—History—21st century.
3. Aesthetics.
I. Title.
HT147.C48V57 2010
307.760951′0905—dc22   2009047828